AIRCRAFT
OF WORLD WAR II
IN COMBAT

AIRCRAFT
OF WORLD WAR II
IN COMBAT

GENERAL EDITOR: ROBERT JACKSON

amber
BOOKS

This edition first published in 2008 by
Amber Books Ltd
74–77 White Lion Street
London N1 9PF
United Kingdom
www.amberbooks.co.uk

ISBN 978-1-905704-88-0

Project Editor: James Bennett
Design: Colin Hawes

Previously published in a different format as part of the reference set *World Aircraft Information Files*

All images courtesy of Aerospace/Art-Tech

Printed in Thailand

Contents

Special Features: Aircraft Profiles

Introduction

Between 1939 and 1943, huge advances were made in the capability of combat aircraft. From Britain and the United States came the heavy bombers that would take the war to the heart of Germany: the Lancaster and Halifax, the B-17 Flying Fortress and the B-24 Liberator. Between them, they would pound the Third Reich around the clock, the RAF by night and the USAAF by day.

In North Africa, decisive battles were being fought, culminating in the last stand of the Axis forces in Tunisia early in 1943. The conflict between the Junkers Ju 52 transports and Allied fighters such as the Curtiss P-40 Warhawk was swift, brutal and one-sided.

Elsewhere, on the great plains of Russia, a combination of winter weather and bitter Soviet resistance had brought the triumphant German offensives to a standstill. The Soviet aviation industry was now beginning to produce excellent combat aircraft in huge numbers; types like the MiG-3 and Yak-9, which could at least hold their own against the Luftwaffe's formidable Messerschmitt Bf 109 and Focke-Wulf Fw 190.

But it was in the west that the decisive air battles were fought. The RAF's immortal Supermarine Spitfire and Hawker Hurricane fought the Luftwaffe to a standstill in the Battle of Britain, but it was an American fighter, the North American P-51 Mustang, that took the war to the enemy, with its ability to escort the bombers of the USAAF all the way to Berlin and back, and face the sternest challenge of the last months of the war – the Messerschmitt Me 262 jet fighter, deployed in increasing numbers from the autumn of 1944.

This comprehensively illustrated book provides an excellent insight into the use of air power in every theatre of World War II, from Germany's Blitzkrieg on Poland to the atomic bombing of Hiroshima and Nagasaki in 1945.

Above: The Junkers Ju 87 Stuka dive-bomber was hated and feared by Germany's enemies in the early part of the war, but was easy prey for fighters.

Left: Armourers manhandling an 1800kg (4000lb) high-capacity blast bomb, nicknamed a 'Cookie', towards the bomb bay of a Vickers Wellington.

Blitzkrieg!
Poland attacked

Having annexed Austria and Czechoslovakia, the German war machine annihilated Poland in a new lightning war, the Blitzkrieg, and thus unleashed the 20th century's most destructive conflict.

Hitler was issuing plans for the subjugation of Poland as early as 3 April 1939. His Fall Weiss (Plan White), a secret directive to the Wehrmacht (German armed forces), stated that: "The task of the Wehrmacht is to destroy the Polish armed forces. To this end a surprise attack is to be aimed and prepared."

At 04.45 (Central European Time) on 1 September 1939, without any prior declaration of war, Blitzkrieg (Lightning war) was unleashed. The ground forces of the Wehrmacht struck out eastwards across Poland's borders from the north and south. The Luftwaffe was used in an offensive capacity to achieve two objectives: the first was the neutralisation of the Polish air force on the ground and in the air. With this task completed, its second role would be direct close support of the army.

A force of approximately 1,580 first-line aircraft was committed to the campaign. Some limitations were imposed on the size of the Luftwaffe forces, since a considerable strategic reserve was held in Germany to defend against any intervention from the west by France and the UK.

Luftwaffe strength

General Albert Kesselring's Luftflotte I, with 1. Fliegerdivision, the Lehr-Division and Luftwaffenkommando Ost-Preussen subordinated, supported von Bock's Army Group North. To the south, Löhr's Luftflotte IV, consisting of 2. Fliegerdivision and the Fliegerführer zur besonderen Verwendung (zbV), operated from bases in Silesia in support of Army Group South.

Against these highly trained Luftwaffe units, the Polish air force could field 15 fighter squadrons of P.Z.L. P.7s and

Above: Having just released its clutch of one SC250 and four SC50 bombs, this Ju 87 engages its target in a typical dive attack. The screaming 'Jericho sirens' on the Stuka's undercarriage legs added to its demoralising effect on enemy troops.

Above: Crews of II./StG 77 perform maintenance between operations. The unit was one of five Stukageschwader serving under Luftflotte IV in the south, the others being III./StG 151, I./StG 77 and I./StG 2. A similar number of units were attached to Luftflotte I and all were used intensively, especially in support of the army.

P.11s, 12 reconnaissance-bomber units with P.Z.L. P.23s and P.37 Lós, and a similar number of units earmarked for army co-operation duties. In all, there were about 150 single-engined fighters and a comparable number of bombers available for operations. The Polish pilots and crews were well trained, and were to prove courageous and resilient in combat, but nothing could make up for the obsolescence of their aircraft, which were to have been replaced in a re-equipment programme during 1941-42.

Now it was too late. Attacks by the Luftwaffe started at 04.26 on 1 September 1939, when Oberleutnant Bruno Dilley's Kette (section) of three Junkers Ju 87B-1 dive-bombers from the 3rd Staffel (squadron) of Stukageschwader 1 (3./StG 1) attacked the Dirschau bridge, a major link across the Polish corridor. Similar raids followed, and within 48 hours of the initial assault Luftflotten I and IV had flown 1,250 sorties, crippling the Polish air force in the air and on the ground in the most efficient and devastating air superiority action launched to date.

Although a number of Do 17M-1 bombers were involved in the action against Poland, the majority of Do 17 units flew the improved Do 17Z. A redesigned forward fuselage, more armour and heavier defensive armament were incorporated in the light of combat experience over Spain. Reconnaissance Do 17P-1s were also active.

AIR WAR FOR POLAND: 1 SEPT 1939 - 6 OCT 1939

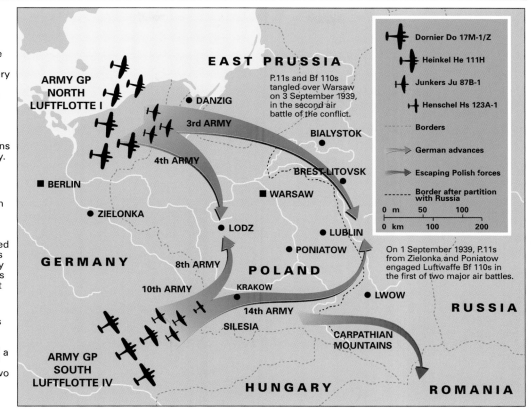

Strategy
According to Generalfeldmarschall Goering, commander-in-chief of the Luftwaffe, the German air force was "...ready to carry out every command of the Führer with lightning speed and un-dreamed of might." The Blitzkrieg on Poland was indeed devastating, with the Luftwaffe soon operating under conditions of absolute air superiority.

Luftflotte I
German air power was divided into two groups, dedicated to operations in the north and south, respectively. Flying in support of Army Group North, Luftflotte I consisted of three subordinate units and mounted the majority of its missions from bases in east Germany and East Prussia.

Luftflotte IV
Although smaller than its northern counterpart in terms of subordinated units, Luftflotte IV played a similar role in support of Army Group South. Its two constituent units flew mostly from bases in Silesia.

On the map:

EAST PRUSSIA

P.11s and Bf 110s tangled over Warsaw on 3 September 1939, in the second air battle of the conflict.

ARMY GP NORTH LUFTFLOTTE I

- DANZIG
- 3rd ARMY
- BIALYSTOK
- 4th ARMY
- BREST-LITOVSK
- BERLIN
- WARSAW
- ZIELONKA
- LODZ
- LUBLIN
- 8th ARMY
- PONIATOW
- GERMANY
- POLAND
- 10th ARMY
- KRAKOW
- 14th ARMY
- LWOW
- SILESIA
- RUSSIA
- ARMY GP SOUTH LUFTFLOTTE IV
- CARPATHIAN MOUNTAINS
- HUNGARY
- ROMANIA

Legend:

- Dornier Do 17M-1/Z
- Heinkel He 111H
- Junkers Ju 87B-1
- Henschel Hs 123A-1
- Borders
- German advances
- Escaping Polish forces
- Border after partition with Russia

0 m   50   100
0 km   100   200

On 1 September 1939, P.11s from Zielonka and Poniatow engaged Luftwaffe Bf 110s in the first of two major air battles.

Stuka supreme

On the first day the Luftwaffe had around 384 Ju 87s in the Polish theatre, with approximately 288 in a combat-ready state. Targets selected for attack by the Stukagruppen included airfield installations, bridges, rail sidings and troop concentrations. It was here, in Poland, that the Stuka gained its legendary and terrifying reputation. Tactics called for the dive to be commenced at an altitude of between 11,480 and 13,945 ft (3600 and 4250 m) at an angle between 65° and the vertical, with dive-brakes extended. The accuracy of the dive attack was phenomenal, with an average pilot able to regularly place a 551-lb (250-kg) SC250 bomb, and four 110-lb (50-kg) SC50s, within a 60-yd (55-m) radius. The effect of dive-bombing attacks on troops was to cause a state of

Easily overlooked since it was present in only small numbers, the Henschel Hs 123A-1 served with only one squadron within Luftflotte IV. The aircraft proved extremely effective in the close-support role and was able to keep pace with the rapid German advance by moving between a succession of airfields. Used mostly against troops and other soft targets, the Hs 123A-1 carried two 7.9-mm machine-guns and up to 200 kg of bombs.

demoralisation that had no precedent. The Stukagruppen encountered scant opposition over Poland and only 31 Ju 87s were lost during the campaign.

Alongside Luftflotte IV's Stukas, a specialist ground-attack unit – II (Schlacht)/LG 2 equipped with Henschel Hs 123A-1 biplanes – played a key part in the implementation of Fall Weiss. Some 37 Hs 123s were despatched from Alt-Rosenberg, initially for strafing

attacks on Polish troop concentrations. This highly mobile unit flew from at least seven different airfields during the brief campaign. Ground crews, spares, fuel and ammunition were transported to each forward base by Ju 52/3m transports in the wake of the German advance.

In addition to its tactical attack assets, the Luftwaffe fielded a large medium-bomber force, which was directed against both tactical and strategic targets. Nine Kampfgruppen (bomber wings) equipped with Dornier Do 17s (mostly Do 17Z-1 and Z-2 variants, with a number of Do 17M-ls) were joined by 15 Gruppen of Heinkel He 111Hs, split between four units under Luftflotte I, and a single unit under Luftflotte IV.

Left: Only a handful of P.37 Lós were available to the Poles at the opening of hostilities. The machine was a capable bomber, but was unable to make any impact on the invaders. A few P.37s escaped to Romania.

Right: Although outdated and lightly armed by comparison with the Bf 109s and Bf 110s of the Luftwaffe, the gull-winged P.Z.L. P.11 fighter nevertheless gave a good account of itself.

Poland crushed

Poland stood little chance of survival against the overwhelming weight of Germany's invading air and land forces, and all organised resistance had collapsed within five weeks.

Left: As soon as the Bf 110 crews had mastered their dive-and-climb tactics for engaging the nimble P.11s, the Polish fighters were doomed in the air. Bombing and strafing attacks on airfields accounted for many more aircraft, such as this P.11, on the ground.

A Staffel of Do 17Z-2s launched from Heiligenbeil in East Prussia at 05.30 on 1 September, for a strike on the approaches to the Dirschau bridge. Warsaw, Poland's proud capital, was attacked on the first morning. Heavy raids were mounted by Prussian-based bombers, and by He 111Hs operating some 465 miles (750 km) from their base in East Germany. Krakow, Lwow and various naval installations, ports and shore batteries situated on the Baltic coast, were also bombed during the opening hours of the invasion. Polish opposition to the raids was again minimal, and

only 78 medium bombers were lost, the majority falling to anti-aircraft fire.

Having performed excellently during the Spanish Civil War, the Bf 109 was forced to operate at extreme ranges during the Polish campaign. Those reaching the action proved vulnerable to ground fire and after an inauspicious introduction to World War II, most of the aircraft were withdrawn to Germany. The Bf 109 units gained invaluable experience in operating from forward strips however.

In addition to flying bomber-escort missions, the Luftwaffe's Jagdgeschwader (fighter squadrons) had the task of

intercepting and countering the reaction of the Polish air force during the first two days of the assault. Making its combat debut, the far-ranging Messerschmitt Bf 110 Zerstörer (Destroyer), achieved considerable success over Poland, although its slow rate of roll and poor turning characteristics made it vulnerable against the nimble Polish P.Z.L. P.11 fighters.

Messerschmitts in force

On the first morning, Bf 110s accompanied raids on Warsaw, Krakow and other targets. Polish fighters were engaged in the afternoon of 1 September, when the fighter brigades based at Zielonka and Poniatow rose to challenge German bombers. Escorting Bf 110s made the initial error of trying to turn with the small P.11s, but later redressed the situation by using dive-and-climb tactics. Five P.11s were

Heinkel He 111s and Dornier Do 17s pounded Polish targets with incendiaries and high explosives. A particularly heavy period of bombing led to the surrender of Warsaw on 27 September. The inadequacies of Germany's medium-bomber force were not yet apparent.

downed for no loss. On the afternoon of the following day the 1. and 2./ZG 76 lost two Bf 110s over Lodz, in return for three P.Z.L. fighters destroyed. A second air battle over Warsaw on 3 September saw five more Polish fighters destroyed for the loss of one Bf 110. Polish fighter reaction now fell to such an extent that the German Jagd- and

┌ Invading German airpower ┐

In the years immediately prior to World War II, Germany had established a modern and powerful air force. In 1939, no other European nation could boast an air force of

similar striking power or mobility. The Luftwaffe's bombers and fighters were easily a match for those in service with the Polish air force.

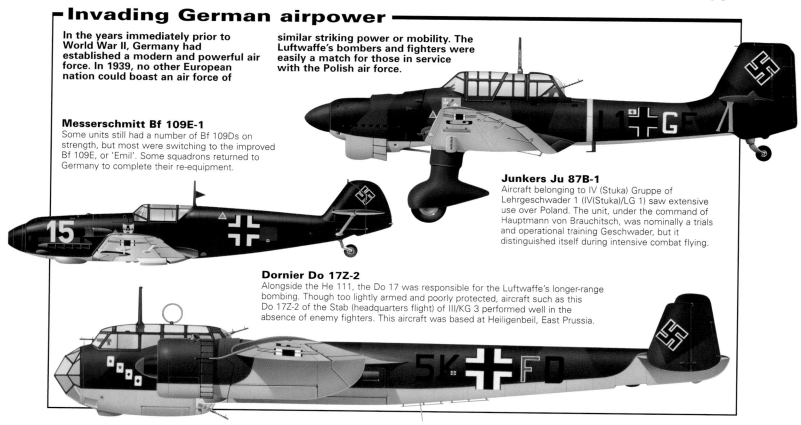

Messerschmitt Bf 109E-1
Some units still had a number of Bf 109Ds on strength, but most were switching to the improved Bf 109E, or 'Emil'. Some squadrons returned to Germany to complete their re-equipment.

Junkers Ju 87B-1
Aircraft belonging to IV (Stuka) Gruppe of Lehrgeschwader 1 (IV(Stuka)/LG 1) saw extensive use over Poland. The unit, under the command of Hauptmann von Brauchitsch, was nominally a trials and operational training Geschwader, but it distinguished itself during intensive combat flying.

Dornier Do 17Z-2
Alongside the He 111, the Do 17 was responsible for the Luftwaffe's longer-range bombing. Though too lightly armed and poorly protected, aircraft such as this Do 17Z-2 of the Stab (headquarters flight) of III/KG 3 performed well in the absence of enemy fighters. This aircraft was based at Heiligenbeil, East Prussia.

Zerstörergeschwader switched to ground strafing duties. During the course of the five-week campaign the Zerstörergruppen claimed 68 Polish aircraft destroyed, with Bf 110 losses numbering only 12 over the period 1 to 28 September 1939.

Polish resistance

By 3 September, whilst destruction of the Polish aircraft industry and air force remained the top priorities of the Luftwaffe, a secondary effort was directed at eliminating any surviving bastions of Polish resistance left behind by the rapid German advance. Such was the efficiency of the bombing campaign, that the full weight of the Luftwaffe was soon turned to the support of the German armies pushing mercilessly on towards Warsaw.

On 9 September 1939, the relentless German advance was checked briefly on the Bzura River, some 50 miles (80 km) to the west of Warsaw. Wehrmacht reinforcements soon proved too much for the Polish armies and elsewhere the advance had

continued unabated. At 07.00 on 9 September 1939, just as the Battle of the Bzura was beginning, the 4th Panzer Division launched its first assault on Warsaw. After a brave resistance which suffered under an exceptionally heavy attack involving 1,150 sorties by the Luftwaffe on the 24th, Warsaw surrendered on 27 September 1939.

Polish retreat

The remnants of the Polish army and air force, including 90,000 men and some aircraft which flew over the Carpathian Mountains, escaped to Rumania and Hungary. Eventually these survivors were to continue the fight alongside the Franco-British alliance. But Poland was lost: the last pockets of resistance ceased fighting on 6 October 1939.

For the Germans the success of the campaign was overwhelming, and the speed at which a military victory was achieved surpassed their wildest dreams.

For the Luftwaffe the outstanding success of the

campaign was the successful use of the Ju 87 dive-bomber, and the demonstration of the far-ranging capabilities of the Messerschmitt Bf 110 fighter. "Beyond all other military arms," wrote Generaloberst Albert Kesselring, "the Luftwaffe, by virtue of its mobility in space,

accomplished tasks which in former wars had been inconceivable…" The Polish campaign demonstrated the potential of the Luftwaffe and allowed it to mature into a powerful, battle hardened force. By April 1940, this force was unleashing Blitzkrieg on Norway.

ROLE	AIRCRAFT TYPE & NUMBER IN SERVICE	
	GERMANY	POLAND
Bomber	400 x Dornier Do 17M/Z 300 x Heinkel He 111H/P	36 x P.Z.L. P.37 Lós
Dive Bomber	384 x Junkers Ju 87 Stuka	
Light Bomber		118 x P.Z.L. P.23 Karás
Fighter	200 x Messerschmitt Bf 109E	51 x P.Z.L. P.7 108 x P.Z.L. P.11
Heavy Fighter	95 x Messerschmitt Bf 110B-1/C-1	
Ground Attack	37 x Henschel Hs 123	
Liaison/Observation		120 x miscellaneous types
Observation		49 x Lublin R.XIII
Reconnaissance, etc	164 x miscellaneous types	
Transport. etc	400 x Ju 52/3m & other types	
Total	**1980**	**482**
Aircraft Lost	**116**	**333**

GERMAN AND POLISH AIRPOWER COMPARISON

Many of the lessons learned by the Luftwaffe's Legion Condor during the Spanish Civil War were put to the test over Poland. Under conditions of almost total air superiority, the Ju 87 Stuka gained a legendary reputation which preceded it as the German Blitzkrieg swept across Europe.

Poland's doomed air force

The Polish air force fielded 433 first-line aircraft, divided between the Dispositional Air Force (159 aircraft) and Armies' Air Force (274 aircraft). Outnumbered and materially outclassed, the Poles fought with extreme courage and tenacity before being crushed.

P.Z.L. P.37 Lós B
The P.37 Lós (Elk) bomber was the most modern strike aircraft in Polish service, a total of 36 being distributed between four squadrons (Nos 211 and 212 of the X/1 Wing and Nos 216 and 217 of the XV/1 Wing) of the Bomber Brigade. The Lós B (illustrated) featured twin fins and rudders.

P.Z.L. P.11
Four 0.303-in (7.7-mm) KM Wz 33 machine-guns gave the P.11 gullwing fighter respectable firepower, although it was no match for the cannon-armed Bf 109E-1. The P.11 mostly joined battle with the Bf 110 however, and was the most feared of Polish aircraft amongst the German crews. This P.11C belonged to No. 121 (Winged Arrows) Squadron.

P.Z.L. P.23b Karás
Polish flying units were strictly assigned to individual army divisions, but at the start of hostilities all units, except those flying the P.23, broke away from this restrictive strategy. This P.23b was attached to No. 42 Sqn of the Pomorze Army. The Karás (Crucian Carp) was numerically Poland's most important light-bomber/reconnaissance type.

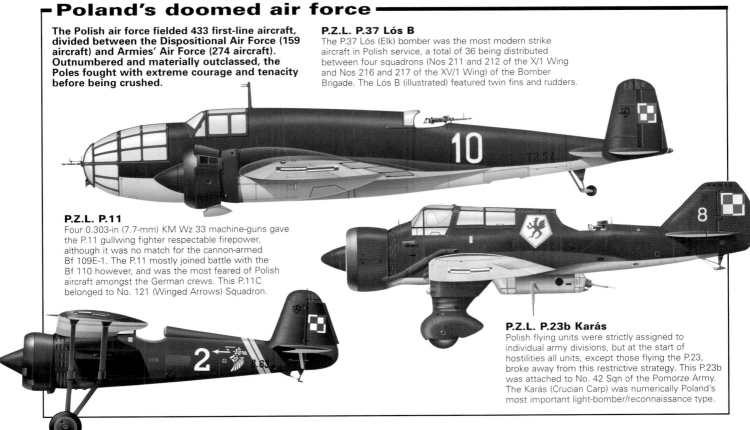

Junkers Ju 87
'Stuka' dive-bomber

Few aircraft have ever caused such terror, to seasoned troops and helpless civilians alike, as the ugly Junkers Ju 87 dive-bomber. Widely known as the Stuka, from the German word for dive-bomber (Sturzkampfflugzeug), the Ju 87 also sank more ships than any other aircraft type in history.

A pair of Ju 87R-2s of 2./StG 3 is pictured returning from a patrol in the Mediterranean in early 1941. The Med was a region in which the 'R' was repeatedly used against British convoys. The aircraft carry 66-Imp gallon (300-litre) drop tanks under their wings.

The technique of dive-bombing was familiar in World War I, but no aircraft designed for the job existed until the 1920s. One of the first was the Junkers K 47, of which two were flown in 1928 with Jupiter engines, and a further 12 with Pratt & Whitney Hornet engines were later sold to China. Extensive research was carried out on the K 47s and revealed that a 90° dive is the most accurate, although such a dive demands a strong aircraft and a resolute pilot, as well as the existence of an indicator of dive angle. At this time, many who later were to head Hitler's Luftwaffe became convinced of the importance of a dive-bomber as a central weapon in an air force dedicated to the close support of ground forces.

When plans for new combat aircraft for the Luftwaffe were made in 1933, the immediate need was met by a trim biplane, the Henschel Hs 123, while Junkers continued to work on the definitive Stuka. The design staff under Hermann Pohlmann adopted the same configuration as that of the K 47, a single-engined low-wing monoplane with prominent fixed landing gear and twin fins and rudders. This was later changed to a conventional single-fin design during development as, during an early dive test, the twin fins collapsed and the aircraft crashed. Another change was to the powerplant; the prototype had originally flown with a British built Rolls-Royce Kestrel engine, but this was later changed to a German-built Jumo 210Ca when the Stuka entered Luftwaffe service in 1937.

Into combat

Stukas were first to see action with the Légion Condor in Spain, where the type proved outstandingly effective. Despite the Stuka's remarkable combat debut, however, Junkers continued to refine and improve the design. One notable addition was to fit sirens – called 'Trumpets of Jericho' – to the landing gears. As the aircraft entered its dive, the flow of the wind through the sirens would cause them to screech and so strike extra terror into people near the target.

By mid-1939, Stuka production had reached up to 60 a month, and these improved 'B' models

The Ju 87 V4 is seen in its original form, with smooth cowling side panels, and before the rearmost windows of the canopy were installed.

Above: A Ju 87A-2 serving with StG 165 in 1938 displays a not-uncommon variety of camouflage finish – usually obtained by switching the basic colours and splinter pattern. The red tail banner and white circle behind the Swastika were soon eliminated on operational aircraft, as illustrated.

Left: Flanked by a 500-kg (1,102-lb) SC500 bomb, this Ju 87B Stuka is seen parked on a Greek airfield during the continuation of the Blitzkrieg campaign through the Balkans. This was the last campaign in which the Ju 87 was able to demolish its targets while encountering little opposition.

Above: The water-soluble white distemper used as snow camouflage by Luftwaffe aircraft in Russia weathered rapidly, becoming heavily stained by exhaust gases. Here, five Ju 87Ds from an unidentified Geschwader turn in for an attack against Soviet armour.

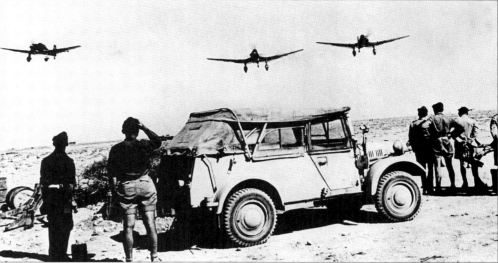

Above: German troops watch as a flight of Stukas return from a mission. Stukas flew in support of Rommel's Afrika Korps, providing close-air support throughout the early years of the campaign in North Africa.

were soon in combat supporting Hitler's blitzkrieg across Europe. Stukas flew the first combat mission of World War II when three B-1s took off on 1 September 1939 to attack the Dirschau Bridge over the Vistula river, some 11 minutes before the Nazis declared war on Poland. Later, Stukas were to prove equally effective in the campaign against Poland, sinking all but two of Poland's warships and attacking numerous troop concentrations.

Alongside the developing ground-attack models, Junkers proposed the Ju 87C, equipped with folding wings and hooks, and incorporating many other changes to enable the type to be used aboard the carrier *Graf Zeppelin*, which was ultimately never completed. Other models were to feature overwing-mounted personnel pods to serve as transport aircraft.

Having wrought havoc throughout Europe in the first year of World War II, over Britain Stuka losses were to prove unacceptably heavy. At the height of the Battle of Britain – from 13-18 August 1940 – RAF Spitfires and Hurricanes shot down 41 Stukas, with the result that, from 19 August, the aircraft were withdrawn from attacks against UK targets.

The Stuka had been designed on the basis of good fighter protection by Bf 109s and Bf 110s and, in such conditions, it had demonstrated its devastating effectiveness. However, the Luftwaffe's inability to achieve air superiority over the UK caused huge losses to be suffered by Stuka units.

Basic design

By early 1941 what was to become the definitive Stuka variant, the Ju 87D, had entered combat on the Eastern and North African Fronts. The entire aircraft was refined to reduce drag, the most visible improvement being the deletion of the large radiator intake and its replacement with a smaller armoured design.

No longer viewed as purely a dive-bomber, Stukas were increasingly used as close-support aircraft, dropping bombs within 330 ft (100 m) of friendly troops.

Other roles extended to glider-towing, anti-partisan attacks and general utility transport with a diversity of loads.

Developed from the Ju 87D were a succession of sub-variants, including the '-5' with extended wingtips to counter the increasing weight of the Ju 87D versions; the '-7' night variant (reflecting the increasing peril of day operations) with long exhaust pipes extending back across the wing to hide the exhaust flames; and the Ju 87D-8 which was the last version in production. The total number of Stukas built by late September 1944 – when almost all aircraft production other than fighters had been

terminated – is generally accepted as 5,709.

The Ju 87 was widely used by all the Axis air forces, including those of Italy, Hungary, Slovakia, Romania and Bulgaria, although it was with the Luftwaffe that the aircraft achieved its well-deserved reputation.

Even at the outbreak of war, the Ju 87 was recognised as a somewhat dated design, but this fact was masked by its fantastic successes. Like so many other Luftwaffe types, it continued to be operated long beyond its original termination of production date, due to the lack of a replacement. Ju 87 crews, like those of the Messerschmitt Bf 110 and He 111, were subjected to flying combat missions in an outdated aircraft, and so the results achieved stand as a testament to the skill of the crews and the durability of the Ju 87 Stuka.

Above: A Ju 87D-3 is seen with experimental personnel transport pods overwing. They seated two passengers in tandem, and were designed to be released in a shallow dive, descending to the ground on the end of a massive parachute.

Left: The Ju 87G-1 anti-tank aircraft was the last Ju 87 variant to become operational (apart from the Ju 87H trainer). Converted from earlier Ju 87Ds, the aircraft were adapted to carry a pair of massive Flak 18 (Bk 3,7) 37-mm cannon pods under their outer wing panels.

Hitler strikes north

Norway was considered to be a vital stronghold by both German and Allied forces. A naval element based in northern Norway could control access to the north Atlantic, and Hitler was keen to ensure that this advantage did not go to the British. In a decisive action, he saw that Norway and Denmark were crushed in days.

Below: He 111s were initially used to demonstrate the strength of the Luftwaffe, by flying over key Norwegian cities and towns while the German landings were underway. In addition, leaflets were dropped over Copenhagen. Three He 111 units were committed – **KG 4, KG 26** *and* **KGr 100** *– with* **KG 26** *later flying from Norwegian bases.*

Above: A stick of Luftwaffe paratroops falls toward Norwegian soil. The largest airborne assault yet attempted came as a devastating blow to the Allies.

A victim of its own geographical position, Norway suffered the horror of Germany's Blitzkrieg in the late spring of 1940. Both Norway and Denmark were spared the devastation that swept Poland, but experienced the speed and efficiency of the Luftwaffe's Fallschirmjäger airborne troops.

Germany's Kriegsmarine (navy) had learned from its experiences against the British fleet during World War I that a powerful naval blockade could be almost impenetrable. In 1929 Admiral Wegener stated that the British blockade of German ports during the earlier conflict could have been negated if ports along the west coast of Norway had been used. Britain too had

realised the strategic importance of Norway, and at the time of the German invasion on 9 April 1940 the Royal Navy was already steaming toward the north of the country.

Hitler's second interest in Norway lay in securing a route for iron ore deliveries from Sweden to Germany's industries in the Ruhr. It was British mining of Norwegian ports to prevent ore shipments, combined with the *Altmark* incident, which triggered the German invasion.

Cossack in action

On 16 February 1940 the crew of the 'Tribal'-class Royal Navy fleet destroyer HMS *Cossack* boarded the German naval auxiliary ship *Altmark*. The Axis vessel was carrying British prisoners of war and was sheltering in the neutral Norwegian waters of Jösenfjord. Hitler saw the act as one of open piracy, achieved with Norwegian co-operation. On 1 March 1940, he issued the formal war directive for Weserübung, the invasion of Norway and Denmark.

While German naval units were heavily involved in the fighting, the Luftwaffe again played a key role. The extreme ranges involved in operations over Norway all but eliminated the Ju 87 Stuka from the air war. Some 40 of the longest-ranged Ju 87R model joined 70 Bf 110C heavy fighters to form the Luftwaffe's ground-attack

Below: Although the deployment of Fallschirmjäger proved highly successful both tactically and in terms of propaganda value, casualties were heavy. The troops could be deployed by glider, parachute or transport, arriving in the field ready to fight.

Left: The Luftwaffe was obliged to make considerable use of reconnaissance seaplanes, such as the He 115, for patrols and offensive operations along Norway's rugged coastline.

Above: German aircraft soon began operating from overrun Norwegian airfields. Dated 15 April 1940, this picture shows Ju 52/3ms dispersed on Oslo's airfield as a destroyed aircraft (possibly a Norwegian Gladiator) burns in the background.

Below: These He 111s of 2./KG 26 operated from a forward base in Norway. The unit remained in the country after its occupation, flying missions against British bases during the Battle of Britain.

Above: KG.z.b.V. 108 See was hastily formed in time for Weserübung. The unit flew transport missions with a range of seaplanes, including Heinkel He 59 biplane floatplanes.

force. Bombing capability was provided by 290 He 111Hs and Junkers Ju 88s; the almost total lack of Danish and Norwegian fighters meant that only 30 Bf 109Es were deployed to provide cover for the bombers. In addition, maritime aircraft proved invaluable around Norway's rocky coastline.

By far the most important Luftwaffe type, both numerically and tactically, was the Junkers Ju 52/3m transport. Around 500 of these aircraft sustained a continuous assault during the first 10 days of action, delivering waves of Fallschirmjäger and assault troops into the beleaguered countries.

This huge and hard-worked transport fleet delivered vast numbers of troops by parachute and directly into the field, along with a constant stream of supplies and equipment. The air forces of Denmark and Norway could offer only token resistance, with the Danes fielding a fighter force of Hawker Nimrod and Gloster Gauntlet biplanes and Fokker D.XXIs, while Norway could muster a force of just 12 Gloster Gladiator Mks I and II.

On the morning of 8 April 1940, British reconnaissance aircraft noted German naval activity; the Luftwaffe's He 111s and Ju 88s were also unusually active. Since no troop transport ships were noted, the British did not consider an invasion imminent, and kept their forces back until it was too late.

Air power unmatched

Germany's invading forces were supported by some of the Luftwaffe's most modern equipment, including the formidable Fw 200 Condor. By comparison, the Royal Norwegian Air Force was poorly equipped and desperately weak.

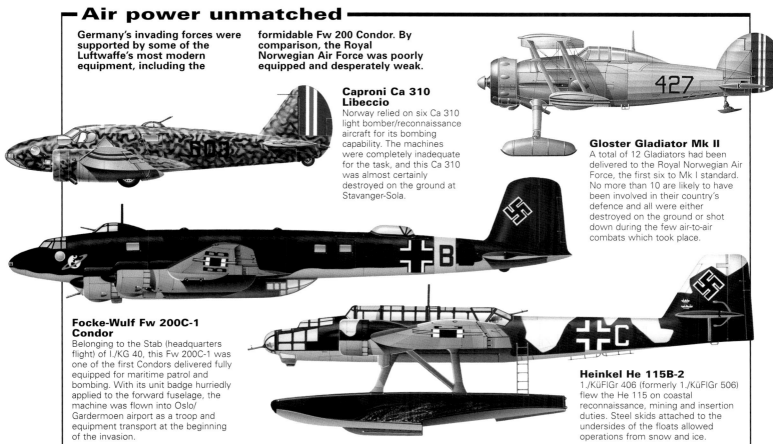

Caproni Ca 310 Libeccio
Norway relied on six Ca 310 light bomber/reconnaissance aircraft for its bombing capability. The machines were completely inadequate for the task, and this Ca 310 was almost certainly destroyed on the ground at Stavanger-Sola.

Gloster Gladiator Mk II
A total of 12 Gladiators had been delivered to the Royal Norwegian Air Force, the first six to Mk I standard. No more than 10 are likely to have been involved in their country's defence and all were either destroyed on the ground or shot down during the few air-to-air combats which took place.

Focke-Wulf Fw 200C-1 Condor
Belonging to the Stab (headquarters flight) of I./KG 40, this Fw 200C-1 was one of the first Condors delivered fully equipped for maritime patrol and bombing. With its unit badge hurriedly applied to the forward fuselage, the machine was flown into Oslo/Gardermoen airport as a troop and equipment transport at the beginning of the invasion.

Heinkel He 115B-2
1./KüFlGr 406 (formerly 1./KüFlGr 506) flew the He 115 on coastal reconnaissance, mining and insertion duties. Steel skids attached to the undersides of the floats allowed operations from snow and ice.

Norway defeated

After successfully defeating Denmark, German forces turned their attention to Norway. Airborne troops were used for the first time during the campaign.

Such was the urgency of the Scandinavian operations that all aircrew, including the pilot shown here, were pressed into service for tasks such as refuelling. Only thus could a rapid turn-around be ensured.

By the end of April 1940, the bulk of Norway was in German hands and Luftflotte V could settle down to conduct four main tasks:
1 supply and reinforcement;
2 reconnaissance of the North Sea and attacks on British naval units;
3 support of ground forces in Norwegian valleys;
4 protection of areas won, by flak and fighters.

Map legend:
- German naval landing
- German paratroop assault
- Allied counter attack
- Naval action

NORWEGIAN SEA · SWEDEN · Halstad · Narvik · Namsos · Trondheim · Åndalsnes · NORWAY · Lillehammer · Bergen · OSLO · Stavanger · Arendal · Oslofjord · Egersund · Kristiansand · Aalborg · NORTH SEA · JUTLAND · DENMARK · FUNEN · COPENHAGEN · Åbenra

ASSAULT: APRIL 1940

With a long, highly exposed coastline, and only limited inland communications, Norway was well suited for the type of combined ground and naval attack that the Germans could launch with massive air support. Although the outcome was never really in doubt, the Germans met stiff resistance and suffered heavy losses. Key to the German plan was the rapid capture of airfields in Denmark and Norway, from which further operations could be mounted. The campaign marked the first use of Fallschirmjäger (paratroops) dropped from Ju 52/3m transports.

For Norway, the failure of Britain's Royal Navy to intercept the Kriegsmarine (German navy) units steaming towards its shores spelled disaster. Troops landing from ships were combined with forces deployed from the air to overwhelm Norway's meagre defences in a devastating show of power.

For Denmark, Hitler's ambitions for Norway were equally disastrous. The Luftwaffe needed the airfield at Aalborg in Jutland as a forward base for its combat aircraft and the many transports required to execute the invasion and maintain its momentum.

Bloodless surrender

Early in the morning of 9 April 1940, the first German troops were successfully landed by sea at Trondheim, Bergen, Egersund, Arendal, Kristiansand and Oslo. Simultaneously, at a little after 05.00, German troops crossed the Danish frontier at Åbenra, while seaborne landings were made on Fünen and other Danish islands.

German air power was also active over Denmark. Within 90 minutes of the seaborne landings

Ju 52/3ms dropped paratroops over the airfields at Aalborg-Ost and -West. Some 20 minutes later airborne infantry was landed by relays of Ju 52/3ms to secure these vital airfields. Top cover was provided by escorting Bf 110 fighters of I/ZG 1. Aerial assault on such a grand scale led to Denmark's bloodless surrender. The whole of Jutland, along with Denmark's capital, Copenhagen, was in German hands by the end of the day.

Meanwhile, the invasion of Norway continued. The initial seaborne landings were followed at 08.30 by strafing attacks on the airfields at Stavanger-Sola and Oslo-Förnebu by I/ZG 76. A brief combat between the He 111s of III/KG 26, a number of Bf 110s and the Norwegian

An He 115 circles over a naval encounter. The capture of Norway gave the Luftwaffe a vital base from which to conduct reconnaissance and attacks on British naval units.

Danish air power: out-numbered and out-fought

Danish military aviation faced a similar predicament to Poland's air force in September 1939. It stood little chance against the overwhelming superiority of the Luftwaffe in terms of numbers of modern combat aircraft, logistics and tactics.

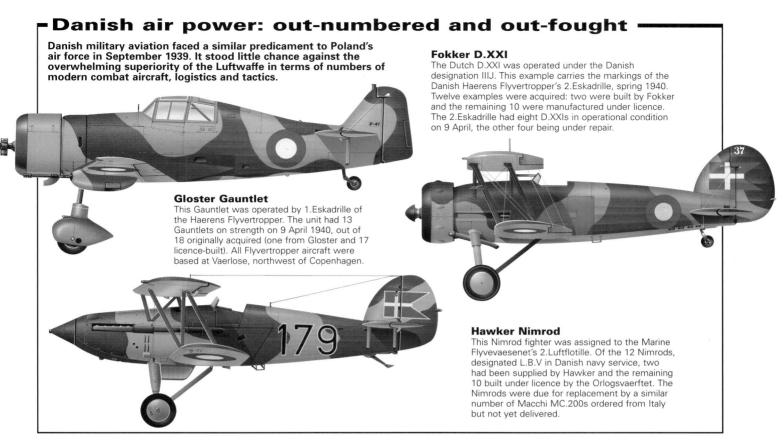

Fokker D.XXI
The Dutch D.XXI was operated under the Danish designation IIIJ. This example carries the markings of the Danish Haerens Flyvertropper's 2.Eskadrille, spring 1940. Twelve examples were acquired: two were built by Fokker and the remaining 10 were manufactured under licence. The 2.Eskadrille had eight D.XXIs in operational condition on 9 April, the other four being under repair.

Gloster Gauntlet
This Gauntlet was operated by 1.Eskadrille of the Haerens Flyvertropper. The unit had 13 Gauntlets on strength on 9 April 1940, out of 18 originally acquired (one from Gloster and 17 licence-built). All Flyvertropper aircraft were based at Vaerlose, northwest of Copenhagen.

Hawker Nimrod
This Nimrod fighter was assigned to the Marine Flyvevaesenet's 2.Luftflotille. Of the 12 Nimrods, designated L.B.V in Danish navy service, two had been supplied by Hawker and the remaining 10 built under licence by the Orlogsvaerftet. The Nimrods were due for replacement by a similar number of Macchi MC.200s ordered from Italy but not yet delivered.

Gladiators sent to intercept them over Oslofjord, finished when all of the Gloster fighters were shot down. Remaining Gladiators were then destroyed on the ground by German strafing. Staffeln from three Luftwaffe bomber wings bombed Oslo-Kjeller airfield, anti-aircraft sites on Holmenkollen and coastal batteries on the islets of Oslofjord.

Airfields assaulted

As they had been in Denmark, paratroops were instrumental in the seizure of vital airfields, including Stavanger-Sola. Förnebu and Kjeller were soon in use as forward bases for I/ZG 76 and the Ju 87s of I/StG 1, and, by the end of the first day, Sola had received 180 troop-carrying Ju 52/3ms. During the following day, He 111, He 115, Ju 87, Ju 88 and reconnaissance units had all moved to Sola. Further south, Kristiansand had become a temporary home for II/JG 77 and its Bf 109E-1s, with detached flights being sent to a number of other locations.

Poor weather and short range combined with other operational problems to allow the Bf 109 only a minor role, with the Luftwaffe's bombers ranging widest over Norway's difficult terrain. In contrast, some 250 Ju 52/3ms were pushed to their limits in the first week. During 3,018 sorties they transported 29,280 troops and supplied the captured airfields with 2,376 tons (2415 tonnes) of cargo and 259,300 Imp gal (1178778 litres) of aviation fuel.

On 11 April 1940, General Otto Ruge was appointed Commander-in-Chief of the Norwegian forces and his leadership, along with the arrival of British reinforcements, effected a temporary reversal in fortunes. On 10 April, Fleet Air Arm Blackburn Skuas of No. 803 Sqn sank the German light cruiser *Königsberg* at Bergen. Further shipping losses at the hands of both Norwegian coastal batteries (including the heavy cruiser *Blücher* in Oslofjord) and the Royal Navy led to an acrimonious dispute between the Kriegsmarine and the Luftwaffe over the latter's apparent inability to defend German naval assets from the Royal Navy. Bad weather and poor communications had prevented Luftwaffe intervention in the naval battles. On the ground, British forces landed between 16 and 18 April at Harstad, Namsos and Åndalsnes: the objectives were the recapture of Narvik and then Trondheim, and to link up with Ruge's forces north of Oslo.

With Allied troops providing fierce resistance at Lillehammer and the Steinkjer Pass, the Luftwaffe turned its He 111s, Ju 88s and Stukas against them, and also set about the destruction of the supply ports at Åndalsnes and Namsos. In order to counter this aerial bombardment, the RAF's No. 263 Sqn was despatched from the carrier HMS *Glorious*, landing its 18 Gladiator Mk IIs on the ice of Lake Lesjaskog near Åndalsnes at 18.00 on 23 April. Serviceability proved low and German bombing destroyed most of the aircraft, but not before 40 sorties could be flown. By 26 April the squadron had ceased to exist, however, and the Germans had completely destroyed Åndalsnes.

Allied withdrawal

Throughout late April, the Luftwaffe had been massively reinforced and now fielded 710 aircraft, including 360 bombers. Faced with overwhelming German air power, the decision was taken to begin an Allied withdrawal. The retreat from Andalsnes on 30 April was followed by retreat from Namsos on 2 May.

The Allies then moved against the German stronghold at Narvik, supported by a re-equipped No. 263 Sqn with Gladiators and No. 46 with Hurricane Mk Is. Heavy fighting following an Allied assault on 28 May included both units, but increased Luftwaffe bombing and supply missions repulsed the advance. On 8 June 1940, the Allies withdrew from Narvik and Norway was lost.

Norway became an important area of operations for He 115 seaplanes during World War II. Ironically, Norway's Marinens Flyvevåben also operated the type, and a few enemy He 115s were captured by both sides during the fighting. Six Norwegian-flown He 115s bombed German positions during the battle for Narvik.

Descent on the Low Countries

Above: The Bf 109E was able to establish itself as a fine fighter over the Low Countries. Units such as JG 53 were instrumental in gaining German superiority.

Left: A German paratrooper leaves a Ju 52/3m transport flying at low-level over the Netherlands as the blitzkrieg sweeps the Low Countries.

With Poland, Denmark and Norway having fallen to German military might, Hitler turned his attention to western Europe and moved towards France.

With its armed forces occupied to the north, the Wehrmacht had maintained a position of stalemate to the west. By May 1940, however, Hitler was ready to strike out across the Low Countries of Belgium and Holland and into France. Just as Denmark had suffered as a staging post to Norway, so the Low Countries would suffer as a stepping stone to France and ultimately to Great Britain.

Fall Gelb revealed

Fall Gelb (Plan Yellow) had been formed as early as 19 October 1939. In its final form it detailed an armoured thrust, with heavy air support, through the densely wooded and hilly Ardennes region and across France to the Channel coast.

This daring campaign was designed to divide the armies of Belgium, and the Netherlands, along with the northern armies of France and the troops of the British Expeditionary Force (BEF) to the north, from the French armies to the south. The attack was to come from the direction thought the most unlikely by Allied commanders for an armoured assault.

In a repeat of the highly successful airborne landings against key airfields and installations in Denmark and Norway, the first attacks against the Low Countries saw the Fallschirmjäger in action during

Amongst Belgium's meagre force of fighters, 23 Italian-supplied Fiat CR.42s were some of the most effective. They were hopelessly outclassed.

the early hours of 10 May 1940. Bridges deemed vital for the progress of the invading armour were the principal targets and all were taken in the face of fierce resistance.

Further troops were landed by DFS 230 assault gliders, towed aloft by Ju 52/3ms, while the Luftwaffe was also engaged in offensive operations. Wherever required, Ju 87s and Hs 123s provided close support to the Fallschirmjäger, while a force of some 300 Do 17 and He 111

bombers mounted co-ordinated attacks against airfields in Belgium, Holland and northern France. Against this formidable aerial onslaught, the Belgian and Dutch air forces offered exceptionally brave, but ultimately ineffective resistance.

Opposing air power

In addition to a large force of bombers and close support aircraft, the Luftwaffe committed 1,106 fighters to Fall Gelb. The air campaign was to be one of the largest staged by Germany during World War II and the Allied forces which rose against it were rapidly overcome.

The cutting edge of Dutch airpower was represented by Fokker's D.XXI and G.1A fighters, with 62 out of a total serviceable force of 125 being lost on 10 May. Belgium's small

Facing the onslaught

A mixed force of fighters was fielded by Belgium and the Netherlands, with no single type available in large numbers. The Fokker G.1A and Hurricane Mk I were by far the most

effective fighters available, and both saw intensive, but brief combat. Even with the addition of the BAEF and units operating from the UK, this combined fighter force could not

match the potential strength of the French air force, which was thought likely to offer stiffer resistance. In the event, nothing could overcome the all-conquering Messerschmitts.

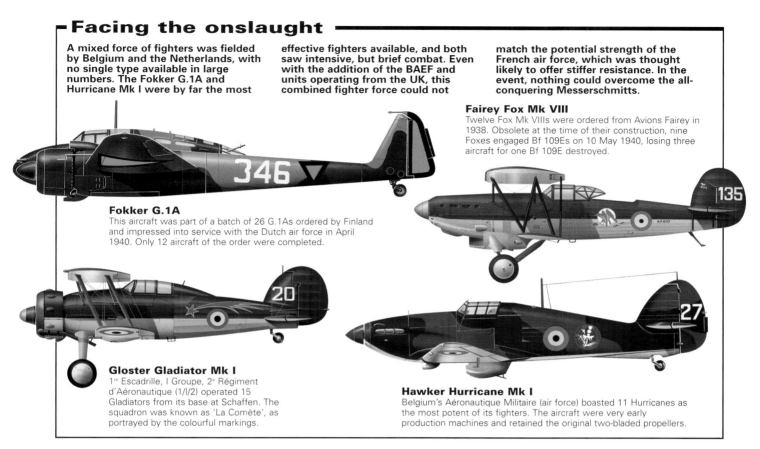

Fokker G.1A
This aircraft was part of a batch of 26 G.1As ordered by Finland and impressed into service with the Dutch air force in April 1940. Only 12 aircraft of the order were completed.

Fairey Fox Mk VIII
Twelve Fox Mk VIIIs were ordered from Avions Fairey in 1938. Obsolete at the time of their construction, nine Foxes engaged Bf 109Es on 10 May 1940, losing three aircraft for one Bf 109E destroyed.

Gloster Gladiator Mk I
1re Escadrille, I Groupe, 2e Régiment d'Aéronautique (1/I/2) operated 15 Gladiators from its base at Schaffen. The squadron was known as 'La Comète', as portrayed by the colourful markings.

Hawker Hurricane Mk I
Belgium's Aéronautique Militaire (air force) boasted 11 Hurricanes as the most potent of its fighters. The aircraft were very early production machines and retained the original two-bladed propellers.

fighter force of Hurricane Mk Is, Gladiator Mk Is and Fiat CR.42s, fared little better, in spite of the intervention of the RAF. The Hurricanes and Gladiators of the British Air Expeditionary Force (BAEF) were augmented by a number of aircraft operating from the UK. Boulton Paul Defiants, Bristol Blenheims, Hurricanes and No. 66 Squadron's Spitfire Mk IAs were all in action, and receiving their first real taste of combat against the Bf 109E.

Retreat from Rotterdam

Even with the involvement of the RAF, the Dutch considered that the Luftwaffe had gained air supremacy from 11 May 1940. The war in the air was lost, but fighting on the ground continued. Fighting between Katwijk and the Hague proved heavy, and the Willems Bridge was the subject of fierce defensive action. It took the advance of the 9th Panzer Division combined with tactical air strikes against the region of Rotterdam just north of the bridge, to force the Dutch into retreat on 14 May 1940.

During the heat of this final battle, the situation on the ground became very confused, with crossed signals and a general lack of clear communication among the German units. With Dutch resistance proving so strong, Hitler and Göring ordered a massive bombing raid against Rotterdam to bring the campaign to its conclusion. Without realising that the ground forces were already negotiating the Dutch surrender, the Luftwaffe committed its bombers. Some 814 people lost their lives and 78,000 were rendered homeless. The centre of Rotterdam was destroyed, the Low Countries had fallen and the possibility of a German defeat in France was non-existent.

Above: Along with the Bf 109E, the Bf 110C played a major role in Fall Gelb. Here crews of I/ZG 52 (later II/ZG 52) receive a briefing.

Right: 10 May 1940 and Fallschirmjäger streaming from their transports symbolise the end of peace in the Netherlands.

Junkers Ju 88

The Ju 88A formed an important part of the Luftwaffe's triumvirate of medium bombers, seeing action in this role in every German campaign of the war. The good performance and manoeuvrability of the type rendered it more survivable in the face of fighter opposition than the Do 17/217 or He 111.

The Ju 88 V1 first prototype featured large chin radiators for the DB 600 engines, removed on subsequent aircraft. Here, the aircraft is seen with an aft-facing test camera installation above the cockpit.

With the exception of close dogfighting, it is difficult to think of any military duty in World War II for which the Ju 88 was not adapted. The original missions were level- and dive-bombing, but to these were added night-fighting, intruder, anti-ship, reconnaissance, anti-armour, and many more.

Versatility was the last thing considered at the start of the Ju 88 programme. By 1935 the RLM (German air ministry) was doubting the viability of a multi-role aircraft and issued a requirement for a simple *Schnellbomber* (fast bomber) which could fly at 500 km/h (311 mph) carrying a bombload of 1,765 lb (800 kg). Junkers went flat out to win the competition, even hiring two designers from the USA who had pioneered stressed-skin construction (even though Junkers had, by that time, already moved on from its traditional corrugated skin structures). In early 1936 two proposals were tendered, with twin (Ju 85) and single (Ju 88) fins. The Henschel Hs 127 and Messerschmitt Bf 162 were also offered.

Work on the Ju 88 began in May 1936, leading to the first flight of the prototype (D-AQEN) on 21 December, with Flugkapitän Kindermann at the controls. The V1 was powered by two Daimler-Benz DB 600Aa 12-cylinder engines, each rated at 1,000 hp (746 kW), housed in annular cowlings which gave the engines the impression of being radials.

Initial trials proceeded smoothly, the V1 demonstrating a good turn of speed and fine handling. It was lost in a crash in early 1937, shortly before the second prototype, D-AREN, flew for the first time on 10 April. This retained DB 600 power, and differed in only minor detail from the V1.

Jumo power

However, the third prototype (D-ASAZ) was considerably altered. Firstly, it was powered by Junkers' own Jumo 211A engine, of the same power output. It also introduced a raised canopy line to permit the installation of a rear-firing 0.311-in (7.9-mm) MG 15 machine-gun. It also had a more rounded rudder of greater area and a bombsight added in a blister under the nose. The performance of the V3 was very impressive, to the point that three more prototypes were ordered and plans drawn up for a massive dispersed production effort, involving not only Junkers plants at Schönebeck and Aschersleben, but also involving Arado, Dornier, Heinkel, Henschel and Volkswagen factories. Final assembly would

Above: The V3 was the first Ju 88 with Jumo power, and the first to have gun armament in a raised cockpit. Note the bombsight fairing under the nose, offset to starboard.

Left: The V4 introduced the 'beetle eye' nose glazing, which consisted of 20 flat panels. The long engine nacelles, which reached nearly as far forward as the nose, led to the nickname 'die Dreifinger' (three-finger).

Speed record

Although initially completed as a standard bomber prototype, the Ju 88 V5 (D-ATYU) was modified for speed record work as part of Germany's propaganda effort. With ventral cupola removed, cockpit glazing lowered and a solid, pointed nose added, the V5 achieved a 621-mile (1000-km) closed-circuit speed record, carrying a 4,409-lb (2000-kg) payload at 321.25 mph (517 km/h) in March 1939. In July it set another record by carrying the same load for 1,243 miles (2000 km) at 311 mph (500 km/h).

Sporting the four-bladed propellers also fitted to the Ju 88A-0 series, the V6 was an important prototype in that it introduced the remarkable single-strut mainwheel undercarriage. The wheels rotated through 90° during retraction to lie flat at the rear of the slimmer nacelles. Shocks were absorbed by the Ringfeder system, which employed a series of high-tensile steel rings of tapered profiles. These expanded radially under compressive loads, bounce being prevented by the friction as the rings pushed their way apart.

be at Junkers-Bernburg and by other companies (notably Arado at Brandenburg).

Changes specified for the Ju 88 included the addition of a fourth crew member, increased armament and dive-bombing capability. The first two requirements were incorporated in the V4, which flew initially on 2 February 1938. This incorporated the characteristic 'beetle eye' crew compartment with ventral bomb-aiming cupola, which had a rear-facing MG 15 at its aft end.

The Ju 88 V5 (D-ATYU) was similar, but introduced 1,200-hp (895-kW) Jumo 211B-1 engines. This aircraft was then modified for speed record attempts. D-ASCY, the V6, was considered as the first pre-production aircraft for the Ju 88A bomber, featuring four-bladed propellers for the Jumo 211B-1s and a redesigned main undercarriage/ engine nacelle arrangement. The similar

V7 followed on 27 September 1938, after which came the V8 and V9, which introduced dive-bombing capability through the use of slatted divebrakes housed in the wings outboard of the engine nacelles. The final prototype was the V10, which tested external bomb carriers between the fuselage and the nacelles.

A batch of 10 pre-production Ju 88A-0 aircraft followed the prototypes, these incorporating the divebrakes and bomb carriers. All had four-bladed propellers, initially at least. They were issued to a specially-formed unit, Erprobungskommando 88, from March 1939, this unit being charged with service evaluation, the development of tactics and the provision of a nucleus of crews for the first operational unit.

Into service

This first unit, I. Gruppe/ Kampfgeschwader 25, was formed in August 1939, shortly before redesignation as I./KG 30 on 22 September. At the same time a training unit, the Lehrgruppe-88, was established at Greifswald.

Ju 88s were considered operational early enough to just see action during the last days of the Polish campaign. I./KG 30 flew the type's first mission on 26 September 1939, and continued in operation to the final fall of Poland on 6 October.

Among its inventory were several of the pre-production Ju 88A-0s, interspersed with full-production Ju 88A-1s. These differed little from the earlier aircraft, but reverted to three-bladed propellers, setting the basic configuration for all subsequent bomber aircraft.

The crew of four were all housed forward of the wing, the pilot sitting offset to port, with the bombardier behind and to starboard. From this position he could access the ventral cupola for bomb-aiming. Behind the pilot sat the flight engineer, facing rearward so that he could operate the upper gun. Alongside him, but lower, was the radio operator, who could squeeze into the rear of the cupola to operate the ventral gun. The pilot operated a single MG 15 mounted in the starboard side of the windscreen.

As a result of initial combat experience, the A-1's defensive armament was soon increased. The ventral position was revised to accommodate two MG 15s, while further weapons were fitted to fire laterally from the cockpit sides. The maximum bombload consisted of 28 110-lb (50-kg) bombs carried in the two internal bays, with four 220-lb (100-kg) bombs carried externally. Maximum speed was a creditable 280 mph (450 km/h).

Above: This is one of the 10 Ju 88A-0 aircraft, completed with four-bladed propellers. Visible under the wing is the airbrake.

Left: Production of the Ju 88 was undertaken at a massive level from the outset. This is the scene at Aschersleben, where Junkers built fuselages before shipment to Bernburg for final assembly. Other Junkers plants were Halberstadt (wings) and Leopoldshall (tails).

Believed to be the fourth production aircraft, this Ju 88A-1 is seen at Bernburg, with a Ju 86G in the background. The aircraft has yet to be fitted with its defensive armament.

Into France

The German forces moved at lightning speed across the low countries towards France, as they had done in Poland, Denmark and Norway. Using gliders and paratroops, they were able to capture key defences and penetrate France's much-vaunted Maginot line.

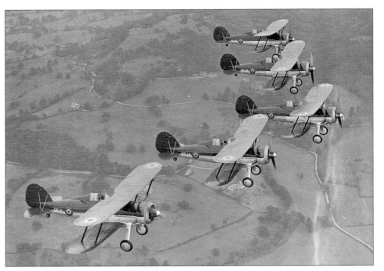

The Belgian air force had little modern combat aircraft with which to counter the Luftwaffe. The most capable fighters available to the Aéronautique Militaire at the time of the German invasion were a handful of Gloster Gladiator biplanes.

Luftwaffe operations in the west began early on 10 May 1940, in support of Operation Fall Gelb (Operation Yellow). Primary attacks began with medium bombers Dornier Do 17s, Heinkel He 111s and Junkers Ju 88s attacking airfields and other key targets around the Hague and Rotterdam in The Netherlands.

The key to success

In order to crush Allied resistance, the Germans first had to capture the heavily armed fortress at Eben Emael in Belgium. The fortress had massive armoured turrets with 4½-in (120-mm) guns and a multitude of anti-aircraft guns. Some of these weapons could fire at distances of more than 12 miles (20 km) and thus it was essential that the fortress was taken if the Germans were to obtain superiority.

For this daring operation, new tactics had to be adopted, a fact recognised by Hitler himself. The answer was to use gliders – the key

to surprise and, ultimately, success.

At dawn on 10 May, a force of Junkers Ju 52/3m transports towing gliders took off and headed towards the fortress. Although outnumbered, the German paratroops quickly captured the bridges surrounding Eben Emael and, using hollow charges, blasted its gun emplacements. The fortress fell the next day with the remaining 1,100 men inside being captured – the Germans had lost only six men. Belgium was now wide open to a German invasion.

The Dutch and Belgian Air Forces tried to stave off the Luftwaffe as much as they could. However, the Dutch Fokker D.XXIs and G.Is, and the Belgian Gloster Gladiators and Fiat G.42 Falcos proved no match for the Bf 109s and 110s of the Jagdgruppen.

Britain had sent reinforcements of the British Expeditionary Force (BEF) to France in an attempt to bolster the already weak Allied forces. The RAF

had also sent an Advanced Air Striking Force (AASF) component, made up mainly of Hawker Hurricane Mk I fighters, Bristol Blenheim and Fairey Battle light bombers and Westland Lysander support aircraft.

RAF involvement

The AASF was in the thick of the fighting from day one and, operating in conjunction with the French Armée de l'Air, managed to achieve some success.

With the Germans having captured Eben Emael, the AASF sent a squadron of Battle Mk Is to attack the bridges on the Albert Canal, near Maastricht, where General Koch's glider troops were located. The raid proved a total disaster with every single Battle being shot down, and only one of the bridges being hit.

With Eben Emael in German hands, Bock's Army Group B continued to press westwards across northern Belgium and The Netherlands. Meanwhile,

THE LUFTWAFFE SMASHES WEST - 10 MAY 1940

In the winter of 1939/40, having drawn both Britain and France into war due to the invasion of Poland, Hitler began to make plans for a westward invasion. He harboured a considerable grudge (dating from the Treaty of Versailles) against the French and was determined to humiliate and crush Germany's western neighbour once and for all. In early May 1940, the Germans' western thrust,

known as Operation Fall Gelb (Operation Yellow), commenced. The Luftwaffe was loosely employed in two Luftflotten, supporting Army Group B (The Netherlands and northern Belgium) commanded by General von Bock, and Army Group A (southern Belgium and France) under General von Rundstedt. Attacks were directed at airfields and communications.

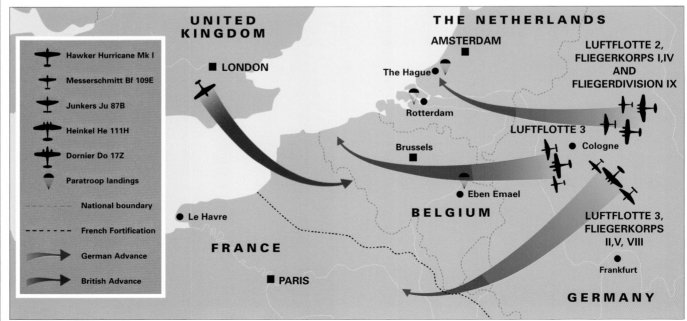

Right: Dornier Do 17s were one of three medium bomber types employed by the Luftwaffe during the offensive in the west. They bombed airfields and Allied communications, gradually whittling away the Armée de L'Air and AASF units.

Below: Although The Netherlands possessed only a small number of aircraft, they fought valiantly against the invaders. Fokker G.1 heavy fighters were among the most capable aircraft available, but were too few in number.

further south, Generaloberst von Rundstedt's Army Group A (comprising the Fourth, Twelfth and Sixteenth armies) marched forward across the Ardennes and Luxembourg towards the French fortifications at Sedan and Montherme just north of the supposedly 'impregnable' Maginot Line.

Along with the advance of ground forces into France, the Luftwaffe mounted further attacks, concentrating primarily on airfields, barracks railway marshalling yards and roads. On 13 May, the Germans emerged from the Ardennes, and two Panzer divisions crossed the River Meuse near Sedan. Operating with them were Ju 87B Stukas of Fliegerkorps VIII, which wrought havoc on the French artillery positions.

Heavy losses

By 14 May, The Netherlands had capitulated and the monarchy had fled into exile. Belgium had been almost completely overrun and the Aéronautique Militaire virtually annihilated.

Both the AASF and the Armée de l'Air put up what brave resistance they could in the face of a resilient enemy. The Bristol Blenheim and Fairey Battle crews proved easy targets for the agile Bf 109s, suffering horrific fatality rates. The fighter units fared little better. Two squadrons of Hurricane Mk Is, Nos 1 and 73, had formed the most modern element of the AASF, but even they suffered heavy losses, with 19 aircraft destroyed and a total of 12 pilots killed in just seven days.

Heavy French losses

Although the French could field close to 1,000 aircraft, the vast majority of them were approaching obsolescence. The Armée de l'Air's primary fighter strength lay in the Morane-Saulnier MS.406, a tough little aircraft which equipped no fewer than 11 Groupes de Chasse. Based alongside these aircraft were American Curtiss Hawk 75As, although in fewer numbers. In the air, they were slow and lumbering, and proved no match for the faster and better turning Bf 109s. Franch bomber and reconnaissance missions were flown by Bloch 174s and Potez 63 aircraft which both suffered heavy casualties. Some 225 of the latter were shot down during that difficult May, the single greatest loss of a sole Armée de l'Air type.

The end in sight

Within a week, von Rundstedt's leading panzer units had firmly established a bridgehead across the lower Somme between Amiens and Abbeville, virtually cutting off from the rest of France what was left of the Seventh Army British Expeditionary Force. What little Allied air power remained began to move backwards towards the coast, leapfrogging from airfield to airfield. Some successes, notably the downing of seven German aircraft by No. 607 Squadron's Gloster Gladiators, had been achieved by the RAF, but such events were proving few and far between.

Facing the German onslaught

The Armée de l'Air was the largest of the air arms facing the Luftwaffe, able to muster nearly 1,000 aircraft. Although courageous, its pilots were mostly poorly trained and ill-equipped to deal with the Germans. The RAF's AASF was a much smaller force, possessing only 60 fighters (including 40 Hurricanes) at the beginning of May 1940.

Morane-Saulnier MS.406

Of all the fighters available to the Armée de l'Air, the MS.406 was available in greatest numbers. Powered by a 860-hp (641-kW) Hispano-Suiza V12 piston engine, it was underpowered, slow, and no match for the Luftwaffe Bf 109Es. During the Battle of France, the MS.406 was credited with the destruction of 175 German aircraft, although more than half of all MS.406s on the Western Front were lost in the process. The fighter illustrated carries the stork emblem of GC1/2, based at Toul/Ochey.

Hawker Hurricane Mk I

At the time of the German invasion in the west, the Advanced Air Striking Force only possessed two squadrons of Hurricanes, Nos 1 and 73 (illustrated). These aircraft were among the best fighters available to the Allies and the only ones really capable of matching the Bf 109s on even terms. The Hurricane's wide-track undercarriage and sturdy design made it ideally suited to operations in France.

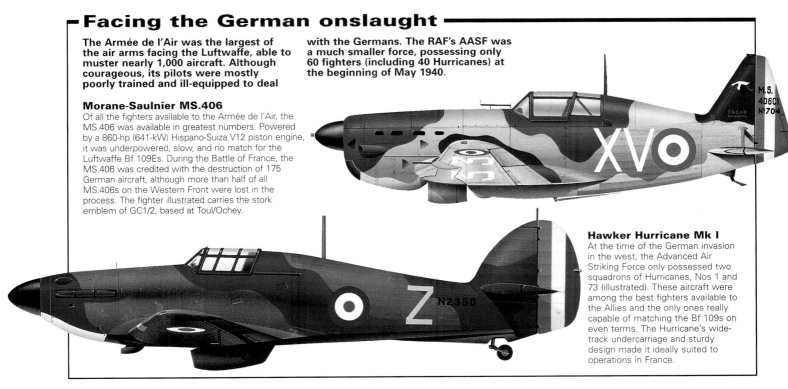

The Fall of France

With the Germans driving deeper into northern France, it became apparent that defeat of the Allied forces was inevitable. The British were beaten back to the coast, where one of the greatest military evacuations in history took place.

Messerschmitt Bf 109Es remained victorious during the invasion of France, as they had done in Poland. Opposition from the British and French air arms was sporadic at best.

By 19 May 1940, it was clear that the AASF could no longer operate safely from French airfields and the decision was taken to return the surviving squadrons to the UK. Although in the first ten days of the German invasion of the West, the AASF had lost only 117 aircraft compared to the Luftwaffe's total of 806, the Germans had a greater number of aircraft available for further combat.

As the remnants of the Allied air component did their best to stave off attacks from Luftflotte 3, General von Rundstedt's panzers reached Abbeville on 20 May. Realising that the Germans were unstoppable, the newly-appointed British Prime Minister, Winston Churchill, ordered Operation Dynamo – the evacuation of all British forces from Belgium and Northern France.

The Admiralty was given the task of planning and organising one of the greatest evacuations in history. Every available vessel, both merchant and military, would be required for the operation, which would be conducted from the beaches at Dunkirk.

The French Prime Minister, Paul Reyaud, had already realised the gravity of the situation following the establishment of the bridgehead over the Meuse by General von Rundstedt's army. On 14 May, Reyaud urgently requested that more British aircraft be sent across the Channel to help bolster the Allied effort. Churchill and the new British War Cabinet agreed, and went as far as to give instructions for despatch of the aircraft. However, the RAF Chief of Fighter Command, Air Chief Marshall Hugh Dowding, disapproved of the idea, realising with considerable foresight that as many aircraft as possible would be needed for the forthcoming German attack on Britain. He was permitted to argue his case before the Cabinet on 14 May, and wrote his now famous and uncompromising letter. This stated that if more fighters were to be sent across the Channel, and if the current loss rate continued, Britain would lose its entire air defence element within a fortnight.

At first, Churchill was unable to understand the situation and, on 16 May, went to France. He soon realised that nothing short of a miracle could save the French. The mood in Paris was one of defeatism and little hope; the French armies were in retreat and morale had completely collapsed.

The effect of Churchill's experience in France was to underline the relevance of Dowding's arguments. British Air Staff were soon convinced that no more British aircraft or pilots should be involved in the Battle of France.

Meanwhile, the 2nd Panzer Division, an element of von Rundstedt's army under the command of General Guderlian, was spearheading further German attacks on France. The speed with which German tanks were rolling across the country was astonishing, and they were accompanied by fresh infantry, thrown into the front line to combat a counter attack by the French. The attack never came. It was cancelled when General Maurice Gamelin was replaced by the elderly General Maxime Weiland, which resulted in the loss of an excellent tactician.

On 26 May, the evacuation of British forces from Dunkirk began, in an operation which would last nine days. By this stage, the Luftwaffe was roaming at will across northern France, the AASF having been withdrawn from the conflict and the few aircraft still possessed by the Armée de l'Air posing no serious threat to the Bf 109s and Bf 110s of the Jagdagruppen. At first light on 27 May, bombers of KG1 and KG4 attacked the beaches and harbour at Dunkirk in continuous waves, managing to sink the 8,000 ton (8128 tonne) *Aden*, while inflicting considerable damage on the docks.

Evacuation begins

By midday, Vice Admiral Bertram Ramsay, leading the Allied withdrawal, managed to commence evacuation of the

ROLE	GERMANY	BRITISH	FRENCH
COMPARISON OF GERMAN AND ALLIED AIRPOWER			
Medium bomber	1,300 x Do 17, Ju 88, He 111	72 x Blenheim Mk IV	221 x Bre.693, 167F, Am.351, F.222, DB-7
Dive-bomber	380 x Ju 87, Ju 88		
Light bomber		84 x Battle Mk I	
Reconnaissance	300 x miscellaneous types		156 x Pz.63.11
Fighter	860 x Bf 109	60 x Gladiator Mk I, Hurricane Mk I	764 x M.B.152, M.S.406, D.520, Hawk 75A
Heavy fighter	350 x Bf 110		26 x Pz.631
Liaison/Observation		82 x miscellaneous types	360 x miscellaneous types
Total	**3,190**	**298**	**1,527**
Aircraft Lost	**1,254**	**193**	**375**

One of the most enduring symbols of Blitzkrieg was the Junkers Ju 87B Stuka. A symbol of Belgium's fate, this machine is parked between two wrecked Belgian CR.42s.

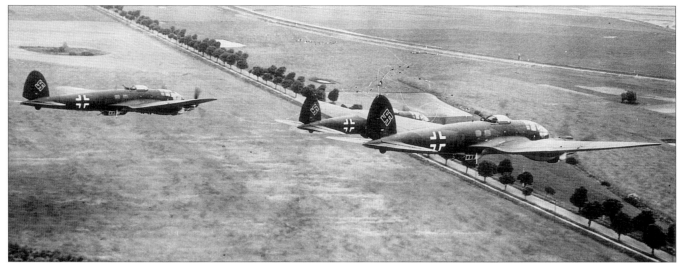

Above: A trio of Heinkel He 111Hs in flight over France. One of three heavy bomber types employed by the Luftwaffe during Blitzkrieg, He 111s played a major part in the bombing of cities, airfields, ports and other key installations. The He 111H variant was to remain the backbone of Luftwaffe bomber units until 1944.

Left: Although the vast majority of France's Groupes de Chasse were equipped with obsolete types, two units of Dewotine D.520s were available in time for the Battle of France. The D.520, powered by a Hispano-Suiza 12Y and armed with a single cannon and four machine-guns, was equal, if not superior, to the Bf 109.

troops. Further attacks by medium bombers (Do 17Zs, He 111s and Ju 88s) continued into the afternoon. At 07.30 the Stukas of VIII Fliegerkorps arrived, eventually putting the quay out of action.

RAF No. 11 Group was able to send a number of Hurricanes and Spitfires to the scene from southern England, although only one squadron at a time appeared over Dunkirk. Nevertheless, the RAF machines managed to destroy a number of German aircraft – nine Hurricanes of No. 601 Squadron managed to fend off a swarm of 20 Bf 109s.

The following day, the weather took a turn for the worse, much to the relief of the British. With very low cloud covering the coast at Dunkirk, the Luftwaffe was unable to conduct successful attacks on the beach head and 17,084 troops were evacuated.

On 29 May, visibility improved and the Ju 87B Stukas of VIII Fliegerkorps recommenced their attacks. They were supported by the Ju 88As of KG30 and LG1, which carried out dive-bombing attacks on the huge number of vessels waiting to transport the BEF across the Channel. The Luftwaffe managed

to sink three escorting destroyers, as well as damaging seven other ships. No. 11 Group was again in action over Dunkirk, committing four squadrons to the battle. Again they were successful, No. 264 Squadron – equipped with Bolton Paul Defiants – managing the destruction of 15 Bf 109Es and a single Ju 88.

On 31 May, the weather began to worsen once more and, with the Stukas of VIII Fliegerkorps grounded due to fog, 47,310 soldiers managed to get away. For the next few days, the bad weather continued to hamper Luftwaffe operations against the Dunkirk beaches and prevented further attacks on Allied ships.

Early on 4 June, the British Admiralty announced the completion of Operation Dynamo. With the British Forces now departed, the Luftwaffe turned its attention to what was left of the French forces. The Armée de l'Air had regrouped on 31 May and now had 16 fighter groups operating in northern France. General Bock's Army Group B began pushing towards Paris, while von Rundstedt's Army Group A marched southwards towards the Alps. By 13 June, French troops had withdrawn from Paris and, the following day, the capital was in German hands. By 21 June, the Battle of France was finally over, and the Luftwaffe began preparing for the Battle of Britain.

Victorious fighters

Throughout the Blitzkrieg campaign in the West, the Messerschmitt Bf 109 had proved virtually unstoppable. Many of the single-seat pilots were veterans of the Legion Condor and had seen considerable action during the Spanish Civil War. The tactics employed by the Luftwaffe pilots exploited the Bf 109's strengths, almost always enabling it to gain the advantage over French and British fighters.

Messerschmitt Bf 109E-3
This particular machine wears the markings of Jagdgeschwader 2 Richthofen, one of the most famous German fighter units of all time. Named after the famous 'Red Baron' himself, JG2 saw much action, claiming to have destroyed 286 enemy aircraft by the end of the campaign in mid-June 1940.

Messerschmitt Bf 109E-3
During winter 1939, the Luftwaffe began adopting this distinctive two-tone splinter camouflage for its fighters. This example, a Messerschmitt Bf 109E-3, belonging to Jagdgeschwader 53 'Pik-As' during the Battle of France, was the mount of then Hauptmann Werner Mölders, possibly the greatest exponent of the legendary Bf 109.

Battle of Britain

Introduction

Having proved unstoppable on the continent, in the next phase of war the Luftwaffe turned on Britain and the RAF's Fighter Command.

Even before completing the French campaign, German strategists were planning the next phase of war against the UK. A speedy conclusion of the war in the west was essential to German strategy. Rather than the Blitzkrieg tactics that had served the Germans so well in Europe, a seaborne invasion of the southern coast of England was planned, preceded by the Luftwaffe achieving air superiority over the south of the UK.

Hitler called for 'unlimited freedom of action' in attacks against Britain when military strength had been regained. Plans for a general air offensive took form. On 30 June 1940 Goering ordered the Luftwaffe to build up bases in northern Europe; test the resilience of RAF Fighter Command's air defences by attacks with small formations of escorted bombers and dive bombers against British shipping; begin a full-scale counter air offensive against the RAF in the air and on the ground; and an aerial blockade of ports and sea communications to prevent the supply of oil, arms and supplies.

Dowding's Fighter Command was organised on a territorial basis, and its force of interceptors operated with a unique system of fighter control based on a line of long-range early-warning radar stations backed by shorter-ranged

stations to pick up elusive low-flying aircraft. Its backbone was 26 Hurricane Mk I squadrons, plus 19 with the Spitfire Mk IA, two with Defiants, and six squadrons with the Blenheim Mk IF fighter.

The Luftwaffe commenced nocturnal operations on the night of 5 June as 30 Ju 88A-1s and He 111H-1s attacked mainland targets. The following night a similar force was sent. Airfields were attacked on 18 June, and thereafter 60 or more bombers operated nightly over the UK. German losses were due mostly to the effects of anti-aircraft fire, despite the average of 40 sorties flown by Fighter Command. Airfield attacks were prompted by Bomber Command's first strategic bombing offensive, on the night of 15/16 May, when 90 Wellingtons, Whitleys and Hampdens attacked the Rühr.

Meanwhile, two Fliegerkorps were assigned to establish air superiority over the English Channel and close it to shipping – tactics employed consisted of freelance sweeps in which the speed and manoeuvrability of the Bf 109E was used to advantage. For the Luftwaffe, no form of ground-to-fighter control existed, and communication between fighters and bombers was unreliable.

Above: A. V. Clowes, DFM climbs aboard his No. 1 Squadron Hurricane with its distinctive wasp markings, in a Wittering blast pen, October 1940. The unit was at Northolt during the summer.

Top: Boulton Paul's Defiant proved itself a failure in the day fighter role as the Luftwaffe quickly came to terms with the limitations of the aircraft's turret-mounted gun armament.

On 2 July 1940 Adolf Hitler issued his first directive concerning the invasion of Britain: "The Führer and Supreme Commander has decided … a landing in England is possible, providing that air superiority can be attained … All preparations to be begun immediately."

An escalation in Luftwaffe activity was evident on 3 July, when a single Do 17Z-1 and a Ju 88A-1 made daylight attacks. Early the following day 39 Ju 87B-2s attacked shipping and naval installations at Portland, and at 14.00 bombers attacked a convoy traversing the Straits of Dover. Inland, single bombers attacked the Aldershot barracks. Convoy and inland attacks by single bombers formed the daily pattern. The most important raids were those on ports during the period 2-9 July 1940: in this week, Dowding sent fighters to defend coastal airfields.

The first major action took place on 10 July 1940: at about 10.50 a Dornier was intercepted by six Spitfires of No. 74

Squadron. At the same time, No. 610 Squadron's Spitfires were engaged over the Channel. At 13.31 radar plots indicated the build-up of a heavy raid. It materialised as some 26 Do 17Z-1s escorted by Bf 110C-2 heavy fighters; a major dogfight involving over 100 aircraft took place off North Foreland, near Ramsgate, when Nos 32, 74 and 111 Sqns intercepted. The fighting on that day is regarded as the first of the opening phase of the Battle of Britain, despite previous operations.

The RAF was forced to defend strategically unimportant convoys, and as a result the Luftwaffe held the initiative: the theatre of fighting was the Channel, where RAF fighter squadrons were disadvantaged, engaged in greater numbers by the Bf 109E holding the tactical benefit of superior altitude. In major battles over the Channel (10 July to 7 August), Fighter Command lost 49 Hurricanes, Spitfires and Defiants, with 30 pilots lost, for combat claims of 108 enemy aircraft destroyed.

13 GROUP (HEADQUARTERS NEWCASTLE)

BASE	TYPE OF AIRCRAFT IN SERVICE/SQN			
	BLENHEIM	DEFIANT	HURRICANE	SPITFIRE
Castletown			504	
Wick			3	
Dyce				603 A
Montrose				603 B
Turnhouse			232, 253	
Drem			605	
Acklington			79	72
Usworth			607	
Catterick	219			
Prestwick		141		
Aldergrove			245	
Sumburgh			232	

12 GROUP (HEADQUARTERS WATNALL)

BASE	TYPE OF AIRCRAFT IN SERVICE/SQN			
	BLENHEIM	DEFIANT	HURRICANE	SPITFIRE
Church Fenton			73, 249	
Leconfield				616
Kirton-in-Lindsey		264 B		222
Digby	29		46	611
Coltishall			242	66
Wittering			229	266
Collyweston	23			
Duxford				19
Ringway	264 A			

11 GROUP (HEADQUARTERS UXBRIDGE)

BASE	TYPE OF AIRCRAFT IN SERVICE/SQN		
	BLENHEIM	HURRICANE	SPITFIRE
Debden		17	
Martlesham Heath	25	85	
North Weald		151	
Hornchurch			41, 54, 65 & 74
Gravesend		501	
Biggin Hill		32	610
Kenley		615	64
Croydon		111	
Westhampnett		145	
Tangmere		43, 601	
Manston	600		
Northolt		1, 257	
Rochford		56	

Gladiator Mk II
By the time the Battle of Britain began, only one squadron of the Gladiator biplane remained in the UK, this being No. 247 Squadron, at Roborough.

Airfield attack
Sheltered by its armoured blast pen, this No. 64 Squadron Spitfire was in the midst of one of the Luftwaffe's strikes on Kenley airfield.

DEFENCE OF BRITAIN, 1940

Dowding's Fighter Command operated in separate groups to defend allocated parts of the British Isles. Each group was in turn divided into sectors. The squadrons and bases are shown as they stood on 8 August 1940, the opening of the Battle of Britain.

Blenheim Mk IF
The Bristol Blenheim 1F was a night-fighter armed with a ventral pack of four 7.7-mm machine-guns. This model pioneered the use of AI (Airborne Interception) radar, and scored the RAF's first AI victory on the night of 2/3 July 1940.

10 GROUP (HEADQUARTERS BOX)

BASE	TYPE OF AIRCRAFT IN SERVICE/SQN			
	BLENHEIM	GLADIATOR	HURRICANE	SPITFIRE
Roborough		274		
Pembrey				92
St. Eval				234
Exeter			87, 213	
Warmwell				152
Middle Wallop	604		238	609

MAP KEY

- ○ Airfields
- ● Towns & Cities
- ⋯⋯ Borders
- – – – Group boundaries

Hawker Hurricane

Overshadowed by the Spitfire, the Hurricane was slower, less manoeuvrable and half a generation older in terms of technology. What mattered was that it was available in numbers and could be adapted to a variety of roles. In terms of victories over enemy aircraft alone, it is undoubtedly the most successful of all British fighters.

Four months before the Spitfire, the Hawker F.36/34 prototype took to the air for the first time on 6 November 1935. Within a month, it had exceeded 300 mph (482 km/h) in testing. By the time war was declared in September 1939, 497 of these aircraft – the RAF's first monoplane fighter – had been completed.

Thrown into action in France in support of the British Expeditionary Force, Hurricane Mk Is suffered heavy losses, but the fact remains that Hurricanes destroyed enough enemy aircraft to make it the most successful British fighter ever built.

At home and abroad

Refined with a variable-pitch Rotol propeller and metal-skinned wings, the Hurricane came into its own during the summer of 1940. It was available in larger numbers than the Spitfire and, by virtue of its simple construction, was better equipped to sustain battle damage from Luftwaffe fighters. More docile, and more forgiving of the novice pilot, the Hurricane was less difficult to fly in poor weather and, in addition, better suited to night operations.

It has been said that the Hurricane served in more theatres than any other combat aircraft of the war, from the Eastern Front to North Africa, Iraq and the Far East. With Spitfires hard-pressed in operations from bases in the British Isles, it was the Hurricane

Above: Soon hard-pressed in the fighter role, the Hurricane was quickly adapted for ground-attack duties, equipped with bombs and rockets. Fitted with twin Vickers 40-mm cannon, the Hurricane took on a 'tank busting' role. So-equipped, the Mk IID, of which 300 were built, entered service in the Western Desert in mid-1942.

Above: Rifle-calibre machine-guns, as fitted to the first Hurricanes, were never very effective against the Luftwaffe bombers' self-sealing fuel tanks. Consequently, cannon soon found their way into British fighters. In the Hurricane Mk IIC, these proved equally effective as ground-strafing weapons.

Left: Mk I L1550 was the third production Hurricane delivered to the RAF. No. 111 Squadron at RAF Northolt was the first unit to equip with the type in January 1938, and helped to defend south-eastern England in 1940.

that was shipped abroad to provide air cover and support for ground forces.

These aircraft not only equipped RAF units overseas, but were also supplied to the Allies. More than 2,800 were shipped to Russia directly from the UK alone; others came from Canada and RAF stocks in the Middle East. After Russia, the Indian Air Force received the largest batch of Hurricanes, over 200 reaching the sub-continent in 1943.

While it lacked the development potential of the Spitfire, the Hurricane was nonetheless progressively improved to take advantage of engine enhancements and the demands of new roles. The Mk II introduced a Merlin XX powerplant with two-stage supercharging and, in successive sub-variants, heavier armament. Many of the latter changes helped to refine the design for the ground-attack role which grew in importance as the Hurricane's shortcomings as an interceptor became more apparent when faced with increasingly modern German opposition.

Bombs and cannon

The Mk IIB, fitted with no fewer than 12 machine-guns, was the first Hurricane mark to carry bombs and gained a suitable nickname – 'Hurribomber'. In common with other British fighters, the Mk IIC gained 20-mm cannon armament, and the Mk IID was equipped with a pair of 40-mm Vickers 'S' guns, ideal for anti-tank work.

The other important weapon associated with the Hurricane was the rocket projectile. This appeared on the Mk IV, a dedicated ground-attack aircraft able to carry a variety of underwing stores, including the 40-mm cannon under a so-called 'universal' wing. Most served in the Mediterranean and CBI theatres.

Night-fighter/intruder operations and tactical reconnaissance were among other roles carried out to a lesser extent by suitably-modified Hurricanes, both at home and overseas.

The Royal Navy, lacking suitable fighter designs of its own, was forced to adapt both the Hurricane and Spitfire for shipborne use, mainly aboard convoy escort carriers. Neither was particularly suitable, but the Sea Hurricane proved more robust than its fragile Seafire counterpart.

After hostilities ceased, Hurricanes found new export customers, including Portugal, Ireland and Iran. For the latter, a unique, two-seat trainer variant was developed. The RAF, meanwhile, quickly withdrew its remaining Hurricanes from front-line service after 1945.

That the Hawker Hurricane occupied a vital place in Britain's history cannot be denied, no less seminal than the introduction of the dedicated fighter in World War I. Put simply, the Hurricane saved Great Britain in 1940; it was the right aircraft, at the right time, and flown by the right pilots.

Britain's saviour

No-one can deny the excellence of the Supermarine Spitfire, nor that it was one of the great fighting aircraft of World War II. Yet, outdated though the Hurricane may have appeared by comparison, its simplicity of concept and operation was such that it could be – and was – despatched to any of the danger spots that spread like cancer during those first three years of the war when events threatened to engulf the Allied nations with disaster.

Flying not only in the great Battle of Britain, but in France, Norway, the Middle East, the Balkans, Malta, El Alamein, Singapore, and off the North Cape, the Hurricane – often arriving two years before the first Spitfires – was able to make its unique contribution to the ultimate victory. When the final analysis was compiled, it transpired that Hurricanes had, by a wide margin, destroyed more enemy aircraft in air combat during World War II than any other Allied fighter and, in fact, more than all other British aircraft put together.

After 1945, most Hurricanes were simply scrapped. Obsolete compared to late mark Spitfires, their usefulness in the post-war RAF was limited. For this reason, few have survived and only a handful of airworthy examples may be seen today. One of these is the last Hurricane built – PZ865. A Mk IIC completed in 1944, it was retained by Hawker, named Last of the Many, and registered G-AMAU. In 1972, it was donated to the RAF's Battle of Britain Memorial Flight, with which it continued to fly in 1998.

The Attack of Eagles

A Bf 110C of Stab I/ZG 52 seen over France in the summer of 1940. Although the big Messerschmitt was a success in mainland Europe, the RAF's nimble fighters were more than a match for the aircraft during the Battle of Britain.

Germany would need to adopt a change of tactics before an invasion of the British Isles could be contemplated. For the invasion to succeed, it was vital for the Luftwaffe to attain air superiority.

The immediate task of the Luftwaffe was to defeat Fighter Command's defensive assets prior to the launch of Operation Seelöwe (sea lion). After Fighter Command's demise, the Germans would be free to engage the home fleet off the coast and, with air bases secured in the south, the Luftwaffe would be able to move up the country. The central objective became confused, however, as various directives and counter-directives weakened the Luftwaffe's essential strategic task.

On 21 July 1940, Goering announced the achievement of his first two aims – the establishment of airfields in Northern Europe and the testing of the UK's air defences. An all-out campaign to win aerial superiority would begin in conjunction with air assaults on sea commerce. However, air strategy was planned on

erroneous intelligence, and the strength of Fighter Command had been underestimated – Goering was confident of its defeat within four days.

Plans for the assault, termed Adlerangriff (Attack of Eagles), were finalised and the date of 13 August 1940 was set. From Scandinavia, the Luftwaffe would attack Scotland and the east; from Belgium, the Netherlands and northeastern France, southern and central England would be targeted; and from northwestern France, the west of England would be attacked. At this time, the Luftwaffe had 3,528 combat aircraft deployed against the UK, including 805 Bf 109E-1 fighters.

The great air battles over the English Channel on 8 August 1940 marked the end of attacks against coastal convoys, as the Luftwaffe turned its attention towards Fighter Command. The

activity of both air arms rose to its highest level as a second phase of action began. E-boats attacked a convoy, destroying three ships and damaging others, under the watchful eye of reconnaissance Do 17s, as Ju 87s clashed with Nos 10 and 11 Groups. At midday, 57 Stukas with Bf 110 escorts and Bf 109 top cover were engaged by four and a half squadrons of Hurricanes and Spitfires. As the convoy reassembled, a further 82 Ju 87s launched another strike, as a full seven RAF fighter squadrons became committed, with Nos 43, 64, 65, 145, 152 and 238 Sqns bearing the brunt of the combat. The RAF suffered 19 losses, but claimed 24 bombers and 36

fighters. Luftwaffe intelligence staff described 'crippling' losses for the RAF, yet German signals intelligence became aware of the capability of the UK's radar defences. The resilience of Fighter Command was also a cause for concern, as was the failure of the Luftwaffe's Bf 110 Zerstörer (destroyer) concept. Furthermore, the potent Bf 109, even in its latest E-4 guise, was hampered by a lack of range.

On 11 August, as bad weather delayed the start of Adlerangriff, docks and shipping were attacked and diversionary attacks launched to confuse radar stations. The RAF lost 32 fighters and claimed

Right: He 111s, blooded over Poland, bore the brunt of Germany's offensive air effort over Britain.

Below: This Do 17 crash-landed at Cormeilles-en-Vexin in September 1940, following a raid over the UK.

This Bristol Blenheim Mk IF of No. 25 Squadron was based at North Weald airfield in early 1940. During the first phase of the Battle, however, the squadron flew from Martlesham Heath, under the command of Squadron Leader K. A. K. McEwan.

38. By 12 August, the Luftwaffe had begun to attack airfields, and radar installations were singled out for dive-bombing and strafing.

Adlerangriff got off to a false start, hampered by bad weather on the 13th, as a first wave of Do 17Z-2s arrived without their escorts. Later that day, large-scale attacks were made, preceded by 30 Bf 109E-4s. Savage combat ensued as the RAF met a mixed fleet of Ju 88A-1s, Ju 87B-2s and Bf 110Cs. Serious damage was inflicted upon Southampton, Stukas hit airfields, and Adolf Galland's III./JG 26 caused losses to the defending RAF. Fighting continued through the night, as Bomber Command hit Milan and Turin and, in turn, the Luftwaffe bombed Belfast. The Germans lost 45 aircraft during 1,435 sorties, downing 13 RAF aircraft in combat.

The following day,

Adlerangriff was conducted on a reduced scale due to poor weather, with strikes taking place on communications, RAF and FAA airfields in the west of England.

The decisive operations of 15 August 1940 marked the first and only entry of Luftflotte V. Its 72 He 111H-1s attacked targets of No. 13 (Fighter) Group, covered by Bf 110D-0 Zerstörers. Additionally, 50 Ju 88A-1s joined in the attack, and all aircraft suffered heavy losses against Fighter Command. The losses of Luftflotte V exceeded half of its total number of aircraft despatched; in all, on this day, the Luftwaffe lost 79 aircraft in return for 34 of Dowding's aircraft.

The losses of *shwarze Donnerstag* (black Thursday) proved that air superiority was necessary if an all-out bomber offensive was to be successful. Diversionary tactics had failed,

the Bf 110D and Ju 87B were proven unsuitable for their tasks, and bombing operations were forced south where Bf 109Es could provide cover.

The RAF discovered that, even though the German bombers had an altitude advantage, they were lightly armed and defended and so were easily shot down. On 16 August, the RAF reported a tactical change by the Luftwaffe, with Bf 109Es flying ahead and alongside the bomber stream, weaving to remain with them. The Luftwaffe attacked southern airfields, with Stukas badly mauled over Tangmere. On that day, the Luftwaffe lost 45 aircraft in 1,715 sorties; of the RAF's aircraft, 22 were destroyed.

After a lull, attacks resumed on 18 August. Dorniers made low-level attacks on Kenley and Biggin Hill, Stukas struck Ford and Thorney Island, while Ju 88s made for Gosport. Nos

10 and 11 Groups battled with the bombers over Sussex, Surrey and Kent. Fighter Command lost 71 aircraft on one of the hardest days of fighting which, together with worsening weather, brought about the closure of the second phase.

During the period 8-18 August, the RAF lost 90 pilots, with 60 wounded. In all, 54 Spitfires and 121 Hurricanes were destroyed, 65 aircraft badly damaged, and 30 destroyed on the ground. Fighter Command was short of 160 pilots, and needed to increase its size. As a result, pilots were taken from OTUs and the squadrons of No. 22 (Training) Group. These pilots, together with those with as little as six hours' flying experience, succumbed to predatory fighters. In the air battles to come, success would rest on the maintenance of pilot numbers.

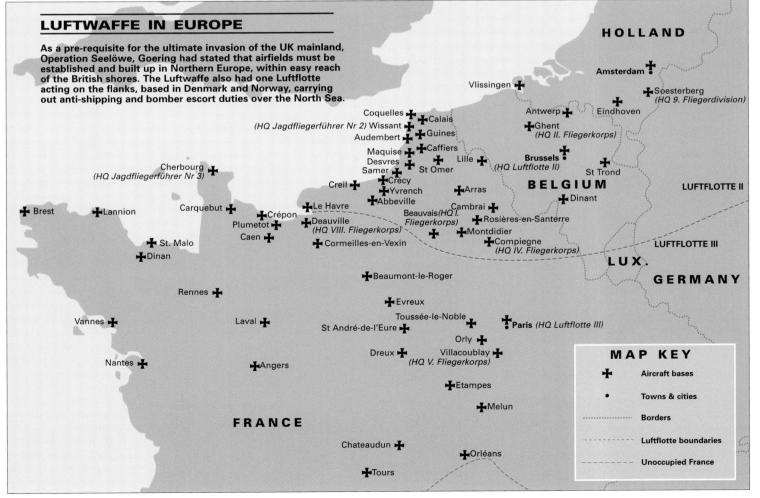

LUFTWAFFE IN EUROPE

As a pre-requisite for the ultimate invasion of the UK mainland, Operation Seelöwe, Goering had stated that airfields must be established and built up in Northern Europe, within easy reach of the British shores. The Luftwaffe also had one Luftflotte acting on the flanks, based in Denmark and Norway, carrying out anti-shipping and bomber escort duties over the North Sea.

HOLLAND

Amsterdam ✠
Vlissingen ✠
✠ Soesterberg (HQ 9. Fliegerdivision)
Coquelles ✠
(HQ Jagdfliegerführer Nr 2) Wissant ✠ — ✠ Calais
Antwerp ✠ — Eindhoven
Audembert ✠ — ✠ Guines
✠ Ghent (HQ II. Fliegerkorps)
Maquise ✠ — ✠ Caffiers
Desvres ✠ — Lille ✠
Brussels ✠
Samer ✠ — ✠ St Omer
(HQ Luftflotte II) — St Trond ✠
Cherbourg ✠
(HQ Jagdfliegerführer Nr 3)
✠ Crécy
Creil ✠ — ✠ Yvrench
✠ Arras
BELGIUM
LUFTFLOTTE II
✠ Abbeville
✠ Dinant
✠ Brest
✠ Lannion
Carquebut ✠
✠ Le Havre
Cambrai ✠
Beauvais (HQ I. Fliegerkorps)
✠ Rosières-en-Santerre
✠ Crépon
Plumetot ✠ — ✠ Deauville (HQ VIII. Fliegerkorps)
✠ Montdidier
LUFTFLOTTE III
Caen ✠
✠ Compiegne (HQ IV. Fliegerkorps)
LUX.
✠ St. Malo
✠ Dinan
✠ Cormeilles-en-Vexin
GERMANY
✠ Beaumont-le-Roger
Rennes ✠
✠ Evreux
Vannes ✠
Toussée-le-Noble ✠
Laval ✠
✠ Paris (HQ Luftflotte III)
St André-de-l'Eure ✠
Orly ✠
Nantes ✠
Dreux ✠
Villacoublay ✠ (HQ V. Fliegerkorps)
✠ Angers
✠ Etampes
✠ Melun
FRANCE
Chateaudun ✠
✠ Orléans
✠ Tours

MAP KEY
✠ Aircraft bases
• Towns & cities
.... Borders
- - - - - Luftflotte boundaries
- - - - - Unoccupied France

Battle of Britain
Fighter Command at bay

Above: The biggest problem faced by the Luftwaffe proved to be massed formations such as this one, comprised of Hurricanes. These fighters were the most numerous in the RAF's inventory.

Left: Based at Carquebut, northern France, the Bf 109E-4s of III./JG 27 flew as part of Jagdfliegerführer Nr 3 on the Central Front during the Battle of Britain.

Luftwaffe losses in the early part of the Battle of Britain prompted a change of tactics from Goering. This presented Dowding with a new threat and Fighter Command soon began to show the strain.

Following the Luftwaffe's massed daylight raids of 8-18 August 1940, the RAF was forced to take into account two crucial factors: a lack of trained pilots, and recent airfield attacks. Although the Luftwaffe's lack of air intelligence had meant that few vital bases had been attacked, some crucial airfields in Nos 10 and 11 Groups had been damaged.

It was clear that the Luftwaffe had abandoned its policy of securing air superiority in fighter-versus-fighter battles over the English Channel, instead turning its attention towards RAF fighters and their vulnerable bases

inland. The Luftwaffe appeared desperate to draw Fighter Command into vast air battles over southeast England.

The first priority for the RAF, therefore, was the defence of prominent sector airfields, most of which lay within the range of the Bf 109E. Costly air-to-air combat was to be avoided.

Meanwhile, Goering was attributing the underperformance of his fighter pilots to a lack of aggression, and charged the aces Mölders and Galland to put the matter right. To improve survival rates and success, the ratio of fighter escorts to bombers would now have to be increased to a ratio of

three to one. Bomber leaders insisted on the escorts remaining close at constant speed, while the fighter leaders believed this would counter the effectiveness of the Bf 109E.

The outcome of the Battle of Britain was to depend on the performance of the opposing fighter organisations. Fighter Command lacked skilled pilots; the Luftwaffe had plentiful numbers of superb pilots, but they had differences of opinion with the bomber crews over tactics.

Both sides were equipped to a similar standard. With the Defiant eventually withdrawn from day-fighting, the RAF's Hurricane Mk Is and Spitfire Mk IIs both proved rugged, reliable and easy to fly although, at high level, the Hurricane was at a disadvantage compared to the Bf 109E. From 24 August-6 September, unrelenting attacks on Fighter Command airfields were kept

up. The majority of the aircraft involved flew from Pas-de-Calais, with attacks typically in groups of three or four, with a heavy escort of Bf 109Es and Bf 110Cs. And, in order to keep his fighter leaders happy, Goering continued to deploy low-level *frei Jagd* tactics.

On 24 August, the attacks began to escalate. Fighter Command lost 22 aircraft, and Bomber Command retaliated with attacks on Berlin, to the embarrassment of Goering. On 26 August, major airfields, including Kenley, Biggin Hill and North Weald, were attacked, and 28 fighters were lost in bitter fighting.

A network of smaller control centres fed radar and Observer Corps information on enemy movements to the centre of Fighter Command operations at Bentley Priory in Middlesex.

A Bf 110C of the Stabsschwarm (staff flight) of I./Zerstörergeschwader 2, based at Amiens in July 1940. The Gruppe was commanded by Major Ott until his death in action on 11 August, when control of this Jagdfliegerführer Nr 3 unit passed to Hauptmann Heinlen.

Above: Squadrons of the Auxiliary Air Force flew alongside their regular RAF colleagues throughout the Battle. Here, crew of No. 610 (County of Chester) Squadron, based at Biggin Hill, relax in the summer heat.

Below: Reichmarschall Hermann Goering, Oberbefehlshaber der Luftwaffe (right), was a World War I ace, a ruthless politician and leader, but not adept when it came to the development of the Luftwaffe's tactics during the Battle of Britain.

Following the losses of 26 August, two Fighter Command Air-Vice Marshals, Park and Leigh-Mallory (leaders of, respectively, Nos 11 and 12 Groups) became embroiled in controversy. Park, who advocated the use of small groups of aircraft for swift reaction to airfield attacks (thereby conserving forces) was at loggerheads with Leigh-Mallory, who favoured the use of large wings. In reality, the 'big wing' concept would have been intimidating, but ultimately not cost-effective.

Fighter Command's heaviest losses came on 31 August 1940; 39 fighters were destroyed (14 pilots killed) in return for 41 German aircraft lost. Massed raids hit the Thames Estuary, Kent, Duxford, Debden and North Weald. Both high-explosive and incendiary bombs were used. The attack on Duxford was thwarted by No. 111 Squadron, but the most serious bomber raids came later in the day, when Croydon, Biggin Hill and Hornchurch were all hit, the latter by Ju 88A-1s and Bf 110C-2 attack aircraft at low level.

The attacks on the airfields and sector stations continued over the next six days, when clear anti-cyclonic weather permitted operations from dawn to dusk. On 1 September, aircraft factories were added to the list of German priorities, with the necessary briefings completed two days later. Among those that came in for immediate attack by day were Vickers-Armstrong at Brooklands (Wellingtons), and Shorts at Rochester (Stirlings). From 29 August onwards, Liverpool, Birmingham, Manchester and other selected targets were attacked by night.

The Luftwaffe's concentration on attacking the fighter airfields brought Dowding's command into crisis: at last, Luftwaffe strategists had found the correct targets with which to draw the RAF fighters into combat and so suffer heavy losses. From 23 August–6 September, the RAF lost 295 aircraft, with another 171 seriously damaged. A combination of RAF repairs and new aircraft production managed to produce 269 new or repaired machines over the same period, however, and the loss of 103 pilots, either killed or missing, and the injuring of 128 was a more severe blow. As many as 120 pilots out of 1,000 were put out of action, including several highly experienced men.

The new or refreshed squadrons reaching No. 11 Group were badly mauled, but it was the combat-experienced ones that survived. For example, between arriving in No. 11 Group and retiring to the less busy No. 12 Group, No. 616 Squadron lost five pilots and 12 aircraft between 25 August and 2 September; during the period 28 August to 6 September, No. 603 Squadron lost seven pilots and 16 aircraft. However, the experienced No. 53 Squadron in the Biggin Hill sector lost only four men and nine of their Hurricanes over a similar period.

As a desperate expedient, Dowding introduced the Stabilisation Scheme, wherein squadrons were categorised into classes: Class 'A' were those in No. 11 Group and the Middle Wallop and Duxford sectors which were always kept up to strength with fully-trained pilots. Class 'B' were those in Nos 10 and 12 Groups which were kept up to strength for the relief of No. 11 Group. Finally, Class 'C' were those in a low state of pilot strength and serviceability, posted far from the theatre of action. By using men drained from the Operational Training Units (OTUs) in August, the battered units of Fighter Command kept fighting with an average of only 10 fully-operational pilots out of the usual establishment of 26. Fighter Command was slowly wasting away.

No. 56 Squadron Hurricanes scramble from their airfield at North Weald during the height of the Battle of Britain. The Hurricane outnumbered its more famed compatriot, the Spitfire, and achieved more aerial kills.

Battle of Britain
The Luftwaffe turns on London

With victory over the RAF in sight, political needs forced the Luftwaffe to change its tactics. Instead of targeting Britain's airfields, the Luftwaffe switched its efforts to bombing London, thus providing Fighter Command with the tactical situation it had been waiting for.

In its quest for supremacy over southern England, the Luftwaffe was close to achieving its objective by September 1940. Although the Germans were not to know, attacks on No. 11 Group airfields had had a devastating effect on Fighter Command's ability to continue operations. The ground-controlled fighter interception system was on the verge of collapse, and fighter losses peaked on 31 August 1940 as the RAF was forced to battle against overwhelming numbers of Messerschmitts. Over the period 23 August to 6 September, 466 RAF fighters had been lost or badly damaged, compared to 138 bombers and 214 fighters of the Luftwaffe; and 25 per cent of Dowding's operational pilots had been put out of action (103 killed and 128 wounded). Moreover, one-third of Fighter Command's forces consisted of barely operational Category 'C' squadrons.

By chance, however, events were to change the fortunes of Fighter Command. In response to scattered bombing of the outskirts of London on 23 August, Bomber Command struck Berlin, an event which Goering had declared to be impossible. A decision was therefore made on 3 September

to concentrate the Luftwaffe's forthcoming bombing campaign on London. The following day, Hitler addressed an audience, promising revenge.

On the morning of 7 September, Invasion Alert No. 1 (invasion imminent) was received by Dowding's HQ, indicating, as was thought, that Operation Sealion was about to be launched. Goering personally directed the attacks of this day, which were the first to specifically target London in great strength.

Some 348 Ju 88A-1, He 111H, and Do 17Z-2 bombers advanced in column along a 20-mile (32-km) front up the estuary of the Thames. Surrounding them were 617 Bf 109Es and Bf 110Cs. By 16.30 around 21 Fighter Command squadrons were in the sky, forming a reaction force of about 280 fighters. Although outnumbered, Fighter Command gave a good account of itself. However, heavy damage had been inflicted on eastern London,

Top: Palls of smoke provide a sombre backdrop for Tower Bridge and the Tower of London as part of the city's dock area blazes in the aftermath of a German bomber raid on the British capital.

Above: The Battle over London as seen from the nose gunner's position aboard a Luftwaffe Heinkel He 111; it was this aircraft that bore the brunt of German heavy bombing operations over Britain.

and fires acted as beacons for the follow-up raids throughout the night, with sorties continuing until 04.30. In total, Fighter Command lost 28 aircraft against 41 German machines.

Poor weather the following day restricted operations, but the Luftwaffe put in a strong attack on London after dusk. Weather continued to hamper the Luftwaffe's raids on 9 September; the only attacks occurred when

26 He 111H-4s attempted to bomb Farnborough. Twenty-eight German aircraft were lost over the 24-hour period, and Luftwaffe crews again reported an upsurge in RAF fighter activity.

After a lull, operations were stepped up on 11 September 1940 when the Luftwaffe attacked Portsmouth and Southampton, and sent in three waves to attack London.

He 111 bombers return from a sortie. The close escort of Bf 109Es that accompanied the aircraft to their targets would have departed when they became short of fuel, leaving the bombers at the mercy of England's air defences.

Right: Contrails in the skies over Kent give a dramatic impression of the churning air battles in which the Luftwaffe bomber forces strove to fight their way past the RAF fighters towards London.

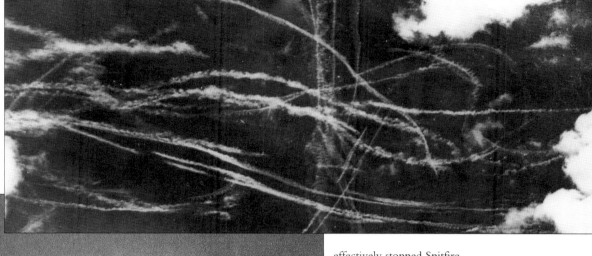

Below: German groundcrew unveil a Kampfgeschwader 26 'Löwen' He 111H from beneath its tarpaulin prior to a mission. Although not a heavy bomber in the mould of the RAF's Lancaster or Stirling, the He 111H could still carry up to eight 551-lb (250-kg) bombs internally, or a single, externally-mounted 4,409-lb (2000-kg) weapon.

Fighter Command losses were high (29 aircraft and 17 pilots), and Luftwaffe raids continued to be launched on London over the next three days, until the weather improved.

On 15 September, radar stations picked up bomber formations as they arrived over the Pas-de-Calais to meet their escorts. The first attack was engaged over Kent, and further mauled as it moved towards London. Scattered bombs fell on London before the bombers retired. Thirty-one Fighter Command squadrons were in the air in the best co-ordinated RAF fighter reaction to date, with furious combat over Kent and Sussex. The day ended with the claim by Fighter Command of a record 185 enemy aircraft destroyed, for the loss of 13 pilots and 26 fighters – a clear victory for the RAF.

Due to the heavy losses that had been encountered on 7 and 15 September, in particular, Goering changed tactics during the following week. Among the changes were reduced formation sizes, attacks that were restricted to London with maximum escort, and the stepping-up of raids on aircraft factories.

By this stage, the preparations for Operation Sealion had been finalised. The continued ability of the RAF to inflict casualties on the Luftwaffe showed, however, that the latter had still not achieved the required air superiority. In addition, Bomber Command and the FAA bombed the invasion fleets at anchor, and the result was that Operation Sealion was postponed.

On 17 September, the Luftwaffe turned its attentions towards oil installations at Thameshaven, preceded by a *frei Jagd* mission by 60 or so Bf 109s over Kent; four raids headed inland, with bombs falling on Chatham. On 25 September, Bristol and Plymouth were attacked during the day, the Filton works being severely damaged. On the following day, the Vickers-Supermarine works were attacked by He 111H-4 bombers, and 70 tons of bombs effectively stopped Spitfire production at this site.

Heavy German losses occurred on 27 September 1940 when new tactics were tried out. Small formations of fast Ju 88A-1s with heavy escorts of Bf 109Es flew *frei Jagd* missions, the high speed of the Ju 88 enabling the Bf 109E to take maximum advantage of its agility. A feint attack failed when it was broken up at Dungeness; a split raid then took place, with 80 or more aircraft making for Bristol, while 300 or more headed across the Channel for London. In the former attack, only the Bf 110C-4s got through, while the latter managed to reach no further than Kent. Fifty-five German aircraft were lost on this day. By the end of September 1940, the majority of the Kampfgruppen within Luftflotten II and III had been withdrawn from daylight operations. After three months and ten days of fighting, the Luftwaffe had lost 1,653 aircraft, with little to show for its sacrifice.

On 1 October, London, Portsmouth and Southampton were attacked, with raids on targets in No. 10 Group meeting stiff opposition. It was noted that the German formations contained many bomb-laden Bf 109Es and Bf 110C-4s. The Luftwaffe's adoption of the Jagdbomber (or fighter-bomber) was now also evident in the raids that streaked across the south to drop their bombs on London that afternoon. The penultimate phase of the Battle had closed.

A Dornier Do 17Z of 4./KG 2 based at Arras in August 1940. The 4. Staffel was part of II Gruppe of Kampfgeschwader 2 'Holzhammer', the Gruppenkommandeur and Geschwaderkommodore being Oberltleutnant Paul Weitkus and Oberst Johannes Fink, respectively.

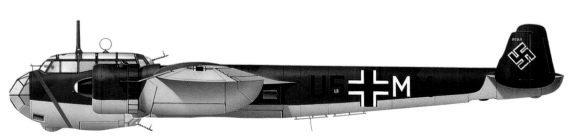

He 111H

A squadron of He 111H-16s maintains a tight formation while returning from a sortie on the Russian front. The H-16 was the third 'standard' production model (following the H-3 and H-6), and was powered by the Jumo 211F-2 engine.

Fitted with Jumo engines, the He 111H became the definitive version of the Luftwaffe's standard bomber. Many sub-variants were produced, and it served from 1939 to the end of the war.

The He 111 V19 (D-AUKY) acted as the prototype for the He 111H, first flying in January 1938. It brought together the rounded nose profile and Jumo 211 engines for the first time.

By the beginning of the Battle of Britain the He 111H had almost entirely replaced the He 111P series. The airframe was essentially unchanged, but the powerplant was the Jumo 211. From the outset, the He 111H, with its 270-mph (435-km/h) top speed, proved a difficult aircraft to shoot down (compared with the Dornier Do 17), and showed itself capable of weathering heavy battle damage. The 17 Gruppen flying the He 111H during the battle operated an average strength of about 500 (compared with He 111P series aircraft, of which some 40 served in the reconnaissance role with the Aufklärungsgruppen), losing some 246 of their number in air combat in the course of the four-month battle. Among the outstanding attacks by He 111s were those by KG 55 on the Bristol aircraft factory on 25 September, and the same unit's devastating raid on Supermarine's factory at Southampton the following day.

The majority of the He 111Hs employed during the Battle of Britain were He 111H-1s, -2s, -3s, and -4s, the latter two initially powered by 1,100-hp (821-kW) Jumo 211D engines. Perhaps the main significance of their losses lay in their five-man crews, whereas the other bombers, the Ju 88 and Do 17, were crewed by only four.

The next variant to join the Kampfgeschwader was the He 111H-5, which incorporated additional fuel tanks in place of the wing bomb cells, and featured two external racks each capable of lifting a 2,205-lb (1000-kg) bomb; its maximum all-up weight was increased to 30,985 lb (14055 kg). He 111H-5s were widely used during the winter Blitz of 1940-41, these aircraft carrying the majority of the heavy bombs and parachute mines to fall on British cities in that campaign. The He 111H-5 could also carry a single 3,968-lb (1800-kg) bomb externally.

Torpedo-bomber

The He 111H-6 came to be the most widely-used of all He 111s, entering production at the end of 1940. With provision to carry a pair of 1,687-lb (765-kg) LT F5b torpedoes, this version was armed with six 0.31-in (7.9-mm) MG 15 machine-guns and a forward-firing 20-mm cannon, and some aircraft featured an MG 17 or remotely-operated grenade launcher in the extreme tail. Despite their torpedo-carrying ability, most He 111H-6s were used as ordinary bombers, the first unit to fly torpedo-equipped He 111H-6s being I./KG 26, flying these aircraft from Bardufoss and Banak in northern Norway against the North Cape

convoys from June 1942 onwards and participating in the virtual annihilation of the convoy PQ 17.

The He 111H-7 and He 111H-9 designations covered minor equipment alterations in the He 111H-6, while the He 111H-8 featured an outsize balloon fender designed to deflect barrage balloon cables to cutters in the wing tips; these were found to be of little use so surviving He 111H-8s were later converted to glider tugs, as He 111H-8/R2s. The He 111H-10 was similar to the He 111H-6 but included a 20-mm MG FF cannon in the ventral gondola and *Kuto-Nase* cable cutters in the wings.

Following the successful use of

He 111Hs as pathfinders by KGr 100, this role featured prominently in subsequent development of the aircraft, the He 111H-14, He 111H-16/R3 and He 111H-18 being specially fitted with FuG Samos, Peil-GV, APZ 5 and FuG Korfu radio equipment for the task; He 111H-14s were flown on operations by Sonderkommando Rastedter of KG 40 in 1944.

As the He 111 was joined by such later bombers as the Heinkel He 177 Greif, Dornier Do 217 and others, it underwent parallel development as a transport; the He 111H-20/R1 was fitted out to accommodate 16 paratroops and the He 111H-20/R2 was equipped as a freight-carrying glider tug.

This black-painted He 111H is seen during the night Blitz of London. The He 111H later proved to be a good platform for the pathfinder mission, with sophisticated navaids.

Above: From the He 111H-5, racks allowed the type to carry large weapons externally. This KG 26 He 111H-6 is seen with an SC 1800 3,968-lb (1800-kg) bomb.

Left: Armourers load two practice LT F5b torpedoes on to an He 111H-6. Although mainly used as a bomber, this variant achieved spectacular success in the anti-ship role while operating with KG 26 in Norway. H-6s were also used for trials of guided weapons such as Fritz-X and BV 246 Hagelkorn.

Nevertheless, bomber versions continued to serve, particularly on the Eastern Front where the He 111H-20/R3 with a 4,410-lb (2000-kg) bomb load and the He 111H-20/R4, carrying 20 110-lb (50-kg) fragmentation bombs, operated by night.

Perhaps the most outstanding, albeit forlorn, of all operations by the He 111H bombers and transports was that in support of the Wehrmacht's attempt to relieve the German 6th Army at Stalingrad between November 1942 and February 1943. As the entire available force of Junkers Ju 52/3m transports was inadequate for the supply task, He 111 bombers of KG 27, KG 55 and I./KG 100 joined KGrzbV 5 and KGrzbV 20 (flying an assortment of He 111D, F, P and H transports) and embarked on the job of flying in food and ammunition to the beleaguered army. Although the bombers were occasionally able to attack Russian armour, bad weather severely hampered the supply operations, and by the end of the Stalingrad campaign the Luftwaffe had lost 165 He 111s, a sacrifice from which the Kampfgeschwader never fully recovered.

He 111H-2

The aircraft depicted here, Wk Nr 3340, 'Yellow B' of 9./KG 53 'Legion Condor' is shown with the wing bars carried (for fighter identification and station-keeping) during the big Luftwaffe daylight raids on London during Sunday 15 September 1940 – the climax of the Battle of Britain. The three white panels have always been said to indicate the III. Gruppe of a *Geschwader*, although so many anomalies exist as to throw doubt on this assumption. This aircraft was in fact damaged in action on that day and force landed at Armentiers with two wounded crew members; recent computerised research suggests that it was probably attacked by Spitfires of No. 66 (Fighter) Sqn.

Armament
The He 111H-2 introduced better defensive armament in the form of five MG 15s, firing through beam hatches, from the dorsal turret and rear of the ventral gondola, and from the Ikaria spherical mounting in the nose. Many aircraft were field-modified with an additional MG 15 in the right upper nose glazing, while the H-3 introduced a 20-mm MG FF in the forward part of the gondola. The next major model, the H-6, often featured an MG 17 in the tailcone. The bombload was carried internally in two ESAC bays, either side of a gangway which led from the forward to the aft crew compartments. The standard load was eight 551-lb (250-kg) bombs, carried vertically with the nose uppermost. The H-4 and H-5 introduced external bomb carriage, the internal bays being used for extra fuel if required.

Structure
The wings were built around a two-spar structure, which carried through the fuselage fore and aft of the bomb bays. Interspar fuel tanks were situated inboard and outboard of the engine nacelles. The rear fuselage was largely empty, providing stowage space for the master compass and emergency dinghy.

Accommodation
The standard crew was five. The pilot sat back in the glazed section, offset to port. The navigator/bombardier sat alongside for take-off, but for operations moved forwards to the extreme nose. In the rear was the radio operator/dorsal gunner. Two further gunners were carried, to operate the weapons in the beams and ventral gondola, which was known to the crew as the 'Stertebett' (death-bed).

Powerplant
The He 111H was the Jumo 211-powered version intended for parallel production with the DB 601-powered He 111P. The first H-0/H-1 aircraft had the Jumo 211A-1 rated at 1,010 hp (753 kW) for take-off, but the H-2 introduced the 1,100-hp (820-kW) Jumo 211A-3.

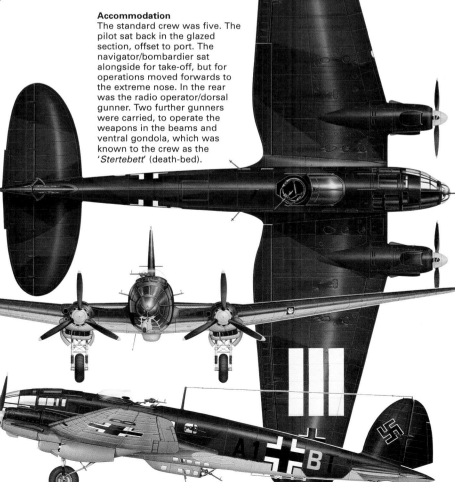

Above: The Defiant in its AI radar-equipped Mk II guise was the most successful of all RAF night-fighters during the winter of 1940-41.

Left: A very hastily night-camouflaged Heinkel He 111 bomber of KG55 is seen flying over France during the night blitz period of early 1941.

Night Blitz

Prompted by the RAF's earlier successes, Goering switched bombers to night operations, thereby losing sight of the very reason for the Battle.

As the fourth phase of the Battle of Britain ended, the limited nature of the Luftwaffe's aerial campaign was realised. The accuracy of *Jabo* raids was minimal; although interception of these raids was difficult, they had little more than nuisance value. The Luftwaffe's massed daylight raids finally ceased on 31 October. Between 1 July and 31 October, the Germans had lost 1,789 aircraft while the RAF had lost 1,603. *Frei Jagds* continued, but failings in policy and tactics meant that the

Luftwaffe was unable to achieve air superiority.

Although the RAF was ahead of the Germans in the acquisition of a radar-aided air defence system, it was far behind them in terms of night operations. During the summer of 1940, when Britain began to come under sustained night attack, defences relied entirely on visual contacts and inefficient sound-locator devices. Unlike the RAF, the Luftwaffe was well versed in the use of radio as a blind-flying aid, all-weather

airfield operations, blind landing and approach, ground control and radio beacons and searchlight aids. Most importantly, they were equipped for blind-bombing with the use of radio.

When the RAF discovered the extent of Luftwaffe night bombing aids, an emergency committee met on 16 June 1940. As a result, a specialist unit, No. 80 (Signals) Wing, was formed in order to jam the bombers' equipment with VHF beams. However, such was the superiority of German all-weather navigation, that the efforts of No. 80 Wing made little impact.

The first main phase of the Luftwaffe's night-time offensive was concerned with bombing London alone, with the aim of bringing the government to the point of surrender. The raids started on the night of 7-8 September 1940 and ended on the night of 13-14 November.

The first wave on 7–8 September comprised 40 or more aircraft and was followed by another two similar waves. Shortly after 20.30, bombs began to fall on Battersea, Paddington and Hammersmith. Two Hurricane Mk IAs on patrol near Tangmere saw nothing as the bombers left; indeed, anti-aircraft

Right: Dornier Do 17Zs set off in the gathering dusk. These aircraft equipped nine Kampfgruppen during the Battle of Britain. Their relative obsolescence is reflected in the high loss rates to nimbler enemy fighters and AAA.

Below: A pair of KG55 Heinkel He 111s taxis from its operating airfield in northern France. Considered the most valuable target by the RAF, these under-defended bombers were targeted by specially-tasked Hurricanes.

Eighty Fiat BR.20M Cicognas, like this one based at Melsbroek in Belgium, were involved in the Battle. In one major raid on 11 November 1940, six bombers and three of their CR.42 escort fighters were shot down after meeting 30 Hurricanes.

artillery (AAA) in the London zone did not start firing until the first bombers had left for home. Thereafter, between 23.20 and 03.15, a constant procession of bombers headed north to strike London. During the night, 327.74 tons of high explosive (HE) and 13,000 incendiaries were dropped. RAF fighters made no contact with the bombers. During this phase, the Luftwaffe directed 57 major raids against London, dropping some 13,140 tons of bombs and incendiaries. The average nightly effort was 200 sorties throughout September 1940, with 38 aircraft lost to British defences.

By September 1940, Dowding's Fighter Command had eight dedicated night-fighter squadrons. At the heart of these were the Blenheim Mk IF and Mk IVF, with smaller numbers of Defiants, and Beaufighter Mk IFs in the trials phase. Several squadrons of Hurricanes were also switched to night work. Prior to this, the AI Mk III radar (with a 2-mile; 3.2-km detection range) had been tested, and the first kill using this radar was achieved on the night of 22-23 July. Meanwhile, the GCI (ground-controlled interception) system was undergoing trials in order to supplement the short-ranged AI Mk III (and later AI Mk IV) devices. GCI would guide night-fighters to their targets before they were within the range of their own radar.

In November 1940, Goering ordered that London should remain the primary target for bombers. The plan was for fighter-bombers to attack during the day; industrial areas to be attacked by night; shipping routes to be mined; Rolls-Royce aero-engine works to be destroyed; Fighter Command to be hit by *frei Jagd* sweeps; and aircraft industry and night-fighter bases to be attacked.

The night assault was intended to destroy the UK industrial base and bring about defeat as the urban population was paralysed. During the night of 14-15 November, London experienced an attack by He 111H-3s before a similar force arrived at Coventry at 20.20. A constant flow of 449 bombers dropped 420 tons of HE and incendiaries over the city until 06.10, with colossal destruction ensuing. RAF night-fighters flew 123 sorties without success.

Major raids

More than 700 bombers attacked Birmingham on 19-20 November, and this raid was followed by others during the remainder of the month, and during December on London, Bristol, Plymouth, Liverpool, Southampton and Sheffield. London suffered huge fires (up to 30 major conflagrations) on the night of 29-30 December, as the Guildhall was burned down.

In November 1940 RAF night-fighter operations by Hurricanes, Defiants, Beaufighters, and Blenheims were complemented by 'cats-eye' Hurricane missions to spot bombers with radio transmission (R/T) guidance and visual contact. The installation of AI Mk IV and GCI stations was proceeding slowly. Although a Beaufighter scored the first AI Mk IV assisted air-to-air victory, only three enemy bombers were claimed by night-fighters by the year's end.

Meanwhile, the RAF was busy with night attacks on German cities and airfields, countering German navigational aids with jamming. It was also experimenting with Douglas Havoc Mk Is fitted with lights for illuminating bomber formations, and attempting to use aerial mines, although without success.

The bad weather of early 1941 curtailed Luftwaffe night operations, and jamming began to take full effect. However, a new phase began on the night of 19-20 February 1941, with the Luftwaffe turning its attention to the blockade of Britain by attacking shipping, and mining, in addition to the continued bombing of cities and industrial sites.

From 19 February to 12 May, there were 61 raids by 50 aircraft or more, the majority focused on ports in the south west of the country. However, RAF GCI stations were increasing – by April 1941 there were 11 such stations operating in key sectors. By March, six squadrons had been fitted with the AI Mk IV.

During the month, the RAF flew 1,005 night-fighter sorties with 48.5 kills. By May, 3,230 sorties had produced 96 kills by night, as the bulk of Luftwaffe operations began to be withdrawn from the UK.

As early as December 1940, Luftwaffe units had been moved to the Mediterranean. In April 1941 bombers were posted to the Balkans, and aircraft in France and Belgium began to be moved for operations in the East. The remaining units flew their last sorties over the UK at maximum strength on 10-11 May 1941 when 550 bombers devastated London with 708 tons of HE and 86,700 incendiaries. By the end of May 1941, only anti-shipping and mining units remained in the West. Germany's accent on anti-shipping by aircraft and U-boats indicated the policy adopted by Hitler and the Oberkommando der Wehrmacht: the UK was to wither through starvation and lack of supplies, and its surrender would follow the successful conclusion of Germany's campaigns in Russia.

Above: Dornier Do 17Zs seen over southeast England, the light-coloured marking on the wingtip probably marking this particular Gruppe's location within the bomber stream.

Left: Such was RAF Fighter Command's success against daylight bomber formations such as this, that the Luftwaffe offensive was quickly switched to night operations.

Cross-Channel operations

Offensive in the West

By December 1940, both the Luftwaffe and RAF were exhausted from the fighting of that summer and autumn. Nevertheless, RAF Fighter Command took up the offensive in a campaign that was to lead to it winning air superiority in the West some three years later.

On 20 December 1940, two Spitfires of No. 66 Sqn set off from Biggin Hill bound for France. Arriving in the vicinity of Berck and Le Touquet, they flew unnoticed at low altitude until they reached their target, where they strafed power transformers, camps and traffic on the roads. This mission marked a change in policy by Fighter Command as it was the first offensive sortie flown since June 1940. In the previous months, Britain's fighters had adopted a defensive stance against the prowling bomber forces of the Luftwaffe. An embryonic night-fighter force of Bristol Blenheim Mk IVFs and Bristol Beaufighters had been set up with little success, but daytime raids by the Luftwaffe were practically non-existent. As Great Britain awaited the very real threat of invasion, it was decided that the best form of defence was to go on the offensive.

The original advocate of an offensive ideology had been Air Vice Marshal K. R. Park who, in October, had called for the use of pre-emptive fighter sweeps across the Straits of Dover whenever a Luftwaffe raid was known to be in the process of assembly. However, these tactics were not used until the appointment of Park's successor, Leigh-Mallory, who declared that the Germans were having an easy time on the French and Belgian coast and if British forces could begin to harass them, it would surely begin to erode the morale of the Luftwaffe.

Offensive sweeps were to be carried out by large numbers of RAF fighters which were to scour the French skies for the enemy. Low-level missions that consisted of pairs or sections of fighters operating over enemy territory under cloud cover were called 'Rhubarb'. 'Intruder' operations consisted of Blenheims

and, later, Havocs patrolling the night bomber bases of the Luftwaffe. Then there was the so-called Operation Circus, the objective of which was to provoke the Germans into sending over a few bombers escorted by up to 200 fighters. Over the ensuing months, operations like these became daily routine for RAF Fighter Command.

Initiative taken

On 9 January 1941, Fighter Command launched its first sweep. Hurricanes of Nos 1 and 615 Sqns patrolled Cap Gris-Nez, while Spitfires of Nos 65, 145 and 610 Sqns circled over the Boulogne-St Omer area. However, the Luftwaffe refused to rise to the bait and stayed on the ground. It was then decided that bombers would accompany the fighters in an effort to lure the German fighters into the sky where they could hopefully be picked off by RAF aircraft.

The first of these 'Circus' operations was launched on 10 January, when fighter-escorted

Blenheim Mk IVs of No. 2 Group set off to attack military camps and dispersal pens in the Forêt de Guines in the Pas-de-Calais. The Blenheims had close escort from Hurricanes and high cover from Spitfires. The 'Circus' went according to plan and the forests were bombed successfully. The bombers then exited the area at low level with a few Bf 109Es in pursuit. Several enemy kill claims were made to the loss of one Hurricane. A number of RAF fighters also peeled off to ground level to seek out and destroy targets of opportunity. The essence of this operation had been to draw the German fighters into the air as they were never more vulnerable than when taking off and assembling, and recovering and landing.

Although few opportunities arose for the RAF fighters on this first 'Circus', the use of aggressive tree-top tactics augured well for the future. However, timidity from higher levels called for the practice to stop, claiming that '... we should be wise to go slowly and content ourselves with attempts to surprise

Although part of RAF's Coastal Command, No. 22 Sqn spent the tough winter of 1940-41 flying offensive bombing missions against coastal targets in western France, using the Beaufort Mk I.

Built on the initiative of the Bristol company, the Beaufighter – with its distinctive jutting engines – transformed the RAF's ability to defend southern England against the Luftwaffe's night blitz.

Part of RAF Bomber Command's No. 5 Group Pool, No. 185 Sqn operated Hampdens (illustrated) and also a single flight of unreliable Dagger-engined Herefords. The squadron was nominally a training unit and met with little success during its Hampden/Hereford operations.

and confuse the enemy'. There was neither surprise nor confusion in store for the Jagdgruppen based in France when the second 'Circus' was planned, with the RAF's fighters remaining at height. This order remained in effect until late 1943, the Luftwaffe fighters therefore being able to take off and land with impunity.

Following two sweeps and a bomber attack on Boulogne on 2 February 1941, the Luftwaffe this time reacted. The second 'Circus' on 5 February consisted of 12 Blenheims which were to bomb St Omer-Wizernes (Longuenesse) airfield where elements of Mölders' JG 51 were based. However, the operation did not go as planned, with several squadrons missing their rendezvous. Furthermore, when the bombers reached the base, heavy snowfall meant that target identification was difficult, with the bombers making two passes before dropping their bombs.

Though no major combat engagements took place, 50 Bf 109Es of JG 3 and JG 51 engaged the RAF squadrons in a series of slashing attacks. Ultimately, the mission was considered a failure, with minimal target damage plus the loss of eight fighters.

Offensive problems

Notwithstanding the obvious disadvantage of fighting in enemy airspace, Fighter Command's squadrons were faced with the tactical problem of escorting slow-flying bombers with the Spitfires and Hurricanes which had a small radius of action. There was also the continued excellence of the German fighters to contend with, plus the lack of the element of surprise.

To improve cohesion in the air, from early March 1941 squadrons were organised on the basis of a wing formation in which three or more squadrons operated under a

fighter leader of proven ability. The wings were not specialised and could perform escort, high cover and escort cover missions on rotation. Production of the Spitfire Mk IIA and Mk IIB redressed some of the disparity with the Bf 109E-4 at high altitude, but the lack of range was a continuing bugbear. At present, only non-jettisonable tanks could be fitted and these made the Spitfires and Hurricanes, which had been built for short-range defensive operations, unwieldy in combat. The fighters had a range of only 70-80 miles (113-129 km) inland of the Pas-de-Calais, where there lay few targets of economic and military value.

Operations to June 1941

Following the end of active daylight raids in December 1940, the bulk of the Luftwaffe's fighter force remained in the West. It consisted mainly of Bf 109E-4, E-7 and Bf 110C types. An added defensive commitment came when these were ordered to defend the battle cruisers *Scharnhorst* and *Gneisenau*, as they lay at harbour at Brest, from coming under attack by RAF bombers. In February 1941, the Luftwaffe was bolstered by the appearance of the Bf 109F-1 and F-2 which were faster than their predecessors, but less heavily armed. The Germans could also count on a series of radar systems

that were being built along the German-held coastline.

The failure of the 5 February 'Circus' brought into question Fighter Command's new policy, with Churchill himself questioning the waste of fighters when the threat of invasion still existed. However, the missions continued and, along with the 'Circuses', 'Rhubarbs' and fighter sweeps, anti-shipping missions – known as 'Roadsteads' – were introduced.

'Circuses' number three and four were operated on 10 February, with Mölders' JG 51 providing the opposition. The great ace scored his 56th kill that day, while the first Bf 109F-1 was lost in combat. The results for Fighter Command were not good, with 11 pilots missing for only eight German aircraft claimed to have been destroyed.

Over the next few months the 'Circuses' continued, with the tenth being the final mission. Up to 13 June 1941, the offensive policies of the RAF resulted in claims for 39 German aircraft destroyed, while 50 RAF pilots were posted as missing or killed. In return, the Luftwaffe lost 58 Bf 109s between 1 January and 13 June 1941; the results were about even. A new phase in the West was about to start however, with the movement of the Luftwaffe eastwards for the impending invasion of the Soviet Union.

RAF fighters of 1940-1941

During this period, the RAF operated a range of fighters which had different roles to play. Spitfires and Hurricanes dominated the daylight defensive and offensive fighter sweep roles, while aircraft such as Beaufighters and Havocs took on the Luftwaffe at night with mixed results. Some Hurricane units, such as No. 85 Sqn, were recast as night-fighter units and received matt black camouflage.

Beaufighter Mk I
This is one of the very first production Beaufighter Mk I night-fighters, delivered without radar in September 1940 and assigned to No. 25 Sqn during the winter of 1940-41. Most of these early aircraft were retrofitted, either at the base unit or at Ford or St Athan, with AI Mk IV and other devices.

Spitfire
No. 66 Sqn was one of those to use Spitfires with a single 40-Imp gal (182-litre) non-jettisonable fuel tank on the left wing (Supermarine Type 343 wing). This particular Spitfire was a Mk IIA, built at Castle Bromwich in 1940.

Douglas Havoc
This aircraft was delivered to the RAF as a Boston Mk I, but was converted to a Havoc Mk I night intruder for No. 23 Sqn.

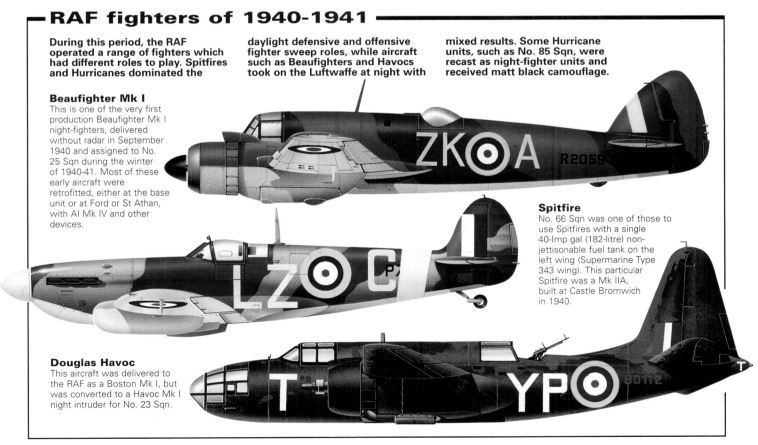

The great fighter offensive

Equipped with Spitfire Mk VBs, No. 81 Squadron became part of the Hornchurch wing. Throughout the summer of 1941 the squadron was heavily involved in aerial battles over France.

RAF Fighter Command's attempts to mount an offensive in the West had hitherto been of an experimental nature, with little strategic value. Nevertheless, Hitler's invasion of the Soviet Union gave the British Air Staff a valid reason for launching a massive operation to keep the Luftwaffe on the alert.

Despite the cloak of secrecy surrounding the transfer of German units to the Russian Front, the British were kept informed by means of 'Ultra', which deciphered coded messages. Apart from supplying arms and materials to the Russians, there was not much that beleaguered Britain could do. Hitler had already indicated that, when the campaign in Russia was completed, the Wermacht would return to face the UK once again; bombing followed by invasion could take place during the spring of 1942. This factor, therefore, explained the reluctance of the RAF Air Staff to part with UK-based squadrons for service overseas. With defence uppermost in their minds the Air Staff nevertheless sanctioned the forthcoming spate of offensive operations by Air Marshal 'Sholto' Douglas's RAF Fighter Command. The arch advocate of the offensive was the volatile and

ambitious AOC of No. 11 (Fighter) Group, Air Vice Marshal Trafford Leigh-Mallory.

On 14 June 1941, the weather proved good enough for the launching of 'Circus' No. 12 after a break of some three weeks; the target was the airfield at St Omer. Twelve Bristol Blenheim Mk IVs of Nos 105 and 110 Squadrons (No. 2 Group) were escorted and supported by nine squadrons of Hawker Hurricanes and Supermarine Spitfires. Much thought had been given to tactics since the start of 'Circus' operations in January 1941. The object was still to drive the Luftwaffe into the air for a fighter battle, and as events in the past had proved that German fighters stayed on the ground in the face of RAF fighter sweeps, the bombers were required to hit 'sufficiently valuable' targets to prompt a reaction. On this day, however, I./JG 26 was caught

Photographed prior to delivery, these Bf 109F-2s demonstrate the unbraced tailplane and retractable tailwheel introduced by this improved Bf 109 variant. This new Bf 109 model, combined with revised tactics enabled German pilots to match their RAF foes.

napping, and Squadron Leader James E. Rankin of No. 92 Squadron shot down and killed Oberfeldwebel Robert Menge near Marquise. Menge had 18 kills to his credit at the time of his death.

Offensive continues

Three days later, RAF Fighter Command launched its greatest offensive operation to date. With zero hour (Z – time of setting course from assembly point) at 19.15, the Kuhlmann et Cie chemical-benzole factory at Chocques was the target for the 18 Blenheims of No. 2 Group. The bombers were to fly at

about 12,000 ft (3660 m) with an escort wing of Hurricane Mk IIAs (Nos 56, 542 and 306 Sqns), a high-cover wing of Spitfires (Nos 74, 92 and 609 Sqns) at 18,000 ft (5485 m), and another five wings acting on freelance sweeps and patrols. 'Circus' No. 13 (as the mission was known) formed up over Manston; Blenheims, Spitfires and Hurricanes, some 120 in all, orbited for position in complete R/T silence. But German radar had already detected the build-up. As the formation made its way across the Channel, elements of JG 26 took on the RAF fighters in a series of running battles near Le Touquet.

Without power-operated gun turrets, the twin-engined Hampden had inadequate firepower against the German fighters. Many fell – to the guns of Bf 109s – during the RAF's early bombing campaign.

Short Stirling Mk Is similar to those above flew their first bombing mission in February 1941. Although agile for their size, the Stirlings suffered from a lack of power when fully laden.

Few dogfights took place – the Spitfires and Hurricanes could out-turn the Bf 109Fs, and so the German pilots adapted their tactics accordingly. Fast, accelerating dives out of the sun, a snap burst of 0.31-in (7.92-mm) MG 17 and 15-mm Mauser MG 151 fire, and a half-roll and away were the accepted tactics of the erstwhile 'Abbeville Boys' and 'St Omer Kids', as the RAF had nicknamed the German squadrons. In all, 11 RAF fighters were shot down (nine pilots failed to return) for claims of 15 destroyed, 7 probably destroyed and 11 damaged. In fact, two Bf 109s were shot down and one Bf 109F-2 was damaged.

Into battle

On 21 June Fighter Command launched 396 sorties on 'Circus' No. 16 (St Omer-Wizernes) at 12.00, followed by 'Circus No. 17 (Desvers) at 16.00; combats were many, with RAF claims standing at 17 for the loss of six aircraft and two pilots. The last 'Circus' resulted in the RAF enjoying a highly successful day, in which the

tactics in use pointed the way forward. The RAF had brought the Luftwaffe into the air and engagements had worked out to the advantage of the British despite the fact that they were operating over enemy ground. And the trend continued. The 'Circus' operations received official Air Staff backing from 19 June 1941, when it was decided that overt assistance must be given to the Russians, and that night bombing of the Rhur communications should be carried out as well as attacks on shipping traversing the Straits of Dover.

In the fighter offensive, Blenheims were to be supplemented by Handley Page Hampdens, and on occasion by the heavy Short Stirling Mk I. The objective was to bring pressure on the Luftwaffe in the West so as to force it to withdraw units from Russia. From this point, RAF operations escalated into an almost daily cycle of sweeps over occupied France.

The British found the Bf 109F-2 to be extremely fast, equalling the performance of the new Spitfire Mk V series that

was rapidly coming into service. However, unknown to the RAF was the impending introduction of the more capable Bf 109F-4, which began combat operations in July 1941.

During July, there was a total of 35 'Circuses' with the RAF losing some 99 Spitfires, Hurricanes and Westland Whirlwinds. Stirlings joined the fray from 5 July to participate in raids on Le Trait. In total, these offensive sweeps over France resulted in the RAF losing around 110 aircraft. This far exceeded the losses of the previous month (56 aircraft) and resembled the daunting losses of summer 1940.

Offensive fails

The whole concept of 'Circus' operations was questioned at a conference held at the Air Ministry on 29 July 1941; much doubt had been voiced over the value of such expenditure for so little gain. Bomber Command felt that Fighter Command was committing exactly the same errors as those of the Luftwaffe in the Battle of Britain. They felt that it was useless to conduct a day bombing offensive unless strategic value could be gained, and that the limited range of the Spitfire VB precluded such an offensive. Operations were allowed to continue, but by this time the balance was turning in favour of the Luftwaffe. Losses occurred throughout August to both sides, but many were to be RAF fighters – the introduction of the new radial-engined Focke-Wulf Fw 190A-1 in July 1941 came as a nasty surprise to the hard-pressed RAF fighter pilots.

At the end of August, Fighter Command's offensive policy was again questioned: losses were high

and results disappointing, and a myriad of commitments was now pressing the RAF in North Africa and the Mediterranean. Only 12 'Circuses' were flown in September, but results were still poor. During the following month, operations continued but often with disastrous results; on 13 October, 10 Spitfires were shot down in a single operation, many falling to the guns of Fw 190s. This was to be the last 'Circus' of the month, although operations against German shipping continued.

In one final bid to validate the 'Circus' operations, Blenheims with an escort of Spitfires crossed the Channel to attack a large troop concentration in France on 8 November. The Blenheims never located the target due to a navigational error and 16 Spitfires, intercepted by German fighters, were quickly shot down. It was an unfortunate end to an offensive that had been bravely fought by the RAF.

On 13 November 1941, a directive from the Air Ministry to both Fighter and Bomber Command ordered the ending of all but the most essential operations in order to conserve strength. During the period 13 June to 31 December 1941, the squadrons of RAF fighter Command had claimed 731 enemy aircraft destroyed (mostly Bf 109s) for the loss of 411 pilots and over 600 aircraft: actual Luftwaffe losses amounted to 135 fighters.

Whirlwinds over France

Holding the distinction of being the RAF's first purpose-built twin-engined fighter, the Westland Whirlwind entered service with No. 263 Squadron in July 1940 and with No. 137 in September. With excellent performance at low altitude, the Whirlwind was at a distinct disadvantage when in dogfights at high altitude. Operations were subsequently restricted to low-level light bombing attacks.

Unreliable engines
Throughout its service the Whirlwind was dogged by problems with its Rolls-Royce Peregrine inline piston engines. Their unreliability in flight caused many pilots to enter a spin, from which few recovered. Only 122 examples were built, serving with two RAF squadrons.

In its day and at low level, the Whirlwind had few equals in terms of speed and armament. This example carries a 250-lb (113-kg) bomb under each wing.

Camouflage colours
Operating with No. 263 Squadron in the winter of 1941-42, this Whirlwind displays the early camouflage scheme of Dark Green and Dark Earth with Sky undersurfaces. The Dark Earth was later replaced by Ocean Grey.

Focke-Wulf supremacy

In December 1941, Japan entered World War II and the conflict became global. Although a German invasion in 1942 seemed unlikely, much of the RAF's strength was dedicated to the defence of the UK.

The Air Staff directive of 13 November 1941, curtailing all but the most important RAF operations over northern Europe, gave both Commands a much-needed respite. Poor results and a lack of accuracy achieved by Bomber Command during 1940-1 had damaged the credibility of a large bomber force. There were calls to reduce the number of missions flown by Bomber Command, and to allocate its bombers to the fight against U-boats in the Atlantic. With a loss factor inflicted by JG 2 and 26 in Pas-de-Calais disproportionate to the results achieved, Fighter Command had been ordered to cease large-scale operations.

The quiet Channel Front was only interrupted by Bomber Command's 'Voracity' missions against the *Scharnhorst*, *Gneisenau* and *Prinz Eugen*. Since the ships' arrival in early 1941 they had faced repeated attacks. In order to protect his capital ships, and fearing an imminent invasion of Norway, in January 1942 Hitler took the decision to move the ships to Germany.

Operation Thunderbolt

Codenamed *Donnerkeil* (thunderbolt) by the Luftwaffe, the movement of the ships to Kiel was to be supported by air cover directed by General Galland, incorporating Bf 109F-4s and the superb Fw 190A-2. Such was the perceived threat as the ships traversed the Straits of Dover that Galland called up Bf 109E-7s from training schools. The night-time sailing

was to be covered by Ju 88C-6 and Bf 110F-4 night-fighters; in total, a force of 280 fighters was to be employed. It was also planned to have 16 fighters flying over the ships in daylight hours, with a relief every 25 minutes, flying below British radar and in radio silence.

Slipping into the night

The ships left on the night of 11 February 1942, unseen by the submarine HMS *Sealion* and Hudson Mk Vs. Later, Fw 190s picked up by radar were dismissed as part of a rescue operation, and the convoy remained unrecognised. Fairlight radar and No. 91 Squadron witnessed the convoy, unaware of its significance, and it was another hour before Operation Fuller counter-attacks began. From Manston, FAA Swordfish were escorted by No. 72 Squadron, RAF Spitfires. Flying low over the waves, the attackers

sighted the ships 20 miles (32 km) south-east of Deal, before the covering Spitfires were engaged by Fw 190s. Further Fw 190s lowered flaps and landing gear to counter the Swordfish, all of which were destroyed. The three ships made port in Germany, with six escort fighters lost. For the Germans the operation was a triumph; for the British, it was a tragedy, with

Above: Demonstrating instant superiority over the best that the RAF had to offer, the Fw 190 came as a rude shock to Allied commanders. This early A was photographed from an Fw 189 Uhu.

Below: Compact, extremely strong and of highly advanced design (with almost entirely electric sub-systems), the Fw 190 became the Luftwaffe's chief tactical attack aircraft, replacing the Ju 87.

Above: Until the arrival of the Mosquito, the Boston Mk III was the RAF's most capable high-speed bomber – it was as fast as a Hurricane Mk IA.

Right: Although more lightly armed than the Bf 109E, pilots generally preferred the Bf 109F because of its agility. This RAF camera-gun sequence shows an unfortunate Bf 109F under attack.

Left: At times hopelessly outclassed, the RAF's Bristol Blenheim soldiered on in its Mk IV guise. Here, a No. 105 Squadron example begins a daylight bombing raid over occupied Europe.

Below: The distinctive radial-engined Fw 190 first appeared on RAF film in September 1941. Previously unknown, the fighter quickly established ascendancy over the RAF.

another 17 Fighter Command aircraft lost.

New offensive – old ideas

The RAF resumed operations in March 1942. 'Circuses', 'Rhubarbs', 'Roadsteads' and 'Ramrods' (wherein the destruction was focused on the target rather than on enemy fighters) commenced. Meanwhile, suffering from attrition and low production, the Luftwaffe was reckoned to be at its weakest point since the war began. Taking advantage of this weakness – in a repetition of the June 1941 plan – the RAF initiated a daylight offensive in the west. The intention was to force Germany to withdraw fighters from the Eastern Front, and relocate them to France and the Low Countries.

Fighter Command strength stood at 1,130 aircraft, with Spitfire Mk Vs, Hurricane

Mk IIB/Cs, Beaufighters, Whirlwinds and Havocs. Overseas theatres received only meagre reinforcements in 1942, as the RAF focused its efforts on the defence of the UK.

From March 1942, No. 2 Group Boston Mk IIIs, together with aircraft from Nos 10, 11 and 12 Groups, began to spearhead missions within the radius of the Spitfire Mk VB. Opposition to the raids on chemical plants, marshalling yards and small industrial facilities in France, Belgium and the Netherlands was light.

In trouble

During the first month of the offensive the RAF claimed a total of 53 aircraft downed in combat, with 32 aircraft lost. Actual German losses stood at 12. In April 1942, resistance stiffened, with small forces of

Bf 109F-4/Bs performing devastating below-radar lightning attacks on the English coast. Additionally, more units had converted to the Fw 190, and a new radar network and interception system was nearing completion. Over France, the RAF was fighting for its life.

Second thoughts

Faster than the Spitfire Mk VB, the Fw 190 was

superior in every mode of combat. In April 'Circus' operations, the RAF lost 103 Spitfires. In the same month, the Luftwaffe lost just 21 aircraft. Hampered by poor weather, the following month the Luftwaffe claimed 61 aircraft for the loss of 13 of their own fighters. On 13 June 1942, RAF operations ended as a direct result of the superiority of the Fw 190 fighter.

Fighters over the Channel

By mid-1942 the formidable nature of the Focke-Wulf Fw 190 could no longer be questioned by the RAF. Up until then, its existence had been doubted, and examples had even been mistaken for captured Hawk 75s. The superiority of the Fw 190 led to the development of the Spitfire Mk IX, dedicated to the countering of the new threat. In Luftwaffe service, the Fw 190 had been intended to replace the Bf 109, but the two remained complementary, the latter being continually upgraded.

Supermarine Spitfire Mk VB
Stanislaw Brzeski, of No. 317 'Polish' Squadron flew *Bazyli Kuick* from Exeter in 1941. Having previously flown with the Polish Air Force, Brzeski downed a Bf 109F and damaged an Fw 190 during a single Circus raid in this machine. Brzeski ended the war with seven victories.

Focke-Wulf Fw 190A-2
One of the earliest Fw 190s to enter service was this A-2. It was flown by the adjutant of II./JG 26, based at Moorseele in late 1941, later at Wevelghem and, in early 1942, at Abbeville. Covering the Channel dash by warships on 12 February 1942, it also saw fierce fighting during the Dieppe landings in August.

Messerschmitt Bf 109E-3
Adolf Galland, the charismatic Geschwaderkommodore of JG 26, had 82 kills recorded on the rudder of this Bf 109 in the autumn of 1941. Later, Galland switched to the Bf 109F (used by JG 26 from March 1941) and, in late 1942, became a general.

Focke-Wulf Fw 190

Introduction

These Fw 190A-0s, seen on the Focke-Wulf test line in the summer of 1941, include a 'small-wing' aircraft (left) and two 'large-wing' machines. In the event it was the latter configuration that featured on production 190s.

When the Focke-Wulf Fw 190 first appeared in the skies over the northern coast of France in the summer of 1941, it was certainly the most advanced fighter in front-line service in the world. The *Würger* (or 'Butcher Bird'), as it was known, was, for a while at least, faster and more manoeuvrable than anything the Allies could put up against it.

Conceived in 1937, contemporaneously with the Hawker Typhoon, to replace the first generation of monoplane interceptors (in the Luftwaffe's case, the Messerschmitt Bf 109), the Fw 190 was tendered with two alternative engines, the Daimler-Benz DB 601 inline and the BMW 139 radial, the latter being selected to power the prototype on account of its assumed higher power potential. The first prototype was flown on 1 June 1939.

The Fw 190 was a small, low-wing monoplane with retractable undercarriage. Its seemingly bulky radial engine was faired into a slim fuselage and a clear-view cockpit canopy provided an excellent view for the pilot. The aircraft was all-metal, with a stressed duralumin skin and sat on a wide-track undercarriage, which provided much improved ground handling compared to that of the Bf 109.

After the BMW 139 was abandoned the Fw 190A entered production with the BMW 801 14-cylinder radial with fan-assisted cooling. The first nine pre-production Fw 190A-0s featured small wings of 161.46 sq ft (15.00 m²) area, but the definitive version had larger wings of 196.99 sq ft (18.30 m²) area.

Service trials at Rechlin went ahead in 1940 without undue problems, although pilots suggested that the proposed armament (four 0.31-in/7.92-mm MG 17 machine-guns) would be inadequate in combat. Production of 100 Fw 190A-1s was completed at Hamburg and Bremen by the end of May 1941, and these were powered by 1,600-hp (1194-kW) BMW 801C engines which bestowed a top speed of 388 mph (624 km/h). The following month the first combats were reported with RAF Supermarine Spitfire Mk Vs, showing the German fighters to be markedly superior, albeit lacking in firepower.

Cannon armament

However, the early criticisms had already led to the Fw 190A-2 version, with two wingroot-mounted synchronised 20-mm MG FF cannon and two MG 17 guns. With a speed of 382 mph (614 km/h), this up-gunned version still had the edge over the Spitfire Mk V.

As the RAF desperately sought to introduce an answer to the Fw 190, production of the German fighter was stepped up. Thus by the time the RAF was ready to introduce its new Spitfire Mk IX and Typhoon fighters to combat over the

Dieppe landings in August 1942, the Luftwaffe could field some 200 Fw 190As in opposition.

Unfortunately, not only had the RAF underestimated the number of Fw 190s available, the British were also unaware that a new version, the Fw 190A-4, had appeared with a top speed of 416 mph (670 km/h), and that a bomb-carrying variant, the Fw 190A-3/U1, was in service. A reconnaissance version of the Fw 190A-3 was first flown in

March 1942 on the Russian Front and Fw 190A-4/Trop ground-attack fighter-bombers appeared in North Africa during 1942. Before the end of that year Fw 190A-3/U1 and A-4/U8 fighter-bombers had embarked on a series of daylight low-level 'tip and run' attacks against cities and ports in southern England, forcing Fighter Command to deploy disproportionately large resources to counter the threat.

An immaculate line of Schlachtgeschwader I Fw 190F-2s pictured at Deblin-Irena in Poland waiting to move off to the front. Several of the aircraft wear the Mickey Mouse badge.

The Fw 190 soon took on a fighter-bomber role, initially in France and later in North Africa and on the Eastern Front. These Fw 190Fs of II Gruppe, Schlachtgeschwader 1 have bomb racks fitted.

Further variants followed, including aircraft equipped with rocket-launchers for use against the growing bomber fleets operated by the USAAF. Other versions carried improved gun armament, extra fuel tanks and even torpedoes.

These were followed by a new fighter variant, the Fw 190A-6, in its standard form with reduced wing structure weight, armed with four fast-firing 20-mm guns inside the wings in addition to the two MG 17s in the nose. The arrival of the Spitfire Mk IX in Fighter Command and its threat to the air superiority of the Fw 190A led to the development of the Fw 190B series, with the GM-1 power-boosted BMW 801D-2 engine

and pressure cabin, and the DB 603-powered Fw 190C, but development snags saw both types abandoned.

The Fw 190D, with 1,770-hp (1320-kW) Junkers Jumo 213A-1 inline engine and annular radiator in a much-lengthened nose proved very successful after it had first flown in May 1944. The first production Fw 190D-9s (widely known as 'Dora-9s' in the Luftwaffe) joined III/JG 54 in September 1944, Dora-9s equipping most Luftwaffe fighter units during the last months of the Third Reich, as the Luftwaffe struggled against overwhelming odds.

Fighter-bombers

Also introduced, in the spring of 1944, was the Fw 190F (*Panzer-Blitz*) armoured assault aircraft, while the Fw 190G fighter-bomber actually entered service long before the Fw 190F. The first of these aircraft were

Designated Ta 152 in honour of Focke-Wulf designer Kurt Tank, the Ta 152 (here in Ta 152H form) was destined for limited service in the closing stages of the war.

sent to North Africa following the Torch landings in November 1942, though the majority served on the Eastern Front.

Mention must also be made of the Ta 152 (its designation finally reflecting Kurt Tank's design responsibility for the whole series). Various prototypes of this 'long-nose' derivative of the Fw 190D series were produced, but it was the Ta 152H-1 version with one 30-mm and two 20-

mm guns and a maximum speed of 472 mph (760 km/h) at 41,010 ft (12500 m) that was selected for operational service; only a handful had been completed when the war ended.

Over 20,000 built

Fw 190 production assumed impressive proportions with no less than 20,087 (including 86 prototypes) being produced during the 1939–45 period and a peak daily production rate of 22 aircraft per day being reached early in 1944. Many Luftwaffe pilots achieved remarkable combat feats on the type. Pride of place must go to Oberleutnant Otto Kittel, the Luftwaffe's fourth highest scoring pilot, of whose 267 air victories some 220 were gained in Fw 190A-4s and Fw 190A-5s. Other very high scorers in Fw 190s included Walter Nowotny, Heinz Bär, Hermann Graf and Kurt Buhligen, all of whose scores included more than 100 victories gained with the guns of the aptly-named 'Butcher Bird'.

This aircraft (now part of the RAF Museum's collection at Hendon, London) is an example of the Fw 190F-8/U1 dual-control conversion trainer – one of a handful converted for the role.

Pictured is a Mustang Mk I of No. II(AC) Squadron. Army Co-operation Command's Allison Mustangs were superb at low level and were used for cross-Channel tactical reconnaissance missions.

From Dieppe to Romilly

During the summer of 1941 and spring of 1942, two RAF fighter air offensives were launched. Both failed, the latter largely due to heavy losses in northern France caused by the formidable Fw 190A. For RAF Fighter Command, there was nothing to do but wait until British fighter development caught up.

When the decision was made to attack the Wehrmacht from northern France rather than in North Africa, it was agreed that a sizeable force would land at the small seaport of Dieppe to test the German forces. The aim of the mission was to put British and Commonwealth troops ashore, aided by tanks and continuous air support. The operation, initially named Rutter, then changed to Jubilee, was to take place on 19 August 1942.

By mid-1942, it was hoped that as many as 60 fighter and fighter-bomber squadrons plus 10 reconnaissance and light bomber squadrons could be assembled to counter the estimated German force of 250 fighters and 220 bombers based in France and the Low Countries. More importantly, it was hoped that a dozen squadrons of the new Typhoons and Spitfires could be fielded to counter the Fw 190A threat.

Operation launched

The operation was finally launched after a number of postponements had served to give the Germans a clue as to the impending attack. Large numbers of Spitfire Mk V fighters took off before dawn to cover the landing areas and provide support for the troops on the beaches as Blenheims and Bostons attacked targets in and around Dieppe. Further afield, Defiants with jamming equipment blinded German radar, while American B-17s

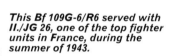

carried out a raid against the Luftwaffe fighter base at Abbeville.

At first, Luftwaffe activity was low, but by mid-morning enemy air activity had increased, with the appearance of Do 217 bombers and a number of Fw 109A-4s which managed to penetrate Allied fighter cover to carry out low-level bombing attacks.

On the ground, things were going badly. Canadian troops and British commandos were unable to capture vital enemy positions overlooking Dieppe, while the new Churchill tanks were not sufficiently armed to knock out enemy strongpoints. Communications blunders meant that Hurricane fighter bombers were called off at a critical point in the battle, resulting in heavy casualties for one Canadian contingent.

The covering fighters did successfully perform their mission in protecting the supporting ships, and only two vessels were hit by enemy

This Bf 109G-6/R6 served with II./JG 26, one of the top fighter units in France, during the summer of 1943.

bombs. Whereas Spitfire Mk V pilots had been briefed not to continue combat too far from Dieppe, Spitfire Mk IXs and Typhoons were given free rein. However, teething problems meant that only a single wing of Typhoons was available at the time of the raid and, even then, the aircraft were governed by a series of flight restrictions. The only time that the Typhoons actually saw any action was when they were accidentally attacked by Canadian-flown Spitfire Mk IXs.

By late afternoon, the assault ships were withdrawing across the Channel, still being supported by Spitfire Mk Vs. It was thought at first, after consultation of RAF pilot reports, that the RAF had come close to victory. Early estimates suggested that up to 100 German aircraft had been downed,

A German soldier surveys Dieppe beach, which is strewn with the bodies and equipment of Allied troops killed in battle. Almost two years elapsed before the Allies finally succeeded in taking and holding the Channel coast. By this time, close support by Allied aircraft was properly planned and far more effective.

Left: The Fw 190 first appeared over northern France in mid-1941 and immediately won the respect of Allied air crew, who suffered at its hands. Superior to the Bf 109 in almost every respect, the Fw 190 had a major impact over Dieppe.

Below: Hawker Typhoons saw their first major offensive action during the ill-fated Dieppe raid. These early aircraft tried valiantly to hold off the Luftwaffe bombers, but air cover for the landings was insufficient to support them.

compared to the loss in combat of 106 RAF aircraft. However, German records later revealed that only 48 Luftwaffe aircraft had been downed.

Lessons learned

The tactical lessons learned at Dieppe were sobering; ground support by fighter- and light-bombers had proved inadequate and there had been little effective communication between ground and air assets. The ratio of fighters to support aircraft had been too high, and the supposed superiority of RAF aircraft had proved unfounded, while control of the fighters had been conducted at radar bases too remote from the actual battle. It was realised in 1942 that Allied forces, their equipment, tactics and training, fell well short of the standard required for a European invasion.

Enter the 8th Air Force

The decision to base the 8th Air Force in the UK had been made in the 'Arcadia' conference between Churchill and Roosevelt in December 1941. However, pressing problems in the Pacific and Far East had delayed the arrival of the first B-17s as part of Operation Bolero Round-up until July 1942. The plan had been to build up a strength of 3,500 bombers and fighters in the UK with the object of supporting an invasion in 1943, but this was

never carried out. After much delay and argument, the British managed to convince the Americans to commit their forces to the invasion of French North Africa (Operation Torch). All the previous plans to establish the 8th Air Force in the UK were changed.

The units that eventually did arrive in the UK from August 1942 included B-17Es, P-39D Airacobras, P-38Fs and Spitfire Mk VBs. However, the majority of the fighters was soon redirected to the Mediterranean. The US VIII Bomber Command began practice-bombing, although its daylight bombing plans horrified the RAF which believed that such a tactic was suicidal. The RAF, however, failed to appreciate the full extent of the ability of the B-17, or indeed of the improved B-24D.

For the Jagdflieger and the pilots of RAF Fighter Command, Dieppe heralded the end of an era on the Channel front. For two years, Luftwaffe forces had been held in the defence of Western Europe, but now, with new Bf 109G-1s and Fw 109A-4s, better trained and more experienced pilots, and an efficient radar detection system, the tables had been turned. Lightly-armed Bostons posed little threat while even the newer Spitfires possessed a relatively poor range.

The first mission by VIII Bomber Command was to

Rouen-Sotteville on 17 August 1942 and was relatively successful due to false radar indications being sent out by 'Mandrel'-equipped Boulton-Paul Defiants. Further missions followed and fierce fighting took place across France, with the first B-17s being lost on 6 September. The heavily-armed, high-flying Fortress generally proved to be a formidable opponent for the Luftwaffe.

Preparations were now complete for the invasion of North Africa, and VIII Bomber Command's aircraft were tasked with bombing U-boat bases at Brest, Lorient, St Nazaire, La Pallice and Bordeaux. However, the bases were strongly armoured: the roofs of U-boat pens were 4.5 m (14 ft) thick, impenetrable by the 500-lb (227-kg) and 1,000-lb (454-kg) bombs being dropped. In addition, the bases were well defended and lay outside the range of RAF Spitfires, meaning that the bombers had to fly the mission alone. The U-boat campaign lasted from 21 October 1942 until July 1943 and was generally considered a waste of manpower and effort, with the British Admiralty issuing many spurious requests.

The effects of Operation Torch in North Africa meant that many Luftwaffe fighter groups were pulled from the north to the south of France to counter any attack on Marseilles. This left northern forces relatively under strength but the Allies also faced the same problems.

On 23 November 1942, during a raid on St Nazaire, US bombers encountered 40 or more Fw 190s head-on. This new tactic was an obvious move by the Luftwaffe as the US bombers were relatively lightly armoured to the front, and 20-mm cannon shells entering the cockpit usually signalled the end for a B-17 or B-24. The tactic took a lot of nerve but was very successful and four B-17s were lost on that day.

Allied day-fighter squadrons continued to escort the bombers as far as possible; types in service included Spitfire Mks VB, VC, IX and VI, Typhoon Mk IBs and Whirlwind Mk Is.

Especially noteworthy was the mass Allied low-level attack by No. 2 (Bomber) Group on the Phillips valve and radio site at Eindhoven. Bostons, Venturas and Mosquito B.Mk IVs flew on this mission (Operation Oyster), while Spitfires flew diversionary feints. However, flak and Fw 190s left 14 bombers destroyed and 20 damaged.

The climax of the December raids came on the 20th of the month when 80 B-17s and 21 B-24s bombed the airpark at Romilly-sur-Seine, to the east of Paris. The battle was incredibly fierce and all the forces of Höhrer Jafü West were in the air (170 or more Fw 190s), with some pilots flying two missions. The escorting Spitfires were virtually left out of the battle. Six B-17s were lost, but their gunners accounted for six Fw 190s plus another 10 damaged. The Luftwaffe was being put to the test.

Above: A Westland Whirlwind I of No. 263 (Fighter) Squadron, photographed before being modified for underwing bomb carriage. Operating from Warmwell in Dorset, No. 263 was involved in offensive sweeps over France.

Left: No. 107 Squadron flew Boston Mk III and Mk IIIA light-bombers between January 1942 and January 1944. They were involved in the abortive attempt to land troops at Dieppe, when their mission was to destroy coastal guns. In the process, nine Bostons were severely damaged.

Offensive challenge

Even as late as early 1943, Hurricanes were still boldly flying over Europe on night intruder missions, while a very small number carried radar on Fighter Command night defence duties. These Mk IICs wore an all-black colour scheme.

For two years the offensive aspirations of RAF Fighter Command and No. 2 (Bomber) Group had been unsuccessful, due largely to the technical superiority of German fighters and the Spitfire's lack of range. In August 1942, the US 8th Air Force arrived to give the Command a new lease of life, although it would take some time for the effects of its presence to be felt.

Air Marshal Trafford L. Leigh-Mallory took over RAF Fighter Command from Sholto Douglas on 28 November 1942. It was his firm intention to pursue the policy of offensive operations against the Luftwaffe, based in northern France and Belgium, through various types of mission, notably the 'Ramrod', 'Circus', 'Roadstead' and 'Rhubarb'. Such a policy, as laid down in the original directive of March 1942, had been dependent on gaining a satisfactory ratio of losses to casualties inflicted on the enemy. But this had not been so. The offensive had been conducted with a singular lack of imagination during the spring and summer of 1942, during a time when the requirement for RAF fighters, in particular Supermarine Spitfires, had been pressing. A curtailment of operations was ordered in June 1942, but was followed in August by the highly questionable Dieppe raid. The arrival of the US 8th Air Force, with the Boeing B-17F, had

At low level, the Spitfire Mk VB (illustrated), with the single-stage low-blown Merlin 45, 46 or 50, performed as well as the Mk IX. This example displays its prominent 20-mm cannon.

given Fighter Command's offensive some renewed impetus.

During January 1943 the Allied leaders met at Casablanca to discuss the future war policy in light of improvements on all fronts. As a result of the conference, a new bombing directive was issued on 21 January 1943. This called for attacks by US bombers on targets selected in the following priority: U-boat construction yards and pens; the German aircraft industry; transportation; oil plants; and 'other' targets in the war industry of the Reich. RAF Bomber Command was given a free hand in the adoption of its offensive policy, whilst the US 8th Air Force used the directive as its guideline.

Responding to the increase in Allied operations, Luftwaffe fighter forces in Belgium and France consisted of the Stab, II. and III./JG 26 based in the Lille-Vitry sector, and the Bf 109G-4s

of III./JG 54. German squadrons based in France and Belgium were probably at the peak of their efficiency in the spring of 1943, and the continued supremacy of the redoubtable Fw 190A-5 was evident. Mute testimony to this fact occurred on 3 February 1943, when eight Spitfires were shot down on 'Circus' no. 258. Other fighter operations went the same way, often with the Allies being on the receiving end of the highly experienced Luftwaffe aces.

Tip-and-run raids

Throughout the following months, Fighter Command was put under incredible pressure, often with several squadrons remaining on alert throughout the day. However, losses to the German fighter-bomber units were on the increase, mainly as a result of the fast Typhoon Mk IBs and Spitfire Mk XIs which entered service in April

Although the technology of sprayed-on Cocoon coatings was in its infancy, thousands of US warplanes crossed the Atlantic (if they were not sunk) and reached the UK in fully serviceable condition. This P-38F, complete with new drop tanks on its pylons, reached Queen's Dock, Liverpool, on 9 January 1943.

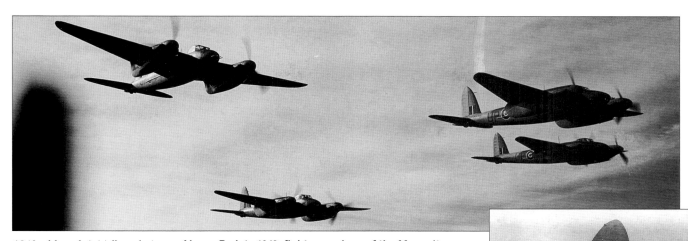

1943, although initially only in limited numbers These improved British aircraft were operated alongside American-supplied machines, which included North American Mustang Mk IAs and Curtiss Tomahawks.

Tribulations of May

Operations during May 1943 intensified with the onset of reasonably fair weather, and the reinforcement of US VIII Bomber Command; by the end of the month, its strength had risen from four to 10 groups, including Liberator-equipped squadrons. Fighter groups were now equipped with P-47 Thunderbolts, although the fighters were restricted in operational range due to the lack of sufficient drop tanks.

B-17s flew their first escorted raid on 4 May, with 79 bombers under a heavy escort from Spitfires and Thunderbolts. Despite being intercepted by over 70 aircraft from JG 26, the good use of tactics and defensive

Above: By late 1943, fighter versions of the Mosquito were transforming the RAF's long-range air combat capability. These NF.Mk II (Special) fighters of No. 605 Sqn carried no radar and were used in day fighter camouflage as intruders. Later, using the more versatile FB.Mk VI, No. 605 operated all over Europe.

Right: One of the first Spitfire Mk VBs produced, R6923/QJ-S was converted from a Mk IB and issued to No. 92 Squadron in early 1941. No. 92 was active throughout the offensive.

fire ensured that not one bomber was lost.

Spring campaign

For the Luftwaffe, the increase in Allied operations was beginning to tell. A period of fair weather permitted the Allies to open a small air campaign aimed at bringing the Luftwaffe to battle. The air battles started on 13 May 1943 when, following a 'Circus', B-17s bombed SNCA du Nord at Albert-Meaulte. RAF and US fighters were now controlled by a new radar system (Type 16 Mk III) which covered the tactical area almost as far inland as Paris. Ten German fighters were shot down by P-47

Thunderbolts and Spitfires the following day.

Despite these successes, the Allies still encountered heavy losses. One of the most notorious incidents in USAAF operations occurred on 17 May 1943. Lt Col Robert M. Stillman led the 322nd Group's Martin B-26 Marauders on a mission to Haarlem and Ijmuiden – it was a low-level attack which was to end in disaster. Light flak and Messerschmitt Bf 109Gs accounted for the loss of 10 B-26s out of the 11 that had taken off (one returned to base due to technical difficulties).

May 1943 represented a serious challenge to the Luftwaffe's superiority in the West, both in the form of bomber/fighter attacks on targets in the Reich and in France. The Luftwaffe, losing many of its aces, encountered its highest casualty rate since the Battle of Britain in 1940, and this set the pattern for the future.

Deadly foes

The RAF had born the brunt of the aerial combat during the early years of the war, and the arrival of the USAAF was to lead to even more vicious fighting. Nowhere was this more apparent than during the daylight bombing raids by the B-17s of the VIII Bomber Command. Lacking fighter protection near their targets, the B-17s were easy prey for the Luftwaffe. As the offensive progressed, however, it was the Luftwaffe that was ultimately unable to sustain the losses of its pilots and aircraft.

B-17F Flying Fortress

42-5177 was a Boeing B-17F-40-BO of the 359th Bomb Squadron. It was typical of the 303rd Bomb Group which, by summer 1943, was contributing to missions in which up to 300 aircraft were flown. This aircraft's insignia was that used from July 1942 until July 1943, when red-bordered rectangles were added.

Focke-Wulf Fw 190A-4

Far more heavily armed than the Messerschmitt Bf 109F and early Bf 109G, the Focke-Wulf Fw 190A-4 and its close relatives operated in large numbers in 1942 in the hands of the outstandingly skilled and experienced pilots of JG 2 and JG 26. Against the RAF, the aircraft scored, on average, five kills for every loss sustained. This A-4 served with 2./JG 2 at Abbeville in May 1943.

Victory over France

Above: A number of RAF Boston IIIs was used in the night intruder role. A gun pack, containing four 20-mm cannon and fitted beneath the fuselage, supplemented the standard Boston III armament.

Left: Serving with the 379th FS, 362nd FG, of the 9th Air Force, this P-47D-11 carries a pair of 150-US gal (568-litre) drop tanks to increase its range.

The defeat of the Wehrmacht started in 1942 with El Alamein, followed by Stalingrad and Tunisia and, in the summer of 1943, by Kursk and the invasion of Sicily. By August 1943 the priority of the Luftwaffe had become the defence of the Reich against the RAF by night and the 8th Air Force by day.

Until April 1943, the German fighters based in northern France, Belgium, Germany and the Netherlands had accomplished their defensive task efficiently. However, since January 1943, US 8th Air Force B-17s and B-24s had been raiding Wilhelmshaven. Although the bomber formations rarely exceeded 60 to 70 in number, the well-defended and tough Liberators and Flying Fortresses were difficult to shoot down, despite the absence of Allied fighter escorts.

Initially, the problem for the Germans was that of strength, with only one Geschwader (JG 1 with four Gruppen) being scattered across bases in northwest Europe. In April 1943, the Geschwader was strengthened by an influx of experienced fighter leaders, splitting up to become JG 1 and JG 11, each with four Gruppen. However, soon after this, the defence of the Reich began to take precedence and crews were withdrawn from French units and moved back to Germany. This left the existing Gruppen in France and Belgium seriously weakened at a time when Allied offensive operations were on the increase.

The fighter losses suffered by Luftflotte III soared from 27 in April to 61 destroyed in the course of the following month; for RAF Fighter Command, it was the first month since 1940 that its own casualties had been exceeded by those of its foes across the Channel. While the Luftwaffe's equipment was technically proficient – the Fw 190A-5 and A-6 were manoeuvrable and strong, and the 'clean' Bf 109G-6 was formidable – the aircraft were being weighed down with extra armament and drop tanks, which rendered them slow and unwieldy. By June 1943, there were as few as 250 single-engined fighters in northern France as units and crews were constantly drawn back to Germany to protect against the US VIII Bomber Command.

Pointblank directive

By April 1943, the Allies were becoming concerned about the number of fighters they were encountering over Germany. The plan therefore, under the auspices of Operation Pointblank, was for British and American bomber commands to carry out attacks on the German day and night fighter forces, and against the industries upon which they depended.

Other tasks remained for the B-17s and B-24s, most notably the attacks on the U-boat pens in the Bay of Biscay, on oil targets, ball-bearing concerns and aircraft component factories. But the priority was the defeat of the German fighter arm in the skies over the Reich, and closer to home. The eventual objective was to secure air supremacy in the West as the prerequisite for the invasion of France, soon to be codenamed Operation Overlord.

Throughout June 1943, RAF Fighter Command underwent reorganisation for Operation Overlord. On 1 June, No. 2 Group was placed under the operational and administrative control of Fighter Command. The Army Co-operation Command was also disbanded. On 14 June, the RAF 2nd Tactical Air Force was formed, to train close support aircraft

Above: During the early stages of the war, the Arado Ar 196A-3 served well on several fronts. However, the units operating on the Channel front found the sky increasingly perilous from 1943.

Left: The Typhoon Mk IB proved a most valuable low-level aircraft in both fighter and attack roles, its reputation for structural failure being due to an aerodynamic tailplane/elevator fault which caused severe flutter. Here, one of the early Mk IBs, with car-type doors, is serviced by No. 56 Sqn.

Left: The Dornier Do 217 was never very successful as a night-fighter and total production for this role was a mere 364. The 1943 production total of just over 200 consisted almost entirely of the Do 217N-2 type, with liquid-cooled DB 603A engines.

Above: Despite banking sharply, this Bf 109G cannot escape the gunfire from a pursuing American fighter. The sheer weight of numbers of the US forces, coupled with the aircraft of the RAF, eventually managed to wear down the Luftwaffe in the West.

squadrons for tactical operations during Overlord. Hawker Typhoon Mk IBs were equipped with bombs and rockets and they gradually began to replace the Hurricane Mk IV in the close support role. The remainder of the 2nd TAF's inventory included Spitfire LF.Mk VBs and Mk VCs, Mk IXBs and a growing number of the more efficient Merlin 66-engined Spitfire LF.Mk IXs. However, range was still a problem, the only solution being a series of often inefficient underwing fuel tanks.

June 1943 was the last month in which the US VIII Fighter Command came under the control of RAF Fighter Command. The most pressing task for the Americans at this time was the development of a drop tank for the P-47 units. Tactically, the P-47D had matched the Bf 109G-6 and Fw 190A-5 fighters of the Luftwaffe, but the Germans had the edge in terms of combat experience. Although the 56th Group claimed its first German aircraft on 12 June 1943, throughout June and July the

P-47s were suffering at the hands of aces such as Adolf Galland.

By August, however, US fighter pilots were getting to grips with the skilful German Jagdflieger, and gaining valuable experience. On 16 August, during 'Ramrod' no. 203 to Le Bourget, the 4th, 78th and 56th Groups, aided for the first time by the 353rd FG, claimed a minor victory over the Luftwaffe by claiming a record of 17 kills for the loss of one of their own.

V-weapons

Owing to the large number of Allied fighters now roaming over Northern France and Belgium, it was expected that the remaining Luftwaffe fighter units would be withdrawn to Germany. However, they were kept in-theatre to defend the construction sites intended to host the new V-weapons ('V' for *Verweltung*, or revenge). Development of the V-1 and the V-2 was still a secretive business but, as early as August 1943, RAF Lancasters had pounded the main test establishment at Peenemünde on the Baltic coast. As the Germans began to build

further launching sites across France, they attracted more interest from the Allies and among the first to suffer attacks was the site at Watten as part of Operation Starkey. Between 25 August and 9 September, the whole of RAF Fighter Command and elements of Bomber Command and the US 8th Air Force attacked sites and tried to achieve air superiority over the Luftwaffe. However, Allied losses were high and the operation was relatively unsuccessful. No Luftwaffe units were withdrawn to Germany or from any other front and it was a relief for Allied air commanders when the operation was terminated.

October 1943 saw the US 9th Air Force re-established in the UK and the US IX Bomber Command took control of the B-26-equipped 322nd, 323rd, 386th and 387th Groups. The IX Fighter Command absorbed the 354th Fighter Group – the first unit to be equipped with the P-51B-1-NA Mustang.

The Luftwaffe's fighter arm was reorganised and a new I Jagdkorps (with subordinate 1, 2, 3 and 7 Jagddivisionen) was set up under Generalmajor Josef Schmid. In northern France, II Jagdkorps was formed from Stab/Hoherer Jafü Brittany, and JG 2 and 26 were enlarged to a complement of four Staffeln per Gruppe.

The air fighting was continuous, with skirmishes occurring whenever weather permitted. The nimble Spitfire Mk XIIs from Tangmere were some of the most successful, claiming 9 Bf 109Gs of I. and II./JG 2 destroyed on 20 October. Elsewhere on this day, German fighters were suffering at the hands of P-47s and P-38H Lightnings and the high attrition rate of experienced pilots was being felt.

Construction of the mysterious 'ski sites' in northern France continued and, when photo-reconnaissance slides taken on 28 October revealed that the axis of a ramp at Bois

Carré was pointing at London, action was demanded. As part of Operation Crossbow, the US IX Bomber Command began to attack the sites, nick-named 'Noballs', at Sottevast and Martinvaast on the Contentin peninsular.

In the meantime, RAF Fighter Command had been disbanded and its forces split between the Air Defence of Great Britain (ADGB) and the Allied Expeditionary Air Force (AEAF), the latter controlling the RAF 2nd TAF and the US 9th Army Air Force. The Allied forces were gathering, and Germany was under sustained attack by RAF Bomber Command at night although, by day, the Jagdgruppen had won a temporary respite with its victory over the US VIII Bomber Command at Schweinfurt in October. However, already there was a new threat from the US 15th Air Force, which threatened the Balkans, the Ploesti oilfields and the southern reaches of the Reich from bases round Foggia in Italy.

In the skies over northern France and Belgium, the few Jagdgruppen committed were now under continual pressure. Both JG 2 and JG 26 contested Allied efforts to bomb the V-1 sites in December 1943 and were severely beaten in the process. They had received few reinforcements and had been robbed of their best Staffeln for defensive duties over the Reich. JG 2 and JG 26 had been the first to feel the brunt of the RAF's fighter offensives, first in 1941 and then in 1942. In that year, they had pioneered methods of combating the B-17s and B-24s of the 8th Air Force, and had held the front line until July 1943, when commitments exceeded their resources. By December 1943, they were being conserved only for action against the 8th Air Force. Now, for the first time since 1940, the skies over northern France were relatively safe from German fighters.

The Lockheed P-38 Lightning was deficient in rate-of-roll and rather too large for close combat, but its long range, significant bombload and generally good flight characteristics made it valuable. This P-38J-10 was one of those assigned to the 55th Fighter Group's 338th Fighter Sqn, based at Nuthampstead, England in late 1943.

With its pressurised cockpit, the Mosquito B.Mk XVI could fly at an altitude of 40,000 ft (12,192 m). This aircraft was flown by No. 571 Squadron, which formed at Downham Market in April 1944 as a light bomber unit with No. 8 (Pathfinder) Group.

de Havilland DH.98 Mosquito

Introduction

The Mosquito was born in an uncertain fashion during the early months of World War II, with few real supporters. Within five years, however, it had become one of the RAF's most versatile and valued assets.

The all-wooden de Havilland Mosquito was possibly the most useful single type of aircraft produced by the Allies in World War II. It owed nothing to any official specification and was created in the face of often fierce opposition by officialdom.

Even after a prototype had been ordered, the limited nature of the programme (a mere 50 aircraft) caused it to be removed entirely from future plans three

times after the Dunkirk evacuation. Each time it was daringly put back by a single believer, Patrick (later Sir Patrick) Hennessy, brought in from Ford Motors by Lord Beaverbrook to help run British aircraft production. Eventually, in November 1940, a single prototype at last took to the air.

Once that had happened, the fantastic performance of de Havilland's Mosquito soon silenced its official detractors.

The first Mosquito (W4050) was secretly built at Salisbury Hall, close to the Hatfield works in Hertfordshire. W4050 received an overall yellow colour scheme, and is seen here covered in tarpaulins in an effort to conceal the aircraft from prowling Luftwaffe aircraft.

The de Havilland Aircraft Company was famed chiefly for lightplanes and rather primitive mixed-construction light transports, but in 1936 it designed the aerodynamically superb (although technically disastrous) DH.91 Albatross airliner, with a structure entirely of wood. A few months later, work was started on a military derivative with two Merlin engines to meet the requirements of Specification P.13/36, but this was not accepted, largely because

of the wooden structure which was not taken seriously. Undeterred, the project staff under R. E. Bishop, R. M. Clarkson and C. T. Wilkins, continued to study a new high-speed bomber able to evade hostile fighters and thus dispense with gun turrets. The concept appeared to make sense. Doing away with turrets reduced the crew from six to two, comprising a pilot on the left with the navigator/bombardier on his right. Either could work the radio. Thanks to the scale effect, in that saving weight enabled the

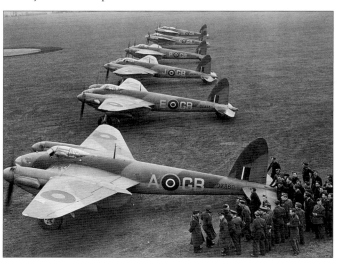

Pilots and ground crews crowd around a line-up of Mosquito B.Mk IVs at their home base of RAF Marham in late 1942. These light bombers of No. 105 Squadron had been on strength since November 1941 and were used for high-speed, long-range bombing raids. Their speed allowed them to fly without fighter escort.

Right: The Royal Navy's Sea Mosquito TR.Mk 33 could carry a wide range of offensive stores, including an 18-in (457-mm) torpedo. It also had radar, four cannon and full carrier equipment. Prior to delivery of this fully-developed, Leavesden-built series, the Fleet Air Arm used 'hooked' Mk VIs.

Left: After the war the Royal Norwegian air force was one of the numerous foreign air forces that operated Mosquitoes. This FB.VI served with RNorAF No. 334 Squadron from Stavanger/Sola. The unit was originally B Flight of No. 333 Sqn, operating the same aircraft with the RAF strike wing at Banff, Grampian, in 1943.

aircraft to be smaller and burn less fuel, it was calculated that the twin-Merlin unarmed bomber could carry 1,000 lb (454 kg) of bombs 1,500 miles (2400 km) for a weight of just over 15,000 lb (6800 kg). In addition, with careful streamlining, the speed could reach almost 400 mph (655 km/h), almost double that of other British bombers.

Full-scale RAF service began with the B.Mk IV series II, the first definitive bomber version, which entered service with No. 105 Sqn of No. 2 Group at Swanton Morley in November 1941. Next came No. 139 Sqn at Marham. The first bomber mission was flown by just one aircraft – W4072 of No. 105 Sqn – at the end of the '1,000-bomber' raid on Cologne on 30-31 May 1942. After various ineffective sorties, a daring attack was made on Gestapo HQ in Oslo, but was thwarted by the performance of the bombs; one failed to explode inside the building, while three others went through the far wall before detonating. For the rest of the war, the original B.Mk IV made daring precision attacks throughout Europe from tree-top height.

Special missions

Mosquitoes proved highly effective in the photo-reconnaissance roles – the PR.Mk IV was a camera variant of the B. Mk IV series II. The FB.Mk VI fighter-bomber, with 2,584 examples completed, was built in the greatest numbers however. With two-stage Merlin engines, wing-mounted drop tanks and underwing racks for two or more 250-lb (113-kg) bombs, which were later replaced by eight underwing rockets, the versatile FB.Mk VI ranged across Europe, hitting such point targets as the walls of Amiens prison, the

Right: The final incarnation of the Mosquito in regular service followed conversion for the target-towing role for the Royal Navy. Known as TT.Mk 39s, the aircraft were fitted with a 'glasshouse' nose which accommodated a cameraman, while the bomb bay housed an electrically-driven winch.

Gestapo HQ at The Hague, Gestapo HQ at Copenhagen, and numerous V-weapon sites. Indeed, the flexibility of the type was such that the Mosquito was not restricted to daylight operations. A host of night-fighter variants was produced, equipped with harpoon-like aerials, or bluff nose radomes.

Foreign operators

Many marks of Mosquito flew with all Allied air forces, including the Red air force and the USAAF, the latter using Canadian-built aircraft as the F-8 reconnaissance version. In addition to 10 civil Mosquitoes used by BOAC on high-priority services with cargo and passengers between the UK and Sweden (and occasionally other places), there were various later marks that did not see war service.

The heaviest and highest-performing of all versions were the closely related PR.Mk 34, B.Mk 35 and NF.Mk 36. All had high-altitude Merlins and broad paddle-bladed propellers. The PR.Mk 34 was the longest ranged of all marks. A PR.Mk 34A made the last RAF's last operational Mosquito flight on 15 December 1955. There were also numerous Sea Mosquito variants, of which the most important was the radar-equipped TR.Mk 33.

The last of 7,619 Mosquitoes was VX916, a night-fighting NF.Mk 38, delivered from Chester on 28 November 1950. It was the 6,33st built in England; Canadian production totalled 1,076 and Australian 212. Post-war air forces using Mosquitoes included those of Belgium, China, Czecho-slovakia, Denmark, Dominica, France, Israel, Norway, South Africa, Sweden, Turkey and Yugoslavia.

By various methods, only some of them legal, the infant Israeli air force (Heyl Ha'Avir) acquired real offensive muscle with Mosquito Mks IV, VI and NF.Mk 36. This colourful FB. Mk6 (post-war designation) was one of a batch bought at a knock-down price from the French Armeé de l'Air.

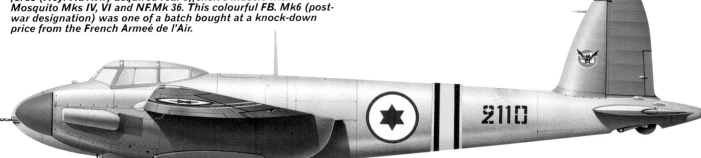

Blitz in the south

Above: The four Greek fighter squadrons had a total of 31 aircraft at the start of the campaign. The 21st, 22nd and the 23rd Mire deployed 25 P.24Fs (illustrated) and P.24Gs, while the 24th Mira had six Bloch MB.151s.

Top: Pictured is an early Macchi MC.200 Saetta, with the relatively low-powered Fiat A.74 RC.38 engine. The Regia Aeronautica first used the MC.200 in action against Malta and then Greece, but it was no match for later fighter types.

Well before the fall of France, on 10 June 1940, Mussolini declared war against the British and the French. Impatient with the scale of German triumph, Il Duce craved a victory – he chose first to attack Greece. The Mediterranean became the scene of major conflict.

It was the worsening of relations between Germany and Russia that first prompted Hitler to secure the vital oilfields at Ploesti, in Romania, to maintain supplies of oil. German pressure on Romania brought about a coup d'état which saw the pro-Nazi General Ion Antonescu take over government, with the deposition of King Carol. Germany moved quickly and occupied Romania on the pretence of instructing the Romanian army.

Meanwhile, Mussolini was furious at being left out of dealings that had occurred within an Italian sphere of influence and decided to uphold Italy's long-standing desire to invade Greece. On 28 October 1940, the Italian army, which comprised several crack Alpini mountain regiments and was backed by 250-300 bombers, crossed the Greco-Albanian frontier. It was widely expected that the Greek army would be unprepared and under strength. The Royal Hellenic air force consisted of some 160-180 obsolescent French and Polish types as well as a few Hawker Horsley torpedo-bombers.

Italy's Regia Aeronautica had the excellent Savoia Marchetti SM.79-II as its primary bomber which came in standard bomber and anti-shipping versions. The remainder of the bomber force was made up of Fiat BR.20M and Caproni Ca.135 twin-engined bombers and Cant Z.506B maritime bombers. Italian fighter units were equipped initially with six squadrons of Fiat CR.32 and CR.42 Falco biplanes.

The attack opens

The attack on Greece was a three-pronged offensive, with

This Bristol Blenheim Mk I of No. 113 Squadron was operational over the Macedonian Front in the early part of 1941. Such bombers could have performed a useful role had they remained in North Africa, but were outclassed by German aircraft in the Balkan campaign.

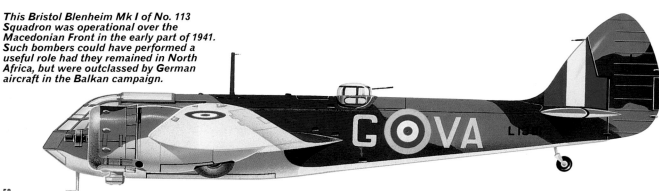

Italian bombers

At the beginning of the conflict, Italy possessed a moderate bomber force which was technologically superior to anything operated by the Greeks.

However, when the British entered the war for Greece, the Italian bombers began to fall prey to RAF aircraft, in particular the Hawker Hurricane.

SM.81 Pipistrello
Pipistrello (bat) bomber/transports of the 202º Squadriglia (part of the 38º Stormo's 40º Gruppo Bombardamento Terrestre) operated over the Greek front in early 1941. Despite its later designation, the SM.81 preceded the SM.79, and about 100 more were in service by June 1941.

Fiat BR.20M
As part of the 277º Squadriglia (part of the 37º Stormo's 116º Gruppo Bombardamento Terrestre), the BR.20M operated over the Greco-Albanian front from its base at Grottaglie in 1940-1. The Cicogna (stork) did not perform particularly well, despite a useful bombload.

thrusts along the Vijosë river to Vovoúsa, the coast of Konispol and north from Koritsa. However, the Italians had underestimated the Greeks' ability and were repulsed at Koritsa and on the coast. Even more disastrous for the Italians was the capture, on 2 November, of 5,000 Italian troops at Vovoúsa. By 22 November, the final Italian troops were ejected from Greek soil.

In response to aggression in the Balkans, Britain upheld its promise to defend the region and a fleet set sail from Alexandria, setting up a base at Suda Bay, Crete. Following this, the RAF began addressing the balance between the Greek and Italian forces, with detachments on Crete of No. 30 Squadron consisting of a flight of Blenheim Mk I bombers and one of Mk IF fighters. Following No. 30 Squadron came Nos 84 and 211 (B) Squadrons with Blenheim Mk Is and Gladiator Mk Is. However, they had little to do and the Gloster Gladiators were eventually turned over to the Greek air force.

The Blenheim bombers made irregular attacks on the Italians, but operations were hampered by poor weather conditions. During November and December 1940, British bombers made 235 sorties and 76 abortive flights due to the weather. In addition, Wellingtons from Egypt and Malta attacked ports on the Adriatic coast. The small RAF fighter force made good use of its Gladiators, claiming several CR.42s, SM.79s and Ro.37s.

On 3 January 1941, the Italians launched a counter-offensive to

the north and west of Koritsa; two fresh Italian divisions were committed to the Klissoura sector on the Valona road to regain the initiative. The counter-offensive failed, however, with the resilient Greeks retaking Klissoura on 10 January. Nevertheless, the Regia Aeronautica still retained air superiority and, what is more, was strengthened with additions including SM.79s and 81s, Fiat G.50s, CR.32s and 42s. It was therefore no surprise that the Greeks urgently requested assistance from the RAF. Chief of the Air Staff Sir Charles Portal then ordered further RAF squadrons to the region. These additional squadrons were made available due to the success of the British counter-offensive in the Western Desert of Africa. However, the supply situation in the Mediterranean had worsened with the sudden arrival of Geisler's X. Fliegerkorps in Sicily which had closed the Sicilian Narrows to British convoys. Simultaneously, there was the threat of German intervention in the Balkan region from the north.

A tactical HQ was established at Ioánnina in Greece, to where No. 80(F) Squadron was transferred along with No. 11 (B) Squadron's Blenheims. Gladiators and Wellingtons were also moved to the area for support. Tactical work in support of the Greek army in its push to Valona was the order of the day for the RAF. In bitter weather, the Blenheims conducted numerous low-level attacks on the Kelcyre-Berat road, and on Italian concentrations at Dukaj, Berat and Elbasan; from 11-18

February, better weather prevailed and the Blenheims flew 108 sorties in support of the Greek attack on Tepelenë.

The prospect of battling MC.200 Saettas, Bf 190Es and Bf 110s with 'museum worthy' Gladiators filled the RAF pilots with despondency, so the appearance of the Hurricane Mk IA in the region proved a significant turning point in the fortunes of the Allies. The first Hurricane sortie saw four Italian aircraft destroyed. The appearance of the Hawker aircraft caused the Regia Aeronautica to withdraw its Fiat CR.42s, their place being taken by the MC.200 Saetta, which acquitted itself well against the Hurricane.

Italy's last effort

Seven Italian divisions launched an attack along the Vijosë river on 9 March 1941, supported by 26 SM.79 bombers and 105 Fiat G.50s and CR.42s; in addition, forces in Italy supplied another 198 aircraft. The battle lasted until 19 March 1941 and, from 9-14 March, RAF Blenheims flew 43 missions on the Buzi-Gllavë road,

supported by 15 Hurricane and 122 Gladiator sorties. The Wellingtons flew four sorties and the Blenheims made 30 anti-shipping strikes off Valona, with other attacks on Lecce and Brindisi. The RAF fighters fought hard in the region and, despite the improved tactics of the Italians, 119 enemy aircraft were destroyed, to eight British losses.

By this time, Hitler, had become incensed with Mussolini's failures in Greece. They had resulted in a British foothold in the area, which had permitted RAF bombers to hit the vital oilfields in Romania – this threatened the planned invasion of the Soviet Union. On 13 December 1940, therefore, Hitler had issued the Füherweisung Nr 20, outlining Operation Marita. This operation called for an army of 24 divisions to be assembled in Romania and to descend through Greece as soon as the weather was favourable. Ground units were to be supported by elements of the Luftflotten II and III, pulled back from the Channel Front and refitted in Germany.

Italy's superior bomber at the start of the campaign was the SM.79-II. Equipping four squadrons, it proved highly effective against the Greek forces.

Operation Marita

Left: As the eyes of the Panzer divisions, the Hs 126 operated free of serious aerial or AA opposition, performing tactical reconnaissance as well as army co-operation duties, which included artillery-spotting.

Below: Outclassed by the Bf 109, the Greeks' 30 Polish-built PZL P-24F/Gs served with three squadrons – the 21st, 22nd and 23rd Mira Dixeos (fighter squadrons). This example was abandoned at Larissa in 1941.

By spring 1941, Hitler's plans for the invasion of the USSR had fallen behind schedule. Five months of frustration had seen the Italians fail in Greece and Libya, and German help was now promised in order to redress the situation in Greece. Meanwhile, events in the Balkans demanded action against Yugoslavia.

By late February 1941, the German military presence in Romania amounted to almost 680,000 troops, who had filtered steadily into the country since General Ion Antoneseu's agreement with Hitler in October 1940. The aim was to cement ties with Hungary and Romania, securing the southern flank of the Axis powers prior to Operation Barbarossa, scheduled to start on 15 May 1941. As far back as December 1940, however, the inability of the Italians to bring about a successful conclusion to the Greek campaign forced Hitler to promise assistance in that theatre when the weather improved. On 13 December 1940 Hitler gave the go-ahead for Operation Marita, a military solution to Greece's intransigence.

Italian assistance

Then came the need to provide additional German air and land forces to stiffen Italian operations in North Africa and the Mediterranean: Rommel's Afrika Korps was established in Libya in February, while Hans Geisler's X. Fliegerkorps started operations in the Sicilian Narrows against the Royal Navy and aided the Axis in Libya. The next stage in the Balkan imbroglio was the annexation of Bulgaria, through whose territory the Germans would stage in the course of Operation Marita; an agreement

for this action was made in a meeting between Feldmarschall Wilhelm List, commander of the 12th Army, and the Bulgarian general staff on 8 February 1941. Two weeks later, German troops crossed the Danube from Romania and took up strategic positions in Bulgaria; on the next day, 28 February 1941, Bulgaria signed the Tripartite Pact to become an Axis ally. Despite delays, all boded well for the Wehrmacht's build-up of forces in the Balkans. There remained, however, the task of bringing neighbouring Yugoslavia into the Axis fold – already there had been moves by the British to goad the Yugoslavs into participating in the campaign in Greece and Albania against the Italians. Hitler exerted pressure upon Prince Paul, and Yugoslavia duly signed the Tripartite Pact on 25 March 1941.

When news of this covert act of liaison was received, a popular uprising, led by senior air force officers, took place in Belgrade on the night of 26-27 March. This caused a furious outburst from Hitler, who made reference to the altered situation caused by the putsch in Belgrade: "Yugoslavia", he asserted, "in spite of her protestations of loyalty, must be considered for the time being as an enemy and therefore crushed as speedily as possible."

Romania became a signatory of the Axis Tripartite Pact on

23 November 1940, and thereafter units of the Luftwaffe were established at Bucharest for the instruction of the Romanian air force; flak battalions were also sent to protect the Ploesti oil complex. During the early months of 1941, the Luftwaffe's strength in Romania grew, and by March 1941 some 400 first- and second-line types were based at Ploesti, Arad, Deta, Focsani and Craiova. Many units moved south on 1 March 1941 following the adherence of Bulgaria to the Axis cause. Deployed on the airfields at Sofia, Plovdiv, Krumovo, Krainitzi and Belitza, these Gruppen, which included both bombers and fighters, prepared themselves for the impending campaign in Greece.

German build-up

Following the putsch in Belgrade, which prompted Hitler's decision to attack Yugoslavia in addition to Greece, the rapid transfer of Luftwaffe units from France, Germany and the Mediterranean to the Balkans took place; the numbers involved were in the order of 600 aircraft.

At the meeting with his commanders in Berlin on 27 March 1941, Hitler stipulated that there were to be no ultimatums presented to the Yugoslav nation: it was to be destroyed utterly, with particular emphasis upon its capital, Belgrade. He charged Goering with the task of mounting a massive attack on the city. At 0500 on 6 April 1941, the skies over Belgrade were clear when the first warning of an air raid was received. A Yugoslavian observer post, some 80 miles

(130 km) north of Belgrade, sighted a formation of 50 or more Dornier Do 17Z-2s and Ju 88A-4s of KG 2, KG 3 and KG 51 flying in from the direction of the Hungarian border; the first German aircraft to arrive were a Gruppe of Ju 87B-2s which circled the city, and peeled off into their dives from 13,945 ft (4250 m) on the nearby airfield at Zemun. The following waves bombed the city centre including the royal palace and the marshalling yards. The attacks continued over the next three days and nights. The city was razed, and some 17,000 civilians lost their lives in what the Luftwaffe termed Operation Punishment.

The small Yugoslav air force fought back valiantly, but was soon overwhelmed; 50 fighters were destroyed at Zemun on the first morning by dive-bomber and strafing attacks. The Jagdgruppen fought Hawker Hurricanes and Messerschmitt Bf 109E-1s which had been imported during 1939-40, and also Dornier Do 17s that were used by the Yugoslav 3rd Bomber Wing. The latter lost many of its aircraft on the ground, but fought back to operate several raids on Sofia and Bucharest, and surrounding airfields.

On 8 April 1941 General Ewald von Kleist's XIV Panzerkorps attacked towards Nis, and struck northwest for Belgrade. Maribor and Zagreb fell on 9 and 10 April 1941 respectively while, the next day, the Germans received the surrender of Belgrade. The final two-pronged assault came from southern Austria and Hungary into Croatia and Slovenia. On 17 April 1941 the Yugoslavian government signed the instrument of surrender.

THE INVASION OF GREECE AND YUGOSLAVIA: HITLER STRIKES SOUTH

HUNGARY

49th German Corps

Klagenfurt

51st German Corps

2nd Italian army

46th German Corps (10 April)

3rd Hungarian army (11 April)

Maribor

Celje

7th Yug. army

Barcs

Szeged

Timisoara

41st German Corps

Trieste
Ljubljana

Zagreb

Karlovac (12 April)

4th Yug. army

Osijek

1st Yug. army

Vrsac (11 April)

ROMANIA

Fiume

Deinice

Brod

Mitrovic

2nd Yug. army

Belgrade (occupied 13 April)

Pula (Italian naval base)

Bihac

6th Yug. army

Zara (Italian naval base)

Valjevo

Kragujevac
Uzice

Krusevac

5th Yug. army

Split

Sarajevo (15 April)

Nis

BULGARIA

Pirot

14th German Corps

Kriva Planka

Sofia

Dubrovnik

Italian infantry division

Prizren

Skopje (8 April)

Vranje

40th German PZ Corps

Scutari

Ekhinos

Durazzo (Italian naval base)

Tirana

Stip

18th German Corps

Strumica (6 April)

Drama

Kavalla

Bitolj

ALBANIA

Edhessa

Valona

Korce

Thessalonika (9 April)

THASOS (16 April)

SAMOTHRACE (19 April)

Kozani

Katerini

LEMNOS

Ioannia (20 April)

GREECE

Larisa (19 April)

Paramitha

Trikkala

Volos

LESBOS (4 May)

Arta

Lamia
Molos

CHIOS (4 May)

Mesolongion (26 April)

Patrai

Thebes

Rafina

Pirgos

Corinth (6 April)

Piraeus

Porto Rafti

Nauplia

Kalamata (28 April)

Monemvasia

Canea

Heraklion

CRETE

→	German advance
⇢	Italian advance
⇠	Hungarian advance
→	Allied evacuation routes

The main attack on Yugoslavia came from List's 12th Army, which was already in position in Bulgaria, and which would also be responsible for the invasion of Greece. German advances from the north, east and southeast were added to by an Italian attack down the Dalmatian coast towards Dubrovnik; in all, the campaign lasted only 10 days. At the time of the German invasion, the majority of the Greek forces were deployed against the Italians on the Albanian front. The balance, together with Commonwealth troops sent from Egypt, held the Metaxas and Aliakmon defensive lines. The German advance through the Monastir Gap forced the surrender of the Greeks in the east and pushed the British back to Thermopylae and beyond to the evacuation of Kalamata. Luftwaffe command of the air meant that troops and equipment could be moved with ease throughout the theatre, the primary transport aircraft being the Ju 52 'Tante Ju'. This was backed up later, in the invasion of Crete, by the DFS 230 glider, carrying elements of the Fallschirmjägerregiment 2 (FJR 2).

The invasion of Crete

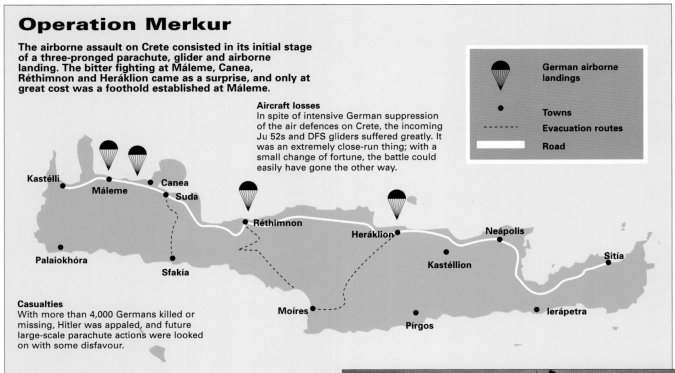

Operation Merkur

The airborne assault on Crete consisted in its initial stage of a three-pronged parachute, glider and airborne landing. The bitter fighting at Máleme, Canea, Réthimnon and Heráklion came as a surprise, and only at great cost was a foothold established at Máleme.

Aircraft losses
In spite of intensive German suppression of the air defences on Crete, the incoming Ju 52s and DFS gliders suffered greatly. It was an extremely close-run thing; with a small change of fortune, the battle could easily have gone the other way.

German airborne landings
Towns
Evacuation routes
Road

Kastélli
Máleme
Canea
Suda
Réthimnon
Heráklion
Neápolis
Sitía
Palaiokhóra
Sfakía
Kastéllion
Ierápetra
Moíres
Pírgos

Casualties
With more than 4,000 Germans killed or missing, Hitler was appaled, and future large-scale parachute actions were looked on with some disfavour.

The battle for Crete was a relatively short and bloody affair. The Allies harassed German forces until a massive combined Luftwaffe/Wehrmacht airborne assault on the island forced the British and Commonwealth troops to evacuate.

British troops began arriving on Crete in November 1940 and the Marine Naval Base Defence Organisation (MNBDO) was set up at Suda Bay with troops and anti-aircraft equipment. No permanent RAF squadrons were situated on the island, but the Fleet Air Arm stationed No. 805 Squadron there, with its reduced strength of Fairey Fulmars, Gloster Sea Gladiators and Brewster F2A Buffaloes.

By April 1941, the RAF Air Staff had concluded that the air defence of Crete was an impossibility. Although the few fighter squadrons available for

RAF Middle East Command had achieved remarkable results over Libya, Greece and Malta, these successes were not to last. Campaigns were soon to be pursued in Greece, Syria, Iraq, Abyssinia and Somaliland in the Western Desert, amid requests by the Mediterranean Fleet for assistance. This was also at a time when Middle East Command was only receiving a trickle of bombers and fighters from the UK and many of these, such as Hurricane Mk Is and P-40Bs (Tomahawk Mk I), were second-best to the Spitfire Mk VBs being retained in Britain. At the same time, while Middle East

Ground crew prepare to load an Rb 50/30 reconnaissance camera into a Bf 110C-5. Operating from Greece, such aircraft failed to discover the true nature of Crete's terrain.

Command was being given more and more tasks, the British Isles did still face the very real threat of invasion.

By the end of April, it was decided that some RAF aircraft

would be stationed on Crete to harass Axis airfields on Rhodes and Scarpanto and to act as escort protectors. Blenheim Mk IFs, Hurricanes and Gladiators were made available

This Junkers Ju 52/3mg4e of the Stabsschwarm (staff flight) of IV/KGzbV 1, based around Corinth and Megara, was under the command of Oberst Buchholz in May 1941. KGzbV 1 suffered from the very real tactical disadvantage of operating from airfields of sand, the effect on aircraft performance being disastrous.

Luftwaffe bombers over Crete

The German forces employed their latest bombers against the Allied Forces entrenched in Crete. The task was deemed so important that aircraft were relocated from other air units around Europe.

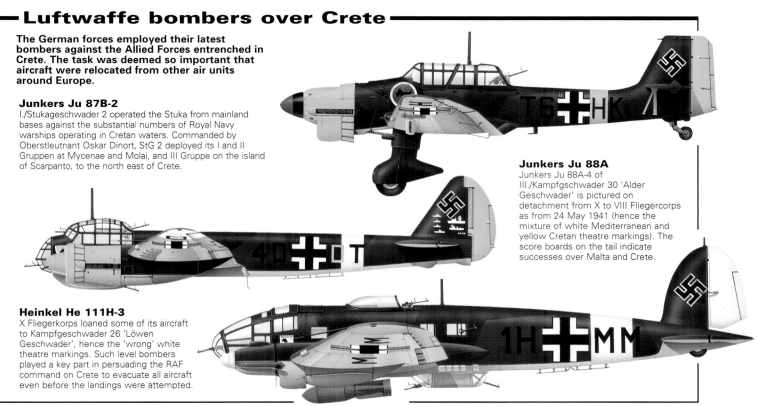

Junkers Ju 87B-2

I./Stukageschwader 2 operated the Stuka from mainland bases against the substantial numbers of Royal Navy warships operating in Cretan waters. Commanded by Oberstleutnant Oskar Dinort, StG 2 deployed its I and II Gruppen at Mycenae and Molai, and III Gruppe on the island of Scarpanto, to the north east of Crete.

Junkers Ju 88A

Junkers Ju 88A-4 of III./Kampfgeschwader 30 'Alder Geschwader' is pictured on detachment from X to VIII Fliegercorps as from 24 May 1941 (hence the mixture of white Mediterranean and yellow Cretan theatre markings). The score boards on the tail indicate successes over Malta and Crete.

Heinkel He 111H-3

X Fliegerkorps loaned some of its aircraft to Kampfgeschwader 26 'Löwen Geschwader', hence the 'wrong' white theatre markings. Such level bombers played a key part in persuading the RAF command on Crete to evacuate all aircraft even before the landings were attempted.

and they soon began to tussle with the Germans.

As a result, the Luftwaffe soon turned its attention away from convoy attacks to attacking airfields on Crete. Swarms of Bf 109Es, Bf 110C, Do 17Z-2s and He 111H-3s pounded the Allied bases and casualties soon mounted. By 19 May, with the prospect of no more reinforcements, it was decided to pull all remaining aircraft out of Crete.

German invasion

By April 1941, German staff had begun to plan how to take Crete, despite some opposition from senior personnel. It was decided that the invasion would take place in the form of a massive assault of airborne troops, with some 22,750 men involved. Troops would either be dropped by parachute, land by assault glider or transport, or invade by sea. It would be a truly massive undertaking, the like of which had never been seen before. The objectives of Operation Merkur (Mercury) were primarily to capture the air bases at Máleme, Canea and Suda in order to secure landing

sites for further troops. The assault was planned for the end of May. However, German intelligence failed to reveal the nature of the terrain, which was a maze of rocky hills and deep clefts that favoured the defenders. Secondly, the great strength of the British, Greek and Commonwealth units on Crete was severely underestimated.

With the end of preliminary bombing on 20 May, the airborne assault of Máleme and Canea began. The DFS 230 gliders came in too high and missed their intended landing place, instead landing near prepared 5th NZ Brigade positions on Hill 107, which effectively neutralised them. A similar fate was suffered by the parachutists of III/FJStR who lost 400 of their 600 troops in a short space of time. Other drops at Canea and Galatas went according to plan, but drops at Réthimnon and Heráklion suffered inordinately high casualties. By the end of the day, the German troops were fighting for their lives. However, over the night, the Germans discovered that the New

Zealanders had retreated, meaning that the hill was now in German hands, therefore ensuring that the Luftwaffe could reinforce that position from the air. Gradually, the Fallschirmjäger units, now bolstered by Generalleutnant Ringel's 5 Gebirgsdivision, consolidated their position. After a savage battle on 25 May, the pressure on Allied forces was such that a withdrawal was the only solution. Allied troops streamed towards Sfakia and the fighting retreat ended on 31 May 1941. However, German casualties were high: 1,990 men were killed, 1,995 missing and 327 drowned at sea. The terrible cost horrified Hitler and never again were the Fallschirmjäger units employed on mass airborne assaults during the war.

Sea battle

Throughout the battle for Crete, the Mediterranean fleet was committed to support, supply and, later, evacuation duties. Air support was minimal, however, the HMS *Formidable* providing 18 Fulmar Mk Is, while RAF Hurricane Mk IAs, Beaufighters,

Blenheims and Marylands gave additional assistance. This lack of support was to prove costly for the Allied forces. The Luftwaffe took a bloody toll: along with 38 RAF aircraft downed, the Royal Navy lost three cruisers and six destroyers, with a battleship, carrier, six cruisers and eight destroyers damaged. About 15,000 Imperial troops were killed or captured. The Luftwaffe lost more than 200 aircraft, of which over half were invaluable Ju 52/3ms. The result was that the Balkan campaign had taken six weeks longer than planned and effectively delayed the start of Operation Barbarossa.

Below: The Curtiss Tomahawk began to enter service with RAF squadrons in North Africa at the time of the Crete campaign, but was just too late for any possible air reinforcement of the island.

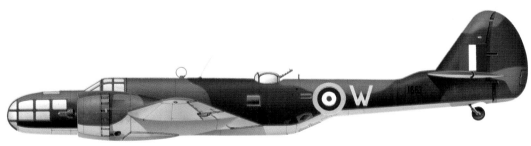

This Martin Maryland Mk II of No. 24 Squadron, South African Air Force, was based at Fuka in Egypt in May 1941. From 23 May, the Squadron was one of those allocated to operations over Crete, bombing the German positions on Máleme airfield in conjunction with six RAF squadrons.

Malta and the Mediterranean

With Mussolini's declaration of war, the Mediterranean became another theatre of conflict, the Italians clashing violently with the Royal Navy. Central to the Mediterranean region lay the small but vital island of Malta.

Malta's position as the nexus of Mediterranean lines of communication was the key to the island's strategic importance and vulnerability. Losses were heavy, as the burning wreck of this Short Sunderland testifies.

In 1940, the threat posed by the powerful Italian fleet of Admiral Angelo Iachino became real. The principal sea route from the UK to its possessions of the Empire and the Commonwealth in the Middle and Far East lay through the Mediterranean, from Gibraltar to the Suez Canal. The alternatives lay around the Cape of Good Hope and through the Indian Ocean. Responsibility for the defence of the British sea lanes in the Mediterranean lay with Admiral Andrew B. Cunningham, headquartered at Alexandria. Due to the French capitulation, an additional naval squadron was needed for the western Mediterranean and this was named Force H.

The balance of power in the Mediterranean was tipped just in favour of the Royal Navy. In June 1940, the Mediterranean fleet and Force H consisted of four battleships, a battlecruiser, two carriers and a number of cruisers and destroyers. The two fleets, separated by almost 2,000 miles (3220 km) of sea, were opposed by the Italian navy's six battleships, 21 cruisers and over 50 destroyers. What is more, its bases in Italy meant that it had significant air cover from the Regia Aeronautica's bombers and torpedo-bombers. The British fleets had the task of supporting convoys and interdicting Italian lines of supply to Albania and North Africa, while the Italians were supporting Marshal Rodolfo Graziani's forces in Libya. These lines of supply, upon which the forces in Libya depended, could only be attacked with effect by air and by naval strike forces based at Malta.

Axis assault

The Italian Regia Aeronautica flew German-built Junkers Ju 87B-2s for attacks on Malta. Although experienced pilots were at the helm, many Ju 87s were lost to defending fighters. Junkers Ju 88A-5s were flown by the Luftwaffe on a daily basis from Sicily on very effective day and night raids against strategic targets in Malta and shipping convoys in the Mediterranean.

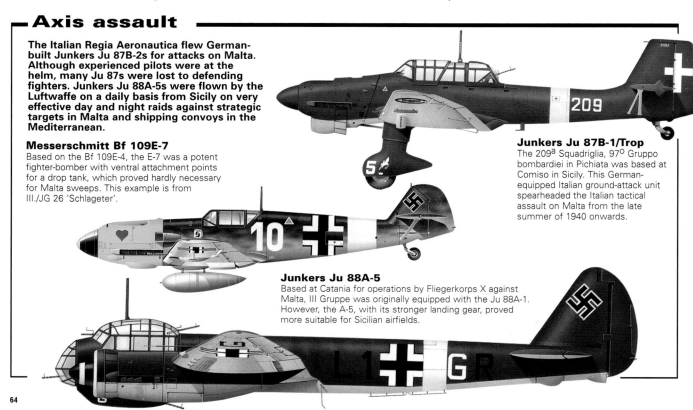

Messerschmitt Bf 109E-7
Based on the Bf 109E-4, the E-7 was a potent fighter-bomber with ventral attachment points for a drop tank, which proved hardly necessary for Malta sweeps. This example is from III./JG 26 'Schlageter'.

Junkers Ju 87B-1/Trop
The 209ª Squadriglia, 97º Gruppo bombardiei in Pichiata was based at Comiso in Sicily. This German-equipped Italian ground-attack unit spearheaded the Italian tactical assault on Malta from the late summer of 1940 onwards.

Junkers Ju 88A-5
Based at Catania for operations by Fliegerkorps X against Malta, III Gruppe was originally equipped with the Ju 88A-1. However, the A-5, with its stronger landing gear, proved more suitable for Sicilian airfields.

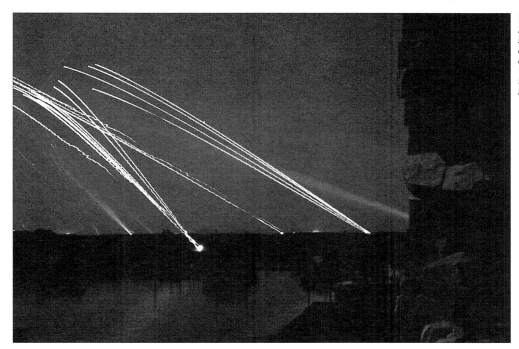

The Italians withdrew their battle fleet from the south, enabling Force H and the Mediterranean Fleet to recommence convoy runs to Malta and Greece.

Enter the Luftwaffe

However, the Royal Navy's supremacy was soon to come under a new threat. With the problems encountered by the Italians in their invasion of Greece on 28 October 1940, it soon became apparent to Hitler that German intervention in the Mediterranean and North Africa would be needed to restore Italian credibility. Planned moves included the invasion of Gibraltar and the intervention of the Luftwaffe against the RAF and RN in the Mediterranean. The Luftwaffe was also charged with closing the Suez Canal, the neutralisation of Malta as a base, the support of Axis forces in Libya, the securing of the Axis sea lanes between Italy and North Africa and attacks on British sea convoys.

Fliegerkorps X was formed in June 1940; by January 1941, its strength had reached 225 aircraft, of which 179 were serviceable. On 10 January, 60 Ju 87s and He 111s attacked a British convoy in the Sicilian narrows, severely damaging the carrier *Illustrious* and the cruisers *Southampton* and *Gloucester*. The carrier limped into harbour at Malta, where it became the target for heavy attacks by the Luftwaffe and Regia Aeronautica for more than a week. With losses increasing among the Hurricanes, and the Luftwaffe achieving almost total air superiority over the island, the Wellingtons now had to be withdrawn to North Africa and Malta was largely disarmed. The Germans were able to send half of Fliegerkorps X to Cyrenaica to support Rommel's counter-offensive in the Western Desert.

The lack of contingency planning and the neglect of Malta's air defence during 1938–40 were soon to prove disastrous. The island, although easily fortified, lay within 15 minutes' flying time from Sicily, meaning that it could be attacked from the air with ease.

At the outbreak of the war with Italy, Air Headquarters RAF Mediterranean Command was at Valletta, with the sole air defence of Malta resting on the unofficial Fighter Flight of four Sea Gladiator Mk Is and some AMES Type 6 Mk I radars. It was to be these Gladiators that faced the Italian S.M.79s, CR.42s and MC.200s that attacked on 11 June 1940. The S.M.79s initially attacked the Grand Harbour and did so unescorted, but the attention of the Sea Gladiators led to further attacks, so that the Italians needed a top cover of CR.42s and MC.200s.

Malta's first strike aircraft arrived on 24 June in the shape of Fairey Swordfish Mk I torpedo-bombers of the newly formed No. 830 Squadron. This unit had been created out of aircraft left behind by HMS *Argus* when it departed the Mediterranean. The exploits of No. 830, operating by night over the next 33 months against Axis shipping, with either 250-lb (113-kg) Mk IV GP bombs or the lethal 18-in Mark XII torpedo, became legendary.

Despite the presence of the Regia Aeronautica and the Italian navy, the supply and reinforcement of Malta posed no great problems for the Chiefs of Staff. *Argus* returned on 2 August 1940 to deliver 12 Hurricane Mk IAs. The sorely-needed Hurricanes were formed into No. 261(F) Squadron at Luqa, but soon came under attack on the airfield from Ju 87s. However, additional Hurricanes continued to arrive throughout the winter.

No. 148(B) Squadron was formed on 14 December 1940 with a view to adding to Malta's offensive capability, and was equipped with 16 Wellington Mk IC bombers. By January, however, Malta's RAF contingent was still weak, consisting of nine Swordfish Mk Is, 16 Wellington Mk ICs, seven Marylands and 16 Hurricane Mk IAs.

Fleet Air Arm offensive

The period of June 1940 to March 1941 saw a number of successful operations carried out by the carriers of Force H and the Mediterranean Fleet. On 9-10 July 1940 Sea Gladiators and Swordfishes from HMS *Eagle* took part in air strikes off Calabria and Augusta.

The Mediterranean Fleet was strengthened with the arrival in August of the *Illustrious*, the latest type of carrier, with heavy armour and armament. It was also the first carrier to operate the Fulmar Mk I fighter, in the shape of No. 806 Squadron, along with two squadrons of Swordfish torpedo-bombers. With support from *Eagle* and *Illustrious*, Cunningham's squadron went on the rampage, attacking airfields on Rhodes, Leros and in Libya. The Fulmars were an immediate success, downing 11 aircraft for the loss of one. The climax to *Illustrious*'s operations was the attack on the naval base at Taranto on 11-12 November 1940. The attack was carried out by 12 Swordfishes, using mines and torpedoes, and the mission was a major success. Three battleships were hit: *Conti di Cavour* never returned to service, while *Caio Duilio* and *Littorio* were out of action for six months. Two Swordfishes were lost but the effect was devastating.

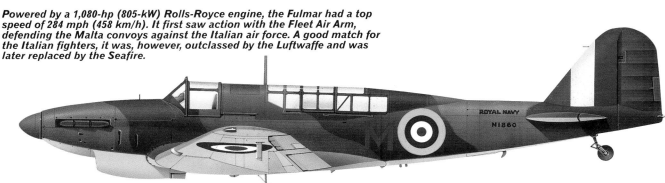

Powered by a 1,080-hp (805-kW) Rolls-Royce engine, the Fulmar had a top speed of 284 mph (458 km/h). It first saw action with the Fleet Air Arm, defending the Malta convoys against the Italian air force. A good match for the Italian fighters, it was, however, outclassed by the Luftwaffe and was later replaced by the Seafire.

War in the desert

In June 1940, war came to the Western Desert, where the Italians faced British Commonwealth troops. Over the next three years the conflict in the desert would be governed by lines of supply and communication.

RAF Middle East Command presided over vast areas of the African continent with many aircraft of a previous era. Almost symbolic of the declining Empire is this Vickers Valentia, flying over Heliopolis, Egypt.

Believing that he would be deprived of the spoils of war when German forces invaded northern France, Benito Mussolini entered the war alongside Hitler on 10 June 1940. At a stroke, the balance of naval power in the Mediterranean swung in favour of the Axis, even more heavily after the French fleet refused to continue operations on the Allied side and was accordingly attacked by the Royal Navy in its North African ports.

Three immediate threats to British strategic interests were posed by Italy's entry into the war: the naval base at Malta would be threatened by Italian air forces in Sicily; Italian forces in Cyrenaica were close to the vital Suez Canal and the British naval base at Alexandria; and a large Italian colonial army and air force threatened British bases in East Africa and the Arabian peninsula.

Little could be done to strengthen Malta's defences immediately and the island was left much to its own devices, recourse being found in a handful of obsolete Sea Gladiators and some Hurricanes with which to provide a measure of air defence.

In the Western Desert, however, the position was more critical and in the face of considerable Italian numerical superiority, the RAF possessed an extraordinary mix of obsolescent aircraft and a huge expanse of territory. Nevertheless, by dint of ingenious deployment and careful use of the resources available, the two Gladiator squadrons managed to exact a considerable toll of Italian aircraft during the early months of the desert war, while General Wavell was able to set about his brilliant campaign which took his army far into Cyrenaica.

Gradually, the RAF was able to send a trickle of reinforcements to the Middle East, at first by convoy through the Mediterranean and later to Takoradi in the Gold Coast for overland flights to the Canal Zone. Vickers Wellingtons and Lockheed Hudsons were flown out directly from the UK, and Hurricanes and Bristol Blenheims arrived by the

Takoradi route; other aircraft were crated and shipped out by the sea route round the Cape of Good Hope.

In East Africa the Italians gained early successes by invading and overrunning British Somaliland and, in doing so, posed a threat to Aden. However, in support of another brilliant counteroffensive by Commonwealth forces, RAF

RAF armourers prepare a Bristol Blenheim Mk I light bomber from No. 113 Squadron for a raid. Large numbers of light bombs were frequently preferred to small numbers of larger weapons, being more effective against unarmoured targets.

The Messerschmitt Bf 109E-4/Trop fighters of I./JG 27 brought a new tactical dimension to air operations over North Africa; they clearly outclassed all available British fighters in the theatre in the spring of 1941.

Vickers Wellesleys and Gladiators, operating alongside aircraft of the South African Air Force, succeeded in defeating elements of the Italian air force in East Africa. In due course, the Italian presence in the horn of Africa was eliminated.

It was at the moment of triumph for Wavell's forces, which reached Benghazi in the first North African desert offensive, that RAF units were called on to go to the assistance of Greece, a critical weakening that was to be compounded by events in Iraq in 1941.

Following a rebellion in support of the pro-Axis Rashid Ali, the large RAF base at Habbaniyah in Iraq came under attack, supported by German and Italian aircraft, a threat eventually overcome by the deployment of Wellingtons,

Blenheims, Gladiators and Hurricanes for defence of the base.

Frustrated by the Italians' inability to gain a decisive victory in North Africa, the Germans moved the advance elements of a major force of aircraft to the Mediterranean (notably a Geschwader, JG 27 of Bf 109Es) early in 1941, and these were quickly followed by Ju 87s and Ju 88s. It was the arrival of this Fliegerkorps in the theatre that first posed a major threat to Malta; for a while, its use as a naval base was severely restricted and it was sustained by sailing aircraft-carriers into the Mediterranean and flying off large numbers of Hurricanes to land on the island's airfields.

On 6 February 1941 Generalleutnant Erwin Rommel, the ex-leader of the successful

7th Panzer Division in France, was appointed to lead the German contingent, which on 2 February had been named the Deutsches Afrika Korps.

The Luftwaffe's intervention in North Africa became apparent from 10 February, when Bf 110s carried out low-level strafing of British troops and motor transport on the roads in the El Agheila/Benin area; Ju 88A-1s, operating from Catania and Gerbini, made daily attacks and prevented the use of port facilities. On 23 February, I and II/ LG 1's Ju 88s sank HMS *Terror*, a monitor en route from Benghazi to Tobruk, in the absence of RAF fighters.

By March 1941, Commonwealth forces were under strength so Rommel began his first offensive on 31 March. Approximately 200 light tanks

and APCs headed east, forcing the British to withdraw. Ju 87s pounded British forces, while small numbers of RAF and RAAF Hurricanes claimed a number of kills.

Rommel had taken Benghazi and Msus by 4 April and the decision was made by British forces to withdraw to Egypt. The Luftwaffe's bombers had been suffering at the hands of the RAF so Bf 109E-4 and E-7/Trops were sent to their defence. The Germans continued eastwards, bypassing the garrison of Tobruk which was reduced to a state of siege. On 25 April the Afrika Korps struck hard and pushed the British back onto the line at Sofafi-Buq Buq, from where some four months earlier, the British forces had originally struck out.

Obsolescent adversaries

At the outbreak of the war, both Allied and Axis forces still possessed a large number of aircraft developed many years before. These aircraft were no match for more modern types and soon disappeared from the battlefields.

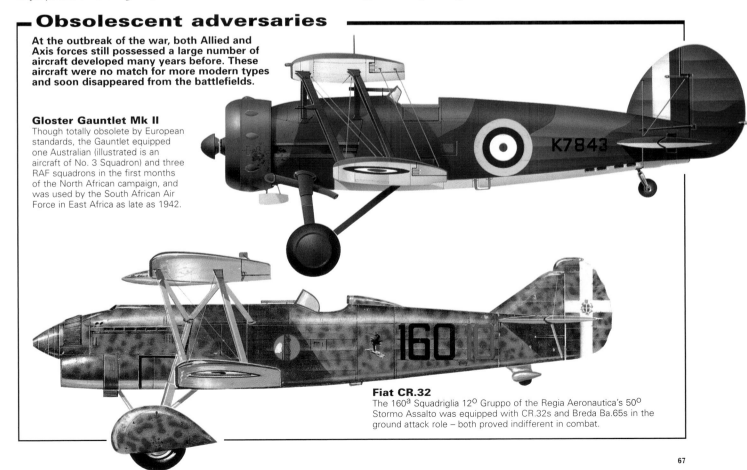

Gloster Gauntlet Mk II
Though totally obsolete by European standards, the Gauntlet equipped one Australian (illustrated is an aircraft of No. 3 Squadron) and three RAF squadrons in the first months of the North African campaign, and was used by the South African Air Force in East Africa as late as 1942.

Fiat CR.32
The 160ª Squadriglia 12º Gruppo of the Regia Aeronautica's 50º Stormo Assalto was equipped with CR.32s and Breda Ba.65s in the ground attack role – both proved indifferent in combat.

Messerschmitt Bf 110
Zerstörer

Despite its successes in the early stages of the war, the Bf 110, with its high speed and heavy armament still found itself outclassed when faced with Spitfires and Hurricanes over the British Isles.

Having proved near-invincible during the Blitzkrieg campaign, the Bf 110 suffered desperately against the fighters of the RAF during the Battle of Britain. Soon, however, it would become the bane of Bomber Command in the night-fighter role.

Speed, acceleration and high manoeuvrability in the cut and thrust of a dogfight were the objectives laid before the fighter designers of all nations following the end of the war in Europe in 1918. Accordingly, it was the single-seat biplane, of high power:weight ratio and relatively low wing-loading, that held the position of pre-eminence in the world's air forces. Then came the monoplane revolution of the 1930s, with monocoque fuselages, retractable landing gear, cantilever tail units, and stressed single- or double-spar wings; the configuration of the fighter remained essentially the same, with armament and fuel tankage carefully restricted so as not to detract from speed and manoeuvrability. However, combat operations over the Western Front during 1917-18 had accentuated the need for fighters with extended range and endurance, and in particular for those with a combat radius of action that could enable them to accompany bombers on missions deep into enemy airspace, either as escort fighters or in order to gain air supremacy in an appointed area.

To design such an aircraft was considered to be well nigh impossible but, in 1934, the idea was resurrected. Whether the long-range strategic fighter concept was to be committed to offensive or defensive tasks is still a matter for argument. For the Luftwaffe at least, the requirement for this type, termed the *Zerstörer* (destroyer), was the pursuit and destruction of enemy bombers operating over the Reich, plus the additional ability to harass over a lengthy period as the bombers withdrew.

Lean design

Attending to the RLM specifications for the development of a heavy strategic fighter, the team at the Bayerische Flugzeugwerke AG (later Messerschmitt AG) started work on the project in the summer of 1935. With their wayward brilliance, they ignored much of the specification data and concentrated their efforts on the design of a lean, all-metal, twin-engined monoplane. Powered by two Daimler Benz DB 600A engines, the prototype Bf 110 V1 achieved a maximum speed of 314 mph (505 km/h) at 10,415 ft (3175 m), considerably

The prototype Messerschmitt Bf 110 V1 first flew from Augsburg-Haunstetten on 12 May 1936, with Rudolf Opitz at the controls. Only four pre-production aircraft were built and their sleek design was very advanced for its day.

in excess of that reached by the single-engined Messerschmitt Bf 109B-2 fighter. Of course, acceleration and manoeuvrability, as noted by the test pilots and later by those at the Erprobungsstelle (service trials detachment) on this and subsequent prototypes, in no way compared with those of

lighter fighters. But Hermann Goering ignored the misgivings of the Luftwaffe regarding the Messerschmitt Bf 110's potentialities, and ordered that production should proceed. The first pre-production model, the Bf 110B-01 powered by two Junkers Jumo 210Ga engines, first flew on 19 April 1938 in the

As a way of destroying large formations of Allied bombers and for ground attack, a number of rocket launching methods was trialled on the Bf 110. This example tested the RZ65 rocket shell, which was fired from a battery of 12 2⅞-in (73-mm) tubes mounted beneath the fuselage. The installation proved unsatisfactory and was ultimately abandoned.

Left: This Messerschmitt Bf 110B-0 fighter reveals the type's slim fuselage and graceful lines. Although the aircraft was hard put to stay the pace with the later single-seat Allied fighters, many German aces claimed high scores on the type. Too vulnerable as a day-fighter, the Bf 110 remained the mainstay of Germany's night-fighter force from 1940 to 1945.

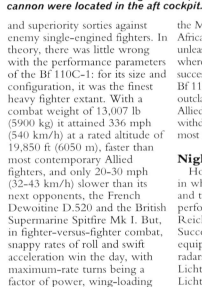

Above: It was as a night-fighter that the Bf 110 finally found major success. There were over a dozen radar-equipped variants and their armament was steadily modified and upgraded. In one type, oblique firing 30-mm MK 108 cannon were successfully installed. Known as schräge Musik (slanting music or jazz), the cannon were located in the aft cockpit.

wake of a major reorganisation of the Luftwaffe's units.

The shortage of Daimler Benz powerplants and the retention of the Jumo 210Ga engines conferred only a mediocre capability on the Bf 110B-1 series that emanated from the Augsburg production lines in the summer. Armed with two 20-mm Oerlikon MG FF cannon and four 0.31-in (7.92-mm) MG 17 machine-guns, the Bf 110B-1 had a maximum speed of 283 mph (455 km/h) at its rated altitude of 13,125 ft (4000 m); the service ceiling was 26,245 ft (8000 m). This version was the first to enter service, equipping a number of schweren Jagdgruppen (heavy fighter wings) in the autumn of 1938.

Early in 1939, the Messerschmitt Bf 110C-0 pre-production fighters were issued to the newly-formed Zerstörergruppen (ex-schweren Jagdgruppen); these featured the modified airframe that was to endure throughout the aircraft's lifetime, and were powered by the 12-cylinder, inverted-Vee direct-injection Daimler Benz DB 601A-1 engines rated at 1,100 hp (820 kW) at 12,140 ft (3700 m). The production Bf 110C-1s were highly effective

long-range fighters, and the crews of I.(Zerst)/ Lehrgeschwader Nr 1, I./Zerstörergeschwader Nr 1 and I./ZG 76, who manned the new type, represented the cream of the Luftwaffe's fighter arm. Just before the outbreak of war, in September 1939, each Gruppe had two staffeln with Bf 110C-1s and a conversion unit with Bf 110B-3 trainers.

Zerstörer at war

The crews used their heavy aircraft well during the short campaign in Poland during September, flying top cover to the Heinkels and Dorniers and conducting sweeps at 19,685 ft (6000 m) and above; they quickly recognised the stupidity of entering turning matches with the nimble Polish PZL P.11c fighters, and adopted climb-and-dive tactics while maintaining good airspeed at all times. Oberst Walter Grabmann's I.(Z)/LG 1 (led by Hauptmann Schleif) downed five PZL P.11s over Warsaw on the evening of 1 September while covering the Heinkel He 111Ps of II./KG 1.

Already it was apparent that the Zerstörergruppen had eschewed what was probably the originally intended role, and were being employed on escort

and superiority sorties against enemy single-engined fighters. In theory, there was little wrong with the performance parameters of the Bf 110C-1: for its size and configuration, it was the finest heavy fighter extant. With a combat weight of 13,007 lb (5900 kg) it attained 336 mph (540 km/h) at a rated altitude of 19,850 ft (6050 m), faster than most contemporary Allied fighters, and only 20-30 mph (32-43 km/h) slower than its next opponents, the French Dewoitine D.520 and the British Supermarine Spitfire Mk I. But, in fighter-versus-fighter combat, snappy rates of roll and swift acceleration win the day, with maximum-rate turns being a factor of power, wing-loading and pilot strength.

Few problems were encountered by the Bf 110 pilots over Poland and Scandinavia, and their early success gave them a sense of security in the aircraft's abilities. Staunch opposition over France and southern England during 1940 destroyed much of that myth, however, for, while the Bf 110 could operate with relative impunity at high level, when it came down to fight with the nimble Spitfires and Hurricanes at medium level, often operating as a bomber escort, it found itself thoroughly out-turned and, as a result, was regularly shot down. At this time, other variants of the Bf 110, including fighter-bombers and extended-range fighters, made their appearance over Britain or in

the Mediterranean and North Africa. Bf 110 units were then unleashed against the Soviets, where they enjoyed mixed success. As the war progressed, the Bf 110 found itself more and more outclassed by the latest series of Allied aircraft and was gradually withdrawn from service in most theatres.

Night-fighter

However, there was one field in which the Bf 110 excelled, and that was as a night-fighter, performing in the defence of the Reich against enemy bombers. Successive series of aircraft were equipped with ever better radars, in particular the FuG 212 Lichtenstein C-1 and FuG 220 Lichtenstein SN-2. Many pilots chalked up a number of kills, in particular Major Heinz-Wolfgang Schnaufer, the last Kommodore of NJG 4 and a recipient of the Diamonds to the Knight's Cross, who claimed no fewer than 121 nocturnal kills during the war.

It should be remembered that few twin-engined aircraft, even those as legendary as the Mosquito, Kawasaki Ki-45 or Lockheed P-38 Lightning, could match the single-seat fighters of the day. Despite its failure as a dog-fighter, the Bf 110 should be remembered as a highly efficient and versatile all-purpose combat aircraft. And, in the Bf 110's original role, as bomber destroyer – particularly at night – it proved highly effective.

A Bf 110C-4b is seen after capture by the Desert Rats of General Montgomery's Eighth Army. The Bf 110 played an important role in the Western Desert, providing fighter-bomber support to Rommel's Afrika Korps.

A trio of Westland Lysanders from No. 208 Squadron cruises over the Suez Canal. To operate effectively the 'Lizzie' needed fighter cover, drawing precious fighters away from more important tasks. Its reconnaissance tasks in the desert passed largely to the Hurricane.

The campaign for North Africa

By April 1941 Rommel's first offensive had pushed the Commonwealth forces back into Egypt. The ensuing campaign to claw back territory, and to relieve besieged Tobruk, was long and bitter.

Italy's inability to stem the advance of General Wavell's forces in the Western Desert in late 1940 resulted in German intervention in the form of the Deutsches Afrika Korps, commanded by Generalleutnant Erwin Rommel. At first the force was small, with only a few aircraft, but its early successes were spectacular, fortunes in this theatre favouring those with short lines of supply. By 30 April 1941 Wavell's forces were back in Egypt, while the Australian garrison at Tobruk was surrounded. Tobruk held, mainly because by this time Rommel's supply chain was too long.

A two-phase counter-attack was launched, coded Brevity and Battleaxe. Operation Brevity opened on 15 May 1941, air cover being provided primarily by Hurricanes and Blenheim

Mk IVs. Other Commonwealth types on charge included Westland Lysanders, Martin Marylands and four squadrons of Wellington bombers. Opposing them were around 150 aircraft under Fliegerführer Afrika (Generalmajor Stefan Frölich) – comprising Bf 110s, Hs 126s, Ju 87s, Ju 88s and Bf 109Es – and the Italian V. Squadra, with SM.79s, SM.84s, Fiat CR.42s and G.50s and Macchi MC.200s. In the air the Commonwealth Hurricane pilots found themselves roughly on a par with the 'Emils' and Italian fighters, the low-level nature of the fighting negating the advantages of the Bf 109 over the Hurricane. Brevity ended after two weeks of stout defence by the Afrika Korps, despite severe fuel shortages.

Battleaxe aimed to relieve Tobruk, and opened on 14 June

The Savoia-Marchetti SM.79 was slower than a Blenheim, but better armed, and made up the bulk of the Regia Aeronautica's bomber force in Libya. These are from the 10ª Squadriglia.

1941. After three days of heavy fighting in which the German 0.35-in (88-mm) guns tore through the Commonwealth armour, Rommel counter-attacked, pushing the Allied force back into Egypt once more.

Tomahawk joins the fray

By this time the Curtiss Tomahawk was in theatre, an aircraft which pleasantly surprised the Commonwealth pilots for its abilities at low level. However, the main opposition was the battle-hardened *Experten* of I./JG 27, who were beginning to compile impressive tallies against their relatively inexperienced enemy. Blenheim bombers, in particular, took a mauling, but the North Africa theatre was considered of low priority in terms of new equipment. The failure of Battleaxe was probably the lowest point in the whole campaign, from an Allied point of view.

In July 1941 Air Vice Marshal Arthur Coningham arrived to take command of the air forces in North Africa. Coincident

with his arrival was a major improvement in terms of aircraft supply, which increased in both quality and quantity. Large numbers of Tomahawks and Marylands arrived, and in September the first of the excellent Douglas Boston Mk III appeared. Beauforts were received for coastal patrols and anti-ship attacks, while two squadrons of Beaufighters arrived. A squadron of Fleet Air Arm Grumman Martlets was deployed ashore.

The Axis, too, was re-equipping, and the new Bf 109F was to prove to be the most capable aircraft in-theatre for some while. II./JG 27 arrived in September with new 'Friedrichs', while I./JG 27 withdrew to Germany for conversion. This new variant, in its F-2 and F-4 forms (suitably tropicalised), was an outstanding

This dramatic shot from the gun camera of an Allied fighter shows the moment when this Ju 52/3m's starboard fuel tanks caught fire during a low-level strafing attack.

The Martin Maryland partnered the Bristol Blenheim in the light bomber squadrons at the start of the campaign. It was mostly operated by South African Air Force squadrons, although this is an RAF reconnaissance aircraft from No. 39 Squadron.

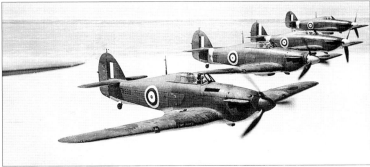

Above: The most valuable commodity for the Allies in the early months of the war was the Hurricane fighter. These three Mk Is are seen during their delivery flight from Takoradi (Gold Coast), prior to fitment of the Vokes dust filter.

fighter, and in the hands of the experienced pilots such as Hans-Joachim Marseille – nicknamed the Star of Afrika – rapidly assumed air superiority over the desert. Nevertheless, the Luftwaffe scarcely ever had enough fighters to fully wrest control of the skies from the Allies, and effective air support for the Commonwealth ground forces was maintained. Another Axis arrival, in November 1941, was the Macchi MC.202 Folgore, which bolstered the Italian fighter force which had hitherto relied on G.50s, MC.200s and a few Fiat CR.42 biplanes.

During the autumn of 1941 the Commonwealth forces built up their air forces to a sizeable strength, and in October embarked on a softening-up phase in preparation for the next major assault. The targets were mostly the Axis airfields and, although the Allies suffered considerable losses at the hands of the Bf 109Fs, the raids severely damaged the Axis air forces, hitting the Stuka dive-bomber force hard.

On the night of 18/19 November 1941, General Sir Claude Auchinleck led the Eighth Army on Operation Crusader. With heavy air cover, the Allies bypassed the Axis defences at the much-fought over Halfaya Pass, and headed for Tobruk. Despite an intense battle at Sidi Rezegh, the Allies prevailed and on 7 December Tobruk was relieved. The advance continued, taking Mechili on 18 December and Benghazi on 23 December. By 6 January Rommel had been pushed back to his original start lines at El Agheila.

In the air Crusader proved to be a triumph of quantity over quality: JG 27's pilots remained undisputed masters of the air, but there were too few to completely disrupt the Allied air cover operations. Recognising the situation, the Luftwaffe dispatched more 'Friedrichs' in the shape of III./JG 27 and, for a brief period, III./JG 53. However, the Allied advance had taken several of the Axis airfields, with the result that many aircraft had to be pulled back to Tripolitania or even Sicily.

Fighter-bombers

Allied air cover consisted of Hurricanes and Tomahawks, the Hurricane operating increasingly in the ground attack role. The British had realised, belatedly, that the fighter was an ideal tool for close support of the army, and that traditional types such as the Lysander could only be used where they were unopposed by enemy fighters. The Hurricane made an admirable fighter-bomber, and was arguably the Allies' most important weapon during the North African campaign. The Blenheim and Boston light-bombers roved ahead of the ground forces, attacking Axis forces which were often well dug-in. The deadly Flak 88 guns, which were proving lethal against the lightly armoured Matilda and Crusader tanks, were prime targets. At night the Wellingtons kept up a consistent bombardment of Axis positions. Photo-reconnaissance was performed by specially equipped Hurricanes and Beaufighters.

Losses had been considerable on both sides. Between 18 November 1941 and 20 January 1942 Fliegerführer Afrika lost 232 aircraft to all causes, while the Italian V. Squadra lost at least 100. During the 12,000 sorties flown by Commonwealth squadrons, over 300 aircraft were lost.

Crusader's success can be attributed to many factors, not least of which were the efforts of the small RAF anti-shipping force based on Malta, which disrupted and destroyed Axis convoys to the point that the Afrika Korps was always short of fuel and ammunition, and operating at the end of a long and flimsy supply line.

For a few short days Crusader had seemed to be a momentous triumph, but Rommel was not a man to be underestimated. British intelligence did not consider that he would break out from his El Agheila stronghold, and certainly not within a matter of days of his retreat. But, on 21 January 1942, that is precisely what happened, and by June Tobruk had fallen and nothing appeared to stand between Rommel and his prize: the Suez Canal.

Figuring in the pre-Crusader build-up of aircraft in the Desert Air Force were the Blenheim Mk IVs of GRB 1, Free French air force. They were based at Abu Sueir, Egypt, from October 1941.

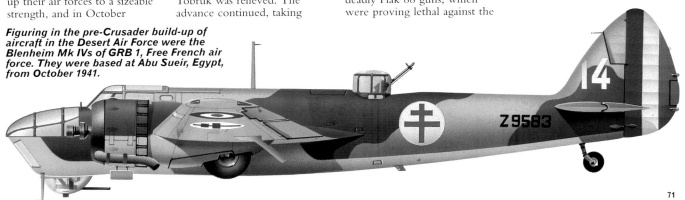

Malta's time of trial

As an FAA pilot scrambles to his aircraft, naval ground crew prepare to swing the prop of Gloster-built Hurricane Mk IIA BG766, armed with a pair of 250-lb (113-kg) bombs for another offensive sweep.

During the summer of 1941, the small Allied force on Malta was given a unique opportunity. It was able to strike the vital Axis supply line from Italy to North Africa and the damage inflicted was massive.

By the end of May 1941, when Crete, the Balkans and Greece had been secured by the Axis, the headquarters of General der Flieger Hans-Ferdinand Geisler's X. Fliegerkorps was transferred from Sicily to the Hotel Bretagne in Athens. Combat units that had served under X. Fliegerkorps in Sicily were posted either to Germany for the impending operations against Russia, or to the airfields of Eleusis, Tatoi, and Kalamaki in Greece, or to Máleme and Heraklion on Crete; the strike forces based in Greece and Crete were primarily of an anti-shipping nature, and consisted of II./KG 26 with Heinkel He 111H-6s and Gruppen of Lehrgeschwader Nr 1 with Junkers Ju 88A-4 bombers. These units kept up pressure on the Royal Navy, and attacked targets around Suez and in the Nile Delta. With the absence of the Germans in Sicily, the garrison on British-held Malta was freed from the constant and damaging air raids that had been the pattern of its existence during the period January–March 1941. Elements of the Regia Aeronautica, notably the SM.79s of the 30° Stormo and 279° Squadriglia, supplemented by the 10° Stormo, and the Cant Z.1007-IIs of the 9° Stormo, maintained a dire threat to the Malta supply convoys from bases in Sardinia and Sicily. But over the island itself the air was relatively secure: raids were frequent but the newly-arrived Hurricane Mk IIAs had no difficulty in dealing with the bombers and their escorts of Fiat CR.42 Falcos and Macchi MC.200 Saettas. Clearly, the time had arrived for Malta to go over to the offensive.

Island replenishment

The relative lull over Malta enabled the passage of supply convoys to take place without hindrance. On 20 July 1941 the convoy 'Substance', consisting of six store ships and a troop-carrier, passed through the Straits of Gibraltar en route to Malta; the convoy was escorted by units of Force H under Rear Admiral E. N. Syfret. Air cover was provided by Fulmar Mk Is from HMS *Ark Royal*, with support by the Beaufighter Mk IFs of Nos 252 and 272 Squadrons detached to Malta. The threat came from the 150 SM.79s and SM.84s of the Regia Aeronautica in Sicily and Sardinia.

The first Axis attack on 'Substance' took place on 23 July, when the convoy was 140 miles (225 km) south west of Sardinia; an air attack took place, with 10 SM.79-Is bombing from 11,800 ft (3600 m), while torpedo-carrying SM.79-IIs of the Aerosiluranti (specialist torpedo units of the RA) ran in from the north. During the attack, Fulmars of the Fleet Air Arm took on the high-level bombers, but the torpedo-bombers managed to sink the destroyer HMS *Fearless*, and damage the cruiser HMS

Manchester. The convoy came under attack from Italian submarines and E-boats during the night, but made it to Valletta harbour on 24 July: in addition to supplies, six Fairey Swordfish Mk Is were delivered from HMS *Ark Royal* to Malta's No. 830 Sqn, FAA.

Steady build-up

Convoys continued to arrive at Malta. Stores and troops from convoy 'Style' were unloaded at Valletta on 2 August: the garrison on Malta now numbered over 22,000 troops in 13 battalions including three of the Royal Malta Regiment, and anti-aircraft defences included some 112 heavy and 118 light guns.

At the beginning of August 1941, AHQ Malta (commanded now by Air Vice Marshal H. P. Lloyd) possessed 15 Hurricane Mk IIs and 60 Mk IIA/Bs in a combat-ready state. The so-called Malta Night Fighter Unit (MNFU) was also formed to counteract the increasing night raids by the Italians.

The 'Halberd' convoy

The decision of the Chiefs of Staff to send another convoy to Malta was taken on 28 August 1941, and it was agreed that Beaufighter strength on the island would be boosted to 22 by the infusion of Nos 252 and 272 Sqns, while five Bristol Blenheim B.Mk IVs of No. 2 Group would be employed for anti-shipping duties; the warships of Forces H and X would escort, with units of the Mediterranean Fleet providing a diversion. Nine freighters, including the *Breconshire*, passed through the

The partnership between Germany and Italy is neatly symbolised by Luftwaffe and Regia Aeronautica Ju 87B dive-bombers returning from a raid on Malta in March 1942. Targets on the tightly-packed island should have been easy prey for the Stukas, but the fighters and AA defences joined forces to down droves of Ju 87s.

An FAA Fairey Fulmar approaches for landing on HMS Illustrious. Naval fighters should have been able to provide convoys with effective fighter escort, but the UK's large and relatively unwieldy carrierborne fighters were able to do little more than hold their own in the Mediterranean.

Baltimores of No. 223 Sqn, based at Luqa, are 'bombed up' and serviced prior to a raid on Axis forces retreating from Sicily. Although the aircraft were a tempting target for Axis bombers, their stay in Malta (20 July to 10 August 1943) coincided with a period of air domination for the Allies over Malta.

Gibraltar Straits on the night of 24-25 September. On 27 September, the battleship HMS *Nelson* received hits from an SM.79-II south-west of Sardinia. The Martin Marylands of No. 69 (GR) Sqn from Malta kept watch for the Italian fleet, but little emanated from this quarter. There followed a well co-ordinated night torpedo attack by SM.79s and SM.84s in which the SS *Empire Star* was crippled, and had to be sunk later. Early on the morning of 28 September No. 272 Sqn's Beaufighters escorted, and kept station, as the convoy entered Valletta shortly after midday. The 50,000 tons of fuel and supplies borne by 'Halberd' was to enable the Malta garrison to last out until May 1942 in theory.

Malta's primary anti-shipping strike force was composed of the Royal Navy's 10th Submarine Flotilla, which was at times reinforced by the Alexandria-based 1st Flotilla. The British submariners operating from Malta proved to be as successful as they were fearless: perhaps the most spectacular sinkings were made on 18 September 1941 when HMS *Upholder* sank the liners *Neptunia* and *Oceania* (each of 19,500 tons) en route to Tripoli with a division of Axis troops. But hand in hand with the forays of the submarines came the efforts of the Malta-based anti-shipping strike squadrons.

Blenheim Mk IV light bombers of No. 2 (bomber) Group had been sent to Malta in small detachments since late April. The Blenheims of No. 2 Group served under AHQ Malta throughout the remainder of the year: No. 82 Sqn arrived on 4 June 1941; next came Nos 105 and 107 Sqns in July and August, and then No. 18 Sqn in October. Primary operations were low-level anti-shipping sorties with four 250-lb (113-kg) GP Mk IV or SAP/HE bombs, a practice that No. 2 Group had become very adept at conducting over the North Sea and in the English Channel. By August 1941 there were, on average, 20 Blenheim Mk IVs at Luqa available for operations; in addition, nine Wellington Mk IC bombers had flown in to total 12 mainly for night work, while the FAA maintained 20 Swordfish Mk Is at Hal Far. Reconnaissance was done by No. 69 Sqn's 10 Martin Marylands, which were assisted more aggressively by six Beaufighter Mk ICs, while some 75 Hurricane Mk Is and Mk IIs were available for defence.

Sinking supplies

Over the ensuing months refinements were added to the anti-shipping strike forces on Malta: in the autumn there arrived three Wellingtons fitted with ASV Mk II radar for detection of shipping up to a maximum of 60 miles (97 km); the Swordfish also received some ASV equipment, while homing equipment fitted to some Wellingtons allowed them to co-operate closely with transponder-equipped Albacores and Swordfish. The 11 torpedo-bombing Albacore Mk IIs carried long-range tanks for distant shipping strikes.

The effects on the Axis supply lines to North Africa were immediate: in June Malta-based aircraft sank two ships totalling 12,249 tons. The Axis was losing some 30 per cent of its supplies on each trip, while total sinkings (June-October 1941) came to 178,577 tons.

Due to the fact that the losses were hampering German operations in North Africa, a request for operations by German U-boats in the Mediterranean was agreed by Hitler. Next came an order to the Luftwaffe for added forces with which to obliterate the troublesome island of Malta. On 29 October 1941 the staff of Luftflotte 11, under Generalfeldmarschall Albert Kesselring and located on the central sector of the Russian front, received orders to proceed to Sicily, along with II. Fliegerkorps under General der Flieger Bruno Loerzer.

The escalation in German air attacks on Malta was evident by December 1941; this occurred at the same time as RAF air strikes from Malta were reduced in intensity as a result of worsening weather. The Axis was now ferrying troops and supplies in warships to Tripoli and Benghazi, which reduced the incidence of sinkings. November was the last month in which the Royal Navy and RAF operated with notable success against the supply lanes: 14 ships, totalling 59,052 tons, were sunk. The arrival of U-boats in the Mediterranean had a catastrophic effect on the Royal Navy, with several warships, notably the carrier HMS *Ark Royal* and the battleship HMS *Barham*, sunk. The arrival of stores and some 66,000 tons of fuel for the Axis in North Africa was instrumental in enabling Rommel to take to the offensive from El Agheila on 21 January 1942. For the moment Malta's teeth had been drawn.

A trio of FAA Albacores cruises over the Maltese countryside. Albacores of Nos 828 and 830 Squadrons amalgamated for operational purposes as Naval Air Squadron Malta from March 1942. By mid-1943 the two squadrons had sunk 30 enemy ships and damaged a further 50.

Once fitted with workable dorsal gun positions, the Martin Baltimore Mk II proved a great asset to the Allies in North Africa in the early part of 1942. The two main operators were Nos 55 and 223 Sqns, RAF, generally operating the type in boxes of 12-18 aircraft.

Rommel's last triumph

Malta's interference with Rommel's supply lines had been instrumental in the success of Operation Crusader, when the Afrika Korps had been pushed back to El Aghelia. But, incredibly, the enigmatic Rommel struck back and this time there seemed to be no way of stopping him.

Despite some successful delaying actions, the Deutsches Afrika Korps had withdrawn to the defensive line near El Aghelia by mid-January 1942. However, the shortage of supplies and fuel and stretched lines of communication that had hindered the Axis forces now applied to the 8th Army. The British force was weak and seriously dispersed following the savage fighting of Operation Crusader, while RAF Middle East Command was outnumbered in the air.

As of 24 January 1942, Luftflotte II consisted of 657 combat aircraft, including 178 Bf 109F-4s and 71 Stukas. A further 200 aircraft were also based nearby in Sicily and Greece. Furthermore, the Italian Regia Aeronautica's strength was 396 serviceable aircraft, based in Libya, Sicily, Sardinia and the Aegean. The Axis retreat from Egypt was coupled with the Luftwaffe restoring the balance in the Mediterranean thanks to newly-accorded priorities: the supply of units and aircraft to sustain the task of Luftflotte II. These new forces were to be skimmed off units in Russia and in Germany.

RAF Middle East's strength was 361 serviceable aircraft consisting of Hurricane Mk I and Mk IIs, Tomahawk Mk IIBs, Kittyhawk Mk Is and Bristol Beaufighters. The army also commanded five squadrons of Hurricane Mk Is. Blenheims and Bostons provided light bomber capability, while Wellingtons and a handful of test Fortresses and Liberators offered a medium- and heavy-bomber force.

Although the Stuka had found itself wanting during the Battle of Britain, it proved successful in the desert and, with escorting Bf 109s, exacted a bloody toll on Allied units.

RAF Middle East was still failing to procure the best equipment; the fear of another Battle of Britain kept Spitfires and heavy bombers in the UK, while the new war in the Pacific and Soviet needs on the Eastern front siphoned off further equipment.

In the air, the Germans definitely held the advantage, with the Bf 109F-4/Trop outperforming all Allied aircraft in-theatre. The best aircraft that the Allies could use in response was the Kittyhawk, which was better than the Tomahawk and Hurricane Mk II, but still had to be flown incredibly well to counter the 'Friedrich'. Meanwhile, the Italians fielded their best fighter of the war, the Macchi C.202 Folgore. Like many Italian fighters, it was light and manoeuvrable, but unlike many, it was also very fast.

Rommel's riposte

Despite the claims by British Intelligence to the contrary, Rommel counterattacked on

Based in North Africa during the summer of 1942 and considered obsolete when compared to Western monoplane fighters, CR.42s were widely used as light ground-attack aircraft, with two underwing guns and provision for a pair of 220-lb (100-kg) bombs.

Mainstay of the British bomber element in the Western Desert was the Vickers Wellington. Seen here is a Mk IC of No. 37 Sqn, one of six Wellington units in the area. This medium-bomber played an important part in deep raids on Axis lines of communication, shipping and supply dumps.

Hurricanes found themselves seriously outclassed by their Axis opponents in aerial clashes and many fell to Bf 109Fs. It would not be until the arrival of Spitfires – which flew top cover – that the Hurricanes were able to concentrate on the attack mission.

21 January 1942 with the Panzerarmee Afrika. Three columns of Pzkpfw IIIs headed alongside the northern side of the Wadi Faregh to threaten British positions. Bad weather had made quagmires of the British Desert Air Force (DAF) airfields and the forward base at Antelat was almost unusable, but the few squadrons there managed to pull out in time. On the first day, Axis forces managed to put up 260 sorties, with the Bf 109Fs and MC.202s flying top cover with CR.42s and Ju 87s bombing Allied positions. Poor weather meant that the DAF was unable to launch any attack on 21 January, but over the following few days, a series of skirmishes between the opposing fighters took place over the desert.

By 28 January, the leading elements of the 15th and 21st Panzer Divisions reached Benghazi. On the way, they had been constantly harried by RAF units, most notably No. 272 Sqn's Bristol Beaufighters with their four cannon and six machine-guns. Axis air units lagged behind the ground forces, but the Panzer units rolled ever forward, crushing all opposition. By 6 February 1942, the 8th Army had lost 1,390 men and 110 tanks and artillery pieces. Rommel had turned failure into success and had dashed any Allied hope of breaking through to Tunisia in 1942.

The spring of 1942 saw a lull in ground activities and both sides took time to build up their forces. This time was also punctuated by a series of aerial clashes involving DAF fighters tangling with the '109s. Major combat took place on 14 February, when 18 RAAF Kittyhawks bounced a flight of Macchi MC.200s. Bf 109s, Fiat G.50s, Ju 87s and Ju 88s also entered the fray, with over 20 Axis aircraft downed.

Following a high rate of attrition after Operation Crusader, the DAF found itself seriously weakened; the Hurricanes Mk Is were outclassed, the Tomahawk supply had dried up, Hurricane Mk IIs were few in number and Kittyhawks fared badly in the desert conditions. The light bomber force was also suffering from a lack of parts and replacements. Plans to build up the forces in the Middle East to 80 squadrons had failed and requests for heavy-bombers had resulted in mixed fortunes. Two squadrons of Halifaxes were earmarked and a detachment of B-24Ds was sent to the region. Tactics for countering the MC.202 and Bf 109F-4 were studied and GCI radar was introduced.

On 14 March, a heavy attack was made on Martuba West, and the Allied escort fought well against JG 27 and several MC.202s. However, it had also been decided at this time that Axis fighter units were to hit DAF raids heavily and maintain air superiority over their bases. This caused an increase in Allied bombers being downed and was coupled with an upsurge in bombing attacks by Ju 87s and Ju 88s on Allied positions, often at night, giving the Beaufighters of No. 89(F) Sqn a busy time.

By May 1942, it was clear that something was afoot. Axis air power had been quietly building up its reserves and in the third week of May, operations were suddenly intensified, with Ju 88s bombing troop positions. In return, the DAF hit JG 27's position with some 160 tons of bombs. On this day the Panzerarmee Afrika started its new offensive – the lull was over.

The attack was largely successful and the 8th Army was soon retreating back to the Egyptian border. During the opening stages, the DAF flew numerous tactical low-level missions, particularly against the advancing Panzer armour divisions, but suffered horrendous losses (50 out of 250 aircraft).

The DAF was also suffering from a failure to receive further Kittyhawks, but it was boosted by the arrival of No. 145 Sqn's Spitfire Mk VCs. These were capable of dealing with the Bf 109Fs and flew top cover for the Hurricanes and Kittyhawks.

As June approached, fighting reached ferocious levels and the Gazala line was bitterly fought over by Rommel and the 1st Free French Brigade under General Koenig. The Axis offensive was supported by continuous air attacks, no fewer than 300 to 350 sorties a day by the Stukas and Jagdgruppen. On the night of 10-11 June, Koenig's forces were forced to withdraw.

The Luftwaffe now turned on Tobruk and continuously pounded it. On 20 June Allied positions were strafed and bombed and, by the following day, the Germans had infiltrated the fort and the Allies had surrendered. In all, 32,220 British and Commonwealth troops were captured, and with this morale-shattering blow, it seemed that nothing could stop Rommel in his all-out drive to Egypt, the Suez Canal and possibly beyond.

This Fiat BR.20M of 13° Stormo Bombardamento Terrestre was based at Bir Dufan, Libya, in February 1942. The early months of the year saw the 13° Stormo suffer very heavy losses and it was pulled back to Italy for re-equipment with the Caproni Ca 313 light reconnaissance bomber.

Malta's last battles

Malta-based aircraft were among the hardest-worked RAF aircraft of the war. Here, a Beaufighter Mk VIC of No. 272 Squadron displays typical wear and tear.

Despite a lack of supplies, aircraft and pilots, the Allied forces on Malta prevented any chance of a German invasion and ensured that Malta remained in British possession for the duration of the war.

In the spring of 1941 salvation for Malta came from two sources. Heavy fighting in Cyrenaica and the invasion of the Balkans by German forces resulted in the redeployment of much of X. Fliegerkorps from Sicily to distant bases. The slackening of Axis pressure in the central Mediterranean encouraged the British Admiralty to sail HMS *Ark Royal* towards Malta on 3 April with 12 Hurricanes, all of which arrived safely. Before the month was out, *Ark Royal* had returned once more, this time with 24 Hurricane Mk IIBs.

Believing that, with the departure of the bombers, Malta's teeth had been finally drawn, the Regia Aeronautica and remaining Luftwaffe units in the Mediterranean left the island largely to its own devices, thinking that significant reinforcement would prove impossible. This belief was proved to be mistaken by the arrival of 46 cannon-armed Hurricane Mk IICs in May and another 143 Hurricane IIBs and IICs in June, in the course of four operations involving HMS *Ark Royal*, *Furious* and *Victorious*. By the beginning of July, the Hurricane Mk II fighter-bombers had started to regain the initiative, with offensive sweeps over Sicily. On 26 July six Italian E-boats, escorted by MC.200s, attempted to attack shipping in Valletta's Grand Harbour; the Hurricanes of Nos 126 and 185 Squadrons were scrambled and set about the

E-boats, sinking four and causing the other two to surrender.

Thus emboldened by the strengthened fighter defences, it fell to Malta's newly-appointed Air Officer Commanding, Air Vice-Marshal Hugh Pughe Lloyd, to make ready for the return of the bomber force. By the end of October Blenheim Mk IVs, Wellingtons plus PR Hurricanes and Marylands were operational.

Throughout the Axis advance eastwards through Cyrenaica, the Germans and Italians contrived to supply their armies by sea. It was such shipping, both in port and on the high seas, that the bombers – as well as the Fleet Air Arm Swordfish based on Malta – constantly attacked, to such effect that roughly three-quarters of all supply shipping available to the Axis in the Mediterranean was sunk or destroyed during the summer and early autumn of 1941 by Allied aircraft and naval forces. Of the 220,000 tons (223520 tonnes) sunk between 1 June and 31 October, about 85,000 tons (86360 tonnes) was accounted for by RAF and Fleet Air Arm aircraft based on Malta.

Early in January 1942 German air attacks on Malta increased rapidly in ferocity, scarcely a day passing on which Valletta's sirens did not sound, often as many as six times. By this time, warning of such raids was provided by two long-range CO and four COL radars. The raids were being flown by elements of Luftflotte 2 under Generalfeldmarschall Albert Kesselring, and General Bruno

Above: Complete with nose art, Baltimore Mk IIIA FA353 of No. 69(GR) Squadron undergoes engine maintenance in its revetment at RAF Luqa in 1943.

A formation of three No. 828 Sqn, Fleet Air Arm Albacore Mk Is cruises over Malta for an official photographer. By mid-1943 No. 828 Sqn, and its sister squadron No. 830, had sunk 30 enemy ships and damaged a further 50.

Engaged, for the most part, in maritime operations, the Beaufighter was popular with crews as it was able to provide concentrated firepower with the added comfort factor of twin engines.

Loerzer's II. Fliegerkorps. As the weeks passed, the latter alone increased in strength to more than 400 aircraft.

Although the Blenheims of Nos 21 and 107 Squadrons managed to make a diminishing number of attacks on enemy bases, even destroying 11 Axis transport aircraft at Castelvetrano on 4 January, it was obvious that large quantities of supplies and reinforcements were succeeding in reaching North Africa, often undetected and seldom attacked. Once more it was decided to reduce the island's bomber force, and on 22 February the Blenheims were flown to Egypt, leaving only the Wellingtons of Nos 40 and 221 Squadrons.

On the brink

By the end of February, Lloyd could seldom put more than a score of fighters into the air to meet the raids on Malta, and low-level sweeps by German fighters rendered even these efforts extremely hazardous. No convoy, with food, fuel, ammunition or aircraft reinforcements, had arrived since November. So essential was it that the island's defences be strengthened once more that, on 7 March, HMS *Eagle* launched 15 Spitfire VBs for Malta – the first such fighters to reach the Mediterranean. Sixteen more Spitfires followed later in the month.

Although the new fighters gave a welcome boost to the morale of the hard-pressed islanders, they could do little to counter the swarms of enemy raiders which now attacked Malta almost daily. Nevertheless, the US, now at war with Germany, was able to send the carrier USS *Wasp* to join HMS *Eagle* and *Argus* in the Mediterranean, with a total of more than 120 Spitfire Mk Vs for Malta during April and May. These reinforcements certainly saved Malta and were, in part, responsible for a reduction in air attacks after mid-May. For their part, the Germans began laying plans to launch an invasion of the island in the autumn, as part of an all-out offensive to drive the Allies out of the Mediterranean. Two Allied convoys, with a total

of 17 merchant ships, had battled their way to the island from east and west during June, but only two merchantmen reached their destination, and those at a cost of one cruiser and four destroyers sunk – despite escorts amounting to two carriers, a battleship, 12 cruisers and no fewer than 43 destroyers. During the first half of July, about 1,000 sorties were flown by German and Italian aircraft against the island, during which 42 were destroyed for the loss of 39 Hurricanes and Spitfires. It was at this time that air command on Malta passed to that supreme fighter exponent, Air Vice-Marshal Keith Park.

If Malta was to survive as an effective offensive base in the run-up to the major Allied operations being planned for the late autumn of 1942, it was imperative that a fresh effort be made to sail another convoy to the island. Operation Pedestal involved the sailing in August of 14 merchant ships through the Strait of Gibraltar. About 100 aircraft (including four Liberators, a squadron of Beaufighters and an additional squadron of Wellingtons) were flown to Malta to increase Park's strength to some 250 aircraft, in an effort to cover the approach of the convoy, whose presence had become known to the enemy almost as soon as it entered the Mediterranean. From 11 August, the convoy came under continuous attack from air and sea forces but, at a cost of one carrier (HMS *Eagle*), two cruisers, a destroyer and 18 RAF and FAA aircraft, five merchantmen reached Malta.

The 55,000 tons (55880 tonnes) of materiel delivered in Operation Pedestal

enabled the defences of the island to be strengthened immeasurably, especially as HMS *Furious* had taken the opportunity to deliver 37 more Spitfires. It was now safe to deploy permanently a squadron of torpedo-carrying Beauforts and one of Beaufighters at Luqa, as Park steadily began to increase his striking power.

By the winter of 1942-43, Malta's aircraft had seized the initiative, and German plans to invade the island evaporated. Now that long-range aircraft were based in Egypt, capable of striking enemy ports throughout the central and eastern Mediterranean theatres, the tasks of Malta's aircraft could be confined to searching for, shadowing and attacking enemy shipping at sea, and it was during the crucial period that Park's aircraft contributed towards cutting off the flow of Axis maritime traffic to North Africa. Moreover, during the vulnerable phase of Allied landings in Algeria (Operation Torch), Malta-based aircraft – particularly the Spitfires – flew sweeps over airfields in Sicily to prevent any serious attempt by Axis aircraft to interfere with the landings.

Cutting supply routes

During the final stages of the campaign in Tunisia, when enemy shipping sailed in frantic efforts to deliver supplies to the Afrika Korps through ports such

as Sfax and Sousse, Allied aircraft, including Malta-based bombers, sank no fewer than 20 supply ships. When the Germans eventually resorted to the use of transport aircraft, such as the vulnerable Ju 52/3m and Me 323, to deliver fuel supplies to the dwindling Axis forces, the Malta-based Spitfires were ideally situated to join the massacre.

Final retribution for the years of trial by fire and explosive was accorded to the people of Malta as preparations were made for the Allied invasion of Sicily. In June 1943, Air Chief Marshal Sir Arthur Tedder started his deployment of an extraordinary concentration of Allied aircraft on the tiny island. By mid-June, in addition to two FAA squadrons and two of the South African Air Force, the RAF deployed 16 squadrons of Spitfires, one of Mosquitoes, a Beaufighter squadron, and two photographic reconnaissance squadrons; to these were added in the next four weeks an RCAF squadron of Spitfire Mk VCs, four Kittyhawk squadrons, one of Baltimores, one of Mosquito night-fighters and air-sea rescue Walrus amphibians – a total of 407 aircraft.

Early on 10 July the first Allied forces went ashore on the southern coasts of Sicily. As dawn approached, Spitfires and Kittyhawks took off from Malta to cover the first great air- and seaborne invasion of Europe.

On 19 April 1942 USS Wasp *dispatched 47 Spitfire Mk VCs to Malta from its crowded deck during Operation Calendar. The carrier was also equipped with F4F-3s of VF-71, US Navy.*

No. 126 Squadron moved from Ta Kali to Luqa and re-equipped with Spitfires in May 1942. This Spitfire Mk VB is believed to have been one of its aircraft and is seen here being guided along an unpaved taxiway.

Supermarine Spitfire

Above: To meet an urgent Fleet Air Arm requirement for a modern carrier-based fighter in 1941, a navalised Spitfire, the Seafire, was produced, initially by converting land-based examples. The Seafire IIC variant, one of which is seen landing aboard HMS Indomitable, was one of the first variants built as such rather than by conversion – these variants did not have folding wings.

Below: The first of the Griffon-engined Spitfires to enter service, the Mk XII was the only variant to have the single-stage engine, asymmetric radiators and four-bladed propeller. This example is seen on a test flight prior to squadron delivery.

By combining superb aerodynamics with one of the best aero-engines ever produced, R. J. Mitchell and his Supermarine team created a pure thoroughbred fighter which became a legend.

If asked to name a British aircraft of World War II, many people would pick the Spitfire. In production and front-line service throughout the war and the subject of constant development, this Supermarine design matured to become one of the greatest fighter aircraft of all time.

Supermarine's chief designer, Reginald Joseph Mitchell, had designed a monoplane fighter, the Type 224, in the early 1930s. However, this failed to win orders, the RAF preferring the Gloster Gladiator biplane. Mitchell then set about developing a new aircraft, the Type 300, this time as a private venture. An all-metal design (apart from its control surfaces),

with a distinctive elliptical wing plan-form, it was to be powered by Rolls-Royce's latest 12-cylinder engine, another private venture, appropriately known as the PV.12. Rated initially at 1,000 hp (746 kW), it offered an excellent power-to-weight ratio, and shared with Mitchell's airframe a great deal of development potential, something that was to be exploited to the full during the forthcoming war. In fact, it was the development of the PV.12 (soon named Merlin) and its eventual replacement, the Griffon, that was to be perhaps the most important catalyst in the Spitfire's development, as the engine lent itself to modification according to the different operational requirements placed

on the aircraft.

Given the rapid development of monoplane fighter designs in Germany, it was clear to the RAF that it needed the new fighter for the home defence interceptor role. Impressed with the Type 300, soon renamed the Spitfire (much to the horror of Mitchell, who commented "It's the sort of bloody silly name they would give it!"), the Air Ministry drew up a specification (F.37/34) around the design and ordered 310 production examples in June 1936. A prototype had flown in March 1936, and the first production Mk Is, fitted with a

Merlin II rated at 1,060 hp (791 kW) and armed with eight 0.303-in (7.7-mm) Browning machine-guns, reached No. 19 Squadron, RAF at Duxford in August 1938.

By the time war had broken out, a total of 1,960 Spitfires was

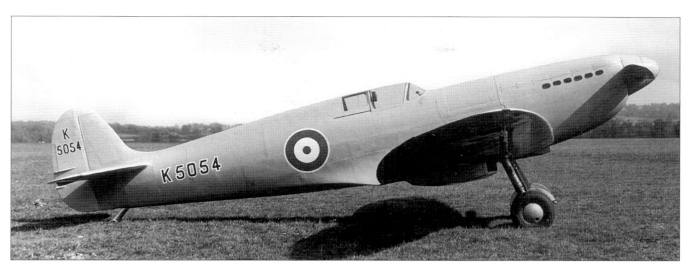

Above: The prototype Spitfire, K5054, first flew on 5 May 1936 from Eastleigh airfield near Southampton, with chief test pilot 'Mutt' Summers at the controls. Over the next three years, the aircraft accumulated about 260 hours' flying time. Its career finally came to an end on 4 September 1939, when Flt Lt 'Spinner' White was killed as the aircraft nosed over onto its back during a landing mishap. The aircraft was not repaired.

Right: Of the 20,000 Spitfires (of all variants) that were built between 1936 and 1948, over 200 survive, around 50 in an airworthy condition. Operating as a flying memorial to former Battle of Britain pilots is this Mk VB, owned by the RAF. The aircraft is displayed throughout the summer at airshows across the UK.

on order, of which 306 Mk Is had been delivered. The Spitfire saw action for the first time on 16 October 1939, when Nos 602 and 603 Squadrons engaged Luftwaffe bombers off the coast of Scotland. Both units were successful in downing German aircraft – the Spitfire's first aerial victories. Nineteen squadrons were operating the type by mid-1940; almost a third of these aircraft were lost to Luftwaffe fighters while covering the withdrawal from Dunkirk during May.

So began the production life of the Spitfire, which was to last 10 years and encompass an almost bewildering array of 22 variants. The aircraft filled not only the interceptor role, but also those of fighter-bomber and reconnaissance, and operated also as the carrierborne Seafire.

In all, more than 20,400 Spitfires were built, from the Mk I to the F.Mk 24, serving for more than 20 years. Not only were they operated by the RAF – which retired its last front-line examples in 1954, 'officially' withdrew the type in 1957, but returned a Mk XIX to service in 1963 to train Lightning and Javelin pilots how to dogfight Indonesian Mustangs – but also by the air arms of at least 20 other nations. Neither was the type's war service limited to World War II. Burma, Egypt, France, India, Israel and the Netherlands all flew the Spitfire in anger during the 1950s.

If the Spitfire had a handicap, it was that it was designed as a home-based interceptor and, while it was fast, agile and possessed an excellent climb rate, it was short on range. This was something that the RAF had to live with and on which Supermarine expended much effort trying to address. (While long-range variants were built, these were mainly specialised reconnaissance aircraft; once deployed overseas, Spitfire fighters and fighter-bombers were obliged to carry belly-mounted fuel tanks almost as a matter of operational necessity.)

It was the constant development of the Spitfire during the 1940s, born of necessity but facilitated by the brilliance of both the airframe's design, and that of its engine, that ensured the longevity of the Spitfire's production and service.

Above: The ultimate Spitfire – the Seafire FR.Mk 47 – served with several Fleet Air Arm squadrons in the Korean War, including No. 800 Sqn. The aircraft was involved mainly in ground-attack sorties, armed with rockets.

Right: Operating in the high-altitude photo-reconnaissance role, the PR.Mk 19s were the last variants to see active service with the RAF. It was not until July 1957 that the one remaining example, PS853, was finally retired.

Alamein and Torch

After the fall of Tobruk and the subsequent Axis advance to El Alamein, the balance of Africa hung on a knife-edge. Rommel seemed poised to strike at Suez and beyond, yet his supply lines were overstretched, a problem that would ultimately lead to defeat.

The redeployment of important elements of the RAF from North Africa to the Balkans in 1941 had left the British fatally exposed following Wavell's brilliant advance into Libya and, with the arrival of the Afrika Korps, supported by Luftwaffe fighters and dive-bombers, the British army in the Western Desert was forced back almost to the Egyptian frontier once more. This was, in turn, followed by an offensive, Operation Crusader (commanded by General Auchinleck), which relieved Tobruk and carried the Eighth Army west once more to beyond Benghazi. Throughout this advance Hurricanes, Tomahawks and Blenheims of the RAF, RCAF, RAAF and SAAF were constantly in action, as were Wellingtons and Baltimores against enemy ports and airfields, maintaining a marginal but vital degree of air superiority over the less numerous aircraft of the Luftwaffe and the Régia Aeronautica.

Auchinleck made a fatal error, however, preferring to concentrate on mopping up enemy resistance and strengthening his positions rather than striking forward at El Agheila before the enemy could counter-attack. It was Rommel who, with shorter supply lines, struck first and quickly forced the Eighth Army back once more, this time beyond the Egyptian border. However, as a result of gallant delaying actions, notably by the South Africans at Tobruk and the Free French at Bir Hakim in May 1942, vital time was gained in which to establish a 'last defence' line before Cairo at El Alamein. It was at Bir Hakim on 6 June that the new Hurricane Mk IID 'tank-buster' was first used to good effect against enemy armour. No. 6 Squadron, later known as the 'Flying Can-Openers', was the first to use the twin 40-mm Vickers 'S' gun-equipped Mk IID. This brought the Hurricane's top speed down but its anti-armour capability was devastating; during one day No. 6 Squadron destroyed 16 Axis tanks.

Last stand

And so it was that, after two years of advance and retreat in North Africa, the famous Eighth Army found itself with its back to the Suez Canal while the victorious Afrika Korps seemed poised for the final thrust. However, by prodigious efforts the Allied Forces had accomplished a massive build-up by the time the Axis forces were brought to a halt at Alamein. In the 18 months since Tedder had assumed command in the Middle East, his air force had undergone transformation, now comprising 96 squadrons, of which 60 were British, 13 American, 13 South African, five Australian, two Greek and one each of Rhodesian, French and Yugoslav. The units comprised a total of 1,500 first-line aircraft, of which 1,200 were deployed in the Western Desert. Among his modern aircraft were Spitfire Mk Vs, Kittyhawks, Beaufighters, Beauforts, Marauders and Halifaxes, as well as 10 squadrons of Wellingtons and five Liberator squadrons. Against them were deployed some 3,000 Axis aircraft, of which only 700 were based in North Africa and only half of these were serviceable.

On the ground, General Bernard Montgomery concentrated a vastly superior army, outnumbering the Axis forces by almost two to one in men, tanks and guns. On 23 October 1942 he was ready to strike at El Alamein, preparing

Above: Despite being relatively slow and unwieldy, Hurricane Mk IID 'tank-busters' operated with conspicuous success throughout the North African campaign, being able to carry up to 500 lb (227 kg) of bombs, or two Vickers 40-mm cannon.

Difficult working conditions did nothing to improve the plight of the Ju 87s used to counter the British armoured thrust at El Alamein, lack of speed making them easy prey for Kittyhawks.

Sent only in small numbers to North Africa, Messerschmitt Bf 110Es were used mainly for shipping protection and defensive duties. This example of 7./ZG 26 at Berka is fitted with 66-Imp gal (300-litre) tanks and wing bomb racks.

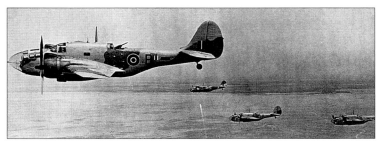

Above: Used exclusively by the RAF in the Middle East, the Martin Baltimore was one of the most successful bombers during the fighting of 1942. It served in two roles, as a medium day-bomber and for anti-shipping reconnaissance.

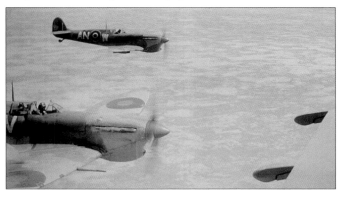

Below: The normally elegant lines of the Spitfire were somewhat disrupted by the heavy Vokes filter fitted to cope with the harsh, dusty conditions. Flying with the cockpit canopies open in the heat, these Mk VCs of No. 417 Sqn patrol over the Western Desert.

his attack with a massive artillery bombardment of German and Italian positions as six squadrons of Wellingtons bombed them from the air. The next day, the fighter-bombers entered the fray and the RAF and SAAF Hurricane Mk IID 'tank-busters' targeted the enemy armoured vehicles. For a week the great battle raged as German Ju 87s joined in attempts to halt the British armoured thrusts, but were almost invariably caught by covering British and American P-40s. On 4 November the 1st Armoured Division broke through the enemy line and at once the Axis began a long westward retreat. At sea, Axis supply ships, desperately trying to bring supplies to the Cyrenaican ports, were subjected to incessant air attacks, no fewer than 18 heavily-laden vessels being either sunk or forced to Italy or Greece on account of damage.

Death of a legend

Almost symbolic of the Luftwaffe's misfortunes at the time was the loss of Hauptmann Hans-Joachim Marseille, the widely-respected fighter pilot and highest-scoring pilot in the West; after attaining the extraordinary total of 158

victories, he was killed while baling out of his Bf 109 after engine failure.

JG 27's Marseille was a 22-year old Berliner who had already claimed seven Spitfires shot down while flying Bf 109Es over the English Channel. When Luftwaffe high command deployed two Gruppen of JG 27 to Libya from the Eastern Front, it had re-equipped with the 'Friedrich' model, and by the beginning of 1942 Marseille's score was around 50 and increasing rapidly. For example, on 3 June, while escorting Ju 87s, his Staffel was attacked by RAF Kittyhawks: Marseille destroyed six in 11 minutes, using the bare minimum of ammunition. A fortnight later, he downed six more aircraft, this time in six minutes. The following day his score stood at 101 and he was awarded Swords to his Knight's Cross.

The first day of September 1942 saw JG 27 at the zenith of its achievements. As Rommel advanced towards El Alamein, daily Ju 87 attacks on the Tobruk garrison were made in the company of escorting JG 27 fighters. Tedder's Middle East Command flew a total of 674 sorties to protect the British Eighth Army; Marseille flew

three times in the course of that day. By the late evening JG 27 had claimed 26 aircraft (20 P-40s, four Hurricanes and two Spitfires) for the loss of one pilot killed, one taken prisoner and one MIA. Marseille had destroyed no fewer than 17 himself. Congratulations came at once from Generalfeldmarschall Kesselring and brought the award of the Diamonds to the Knight's Cross the following day. By 15 September Marseille had reached a score of 150 victories; that day he had shot down seven aircraft in 11 minutes. By dusk on the 30th, by which time he was flying a Bf 109G-2, he was dead – the victim of engine failure and bad luck as his parachute became entangled with his aircraft's tailplane.

As the victorious Eighth Army swept eastwards for the last time, British fighters landed at Gazala, 100 miles (160 km) inside Cyrenaica on 17 November; two days later they were at Matruba, 50 miles (80 km) further on.

As the Axis forces were desperately trying to stand firm in

Tripolitania, the Allies launched their master stroke when, on 8 November, American and British forces (comprising 250 merchantmen and 160 warships) sailed from the West and put ashore in considerable strength (some 107,000 Allied troops) in Morocco and Algeria under cover of carrierborne aircraft and others operating from Gilbraltar. Operational security was good and even when the Germans finally heard of the operation, they had no inkling of the intended point of landings. Opposition was light, with only some Vichy-French forces managing to offer any defence.

The landings, Operation Torch, immediately threatened the whole Axis position in North Africa. Straightaway, Tunisia was occupied by the Germans as air reinforcements from Italy and Sicily landed at airfields in the north. RAF and USAAF fighters and bombers, as well as troop-carrying C-47s, poured ashore at Algerian airfields. The final battle for North Africa was about to begin.

North African opponents

For much of the fighting in the desert, both Axis and Allied forces had to make do with aircraft that were inferior to those fighting over mainland Europe.

Nevertheless, combat was fierce and several pilots, most notably on the side of the Axis, notched up an astonishing number of kills.

F4F-4 Wildcat

Lt Cdr John Raby of VF-9 aboard USS *Ranger* flew this Wildcat during the invasion of North Africa. Standard US Navy markings of the period are carried, with the exception of the yellow ring around the national marking, which was adopted by all aircraft participating in Operation Torch.

Bf 109F-4/Z Trop

'Red 1' was the mount of 'Fiffi' Stahlschmidt, a close friend of Marseille and one of the most successful Luftwaffe fighter pilots in the Western Desert. The 48 kills illustrated here had already won him the Knight's Cross but by 7 September 1942, by which time he had achieved a further 11 kills, he was reported missing in action after being bounced by a formation of Spitfires south east of El Alamein.

Three B-25C Mitchell squadrons serving with the 340th Bomb Group became operational in April 1943 as part of the US 12th Air Force. They played a critical part in the nullification of Axis shipping in its endeavours to reach North Africa.

Riposte in Tunisia

With the Allied landings as part of 'Torch', the balance of power in North Africa swung away from the Axis back to the Allies. However, Anglo-American co-operation started badly, and swift and efficient German countermoves took advantage of the Allies' hesitation.

Prompt German action in Tunisia was to thwart Allied aims at bringing the war in Africa to an end in the immediate future. As early as 8 November, Hauptmann Schürmeyer (a liaison officer) arrived at Tunis-Aouina airfield to supervise the first landings of men and materiel: combat aircraft, 27 Bf 109G-2s of I./JG 53 and 24 Ju 87D-1 Stukas of II./StG 3, arrived on the following day from Sicily. Airfields were in good condition, many with concrete runways and revetments, but at first it was necessary for the Luftwaffe to set up a ground organisation. Relays of transport Ju 52/3ms then flew in, bearing troops: these included two companies of I./Fallschirmjägerregiment Nr 5 and one of Panzergrenadierregiment Nr 104. The first complete army unit to arrive was Generalleutnant Wolfgang Fischer's 10th Panzer Division. Command of air forces in the area was vested in Generalmajor Harlinghausen, as the Fliegerführer Tunis, who now controlled what was essentially a small tactical air force.

Undoubtedly, the most important arrival was the formidable Fw 190A-4 fighter; this came with Hauptmann Adolf Dickfield's II./JG 2 'Richthofen'. The first base of II./JG 2 was Tindja South. Additional fighters of the Fliegerführer Tunis included at first the II./JG 51 'Mölders' with the Stab, and I. and II./JG 53 with the Bf 109G-4. Fighter and dive-bomber elements were III./Schnellkampfgeschwader Nr 10 with Fw 190s at Bizerta-Sidi Ahmed, 5./Schlachtgeschwader 1, also with Fw 190s, at El Aouina, and II./StG 3's bombers at Sebala. The aims of the Fliegerführer Tunis were twofold: firstly to slow down the Allied advance from the West in order to let Rommel recover, and secondly to secure sea and air lines of supply to North Africa.

Initially, there had been no stopping the headlong retreat of the Panzerarmee Afrika following the El Alamein debacle: by 15 November 1942, Rommel had retired to as far back as

During November 1942, the Lightning arrived in-theatre – this was the first appearance in North Africa of the twin-engined P-38. The aircraft's range and performance put it at a premium, but initially it suffered in combat with the seasoned Tunisia-based Jagdflieger due to the inexperience of its American pilots.

Benghazi-Derna, from where the residue of the Fliegerführer Afrika's forces – 4(H)./12 and L(F)./121 for reconnaissance – now operated. Bad weather forced a further retirement to bases at Tamet, Arco and Nofilia by 20 November.

Battle over Tunis

At first it was the Axis which managed to react with vigour; by comparison the Allied advances were slow. After establishing their Tunisian bridgehead, the Germans stemmed the advance of the British 1st Army from Bône along the coastline towards

Bizerta; Allied thrusts to Sidi Nsir, Tebourba, and Medjez el Bab were stopped by strong forces of motorised infantry, tanks and excellent cover by the Fliegerführer Tunis's tactical support aircraft. The campaign now promised to be a long one.

In the period from 8-21 November, during which the Eastern and Western Air Commands made contact with the enemy on the Tunisian border, fighting (including Torch) cost the Fleet Air Arm 34 aircraft destroyed in 702 sorties and the RAF 12 aircraft in 540 sorties; units of the US 12th Air Force lost at least eight aircraft.

A six-engined Me 323D-2 transport lands at a desert airfield in North Africa, having arrived from Trapani with ammunition and fuel. Serving with KGzbV 323 (later TG 5), the Me 323s suffered severely at the hands of Allied fighters and bombers.

Final preparations are carried out on a Ju 87D/Trop of StG 3 from a Tunisian base in 1943. The silhouette of a single large bomb can be seen on the underfuselage 'crutch', while two of the four smaller weapons are visible under the starboard wing. Stuka operations were extremely hazardous by 1943.

Eastern Air Command's arrivals at Bône included the Hurricanes of No. 225 Sqn, the tactical reconnaissance aircraft of No. 253 Sqn at Philippeville, and the Spitfire Mk VBs of Nos 72 and 93 Sqns at Souk el Arba; the US 14th FG's P-38F-1LOs operated from Youk les Bains. Other new arrivals in the US 12th Air Force included the P-39D Airacobra, the B-26C Marauder and the C-47 transport.

During December 1942 and January 1943, bad weather played a large part in reducing operations in the air. Montgomery's 8th Army forced Rommel's Panzerarmee to retreat through Libya and into Tripolitania; on 23 January 1943 Allied troops entered Tripoli, and by 4 February had penetrated across the border into Tunisia from the south east. The advance was halted at Medenine in order to prepare for the assault on the Mareth Line defences. Throughout the advance the Western Desert Air Force and the US Desert Air Task Force struggled to keep up, while at the same time both gave support to the ground forces. In comparison with the speedy advance in the south, the 1st Army's progress on the western Tunisian flank was marked by staunch fighting at Bou Arada, Medjez el Bab and Fondouk, in which the Axis gained the upper hand.

New organisation

In January Air Chief Marshal Sir W. Sholto Douglas took over RAF Middle East Command, while Air Chief Marshal Sir Arthur Tedder became AOC-in-C Mediterranean Air Command (17 February), with responsibility for all air operations. On 18 February 1943 the Northwest African Air Forces (NWAAF), commanded by Major General Carl A. Spaatz, came into existence under MAC.

Combats were frequent, with the opposing air forces being based so close to one another; a recent arrival on the front was the anti-tank Henschel Hs 129B-1, which served with 4. and 8./SG 2, and these and the Ju 87Ds of StG 3 were often in action against Allied troop positions and armour. The top cover of Bf 109Gs and Fw 190A-4s was usually engaged, and fierce dogfights took place over the various battlefields. German fighters were not slow to react against the B-17s, B-24s, and B-26s of the North West African Strategic Air Force (NWASAF), which attacked Bizerta, Tunis, Gabes and airfields in Sicily. The summary for the period from 18 January–13 February 1943 included 5,000 RAF sorties (34 lost), 6,250 USAAF sorties (85 lost), and at least 100 aircraft of Fliegerkorps Tunis destroyed in action.

On 14 February 1943 the Axis launched a strong counterattack in the Gafsa-Sbeitla sector, with forces drawn from the Deutsche Afrika Korps (DAK), and the 10th and 21st Panzer Divisions under Generaloberst Jürgen von Arnim. Stukas, Fw 190s and Hs 129B-1s, covered by fighters, supported the thrust: some 360 to 375 sorties were flown in support of the advance to Fériana and Sbeitla, the total falling back to some 250 per day over the following week. The American effort consisted of 200 sorties per day between 14 and 22 February, for the loss of 58 aircraft (including 38 blown up on the ground at Thelepte). The Axis advance succeeded in capturing a great number of US prisoners and equipment following the swift encirclement at Kasserine Pass.

The strength of Fliegerkorps Tunis was still over 300 when the Allies breached the Mareth Line (16-23 March 1943), but gradually the ring was closing from the south and the west around Bizerta and Tunis. German losses rose as US pilots gained experience.

The end in Africa

By the end of March 1943 the 1st and 8th Armies had linked up, and had forced the Axis to retreat; in the course of April the Allies concentrated their strength in an offensive in the Medjerda valley in a final attempt to crack the Axis front. On 5 April 1943 the Allied air forces commenced a series of interdiction attacks on the German air bridge from Sicily, termed Operation Flax. Flax possibly accounted for the destruction of over 400 Axis transports and escort fighters; the Allies lost 35 aircraft.

By this time, some 200 transport flights per day were arriving from Sicily at the airfields of Tunis and Bizerta: the forces used mainly Ju 52/3m, Ju 90, Ju 290, Go 242, DFS 230, and S.M.82 aircraft. Some 20 Me 323D-1 six-engined Gigants of I. and III./KGzbv 323 (later redesignated TG 5) were also in use.

Final assault

The last Allied push started on 22 April 1943, with armour making progress from Sidi Nsir, Medjez and Pont du Fahs: only at Enfidaville was there a halt. Resistance remained fierce, however, and was professionally handled by the Germans and Italians. But already units of the Luftwaffe were being evacuated from the shrinking perimeter, and combats were frequent. On 13 May 1943 Marshal Giovanni Messe, commanding Axis forces in Tunisia, and von Arnim surrendered to the Allies.

Flt Lt Eugeniusz Horbaczewski was OC of the Polish Fighting Team which was seconded to No. 145 Sqn in Tunisia during spring 1943. Horbaczewski, in a Mustang III, was shot down and killed by Fw 190s on 18 August 1944, his score standing at 16 aircraft destroyed, one probable and one damaged. Most of his kills were scored in Spitfire Mk VBs and IXs (below) in 1942-43.

The Mediterranean

Squadron Leader Russell Foskett is seen at the controls of an early-build Spitfire LF.Mk IX of No. 94 Squadron, RAF in mid-1944 during a bomber escort sortie over the Mediterranean.

After the success in North Africa, the Americans wanted to concentrate on the planned invasion of France, but the British successfully argued the case for continued offensives in the Mediterranean.

Towards the end of April 1943 the campaign in North Africa was virtually over, with the Luftwaffe and remnants of the Italian Regia Aeronautica pulling out of Tunisia, and retiring to Sicily, Sardinia and the Italian mainland. Well before the end of Axis resistance in North Africa, the Allies proceeded with the preparation for the invasion of Sicily, to be named Operation Husky and scheduled for early July 1943.

By May 1943 Air Chief Marshal Sir Arthur Tedder's Mediterranean Air Command (MAC) controlled an establishment of 3,516 aircraft of all categories on stations that stretched from Gibraltar to the Gulf of Aden. The spearhead of MAC was Major General Carl A. Spaatz's Northwest African Air Forces (NAAF), that controlled a force of 2,286 combat aircraft then based in Libya, Cyrenaica, Egypt and Tunisia.

The striking power of NAAF lay in the Northwest African Strategic Air Force (NASAF), commanded by Brigadier-General J. H. Doolittle and consisting of heavy, medium and light bombers plus escort fighters. The tactical and close-support element of NAAF's armoury, and one which had fought with distinction in Tunisia, was Air Marshal Sir Arthur Coningham's Northwest African Tactical Air Force (NATAF). The famous Western Desert Air Force (WDAF), led by Air Vice Marshal Harry Broadhurst, also came under Coningham's command, with No. 211 Group (RAF) subordinated.

The fighter component was concentrated under No. 211 Group with Nos 7 (SAAF) and Nos 239, 244 and 285 Wings (RAF). Lastly, NATAF controlled two strong fighter elements which acted autonomously: Brigadier-General John K. Cannon's US XII Air Support Command controlled the 31st, 33rd and 52nd Fighter Groups.

The remaining components of NAAF consisted of the Northwest African Coastal Air Force with maritime patrol bombers, anti-submarine aircraft and defensive fighters, and the US 51st Troop Carrier Wing, which was disposed under the Northwest African Troop Carrier Command.

Mustering the forces

In the forthcoming campaign in Sicily the NAAF's fighters and bombers were to be the main element directed against the Luftwaffe, but an important part was to be played by Malta Air Command and the United States 9th Air Force. Malta's units, under the overall command of Air Marshal Sir Keith Park, consisted of 15 reconnaissance, anti-shipping and fighter squadrons. The US IX Bomber Command, consisting of two Consolidated B-24 groups and one RAF squadron, was stationed in the Benghazi complex. This was employed in close co-operation with NAAF's daylight attacks on Axis targets in Sicily, Italy, Sardinia, Greece and Crete. Malta's aircraft numbered 218 on establishment, with a further 1,012 on the strength of Middle East Command.

Medium bombers played a prominent part in the campaigns in Sicily and Italy in 1943-44. Here, B-25J Mitchells of the 321st Bomb Group head home following one of the innumerable missions flown against Axis communications in northern Italy.

The plan for Operation Husky called for the seaborne descent of 10 July to be preceded by the invasions of the Axis-held islands of Pantelleria and Lampedusa one month earlier in Operation Corkscrew. Even before the surrender of the enemy in Tunisia, Tedder's command turned to the strategic bombing of Axis aerodromes, installations and communications in Italy, Sardinia, Sicily and Greece; coupled with these operations were widespread reconnaissance missions over the entire Mediterranean theatre, daylight sweeps by fighters, intrusions by night-fighting Mosquitoes and Beaufighters, and anti-shipping strikes by the aircraft of the NACAF. As the primary aim, the defeat of the Axis air forces prior to the invasion of Sicily was carefully planned, and was handled by the bombers of NASAF and US IX Bomber Command. Following Tedder's directive the bombers were to pay no attention to Sicily while conducting an escalating round of operations over the period from 16 May to 5 June 1943; support for the NATAF's fighter-bombers would be provided against Pantelleria during the period 6-12 June; an all-out offensive against operational Axis airfields was to be made over the period between 13 June and 2 July; and from that date onwards, a systematic bombing campaign would be waged against airfields and installations on Sicily.

Airfield attacks

During the last weeks of May, Allied bombers turned their attention to attacks on airfields in the Foggia area, and the transport bases at Pomigliano and Capodochino near Naples, with frequent fighter sweeps by Spitfire Mk VCs and P-40Ls from Malta and Gozo applying pressure on II Fliegerkorps' fighters in Sicily.

Maximum-effort raids on the fortified island of Pantelleria started on 1 June 1943; NASAF's Boeing B-17Fs attacked, backed up by the B-25s and B-26s while P-40 Warhawks conducted

Left: Martin B-26 Marauders from the 310th Bomb Group, USAAF prepare to depart from their base at Berteaux, North Africa for a raid over Sicily in March 1943.

Below: Wrecks found on Tunisian airfields, such as these Junkers Ju 88s, bore testimony to the huge losses sustained by the Luftwaffe, a situation that was to be repeated later in Sicily and Italy.

fighter-bombing and strafing. Over the period 6-11 June, when the island fell without a fight, MAC flew 3,712 bomber and fighter-bomber sorties against Pantelleria, 5,234 tons of bombs being dropped. Luftwaffe opposition was sparse until 6 June, when Messerschmitt Bf 109G-6 fighters of JG 27 and JG 53 tried to head off some of the frequent raids; the heaviest air fighting took place on 10 June, when III./JG 27 lost nine Messerschmitts and six pilots in combat.

Despite the magnitude of the Axis defeats at Stalingrad and in Tunisia, the Luftwaffe aimed to restore the balance of air power in its favour in the late spring of 1943. Russia and the Mediterranean held equal priority in the allocation of aircraft from a booming production industry that, in June 1943, achieved an output of 2,316 aircraft, of which 1,134 were Messerschmitt and Focke-Wulf fighters.

The losses suffered in Tunisia were quickly made good. Excluding a powerful force of

transports, the Luftwaffe's strength in the Mediterranean theatre grew from 820 aircraft in May to an all-time peak of 1,280 combat aircraft on 3 July 1943, of which 975 were based in Italy, Sardinia and Sicily. In all, the Axis could count on some 1,750 operational aircraft to counter Tedder's forces, the additional units coming from the then Regia Aeronautica. The Axis air forces in the Mediterranean to face the invasion of Sicily appeared to be well-balanced and strong, but nothing on paper could sway the course of events when MAC went to work against these forces before the commencement of Husky in its counter-air campaign.

Heavy bombers

Over the period from 18 June to 2 July 1943, the NAAF blasted ports and airfields to blockade the supply of reinforcements to Sicily: the B-17s of NASAF flew 317 sorties with the support of the P-38 Lightnings; the medium bombers contributed 566 sorties, while US IX Bomber Command

flew 107 with its B-24 Liberators. Opposition by the Jagdgruppen of II Fliegerkorps amounted to 50-100 sorties per day, during which casualties were heavy, both in the air and on the ground: the use of 500-lb (227-kg) and 250-lb (113-kg) bombs and the new 20-lb (9-kg) fragmentation bombs by the B-17s and B-24s had devastating effects on parked aircraft. On 15 June III./JG 53 lost eight Bf 109G-6s on the ground at Sciacca. Daily attacks were made by NASAF on airfields in Sicily, Sardinia and in Italy. The battle was not one-sided: on 26 June, over 100 Ju 88s, He 111s, Fw 190s and CANT Z.1007s attacked an Allied convoy, whilst night attacks continued on Bizerta, Bône and Algiers, where the invasion fleets were gathering. The final phase of the bombing campaign started on 2 July with raids on Gerbini by B-17s, with the B-24s visiting Grottaglie, Lecce and San Pancrazio.

Luftwaffe reaction varied, on one day the force did little, and on another it would take part in a

fierce battle, but with the P-38s always gaining the upper hand. During the Gerbini raid on 5 July 1943, over 100 Bf 109G-6s of JG 53 and JG 77, joined by the Fw 190s of III./SKG 10 and the Macchi MC.202s of the 4° Stormo, fought an epic combat. In addition to the major contribution of NASAF and US IX Bomber Command were the constant patrols and fighter sweeps of the Malta-based P-40s and Spitfire Mk VCs, which gave the Luftwaffe in Sicily no respite during the time needed to recuperate after the fighting in Tunisia. The effect of over two months of constant battering and harrying would be seen in the poor showing put up by the Axis air forces following the Sicilian invasion. Luftwaffe losses in the crucial campaign for air supremacy before Husky amounted to 323 aircraft destroyed in the air and on the ground; the Regia Aeronautica lost 150 aircraft on the ground to bombing. The effort of MAC from 16 May until dusk on 9 July 1943 amounted to 42,227 sorties with the loss of 250 British and US aircraft, but its contribution to the success of the establishment of Allied forces in Sicily and Italy can never be overemphasised.

┌ Italian defenders

Spoils of war
This captured Breguet Br.693 was one of many such types which were impressed into service with the Axis for second-line duties. This particular example served with the Regia Aeronautica at Orange-Caratit airfield, situated in the Rhône Valley, in March 1943.

Night attacker
Resplendent in nocturnal camouflage, this CANT Z.1007bis bomber served with the 260ª Squadriglia of the 47° Stormo BT of the Regia Aeronautica during early 1943 in attacks against Allied ports and installations in North Africa. Note the Breda Mk V dorsal turret in place of the more usual Lanciana type.

Above: Lockheed F-5E Lightnings (unarmed and camera-equipped) of the 90th Photographic Reconnaissance Wing were used for pre-invasion reconnaissance operations over Sicily in 1943.

Left: The Martin Marauder Mk I first entered RAF service in August 1942 with No. 14 Squadron. Based in Egypt, this unit flew bombing and maritime strike sorties off the coasts of Sicily and Italy.

Invasion of Sicily

Despite constant harassment by the bombers of Mediterranean Air Command, the Luftwaffe fought with tremendous tenacity, allowing the Axis commanders to extricate the bulk of their land forces.

The seaborne assault on Sicily, codenamed Operation Husky, was scheduled to commence on 10 July 1943; aided by the new, amphibious landing craft, 2,500 ships and landing vessels carried 160,000 combat troops of the British 8th Army and the US 7th Army to the beaches on southern Sicily, covered by 750 warships of the Royal Navy and the US Navy, and by some 2,500 aircraft of the Mediterranean Air Command (MAC). The 8th Army landed its troops on the beaches to the south of Syracuse at Avola, Noto, Pachino and Pozallo, along a coastline that stretched for 45 miles (72 km). The 7th Army put ashore farther to the west, between Scogliatti and Licata. As a result of bad weather the element of surprise was total, and the divisions and brigades went ashore with surprisingly light opposition. However, the presence of hundreds of ships lying offshore, along a stretch of coast that measured in total some 85 miles (137 km), was a tempting target for the Axis air

forces stationed in Sicily and at nearby bases in Sardinia and in the southern portion of the Italian mainland.

The Axis forces actually in Sicily at the time of the invasion were not particularly strong: an average of 289 Luftwaffe aircraft were on strength there, with 143 combat-ready. In addition, there were 145 Italian aircraft (63 serviceable). There were, however, some 775 combat aircraft based within range of Sicily under Luftflotte II, to which II Fliegerkorps was subordinated. The low combat status of Axis air elements in Sicily resulted from the

extremely fierce round of bombing operations that had been carried out over the past few weeks by Northwest African Air Forces (NAAF), and by the Liberators of the US 9th Bomber Command.

In Operation Husky the Allied objectives lay in the capture of the seaports at Palermo and Messina: the British were to advance to Catania, capture the sorely-needed airfields in the Gerbini complex, and thwart the Axis withdrawal by the taking of Messina; the US 7th Army was given the task of striking across country to split the defences, and of capturing the supply port of Palermo. Between these armies lay difficult terrain, defended by 200,000 Italian troops, many of low calibre, but stiffened by 32,000 German troops.

Massed parachute and air landings formed part of the early operations. Through no fault of the paratroops, these operations were conducted very badly. On the night of 9 July, in Operation Ladbroke, 2,075 men of the British 1st Air-landing Brigade set off from Kairouan in 137 Airspeed Horsa and Waco Hadrian gliders. The aim of the landings was the capture of the Ponte Grande Bridge, south of Syracuse, but disaster ensued. No moon and a stiff offshore breeze encountered on the leg from Cape Pessaro to the drop zone foiled the navigators, who were unable to give accurate fixes. Released too early, 69 gliders landed in the sea, while another 59 were strewn over a distance of 25 miles (40 km) from Cape Passero to Cape Murro di Porco. A simultaneous air drop, made by the US 505th Parachute Regiment of the 82nd Airborne Division, suffered a similarly ignominious fate: navigational errors were made by the 226 C-47s of the US 52nd Troop Carrier Wing, which dumped their unfortunate charges at

Italian fighter units fought hard during the preliminary Allied air attacks on Sicily and Italy. This Macchi MC.202 Folgore was from the 369ª Squadriglia, 22º Stormo CT, based at Naples-Capodichino in July 1943.

random in the area between Gela and Syracuse. To the credit of the British and American paratroops involved, many of the objectives placed before them were attained.

German successes

Sporadic attacks by Fw 190A fighter-bombers, Ju 88A-4 bombers, and Bf 109G-6 fighters started at first light. In the British area, one air attack took place in the morning, with a number after midday. The hospital ship SS *Talamba* was sunk. The US sectors received greater attention. The USS *Sentinel* (a picket ship) was hit by an Fw 190's SC250 bomb off Molla, and sank later; at dawn the destroyer USS *Maddox* was dive-bombed, and sank within two minutes. During the day the USS *Murphy* was hit, and LST-313 was sunk by German aircraft. Hurtful accusations were directed by the US Navy over the apparent lack of air cover. Curtiss S03C-1 floatplanes launched by the cruisers USS *Savannah* and *Boise* were badly mauled by aggressive Messerschmitts which killed one crew, and forced the rest down later.

Allied fighter cover was provided from 20 minutes after first light on 10 July, with five Malta-based squadrons of Supermarine Spitfire Mk VCs giving relay protection over Avola, Pachino and Scogliatti, the Spitfires of the US 31st Fighter Group protecting the Gela sector from Gozo and the P-40Ls from Pantelleria covering the Licata area. These fighters were soon receiving assistance from fighter control ships lying offshore. Only one interception was made by the US fighters from Gozo and Pantelleria, but the Malta-based Spitfire Mk VCs had more fortune, and fought several combats: in one of the last battles of the day No. 229 Squadron's Spitfires downed three Macchi MC.202s out of eight encountered. Much of the Luftwaffe's strength was dissipated in battles against the bombers of NATAF (Northwest African Tactical Air Force), NATBF (Northwest African Tactical Bombing Force) and US 9th Bomber Command. In the morning 51 B-17 Flying Fortresses bombed Gerbini; 35

B-25 Mitchells attacked Sciacca, 36 attacked Trapani–Milo, and 60 railyards at Catania and communications at Palazzolo. Vibo Valentia airfield was hit by 21 B-24D Liberators. In all, only four US bombers were shot down by flak and fighters. Luftwaffe losses on 10 July numbered 16 destroyed or missing. According to Axis sources 370 sorties were flown by the Luftwaffe and 141 by the Regia Aeronautica, which lost 11 Macchis in combat.

By 12 July the Allies had established their position in southern Sicily in some strength. As airfields were captured, so the recent lack of close-support and air cover, which at times had become dangerously apparent, was made good. The HQ of the Western Desert Air Force (renamed Desert Air Force as from 21 July) opened at Pachino on 13 July with three Spitfire Mk VC squadrons; a fourth squadron flew in on 14 July with the Spitfire Mk Vs and Mk IXs of No. 324 Wing going to Comiso.

During the period 10-12 July 1943 the Luftwaffe flew 275-300 sorties per day. In the face of overwhelming Allied air opposition, this scale of effort fell to around 150 sorties per day thereafter, largely as a result of the disruption caused at airfields and maintenance units by bombing. For the Luftwaffe conditions in Sicily were soon beyond remedy:

by 16 July only 120 aircraft (of which not more than 30 were serviceable) remained on the island and by 18 July the total had sunk to 25. All that remained of the Luftwaffe and Regia Aeronautica in Sicily were some 1,100 destroyed or damaged aircraft left behind on the various airfields: of these, approximately 600 were German.

The Luftwaffe was virtually eliminated in the land battles: a small force of fighter-bombers, numbering some 50 Fw 190s and Bf 110G-2s and about 65 Bf 109G-6s were stationed in the toe of Italy for tactical operations. Meanwhile, the Allied heavy bombers roamed almost at will. The first attack on Rome's marshalling yards, which handled about 60 per cent of traffic bound for the south, took place on 19 July. From 17-23 July 1943 both NASAF and US IX Bomber Command flew continuous raids on the Luftwaffe fields at Grottaglie, San Pancrazio, Viterbo, Pomigliano, Montecorvino, Aquino, Vibo Valentia, Crotone and Leverano, to which the remnants of II Fliegerkorps had retired. On 25 July II. and III./JG 27 again suffered losses before being withdrawn for refit. Operating off Sardinia on 30 July, Curtiss P-40s and P-38s claimed 21 enemy transport aircraft: five of III./JG 77's pilots were shot down in frantic battles.

Axis fighters over Sicily

During the battle for Sicily the Axis forces came under tremendous pressure both in the air and from Allied bombing raids. During the five weeks of fighting, the German and Italian air forces lost some 1,850 aircraft, compared with the loss of fewer than 400 British and American aircraft.

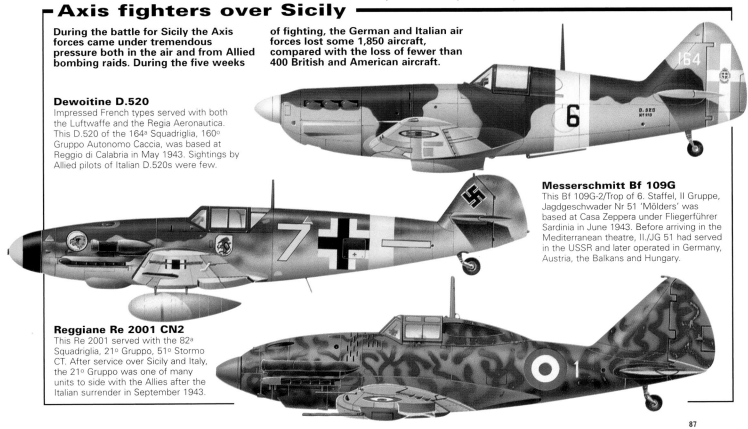

Dewoitine D.520
Impressed French types served with both the Luftwaffe and the Regia Aeronautica. This D.520 of the 164ª Squadriglia, 160º Gruppo Autonomo Caccia, was based at Reggio di Calabria in May 1943. Sightings by Allied pilots of Italian D.520s were few.

Messerschmitt Bf 109G
This Bf 109G-2/Trop of 6. Staffel, II Gruppe, Jagdgeschwader Nr 51 'Mölders' was based at Casa Zeppera under Fliegerführer Sardinia in June 1943. Before arriving in the Mediterranean theatre, II./JG 51 had served in the USSR and later operated in Germany, Austria, the Balkans and Hungary.

Reggiane Re 2001 CN2
This Re 2001 served with the 82ª Squadriglia, 21º Gruppo, 51º Stormo CT. After service over Sicily and Italy, the 21º Gruppo was one of many units to side with the Allies after the Italian surrender in September 1943.

Operation Tidalwave

A 718th Bomb Squadron, 449th Bomb Group B-24D Liberator rides high above a towering column of smoke after dropping its load of bombs on the Astro Romano oil refinery at Ploesti during one of the subsequent raids made in 1944.

The raid on Ploesti

Lauded in the contemporary press as a decisive American air victory, the Ploesti raid was in fact a costly defeat in tactical and strategic terms as well as taking a heavy toll of US aircraft and airmen.

Producing some 3 per cent of the world's refined fuel oil, Ploesti lies some 35 miles (50 km) north of Bucharest in Romania: by 1943 the many Romanian oil refineries were helping to bolster the German war effort to a large degree, with over 60 per cent of their oil output going to the Reich. US plans aimed at attacking Ploesti went back to 1942, when an unsuccessful mission to Ploesti was flown in June. This only had the effect of strengthening the defences and by

the spring of 1943 heavy flak was supported by day- and night-fighter units of the Luftwaffe as well as Romanian units equipped with IAR 80 and Avia B.534 fighters. In April 1943 the plan was hatched to wipe out the Ploesti complex once and for all. The raid was to be a mass low-level strike by B-24Ds of the US IX Bomber Command in an operation named Tidalwave.

The Liberator units involved were the 44th and 93rd Groups (seconded from VIII Bomber Command) and the 98th, 376th and 389th BGs. The planning of Tidalwave was thorough, with much practice of low-flying techniques and navigation before the mission commenced on the morning of 1 August 1943. Loaded with 500-lb (227-kg) and 250-lb (113-kg) GPs with a large proportion of incendiaries, 177 Liberators departed their Benghazi bases on the 1,550-mile (2500 km) round trip which was carefully planned to achieve the maximum level of surprise. Each Group was allocated specific refineries as targets: the 376th BG

in the lead position was allocated the Romana Americana refinery; the 93rd BG Concordia Vega, Standard Petrol and Unirea Speranta; the 98th BG Astra Romana and Unirea Orion; the 44th BG Colombia Aquila and Crédital Minier; and the 389th a target well to the north of the rest, the oil refinery at Campina.

Costly mistakes

Initially the mission went as planned, following a route along the Tyrrhenian Sea. However, as the formations turned to cross the mountains of Albania, heavy thunderstorms gradually reduced their cohesion and the timing of the raid began to go awry. The small town of Floresti to the northwest of Ploesti had been selected as the initial point (IP) for the raid, since it had a railway which led directly to the oil fields. But low-level navigation is notoriously difficult, and once a mistake has been made it is difficult to remedy. The two leading groups (the 376th and 93rd) mistook the town of Tagoriste for Floresti and turned. This track took them straight into the outskirts of Bucharest, where a frantic course change was made to the north once the error had been recognised. By this time the 389th BG was already en route for Campina, and the 44th and 98th Groups were running in on the correct track for Ploesti. The overall effect was a breakdown in the element of surprise. Flak and fighter reaction was prompt and several Liberators were knocked down as they swept over the fields at less than 40 ft (12 m). The losses incurred on Tidalwave were extremely high: only 92 B-24s returned to Benghazi, 19 came down at other airfields, seven landed in neutral Turkey and three crashed into the sea. A total of 54 failed to return and 532 men were lost. The German losses amounted to four Bf 109Gs plus four damaged and two Bf 110s plus five damaged. Despite the raid being heralded

Much effort was put into training the pilots and navigators in low-level operations. Here a squadron of B-24Ds thunders over the Benghazi plains on one such practice mission.

Left: A B-24D of the 9th Air Force emerges from the heavy fires burning at the Astra Romano refinery. Early B-24s had manually operated guns in the nose, which proved a weakness in combat.

Below: Fighter reaction by the Jafü Rumanien (Romanian air force) was prompt, aircraft such as these IAR 80s intercepting the formations and claiming a heavy toll on the raiding force.

as a great success, the damage was easily repaired and the complex was operating at normal output within a few weeks.

Defences strengthened

Less than a fortnight later, on 13 August, the same five B-24 groups were sent to the Messerschmitt assembly plant at Wiener Neustadt in Austria. Due to bad weather only 65 Liberators reached the target, however they encountered little in the way of Flak or fighter defences losing only two aircraft. The effect of the raid was to force the Luftwaffe to strengthen defences against attack by Allied forces in the Mediterranean theatre.

In support of the troops in the field, the Desert Air Force continued to fly maximum effort operations over the Catania area in support of the British 8th Army. Concurrently the US XII Air Support Command supported the American forces'

drive to Marsala, Trapani and Palermo, and the steady push eastwards. During the last week of July the German forces started to pull out of Sicily across the Straits of Messina. The withdrawal was a model of ordered efficiency, and an average of 17,000 men was evacuated each day. The 8th Army finally captured Catania on 5 August, before initiating a plan to traverse around Mount Etna to link up with the US forces approaching from the west. The Allied tactical air forces flew constant missions over the enemy strongpoints during daylight hours: Spitfire Mk VCs, Kittyhawk Mk IIIs and A-26 Invaders dropped 500-lb (227-kg) and 250-lb (113-kg) GP bombs from low-level, strafed troop concentrations and enemy strongholds: Baltimores, Bostons and A-20Bs operated at medium altitude to avoid the worst of the light Flak. Of the Luftwaffe over

the battlefront little was seen after the 17-18 July by day, save occasional Jabo raids by Fw 190A-5s against ports: fighter sorties by Bf 109G-6s averaged about 60 every 24 hours.

Raid on Rome

The few German fighter units still operating from bases in the south of Italy were for the most part committed against the daily raids of NASAF and US IX Bomber Command. On 13 August the Lorenzo marshalling yards near Rome were pounded by 106 B-17s, 66 B-25s and 102 B-26s, escorted by 140 P-38G Lightnings. On this occasion the Regia Aeronautica reacted with vigour, sending up at least 75 MC.202s and Re.2001s along with a handful of the latest G.55 and Re.2005 fighters and a small number of Bf 109G-6s. Heavy damage was inflicted on the yards and although two B-26Cs were

downed the Italians lost five aircraft in combat with the P-38s.

This second major attack on Rome's surrounding airfields and rail facilities was designed more as a propaganda exercise to bring home to the Italian people the hopelessness of the facist cause. By this time Mussolini had been arrested and covert negotiations with the new Badoglio government were in progress with the aim of producing suitable terms for surrender.

Within four days of the Rome attack British and US forces had completed the capture of Sicily, with German forces carrying out their orderly evacuation of troops and equipment to the last. Throughout the last four weeks of fighting Allied air supremacy had been total, and of the once proud forces of Luftflotte II little had been seen save for the occasional sporadic daylight raid, and a number of inconclusive nocturnal attacks.

'Gustav' defenders

During Germany's evacuation from the port of Messina in Sicily the Luftwaffe's small force of Bf 109G-6s flew desperate fighter sweeps to prevent Allied attack. Around 150 sorties were flown per day, the majority by Major Johannes

Steinhoff's JG 77. Four Italian Gruppi also flew the Bf 109G in the Mediterranean theatre during the spring and summer of 1943. The aircraft were used in a defensive role over Sicily and southern Italy.

Bf 109G-6 'White 1'

JG 77 was one of the most active Luftwaffe units in the defence of Sicily. This aircraft was the mount of Oberleutnant Ernst-Wilhelm Reinert who became commander of I. Staffel in August. Previously the top-scorer in the Tunisian campaign, Reinart went on to claim 174 aerial kills.

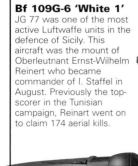

Bf 109G-6/Trop

This particular aircraft was flown by Sottotenente Giuseppe Ruzzin from Comiso, Sicily during July 1943. Attached to 154ª Squadriglia, 3° Gruppo CT, this aircraft carries the 'Diavolo Rossi' ('Red Devil') group badge on the cowling and a plain white Savoia cross on the tail.

Messerschmitt Bf 109

Of the more than 30,000 Messerschmitt Bf 109s built during World War II, none remains airworthy, although several are undergoing rebuild to flying condition. This RAF-owned Bf 109G is now stored at the Imperial War Museum at Duxford, where it remains grounded following a landing accident in 1997.

Without doubt the most famous German aircraft of World War II, the fortunes of the Bf 109 mirrored those of the Luftwaffe itself: total dominance in the early victories, a long hard struggle to retain the superiority achieved, and final defeat in the face of overwhelming numbers.

When chief test pilot, Flugkapitän Hans 'Bubi' Knötsch, lifted the first prototype of a brand-new fighter from the runway of Messerschmitt's Augsburg-Haunstetten field in May 1935, he undoubtedly knew that the machine in his hands represented a quantum leap forward in fighter design technology. What he could not have foreseen was that a decade later, despite having suffered total defeat, it would be accorded a rightful place alongside the Spitfire and Mustang as one of aviation's true immortals.

Although the Bf 109A, as it was initially designated, was not the first single-seat fighter to combine an all-metal stressed-

Above: Leutnant Steindl, the Geschwader adjutant of JG 54, positions his Bf 109E-4B for a wingman's camera during a bombing mission to Stalingrad in spring 1942. The Jagdbomber (fighter-bomber) version of the Bf 109E stayed in front-line service long after the day-fighter version had been replaced by the Bf 109F and 109G.

skin monocoque structure with a low-wing cantilever monoplane configuration, it was the first to add to these a whole raft of extra refinements such as an enclosed cockpit, retractable undercarriage and the then radical combination of automatic leading-edge slots and slotted trailing-edge flaps.

Pioneering design

Messerschmitt's achievement in producing such a pure thoroughbred was all the more remarkable in that it was a first. Comparison is often made between the Bf 109 and its near contemporary, the Spitfire. But whereas the latter drew heavily on experience gained with the earlier Schneider Trophy high-speed racing floatplanes, the Bf 109 had no such illustrious forebears; its immediate predecessor was a four-seat light civilian touring machine.

Operational trials

The Bf 109 was without doubt the most advanced fighter of its time to enter service and see combat. Four prototypes (V3-6) were sent to Spain late in 1936 for operational trials with the Legion Condor. They would be followed by 124 production machines. In an era of fighter biplanes whose design ancestry and tactics dated all too obviously back to World War I, the Bf 109 pilots in Spain rewrote the rule book. Foremost among them was the future fighter ace, Werner Mölders, whose Schwarm, or 'finger-four', formation was later adopted by air forces the world over.

The first major production model, the classic Bf 109E, or 'Emil', marked perhaps the early apogee of the entire 109 line. Not only will it forever be associated with the Battle of Britain, it was popular with the Luftwaffe pilots themselves. It embodied everything that the chief designer – Willy Messerschmitt – had sought to achieve before military necessity

In Spain, Bf 109s were primarily used for bomber escort operations and low-level sweeps. The Messerschmitts proved vastly superior to the Republican fighters.

Above: During the early campaigns of World War II, the Bf 109 proved to be a formidable opponent when pitted against outdated French and Polish fighters. The few that were lost were mostly as a result of ground fire.

Left: Most of the Bf 109's actions were undertaken by day, but the type was impressed into action as a night-fighter. This is a II./JG 54 Bf 109F, flying in the early months of the war in Russia. Note the 19 victory bars on the rudder.

dictated the incorporation of various lumps and bumps to house additional armament and equipment, and the bolting on of performance-sapping weapons packs.

If the Emil had a flaw – apart from the narrow-track undercarriage, which was a weakness in every one of the 30,000+ Bf 109s built – it was its lack of punch: at best, two 20-mm MG FF wing cannon and two fuselage-mounted 0.31-in (7.9-mm) MG 17 machine-guns. The aerodynamically improved Bf 109F, with its uprated DB 601N powerplant, did little to remedy the armament situation. And, while many pilots appreciated the superior muzzle velocity and rate of fire of the single engine-mounted MG 151 cannon which had replaced the Emil's wing guns, others preferred to continue to fly the Bf 109E as long as conditions permitted.

Fighter for all fronts

The mid-war Friedrich had held its own on all flying fronts: the Channel, Mediterranean and Russia. It would fall to those who flew its successor, the Bf 109G, to pay the price for the Luftwaffe's failure to produce and make available an adequate replacement for a design which was already past its peak. By far the most prolific of all Bf 109 variants, the Gustav would soldier on under increasing pressure until the final collapse.

Development of the Bf 109G led to the Bf 109K-4 of October 1944, the final production version. Powered by the highly supercharged DB 605D engine, the K-4 was fast but, by this time, the design had lost most of the fine handling of its early predecessors. It was still a potent weapon: all it needed was fuel to power it and experienced pilots to fly it – both of which items were sadly lacking in the Luftwaffe during the final months of the war.

Post-war service

The ending of hostilities did not see the operational history of the Bf 109 draw to a close. Spain had investigated licence-assembly of the aircraft during the war and afterwards completed Bf 109s utilising its own Hispano-Suiza engines and, later, British Rolls-Royce Merlins (the same powerplant as used in its former wartime adversary, the Supermarine Spitfire). Known as Hispano HA-1112-M1Ls, the Spanish Bf 109s remained in service until the mid-1960s.

Further post-war use of the Bf 109 included a number of S-199 'Mezecs' (Czech-built Jumo 211F-powered 'Gustavs'), flown by Israel against the Egyptian air force in 1948-49. The fighter was disliked by pilots for its poor handling and was dubbed 'the mule' by those unfortunate enough to have to fly the aircraft in combat.

This Messerschmitt Bf 109G is operated by MBB Aircraft/Flugzeug-Union Sud in Germany. The aircraft is something of a hybrid machine, being a Spanish Hispano HA-1112 Buchón fitted with a German Daimler-Benz engine.

Setting foot in Italy

'Yellow 14', a 20-mm cannon-armed Bf 109G-6/R6 Trop abandoned by JG 53, shares Comiso airfield, Sicily, with a Spitfire Mk VC in summer 1943. As the Allies occupied Sicily and moved north through the Italian mainland, they occupied and made use of captured Italian airfields.

The strength of Allied forces in the Mediterranean theatre meant that, even before the Sicilian campaign was over, plans were being made for the invasion of the Italian mainland.

The aims of the three landings scheduled for September 1943 were to force Italy out of the war, to establish bomber bases from where attacks could be made against southern Germany and the Balkans, and to draw German divisions into a battle of attrition in the defence of Rome. Planned for 3 September, Operation Baytown would place elements of the British 8th Army on the 'toe' of Italy at Reggio Calabria, across the narrow Straits of Messina; a more ambitious Operation Avalanche was aimed at cutting off the line of retreat of the Axis forces by putting the US 5th Army down on the beaches of the Gulf of Salerno, south of Rome. Avalanche was to take place on 9 September 1943, with landings by the 8th Army simultaneously taking place at Taranto in Operation Slapstick.

The distribution of strength on 3 September was 3,546 aircraft with NAAF (Northwest African Air Force), 840 with MEAC and

Below: When conditions at Foggia became untenable, II Fliegerkorps moved north, including the Ju 88A-4s of I./KG 54 'Totenkopf' Geschwader, which moved to Bergamo.

184 under Malta Air Command; these totals included a force of 350 transports and 400 gliders. A force of no fewer than 3,280 aircraft, with the addition of B-24 groups sent from England, was allocated to the Salerno landings and the subsidiary operations.

Pre-invasion bombing

Widespread bombing attacks by the medium and heavy bombers of NAAF, in preparation for the invasions at Reggio and Salerno, started on 18 August 1943. During the period 22 August– 2 September forces of 70 B-25s and B-26s attacked rail targets at Salerno, Battipaglia, Benevento,

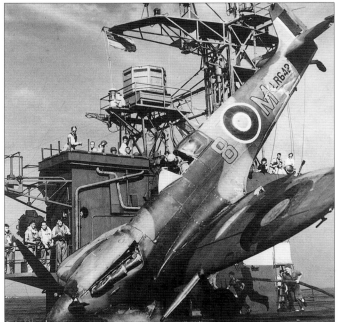

A No. 807 Sqn Seafire L.Mk IIC is seen aboard HMS Battler during the Italian landings in 1943. During the invasion at Salerno, FAA Martlets and Seafires provided vital air cover to enable airfields to be established.

Caserta, Cancello, Averse, Torre Annunziato and Civitavecchia. NASAF's (Northwest African Strategic Air Force) heavies returned to Capua and Foggia airfields on 25 August. Attacks on the Naples airfield complex took place on 26 August, with waves of B-17s, B-25s and B-26s attacking Grazzanise and Capua where stiff opposition from Bf 109G-6 fighters was encountered, but much damage was done to aircraft at these fields. Viterbo, another bomber base, was raided on 30 August. During this time NASAF kept up the pressure on the railheads, bombing Sulmone, Terni, Forli, Pisa, and, on 2 September, the marshalling yards at Bolzano, Trento and Bologna, this time with unescorted B-17s.

Fighters on armed reconnaissance over the 'toe' of Italy flew patrols and strafing

Left: The Italian summer gave rise to surprisingly difficult conditions for this 376th Bombardment Group B-24D Liberator, struggling with flood water at the waterlogged San Pancrazio airfield.

Below: B-25 Mitchells of the NAAF's 487th Bombardment Squadron/340th Bombardment Group ride the flak during a raid on German communication lines in northern Italy.

attacks on motor transport and rolling stock at Scalea, Centraro, Cosenza and in the Sapri areas. Air-to-air combat came to a head on 7 September when about 120 B-17s attacked the Foggia airfields; a Luftwaffe force of 60-70 aircraft entered combat with determination. However, the P-38 escort proved too strong, and in the ensuing battle only two B-17s went down for an estimated enemy loss of 37 fighters. This epic battle witnessed the end of massed German fighter opposition over southern Italy.

Battle of Salerno

In preparation for the invasions, MAC's air effort amounted to over 13,300 sorties from 17 August-2 September; 180 Allied aircraft and about 85 German aircraft were destroyed on operations. Some 3,800 sorties had been directed against the enemy rail system to stop the flow of all traffic south of the line Naples-Foggia. The 8th Army landed at Reggio Calabria at 03.45 on 3 September while, at dawn, Spitfires and Kittyhawks patrolled overhead; opposition both on the ground and in the air was light, and by 11.45 the Canadians entered the port at Reggio. In the period 2-8 September Air Chief Marshal Sir Arthur Tedder's unit flew 7,145 sorties, losing only 25 aircraft, while II Fliegerkorps lost some 16 aircraft on operations.

In Operation Avalanche the greatest problem faced by the Allied air commanders lay in the restricted radius of action of the fighter cover: the distance to Salerno from the Gerbini airfields was 220 miles (354 km), which placed undue pressure on the P-38s of the US 1st, 14th and 82nd Groups. Naval fighter cover was therefore essential. Under Force H, the carriers HMS *Illustrious* and *Formidable* provided Martlet Mk IVs and Seafire LF.Mk IICs. Light carriers of Force V (HMS *Unicorn, Stalker, Hunter, Attacker* and *Battler*)

Marshalling yards, factories and an oil store at Naples were struck by a wave of Wellington bombers, followed by B-25s, B-26s and P-38s in August 1943.

provided further Seafires. The total forces allotted to the air umbrella over Salerno consisted of 110 Seafires and Martlets, nine squadrons of P-38Gs, seven of A-36s, and 13 British and US Spitfire squadrons. H-hour for Avalanche was at 03.30 on 9 September; the British X Corps and the US VI Corps, under the US 5th Army, landed on a 25-mile (40-km) stretch of coastline on the Gulf of Salerno between Amalfi and Paestum.

Resistance inland quickly intensified and, by the evening (when the Italian surrender was announced to the world), the troops were in the thick of battle. Opposition to the Salerno landings was fierce, and over the

period 9-16 September the Allies came close to being pitched back into the sea. It was only the combination of desperate fighting on the part of the Allies and Hitler's agreement for Kesselring to make a strategic withdrawal on 17 September that saved the situation. Luftflotte H's forces made a determined effort to attack shipping in the roadsteads, with the Fw 190A-5 fighterbombers of II Fliegerkorps putting up an average of 170 sorties per day. Over the period 8-16 September MAC flew 21,696 sorties, losing 60 aircraft, as against 81 lost by Luftflotte II and eight by Luftwaffenkommando Süd-Ost.

In comparison with the

Salerno landings, those at Taranto went smoothly and with little opposition. By 20 September, Desert Air Force (DAF) headquarters was at Crotone in southern Italy. Much of the Luftwaffe's strength was dissipated in the Salerno fighting by the withdrawal of units to cover the evacuation of Sardinia and Corsica by the Wehrmacht. On 9 September the Germans decided to withdraw air units and troops from Sardinia to Corsica. On its completion, on 3 October, some 21,107 men and 350 tons of stores had been airlifted out for the loss of 55 transports, which met their end on Italian airfields at the hands of Allied bombers.

A hard winter

German resolve to defend Italy at all costs turned Allied dreams of a speedy offensive into nightmares of attrition in the battles on the Volturno, the Sangro and at Cassino. For once, Allied air supremacy counted for little in the face of stubborn German resilience on the ground.

The early autumn of 1943 was an eventful time for the Allied forces in the Mediterranean theatre of operations. After a bitter struggle at Salerno, the US 5th Army advanced inland to make contact with the British 8th Army, advancing through Calabria, at Auletta on 20 September 1943; to the east, elements of the 8th Army took Bari and then the airfield complex at Foggia on 1 October, the day on which the port of Naples fell into American hands.

Since the surrender of Italy in September, German resolve to stand firm on the Italian mainland had hardened: rather than conduct a withdrawal to Rome, as had been intended originally, Generalfeldmarschall Albert Kesselring was given a directive by Hitler to establish strongly defended lines well to the south of Rome athwart the precipitous Apennines, and along the many deep river valleys: a glance at the topographical characteristics of Italy will show that the country favoured the Germans on every count. Appointed as Oberbefeldshaber Süd West on 21 November

1943, Kesselring was given command of Heeresgruppe 'C' (Army Group 'C') with the 10th and 14th Armies in the south and north of Italy respectively. His appointed task was to sap Allied strength in the Italian sector, to embarrass their preparations for the invasion of northwest Europe, and to baulk any attempt at an invasion of the Balkans.

As the Germans continued their slow withdrawal to the line of the river Volturno, the Allied tactical air forces established themselves at airfields in southern Italy: in essence, the format of the support forces was similar to those that had taken part in the campaign in Sicily. Major-General Edwin J. House

Above: The Allies' tactical bomber force was kept on constant action against Axis lines of communication. Here, a 12th Air Force B-26 Marauder successfully hits a rail bridge at Anastasia.

Above: Armourers load 500-lb (227-kg) GP bombs on to a P-38L Lightning of the 94th Fighter Sqn, 1st Fighter Group, USAAF, prior to a fighter-bomber mission.

Below: Bomb-laden Spitfire Mk VCs of No. 2 Sqn, South African Air Force are seen en route to a target on the Sangro River in eastern Italy. Each carries a 250-lb (114-kg) bomb under its centreline.

B-25 Mitchells parked in revetments in Sardinia await another mission. Ave Maria survived 103 combat missions in the MTO, where the fighter threat was exceeded by that posed by flak.

commanded US XII Air Support Command for the support of the US 5th Army, and the Desert Air Force (Air Vice-Marshal Harry Broadhurst) covered the activities of the British 8th Army in its advance up the eastern coastline of Italy. The Northwest African Tactical Bomber Force was split between the two tactical air forces. The order of battle of Air Marshal Sir Arthur Coningham's Northwest African Tactical Air Force on 4 November 1943 shows its power and tactical flexibility.

Under the Desert Air Force (HQ Lucera-Foggia) were No. 239 (RAF) Wing at Mileni with six squadrons of Kittyhawk Mk IIIs, No. 244 (RAF) Wing at Triolo with a few squadrons of Spitfire Mk VCs and Mk VIIIs, US 57th Fighter Group at

79th Fighter Group with the 99th Fighter Sqn at Salsola-Foggia with P-40Ns, No. 7 (SAAF) Wing at Palata with three squadrons of Spitfires, and No. 285 (RAF) Wing at Capelli-Foggia No. 1 with Nos 40, 255 and 682 Sqns with night-fighter and reconnaissance types. Based under the United States XII Air Support Command (HQ Caserta) was the 64th Fighter Wing with US 31st and 33rd Fighter Groups (Spitfires and P-40s) at Pomigliano and Paestum, US 27th and 86th Fighter Groups with A-36As at Capacchio and Serretelle, No. 324 (RAF) Wing with five squadrons of Spitfire Mk VCs and Mk VIIIs at Naples-Capodichino with the tactical reconnaissance No. 225 Sqn, US 111th Observation Sqn at Pomigliano with A-36s,

A flight of Ju 52/3mg5e seaplanes of 1. Seetransportstaffel, based at Skaramanga (Piraeus), under X Fliegerkorps is seen on a supply mission over the Aegean, autumn 1943.

equipped Beaufighters, and the US 324th FG at Cercola with P-40L Warhawks. Forty-six squadrons of fighters, fighter-bombers, tactical-reconnaissance aircraft and a few night-fighters, therefore, made up NATAF's inventory: an establishment of over 550 aircraft.

Equipped with light bombers based in the Foggia area, the NATBF had its headquarters at Sebezia: the US 47th (Light) Bombardment Group was at Vincenzio with A-20Cs, No. 3 (SAAF) Wing at Torterella with Baltimores and Bostons, No. 232 (RAF) Wing with similar types at Celene, the US 12th (Medium) 13G with B-25C Mitchells at Foggia-Main, the 340th (Medium) BG with B-25s at San Pancrazio, and the four squadrons of B-25s of the 31st (M) Group at Grottaglie. Also in southern Italy, under the Northwest African Coastal Air Force's No. 322 Wing, were three squadrons of Spitfire Mk VCs at Gioia del Colle.

Allied air forces at war

September 1943 saw the departure of the US 9th Air Force to the UK for action over north-western Europe; the B-24s of the 98th and 376th BGs were transferred to NASAF to continue operations in the MTO. The Strategic Air Force (Major-General James H. Doolittle) now controlled nine squadrons of RAF Wellington B.Mk IIIs and B.Mk Xs of No. 205 Group which operated by night. The 2nd, 97th, 99th and 301st Groups of the US 5th (Heavy) Bombardment Wing formed the NASAF's primary strike force with an establishment of 192 B-17F Fortresses: added to this were the 42nd and 47th (Medium) Bombardment Wings with B-26C Marauders and B-25C Mitchells.

Fighter cover for these wings was provided by the P-38s of the US 1st, 14th and 82nd FGs, and the P-40Ns of the 325th Group. Over Sicily and Italy the Lightnings of NASAF had become the scourge of the Luftwaffe. The veteran groups equipped with the Lightning had come a long way from their first missions against the well-handled Messerschmitts of the Luftwaffe over Tunisia. By now, P-38 pilots were imbued with aggressive combat prowess, and made full use of the incredible acceleration and dive-and-zoom capabilities of their big 15,800-lb (7165-kg) aircraft. Their companions over Germany were blighted by icing and foul weather conditions and often met high-quality German

pilots of the Reich's defences. Over Italy, however, German pilots of inferior quality were met increasingly, while the weather posed less of a problem for the tricky Allison engines. Moreover, this aircraft had the range (a radius of 450 miles/725 km) to seek out the Jagdgruppen, whereas the P-40s and the Spitfires of the DAF and the US XII Air Support Command did not.

After the completion of the Salerno operation, the Luftwaffe switched its attention to the Aegean, and so little priority was now accorded to the Italian theatre. The II. and III./JG 53 were so badly mauled that the Jagdgeschwader was sent to Lucca (near Pisa) for refitting; I./JG 53 was given the remaining Bf 109G-6s of these Gruppen and those of IV./JG 3, which was withdrawn to the Reich. By 16 September, I./JG 53 was at Rome-Centocelle, I./JG 77 at Viterbo, and the Fw 190A-5 fighter-bombers of II. and III./SKG 10 were based at Aquino. This small force, under the command of Oberst Hubertus Hitschold (Fliegerführer Nr 2), was now the only tactical organisation in Italy facing the Allied armies and the units of NATAF. By 30 September only 432 German aircraft remained under Generalfeldmarschall Wolfram, Freiherr von Richthofen's Luftflotte 11 in Italy, a marked contrast to the 1,008 based in the central Mediterranean area before the invasion of Sicily. Similarly, the bomber forces dwindled with the transfer of I. and II./ Kampfgeschwader 76 to Istres in southern France, and the Gruppen of KG 1 to Germany; only I. and II./KG 30 at Piacenza and Villafranca, and III./KG 54 at Bergamo, remained in northern Italy.

The offensive by the NASAF's bombers on the Rome airfields started on 16-17 September, transportation and lines of communication coming under attack on the same night. By 1 October 1943 American troops had captured Naples, while the important airfields at Foggia had fallen to the British 8th Army; by that time a total of 832 Axis aircraft (including 410 German) had been found littered on the various airfields. The efforts of MAC between 16 September and 1 October amounted to 13,383 sorties for the loss of 120 aircraft; during the same period the Luftwaffe lost 113 aircraft in the Italian theatre and 12 in the eastern Mediterranean.

The appearance of the P-47 further safeguarded the passage of Allied bombers as they struck strategic Axis targets. Torrid Tessie *was downed by flak on 27 April 1945 over the Po Valley. While the pilot was rescued by Italian partisans,* Torrid Tessie *fell into German hands.*

Advance to the Gothic Line

As the Allied armies struggled in the Italian mud, the air forces kept up a constant pressure on the German lines of communications and took the war further afield to the Balkans, Austria and Germany.

The early onset of low clouds and rain in October 1943 heralded an appalling Italian winter which was to curtail air operations severely. Under Generaloberst Heinrich Vietinghoff's 10th Army, the XIV Panzerkorps faced the US 5th Army advancing from Naples on the western seaboard, with the LXXVI Panzerkorps countering the British 8th Army on the eastern flank along the coastline of the Adriatic. Every mile of ground was now contested as the Germans slowly pulled back to the defences of the Gustav Line. Bitter fighting was experienced before the US 5th Army crossed the Volturno river, and the 8th Army, in the east, breached the defences on the Sangro river. Thereafter, the Allied advances faltered as a result of bad weather and resilient German resistance: in the west the US 5th Army fought on the approaches to Cassino in a series of savage battles that thwarted its attempts to break into the Liri valley and advance northwards to Rome. Resistance of equal severity was encountered by the 8th Army at Palmoli, and in the battles of attrition at Orsogna and Ortona.

In the first week of October 1943 the Northwest African Tactical Air Force flew over 2,600 sorties in support of the armies in the field. German defences were protected by Flak of all calibres and in great quantity on the battlefront and, for the fighter-bombers, the 20-mm Flakvierling and 37-mm Flak 18 guns became the most

serious threat as they dived down through the steep-sided valleys. Enemy fighter opposition was encountered by the heavies on the majority of occasions.

Sporadic raids on ports and shipping were made throughout November and December by the Kampfgruppen of 2. Flieger-division and, to a lesser extent, by those of II Fliegerkorps.

On the night of 2-3 December 1943 German bombers made a devastating attack on Bari, in southern Italy; the port was jammed with shipping, and had been regularly reconnoitred by Me 410A-4s. No night-fighters were stationed thereabouts, and the harbour was defended only by the AA guns of Nos 2862 and 2856 Sqns of the RAF Regiment, while the radar unit of No. 548 MSU was unserviceable. Eighty-eight Ju 88s and Do 217E-5s attacked the port behind a cloud of Düppel (chaff). Strikes on two ammunition ships decimated the surrounding area: 17 ships were destroyed, amounting to some 62,000 tons.

Fortunes of the 15th AF

At the Quadrant conference of September 1943 General H. H. Arnold submitted a report suggesting the splitting up of the US 12th Air Force into two entities: a new 15th Air Force strategic bombing force to carry out the aims of the 'Pointblank' directive against the Reich from bases in the Foggia complex; and the 12th Air Force restructured for tactical operations only, in the guise of the US XII Air

A wrecked Me 410A-3 reconnaissance aircraft lies on the banks of the Sangro river in Italy. The aircraft carries the codes F6+QK and is mottled in blue greys. The unit, 2. Staffel/Fern-aufklärungsgruppe 122, was based at Frosinone.

Support Command and XII Fighter Command. Despite objections, Arnold's plan went through, and on 1 November 1943 the US 15th Air Force was formed under Major General J. H. Doolittle, with its headquarters in Tunis. Composed of six groups of B-17F Flying Fortresses and B-24H Liberators, the 5th

Bombardment Wing (Heavy) included the 14th Fighter Group (P-38H) and the 325th FG. The B-26 Marauders and B-25 Mitchells were withdrawn from the Foggia area and put under the 12th Air Force's command in Sardinia. By January 1944 the US 449th, 450th and 451st BGs had arrived with B-24s, while the Lightnings of the 1st and

Some carrying tanks and some without, a squadron of P-38Js returns to base after an escort mission for 15th AF bombers over Austria. The Lightnings belong to the 1st Fighter Group (27th, 71st and 94th Sqns), based at Salsola in the Foggia complex.

Italian adversaries

After the Italian capitulation on 5 September 1943, the majority of surviving Italian air force pilots either retired or joined the Co-Belligerent Air Force and, with their mounts carrying the new roundel, operated alongside their new allies. However, many fascist pilots joined with Mussolini and flew with the Aviazione della Reppublica Sociale Italiana (ARSI). However, the two forces were kept apart by the Allies and the Axis, thus preventing any civil war.

G.55/1 Centauro
The Squadriglia Complementare Caccia Montefuscq was formed to defend Milan and Turin during 1944-45, flying alongside ARSI-piloted Bf 109G-6s. The Fiat aircraft was a formidable machine and was armed with twin 12.7-mm Breda SAFATs and three 20-mm Mauser MG 151/20 cannon; only 105 were completed, however.

P-39N-1 Airacobra
With the Italians joining the Allies, they received Allied equipment and this P-39 was part of the Italian Co-Belligerent Air Force's 4º Stormo. The unit operated on reconnaissance and air support missions over the Adriatic.

82nd Groups were already ensconced within the 15th Air Force's 5th and 47th Wings.

German fighter defences based in the Po valley were under Jafü Oberitalien, and consisted of the Bf 109G-6s of II./JG 77, III./JG 77, II./JG 53 and III./JG 53. The new US 15th Air Force was to encounter these Messerschmitts with regularity in the following months, with a growing number of Italian fighters flown by pilots of the fascist ARSI.

The first major raid for the 15th Air Force was to Wiener Neustadt on 2 November, in the course of which 11 B-17s and B-24s were shot down by aircraft of 7. Jagddivision and Jafil Ostmark. On 6 December Eleusis and Tatoi were bombed, and a repeat visit to these airfields on 14 December wrecked many German aircraft. The latter mission saw the introduction of P-47s on long-range operations with the 15th Air Force.

Over Italy, the Luftwaffe also proved that it still possessed punch: during an attack on Vincenza on 28 December the 376th BG lost an entire squadron (10 B-24s) to more than 60 Bf 109G-6s. By the end of the month, the transfer of the 15th Air Force's units to the Foggia area had been completed; the headquarters of the 5th and 47th Bomb Wings were established at Foggia and Maduria, in the plains of Apulia.

Anzio-Nettuno invasion
The savage battles of December 1943 and January 1944 were dominated by Allied attempts to breach the Gustav Line at Cassino, and in order to outflank the German defences and break their hold on the Liri valley, a seaborne landing was made at Anzio and Nettuno. The US 5th Army opened its offensive on the Gustav Line on 12 January in appalling weather, with the US II Corps taking Mount Trocchio three days later; on 10 January the British X Corps crossed the Garigliano river, but thereafter German resistance hardened, and the offensive came to a halt. At 02.20 on 22 January some 55,000 troops of the US VI Corps, made up of the British 1st and US 3rd Divisions, landed without opposition on the beaches of Nettuno and Anzio in Operation Shingle. The objective, the city of Rome, lay only 33 miles (52 km) to the north. The invasion achieved complete surprise and only a few reserve battalions were available in the area. However, Kesselring was able to capitalise on Allied caution and inertia, and gather sufficient forces to form a stop-gap defence: German divisions were rushed in from the north and, within a few days of the landings, the US VI Corps was completely surrounded and under severe pressure within a confined perimeter. For the next six weeks the German 14th Army mounted repeated assaults aimed at decimating the beachhead.

In support of Shingle, the Allied air forces could muster between 2,600 and 2,900 combat aircraft to oppose the 450-475 aircraft of the Luftwaffe now pitted against the Anzio beach-heads. But despite this preponderance, the Allies were to be hindered by continuing bad weather, which tended to give the Luftwaffe an element of advantage. For the German air forces the main burden was borne by the anti-shipping Ju 88A-4s and Dorniers, which made nightly attacks in strengths of up to 150 aircraft. During the daylight hours, the DAF and US XII Air Support Command countered numerous attempts by Fw 190s, escorted by Bf 109G-6 fighters, to attack shipping lying offshore. In comparison to those experienced at Salerno, the shipping losses to enemy air attacks were less severe: naval forces lost three ships and five were badly damaged, one merchantman was sunk and seven landing ship tanks (LSTs) were damaged up to and including 19 February. Following the failure of the third German offensive aimed at eliminating the Anzio positions on 29 February, Kesselring decided to go on to the defensive. Nearly 75,000 Allied troops could thus maintain a precarious existence at Anzio-Nettuno, while those in the south faced the Cassino defences.

Denied swift victory in the Mediterranean theatre, the Allies switched their priority to the UK for the preparation of Operation Overlord, which was scheduled for the first week of June 1944. Similarly, the Luftwaffe had shifted the bulk of its forces from the Italian theatre after the static situation at Anzio had materialised on 1 March; maximum priority was now accorded to Luftflotte Reich in the defence of Germany by day and by night against the US 8th Air Force and RAF Bomber Command. Also, there was the need to conserve all available forces for countering Overlord and the anticipated Russian offensive.

The long legs of the Beaufighter Mk X enabled Middle East Air Command's No. 201 Group to venture far into the Balkans and Greece. Here, a flight passes over a de-engined Cant Z.501 at Preveza seaplane base, on a long-range Rhubarb mission.

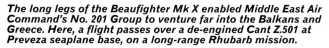

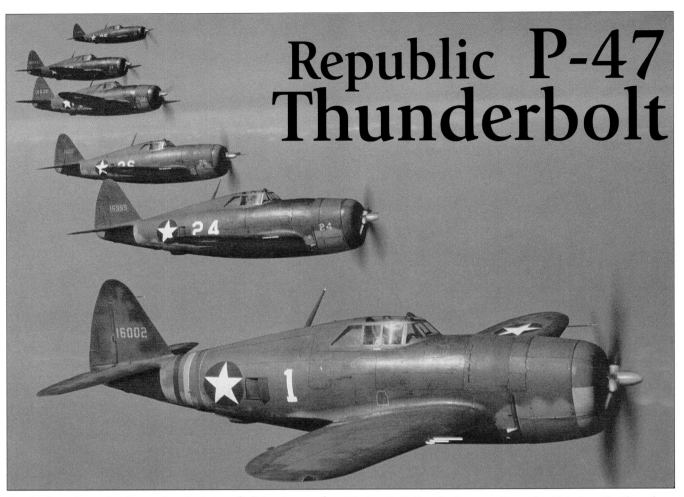

Republic P-47 Thunderbolt

As the heaviest single-engined piston fighter to reach large-scale service, the P-47 is acknowledged as one of the greatest ground-attack aircraft of World War II.

Most early P-47 variants were of 'razorback' design, like those in this formation of six P-47Bs from the 56th Fighter Group in October 1942. The lead aircraft is flown by P-47 ace, Hubert Zemke.

The big, roomy, powerful Republic P-47 Thunderbolt was produced in greater numbers (15,683) than any other American fighter. Yet its career was near an end as early as 1945. The Thunderbolt was one of the top-performing fighters of the war and enjoys a devout following of veteran pilots and vocal advocates. Yet the P-47 was always a paradox, a big aircraft with an air-cooled engine even though the US Army Air Force (USAAF) believed in in-line engines, a superb high-altitude fighter that was often outclassed by other fighters at lower heights, yet was rugged and enduring in air-to-ground strafing and bombing missions.

The P-47 could dive at incredible velocity – giving rise to mistaken rumours that it could

Above: Fitted with eight 0.5-in (12.7-mm) machine-guns and capable of carrying bombs and rocket projectiles, the P-47N was an ideal weapons platform in the ground-attack role.

Right: Armourers of the 318th Fighter Group load and clean the guns of P-47N Thunderbolt Jane at Ie Shima in July 1945. The long range of the P-47N variant rendered it ideal for escorting B-29 Superfortress raids against the Japanese mainland.

approach or even exceed supersonic speed in the dive – but it was sluggish in a climb. In 'clean' condition, there was no better dogfighter, but P-47 pilots were often sent into action carrying hated bomb pylons that slowed the Thunderbolt and impeded its manoeuvrability.

Other Thunderbolt attributes were a comfortable cockpit, a low internal noise level, little vibration, and excellent control response. The large barrel-like nose did, however, protrude far ahead of the pilot, with the result that visibility downwards and to the front was obscured both on the ground and in flight. The firepower of the P-47 was a sight to behold and it was rated the 'best strafer' among US fighters. The aircraft could also withstand considerable combat damage and there was no more glorious an apparition than a P-47 returning safely to its home base after being riddled with hundreds of rounds of gunfire.

Francis Gabreski, Robert Johnson, Hubert Zemke and Neal Kearby were among the aces who flew the P-47 Thunderbolt and swore by it. Luftwaffe ace General Adolf Galland flew a P-47 and said that he initially felt that the cockpit was big enough to walk around in. But on internal fuel alone, the Thunderbolt lacked the 'legs' to enter the war and, even with drop tanks, it never possessed the

range of its slimmer, prettier rival, the P-51 Mustang. Some US officers in Europe thought that the Thunderbolt used up too much runway to take off, was difficult to pull out of a dive, and had weak landing gear. In the Pacific, however, 5th Air Force General, George C. Kenney, liked the performance of the Thunderbolt and requested that more fighter groups be equipped with the big machine.

Misconceptions were many. Contrary to myth, the P-47 Thunderbolt was not especially difficult to fly. It was not even difficult to land, although even a skilled pilot had to be careful not to flare and to bring the aircraft straight down for a solid, thumping reunion with the ground. Nor was it true, as lore had it, that the P-47 was effective only at high altitude – although its air-to-air prowess was greatest at the edge of the stratosphere.

Heavily armed

Contrary to another widely published mistake, the Thunderbolt was not nicknamed the 'Jug' because it was like a juggernaut. The 'Jug' appellation came about because the fuselage of the P-47 resembled an illicit container for home-made whisky.

The company that manufactured the Thunderbolt in Long Island was sometimes called the 'Republic Iron Works'. Founded by Russian immigrant,

Able to take considerable punishment and packing a hefty punch, USAAF P-47s played a vital role in crippling German supply and communication lines. This P-47 from the 406th FG flys through the explosion of an ammunition-filled road vehicle in June 1944.

Major Alexander P. de Seversky – who awarded himself the rank of major and published volumes about the preponderant role of air power – the company dropped Seversky's surname and became Republic just when the first P-47 was taking shape. It was another Russian settler, Alexander Kartveli, who led the engineering design team. Kartveli and his company believed in size and strength, and their aircraft were built accordingly. It was said that if a P-47 pilot could not defeat his foe any other way, he could taxi over the top of the enemy and retract his gear. The sheer inertia

of the 11,600-lb (5261-kg) 'Jug' would do the rest.

As recently as 1990, an extract from a USAF history stated: 'The Thunderbolt first took shape in a sketch made by Kartveli on the back of an envelope. That was at an Army fighter-plane requirements meeting in 1940.'

The legend is heartwarming, but overlooks the step-by-step, 'building block' process whereby the Thunderbolt came into being after a progression of earlier pursuit types from the same shop, among them the lacklustre P-43 Lancer which saw limited action in the China-Burma-India theatre.

To exploit the enormous power of its corpulent R-2800 engine, the Thunderbolt mounted a massive 12-ft (3.65-m) four-bladed, controllable-pitch propeller and, in later models, employed 'paddle' blades that enhanced performance. Its supercharging system was the key to its success and was placed in the fuselage aft of the pilot, with exhaust gases piped back to the turbine and expelled at the rear – ducted air being returned to the engine under pressure. Despite teething problems, the system worked well, ensuring the superb reputation of the 'Jug' at altitude.

Five years after VJ-Day, when the US needed a prop-driven fighter for air-to-ground work in Korea, the Pentagon tried to find enough Thunderbolts for the job. By then however, the most widely-built American fighter was almost out of inventory, so the Air Force had no choice but to give the job to the less enduring and more fickle Mustang.

P-47 Thunderbolt pilots said, then and now, that their aircraft was superior and, on that occasion, there was no arguing with them.

Right: The fastest and heaviest of all wartime variants, the P-47N featured square-cut wingtips and four new fuel cells in the root of each wing. Its gross weight of 20,700 lb (9389 kg) was the highest for a piston-engined single-seat fighter.

Below: Over 800 P-47Ds were allocated to the RAF, under the Lend-Lease agreement, for operations in the Far East. This aircraft was one of four Thunderbolt Mk IIs which underwent operational trials in the UK.

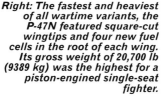

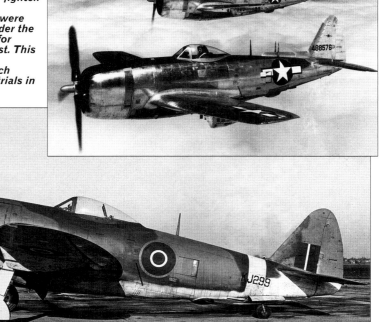

The final round

Used as a fighter-bomber, the P-38 Lightning performed excellently in the Italian theatre. The twin-boom layout produced little drag, enabling the Lightning to be one of the fastest twins of the war.

Stubborn resistance in Italy reduced the Allied advance to a crawl proving that there was no easy way into the Reich from this quarter. The Luftwaffe, however, continued to fight in defence of oil.

Established in the complex of airfields around Foggia and Bari, by early 1944, the B-17s and B-24s of the US 15th Air Force were called upon to conduct tactical operations on the Italian battlefront, and a large number of missions against rail yards, airfields, and industrial targets situated in Romania, Bulgaria, Yugoslavia, Austria, southern France and southern Germany: and it was against the 15th Air Force that the major air battles were fought during 1944.

The Ploesti oil refineries remained as the most heavily defended targets in the Balkans. They were defended by the 5. Flakdivision, in addition to some 100-150 fighters: the guns, of 88- to 105-mm calibre, were provided with radar prediction, while radar for fighter control gave good coverage of the Balkans and the southern Alps.

On the day before Operation Shingle the 15th Air Force's B-17s hammered 2.Fliegerdivision's airfields at Istres and Salon. The presence of many Bf 109G-6s and Ju 88A-4 bombers in the Udine area prompted Twining to send his bombers to Aviano on 28 January, and on a synchronised strafing and bombing raid on Villaorba, Maniago, Lavariano and Udine on 30 January: the devastation on the ground was great, while in the air many kills were claimed.

In the conflict on the ground the offensive actions around Cassino were halted on 22 March 1944 after repeated setbacks: it would not be until 11 May that the Allied 15th Army Group would have sufficient resources to launch a major push aimed at reaching Rome. In the meantime the tactical forces of the MAAF went over to a maximum effort offensive on enemy lines of communication: Operation Strangle started to this effect on 19 March 1944.

By April the Russian armies in the southern Ukraine were threatening Romania, and it therefore became essential for the Allies to do everything in their power to put pressure upon the extensive lines of communication to this theatre.

In the meantime, the 15th Air Force continued to grow till Twining's command fielded 21 bomber and seven fighter groups. The 31st and 52nd FGs had converted to the superb P-51Bs in April, while the 325th FG converted the following month; the 332nd FG continued flying Thunderbolts until June, when it, too, went over to the Mustang. The superb combat radius of the P-51B now enabled the bombers to fly with escorts during the longest of missions.

After receiving a hot reception by more than 50 fighters over

The Germans put up a brave defence against the Allied bombers, this Boeing B-17 Flying Fortress of the 301st Bomb Group being lucky to return after a direct hit by anti-aircraft fire.

No. 5 Sqn, SAAF used the Mustang Mk IV for effective fighter sweeps over Italy and Yugoslavia, the opposing Axis fighters being unable to cope with the type's speed and strength.

Bucharest on 4 April, the 15th Air Force sent 95 B-17s and 135 B-24s to the Ploesti marshalling yards, where 587 tons of bombs were dropped for the loss of 13 bombers. Oil output from the great Ploesti complex was soon on the wane, and production in April dropped from 270,000 tons to 137,000 tons.

Progress on the ground
Before the Allied offensive of May 1944, a small force of

Consolidated B-24 Liberator Burma Bound *of the US 15th Air Force limps away with no. 1 engine smoking and no. 4 shut down after attacking marshalling yards near Munich in late 1944.*

German tactical and reconnaissance aircraft was stationed in the Rome area. This tiny force could do nothing against the might of MATAF during the offensive that broke on 11 May. On 17 May Generalfeldmarschall Albert Kesselring ordered the withdrawal from Cassino, and by 4 June the US 5th Army had reached Rome, and thereafter rapid progress northwards was made. In the meantime, MAAF's forces had covered the invasion of southern France, was fully engaged in the Balkans theatre, and was active in the forlorn effort to supply the beleaguered forces of General Bor-Komorowski's garrison in faraway Warsaw.

Operation Anvil (the invasion of southern France) began on the night of 14-15 August when the first of 400 paratroops was dropped behind Cannes: gliderborne troops followed and by 08.00 the US VI Corps was landing on the beaches of Cavaliére, St Tropez, Agay and Cannes. The landings were opposed weakly, while in the air little was seen of the Luftwaffe. Progress up the Rhône valley was swift, and by 12 September the leading elements of the US 7th Army linked up with the French 2nd Armoured Division at Châtillon-sur-Seine.

MAAF's interest in the Balkans had started as early as October 1943, when it started flying regular missions against shipping off the Adriatic coast and amongst the Yugoslav islands. Tito's partisans received supplies from the RAF at Brindisi, and the C-47s of the US 62nd TCC Group. On 7 June 1944 Air Vice Marshal W. Elliot took over the new Balkan Air Force that at first consisted of a small number of fighters and transports. By the end of the year Elliot's forces included AHQ Greece with three fighter, one bomber and a Special Operations Wing. Supply missions to Warsaw entailed a round trip of some 1,750 miles (2820 km) at great risk from marauding night-fighters. Nos 31 (SAAF), 148 and 178 Sqns joined the desperate attempts to supply Warsaw with their Liberators and Halifaxes: by September 1944, when the Polish uprising had been put down by ruthless action by the SS, 31 aircraft had been lost in the course of 181 sorties to Warsaw.

In the offensive in Italy itself the demands of Anvil and Overlord totally sabotaged Alexander's chances of success against what was now a powerful foe. Despite massive efforts, the MAAF never succeeded in strangling Axis lines of supply.

However, by September 1944 the Axis air forces in Italy had been reduced to a tiny element based in the Udine and Turin areas: on 27 September Richthofen went into retirement and Luftflotte II was disbanded. By the end of August, following the collapse in western Europe, JG 77's aircraft were pulled back to the Reich. Therefore no further attention was paid to the Italian theatre by the Luftwaffe, save for reconnaissance duties for the 10th Army and night harassment attacks on Allied troop positions. By October 1944 the Allied 15th Army Group had once again been halted after making some progress beyond the Gothic Line.

Last battles

Much action was seen by the US 15th Air Force during the summer, despite the Luftwaffe's commitments in Normandy. Savage air battles were fought throughout that hot summer over Austria, Hungary, southern Germany and the Balkans. Despite the efforts of the escorts the 15th Air Force's loss of 318 bombers in July 1944 represented the highest ever in its career. However, during the following month there was evidence to support the fact that the Luftwaffe was feeling the effect of the huge losses suffered on the Western Front. Few enemy fighters were encountered during the last three raids on Ploesti. Due to a chronic shortage of aviation fuel the Luftwaffe was forced to undergo strict conservation in September 1944, and thereon the US 15th AF operated without much enemy interference.

After a long hard winter of stalemate in Italy the Allies launched their final offensive in April 1945: by 25 April Verona, Bologna, Ferrara, and Parma had been taken as the Wehrmacht pulled back across the border into Austria. On 2 May 1945 Field Marshal Alexander accepted the surrender of the Axis, and over 1,000,000 men in northern Italy and Austria laid down their arms.

Focke-Wulf Fw 190F-8s of 1./SG 4 were used in the close-support role over Anzio and Nettuno, operating from bases in Sardinia. Note that the upper part of the white theatre band, the tail swastika and the upper wing surface crosses have been overpainted as protection against ground strafing.

Republic P-47 Thunderbolts hammered German positions in the Brenner Pass and along the front line in conditions of almost total air supremacy. Illustrated here is a P-47D-24RE of the 86th Fighter Squadron, 79th Fighter Group based at Fano in northern Italy in the spring of 1945.

Air war on the Eastern front

Advance to Moscow

The door had only to be kicked, said Adolf Hitler, for the whole rotten edifice of Soviet Russia to cave in. It was an underestimation with unimagined consequence, and one which cost Germany the war.

These Ju 88A-5s of III./KG 77 were operating in the northern sector under I Fliegerkorps. Soviet fighters were not fast enough to deal with the Ju 88s adequately, and occasionally resorted to ramming attacks.

The war in the USSR was confidently expected to last only six to eight weeks. The Blitzkrieg campaigns in the East by the Wehrmacht and its Axis allies broke on 22 June 1941, when Operation Barbarossa, the invasion of the frontiers, took place. The ultimate German objectives were the seizures of Leningrad, Moscow and Kiev (the capital city of the Ukraine), the destruction of Soviet military forces in total, and the establishment of a largely undetermined defensive line from Archangel, on the White Sea, southwards to the Caspian Sea.

The preparations for Barbarossa dated back to July 1940, and its aims were stressed in the Führerweisung Nr 21 of 18 December 1940. During the preparatory period communications, bases, airfields and depots were established in Prussia, eastern Poland and Moldavia under Aufbau Ost (Build-up East), while Luftwaffe reconnaissance units made frequent, and undisturbed, sorties over the Soviet border and

beyond. Movement of troops, tanks, aircraft and artillery to the start lines took place during May and June 1941 under conditions of secrecy.

The shattering blows received by the Soviet forces during the period from June to September 1941 were to exceed the wildest dreams of the Wehrmacht. At a stroke the Luftwaffe decimated the Soviet air forces (Voenno-Vozduzhnoye Sily, or V-VS).

German forces

Of the 3,800,000 men under arms in the German armies on 22 June 1941, no fewer than 3,200,000 were committed to the invasion of the Soviet Union in 148 divisions. The Romanian and Finnish allies were in at the start, being joined after 24 June by the armies of Hungary and Slovakia, supplemented by detachments from Italy and Spain. The Axis echelons were deployed in three army groups (Heeresgruppen) designated North, Centre and South, in 117 front-line divisions. Sixty-five per cent of the Luftwaffe's strength was deployed in support of Barbarossa: 2,770 combat

aircraft in all, including 775 bombers, 310 Junkers Ju 87B-2 Stukas, 830 Messerschmitt Bf 109E and Bf 109F fighters, 90 Messerschmitt Bf 110 Zerstörers, 710 short- and long-range reconnaissance aircraft, and 55 coastal aircraft.

At 04.15 on 22 June 1941 the front erupted in an artillery barrage, while the Luftwaffe took to the air on that fine, hazy summer morning to inflict what was probably the most destructive pre-emptive air strike of all time. At over 66 airfields the majority of the V-VS's units were caught on the ground, uncamouflaged, and parked wing-tip to wing-tip. At 12.00, according to General Franz Halder of OKW, the Luftwaffe had claimed the destruction of over 800 Russian aircraft since the start of the morning's

activities: by the end of the day, the tally stood at 1,811 destroyed (1,489 on the ground and 322 shot down in the air), and to this was added another 1,000 or so by the evening of 23 June, at which point some 150 German aircraft had been lost. A subsequent recount of the Luftwaffe's claims was demanded by Göring, which revealed the destruction of another 300 Soviet aircraft: the vast majority of the claims were verified as the Germans gained ground over Soviet territory. On the first day Oberst Werner Mölders, the Kommodore of JG 51, claimed his 72nd kill to be awarded the *Schwertern* (swords) to the Ritterkreuz (Knight's Cross of the Iron Cross): by 16 July, he had claimed 101 victories to gain the *Brillanten* (diamonds). His success was mirrored by the Jagdflieger as a whole, who ran up enormous tallies in the air fighting of June to August 1941, against gallant but relatively

Being examined by German personnel, this Tupolev SB-2 was one of hundreds crippled by the ferocious opening assault of Barbarossa, in which Luftwaffe aircraft pummelled V-VS bases.

Right: At the time of Barbarossa the Bf 109F was the principle Luftwaffe fighter, and was to claim the majority of kills during 1941. However, the Bf 109E continued to serve in considerable numbers. This Bf 109E-4/B Jabo (fighter-bomber) served with the Gruppenstab, II. Gruppe/JG 54, and was engaged on army support missions on the Leningrad front.

Below: Ilyushin's Il-4 (formerly DB-3F) was a useful light bomber, but could do little to blunt the German onslaught.

Operation Taifun (Typhoon) was ordered on 26 September, and started on 2 October 1941: Kesselring's Luftflotte II was reinforced and some 1,320 aircraft were concentrated in the Konotop and Smolensk-Roslavl areas, including those of I and VIII Fliegerkorps. The approaches to Moscow were defended by only 364 aircraft (half of them outdated).

Desperate defence

In the defence of Moscow, and in the battles of Vyasma and Kalinin, the V-VS flew bravely and in all weathers but its numbers were too few to have a material influence on the outcome of events. It was the winter that stopped the Germans at the gates of Moscow, and the bitter resistance of the Russian ground troops aided by KV-1 and T-34 tanks. After initial successes, the forward elements of Army Group Centre halted in the paralysing conditions of snow, alternating with sleet, impassable roads and temperatures below -4°F (-20°C): by 27 November 1941 the Panzers had penetrated to within 19 miles (30 km) of the northern suburbs of Moscow, but this was the limit of the German advance.

On 5 December 1941, to the amazement of the world and despite their atrocious losses of the summer, the Soviet armies before Moscow went over to the offensive. The strength of the V-VS forces supporting the assaults was pitifully low: only 13 Pe-2s, 18 Il-2s and 52 fighters of the Kalinin FA supported their ground forces on a 155-mile (250-km) front. A mere 199 aircraft lent their support to General Georgi Zhukov's Western Front, while 79 were available for operations with Marshal of the Soviet Union Timoshenko's South West Front.

Throughout the epic Moscow defensive battles the V-VS flew 51,300 sorties, and the Luftwaffe lost an estimated 1,400 aircraft. The Soviets had continued the fight against impossible odds.

unskilled opposition by the V-VS. Mölders' Jagdgeschwader 51 led the way, gaining its 1,000th kill of the war on 30 June and was closely emulated by JG 3, JG 52, JG 53, JG 54 and JG 77; pilots flew six or seven sorties per day, in good weather and from airfields close to the front line, 'trade' being easy to find and confined to heights below 12,000 ft (3660 m) against unskilled Soviet pilots in obsolescent aircraft.

Soviet forces

By June 1941 estimated Soviet air strength stood at between 10,500 and 12,000 aircraft: some 7,500 of these were based in European Russia with the remainder in the Siberia/ Manchuria border regions. By German standards the majority of Soviet first-line types was obsolete: as of 22 June 1941 the V-VS had accepted only 2,739 modern combat aircraft including 399 Yakovlev Yak-1, 1,309 Mikoyan-Gurevich MiG-3 and 322 Lavochkin LaGG-3 fighters, 460 Petlyakov

Pe-2 light bombers, and 249 Ilyushin Il-2 close-support aircraft.

Preponderant Russian fighters in June 1941 were the biplane Polikarpov I-15, I-15bis and I-153 types, and the Polikarpov I-16 monoplane. The ground-support regiments (ShAP, or Shturmovaya Aviatsiya Polk) flew obsolescent RZ, DI-6, SB-1 and I-15bis types, while the BAPs (Bombardirov-ochnaya Aviatsiya Polk, or bomber air regiments) used the medium-capacity SB-2, SB-2bis, Il-4 and DB-3 types. The strength of naval aviation in June 1941 was 1,445 aircraft, including fighters (I-15, I-15bis and I-153), bombers (DB-3, DB-3F, Ar-2 and TB-3), and seaplanes (MBR-2, MDR-2 and MTB-2). The majority of fighters under the IA P-VO (air defence organisation) were MiG-3s, with a small but growing number of Yak-1s and LaGG-3s.

As early as 26 June 1941 Army Group Centre smashed resistance at Brest-Litovsk: on 1 July Guderian's tanks crossed the Berezina, closed the Minsk

pocket on 9 July and took Vitebsk. Between 15 July and 5 August 1941 Army Group Centre encountered tenacious Soviet resistance around Smolensk, but took 330,000 Soviet prisoners following the fall of the city: with pressure reduced in the centre, VIII Fliegerkorps was sent to Luftflotte I's area in the north, where the German forces had penetrated as far as Luga for the final drive to Leningrad. Great battles were now being fought in the Ukraine: during 18-27 September 1941 Army Group South conducted great slaughter, sealing the Kiev pocket and killing or capturing nearly 665,000 Soviet troops in the battles of Kiev, Uman and Chernikov-Korosten. In the north, as early as 15 September, Finnish and German forces encircled and laid siege to the city of Leningrad.

The favourable situations achieved after 12 weeks of heavy fighting enabled the Wehrmacht to launch an all-out drive for Moscow: the offensive, called

The Polikarpov I-16 was the principal fighter with which the Soviet air force attempted to defend the Motherland. Although in general the type was woefully inferior to the Messerschmitt Bf 109, in the right hands its outstanding agility could be put to good effect. Snr Lt A. G. Lomokin of the 21 IAP flew this aircraft to some success over the Gulf of Finland.

A year in the Ukraine

The Red Army's winter offensive of 1941-42 came as a shock to the Wehrmacht, and shattered Hitler's forecast of a short war. However, by the summer Germany was back on the offensive, pushing towards the vital Caucasian oilfields – and Stalingrad.

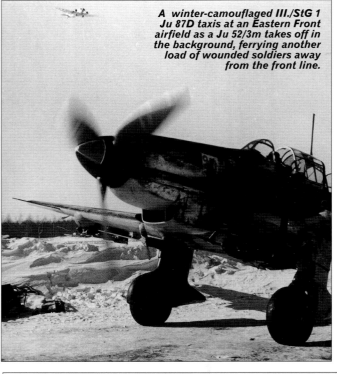

A winter-camouflaged III./StG 1 Ju 87D taxis at an Eastern Front airfield as a Ju 52/3m takes off in the background, ferrying another load of wounded soldiers away from the front line.

The Soviet winter counter-offensive started in the snows before Moscow on 5 December 1941, with other offensives taking place in the north in an attempt to relieve Leningrad, and in the south against Kharkov. In the savage fighting of that winter the Soviet armies made good ground, pushing the Germans back over an average distance of 150-200 miles (240-320 km) on the front of Army Group Centre in Belorussia, and making fair progress in the northern sector, although the attempt to raise Leningrad's siege failed. During March 1942 the Soviet offensives in the centre and north came to a halt, and attention was turned to the Ukraine. With the exception of the naval port of Sevastopol, the Crimea was in German hands. In the course of 1942, when the German army recovered its strength and initiative, the emphasis was to lie in the south.

With the transfer to Sicily of II. and III./JG 27 and I.-III./JG 53 'Pik-As', each equipped with the latest Messerschmitt Bf 109F-4s, the shortage of German fighters on the Eastern Front became acute: similar shortages in bomber and Stuka strengths were evident with the removal of I.-III./StG 3 and elements of KGs 54 and 77, LG 1 and KGr 806, with Junkers Ju 88A-4 bombers. Serviceability rates plunged in bitter cold and rustic airfield conditions, with accurate 20-mm and 37-mm Soviet light flak taking a high toll on operations. Low production rates failed to keep pace with losses, with the training system barely managing to fill the gaps. The transport force of Junkers Ju 52/3m aircraft took heavy losses during January-March 1942 on supply missions over the Kholm and

Demyansk pockets, and hampered operations in the Mediterranean theatre. The Luftwaffe was to survive this first crisis, and rebuild its strength for the campaigns of the summer.

In early 1942 the legacy of the previous summer was still evident in the ranks of the Voenno-Vozdushnoye Sily. To the fearful losses (5,000 aircraft admitted by the Soviets as early as October 1941) were added the lowering production rates as industries pulled back to beyond the Urals: 1,807 aircraft delivered in July 1941, 2,329 in September, but down to a horrifying 627 in November.

Enter the Shturmovik

It was during the winter months that the lumbering but effective Ilyushin Il-2 Shturmovik made its mark. Unsophisticated in its design, easy to fly and maintain, the Shturmovik could take prodigious battle damage. The ShAP (close-support regiment) units operated in all weathers from rudimentary airstrips: cloud bases below 200 ft (60 m) and visibilities of 440-660 yards (400-600 m) were sufficiently good conditions for a strike. The Il-2s operated in formations of 12-20 in number, approached the target in line astern at around 1,300 ft (395 m) and attacked in 20-30° dives firing rockets and guns: alternative approaches could be made just above the tree-tops before pulling up, winging over and making a pass. For German flak crews the Il-2 was a difficult aircraft to shoot down, seemingly impervious to

As important as the T-34 tank was on the ground, it was the Ilyushin Il-2 which epitomised the Soviet fight-back in the air. Like the T-34, the Il-2 was well-designed and rugged, but triumphed primarily due to the huge numbers produced.

20-mm and Flak 18 fire: it was the ideal weapon. And in October 1942 the improved Il-2/m3 two-seater, powered by a 1,760-hp (1313-kW) Mikulin AM-38F, made its debut.

Slowly the Soviet aircraft capable of matching those of the Luftwaffe were entering service: phased out of production by 1942 were the MiG-3, the I-15s and I-16s, and the lumbering SB-2 and TB-3 bombers. But there was a long way to go.

Soviet fighter units were now equipped with a high proportion of Yakovlev Yak-1 and Lavochkin LaGG-3 aircraft, which came somewhere near to upsetting the superiority of the Messerschmitt Bf 109F.

Throughout March and into the early summer of 1942 attention was focussed on the campaign of Army Group South in the southern Ukraine and in the Crimea. On 17 April 1942 VIII Fliegerkorps was moved south for the assaults on Kerch and Sevastopol. Kerch was evacuated by the Russians on 15 May, while a maximum-effort Blitz on Sevastopol opened up with 723 sorties on 2 June 1942, the Junkers Ju 88A-4s of I. and II./KG 51, I. and III./KG 76 and III./LG 1, the Junkers Ju 87D-1s of I.-III./StG 77 plus the newly-arrived III./StG 1, and the Heinkels of I./KG 100 plastered Sevastopol's

The Polikarpov I-16 was still in action long into 1942, especially in the north. This I-16 tip 17 was flown by Mikhail J. Vasiliev (22 kills) of the Baltic Fleet, shortly before he was lost in action on 5 May 1942.

Short-range reconnaissance aircraft played a major part in support of the ground armies on the Eastern Front. This Focke-Wulf Fw 189A-2 served with 1.(H) 31 in the summer of 1942.

Below: Able to withstand great punishment, and to operate in conditions which grounded other Luftwaffe types, the Henschel Hs 123 was employed by ground attack units until mid-1944.

fortifications. Throughout the month an average of 600 sorties per day was maintained: fanatical resistance was overcome on 4 July 1942, and Sevastopol fell to General-oberst Manstein's 11th Army.

The way was now clear for Hitler's major offensive of the summer (Fall Blau, or Case Blue) aimed at the capture of Voronezh on the Don river, a huge manoeuvre of encirclement on the Volga at Stalingrad, and then a lunge deep into the Caucasus to take the oilfields at Maikop: if success attended this mighty offensive the Soviets would be finished. Already the preliminary moves had seen

success: during 17-22 May 1942 the Izyum-Barvenkovo pocket was eradicated.

Luftflotte IV was allocated to the support of Fall Blau. Energetic production had placed Luftwaffe strength in the USSR at 2,750 by June: of these 1,500 were in the south under Luftflotte IV, 600 were in the centre under LwKdo Ost, 375 in the north under Luftflotte I and 200 or so on the Murmansk-Kandalaksha front under Luftflotte V (Ost). New types entering service included the Focke-Wulf Fw 190A-2 with I.-IV./JG 51, the improved Junkers Ju 87D-1 dive-bomber, and the Henschel Hs129B-1/R2

anti-tank aircraft, armed with a single 30-mm MK 101 cannon.

The offensive proper opened at 02.15 on 28 June 1942 with the Panzers rolling through the corn with minimal resistance towards the first objective, Voronezh: three Soviet tank corps were defeated there on 4-7 July. Hitler's influence now came into the course of the offensive. Thinking that he had the Soviets once again in a state of defeat and disintegration, he cancelled the original aims of Fall Blau and split his forces: Army Group South became Army Group A for an immediate drive south to Rostov and the Caucasus, as far as the oilfields at Grozny and Baku, while Army Group B was actually to take Stalingrad, rather than establish a line along the Don. To cap it all Manstein's victorious 11th Army was soon transferred from the northern Caucasus and up to the Leningrad sector. The offensive in the south went well, and by 22 August 1942 the German swastika had been planted on the summit of Mt Elbruz, and the Panzers were within 30 miles (48 km) of Grozny and only 80 miles (128 km) from Batumi on the Black Sea border with Turkey. Now attention was switched to the progress of the weakened Army Group B in its drive down the Don towards Stalingrad.

Stand at Stalingrad

Stalingrad to the Soviets was more than just another industrial city on the Volga: it had a significance in 1942 of untold political and patriotic value. Here the Russians chose to stand.

The outnumbered Soviet air force, already thrown into some

confusion by a headlong transfer to makeshift bases on the east bank of the Don, took heavy losses. New Lavochkin La-5 fighters arrived in time to bolster the depleted fleet: these claimed 97 enemy aircraft in 299 sorties during the period 21 August-16 September 1942. On 19 November 1942 the Soviet armies carried out Plan 'Uranus', an offensive aimed at smashing the weak Italian and Romanian flanks of the German forces: on 23 November the Russian pincers met at Kalach, to encircle the German armies.

Göring promised the supply of at least 500 tons of food, ammunition and weapons per day, but he did not take into account the weather, the poor airfields, and the fierce Soviet flak that surrounded the Stalingrad perimeter.

All available transport aircraft were rounded up for the mammoth airlift, including Heinkels of the bomber and training units. The transports flew 3,196 sorties from 25 November until 11 January 1943: 1,648 tons of fuel, 1,122 tons of ammunition, and 2,020 tons of rations were supplied. The Heinkel He 111H-6s of KG 55 contributed another 3,259.9 tons. It was not enough, and aircraft losses were catastrophic. On 14 January 1943 the airfield of Pitomnik was overrun: the last airfield, Gumrak, fell into Soviet hands on 23 January. On 31 January 1943 Friedrich von Paulus, commanding the 6th Army and recently promoted to Generalfeldmarschall, surrendered his forces: the XI Korps held out in the northern sector before they too laid down their arms on 2 February.

Red Stars in the south

Just as the overall quality of Soviet fighter equipment improved during 1942, so did the tactics and fighting skills of the pilots. Fighter vs. fighter combat became increasingly less

one-sided as the year wore on. This was to be seen over Stalingrad, a battle which also marked the entry into combat of the excellent Lavochkin La-5 fighter.

MiG ace
Aleksandr Ivanovich 'Sasha' Pokryshkin was arguably the most influential Soviet fighter tactician of the war. Flying with the 16 GvIAP, he flew this Mikoyan-Gurevich MiG-3 while serving on the southern front in mid-1942. Pokryshkin was eventually credited with 59 individual kills, and was thrice awarded the coveted Hero of the Soviet Union award. By 1943 Pokryshkin was flying the Bell P-39.

Stalingrad defender
Snr Lt V. Orekhov (19 kills) flew this Yakovlev Yak-7B during the defence of Stalingrad in September 1942. His unit, the 434 IAP, had been moved from the Moscow front to defend the city on the Volga. The Yak-7B was a single-seat fighter version of the two-seat UTI-26 trainer – simplified with and better handling compared to the Yak-1.

Stalemate in the East

The Kuban challenge

This winter-camouflaged Ju 87D-3 flew with I./StG 2. During the summer of 1942, this unit operated in the south, seeing action in the Caucasus and Stalingrad sector.

The German defeat at Stalingrad was a horrendous and unexpected shock to the Axis, but was not the turning point of the war. The Wehrmacht was still strong, while the Luftwaffe held air supremacy.

In November 1942, immediately before the horror of Stalingrad, some 2,450 Luftwaffe aircraft were operational in the East. Opposing these were 7,500 Soviet aircraft of the V-VS distributed between 13 air armies. However, quality was all important and this factor was still firmly held by the Luftwaffe in aircraft, weapons and tactics. But the V-VS was rising slowly from the disasters of 1941, the aircraft and engine industries had been moved wholesale beyond the Urals. The safety of the rear areas, coupled with the strict rules of the Stalin regime, meant that average monthly production of aircraft rose to 2,120 with a total output of 25,436 units in 1942.

The epic Stalingrad campaign bore many Russian heros and aces. Major I. I Kleshchev's

434th IAP claimed 36 kills in the first fortnight of *Fall Blau* in July 1942 while the Pe-2 dive-bombers of the 150th BAP conducted dives of up to 60° in pinpoint attacks; the Il-2s of 26th and 228th ShAD received citations for their work, as did the 220th and 268th IAP. The Yak-1s comprising the fighter cordon around Gumrak and Pitomnik shot down many Ju 52/3m transports, while 17 members of the VA received the award of the Hero of the Soviet Union, the highest Soviet honour. From 19 November 1942 to 2 February 1943, V-VS armies on the Stalingrad front flew 35,929 sorties, often in terrible weather and shot down some 3,000 German aircraft, while Li-2s transported over 31,000 men and 2,587 tons of freight in over 46,000 missions.

This Yak-7B fighter of the 18th GvIAP at Khaizonki was flown by Lieutenant Colonel A.E Golubov during 1943. The 18th Guards was one of 288 V-VS units to receive the 'Guards' title in the war.

Throughout the summer and autumn of 1942 the Luftwaffe, despite the rebirth of the V-VS, still managed to maintain air superiority over the theatre. A new breed of aces notched up their 100th, 150th and 200th kills in Bf 109G-4s and Fw 190A-4s, which still had the advantage over the Yak-1s, LaGG-3s and MiG-3s. Close

support and tactical ground attack was fulfiled by the hardy Ju 87D which with good fighter cover performed well against Soviet fortifications.

However, the Luftwaffe was still faced with the task of knocking out the formidable number of Soviet tanks, most notably the powerful T-34/76. A series of different aircraft and

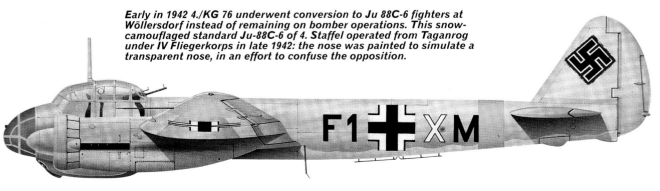

Early in 1942 4./KG 76 underwent conversion to Ju 88C-6 fighters at Wöllersdorf instead of remaining on bomber operations. This snow-camouflaged standard Ju-88C-6 of 4. Staffel operated from Taganrog under IV Fliegerkorps in late 1942: the nose was painted to simulate a transparent nose, in an effort to confuse the opposition.

An He 111, armed with a 2,204-lb (1000-kg) bomb crosses the Don front en route to another raid on Soviet forces. Large bombs like these were carried externally, while the bomb bays could house additional fuel.

Below: Despite the rapid advances made by the V-VS, it still found itself outclassed by its Axis opponents. This Yak-7B was shot down at Pitkäranta on 12 February 1943. Note the sleds under the wings that have been used to transport the wreck.

different weapon fits were used with the 37-mm Flak 18 cannon being the best for detracking T-34s, and destroying KV-1 tanks and SU-76 assault guns.

After Stalingrad, the Luftwaffe found itself in a position similar to that of the winter of 1941-2. No fewer than 488 losses were sustained in the Stalingrad supply mission alone, crippling the bomber force and destroying the Transportverbände for all time. Furthermore, with the Allied offensive in North Africa, some 400 aircraft were drawn from the Eastern Front to bolster Luftflotte II in the Mediterranean. Total Luftwaffe strength in the East by December 1942 was 1,815 aircraft with 900 in the Don-Donets sector and 230 in the Crimea and the Caucasus theatre from which the Germans had started to retreat.

Recovery at Kharkov

Early in January 1943, with the bitter fight at Stalingrad still in progress, the Soviet Voronezh Front launched an offensive west towards the Kharkov area while the South West Front headed due west to cut off the line of German retreat from the Caucasus. By 16 February, Voronezh, Kursk, Kharkov and Voroshilovgrad had been retaken and the German position in the Don-Donets sector was severely threatened by the marauding Soviet tank armies. However, the Soviet lines had

become over-extended and the German Army Group 'South' counterattacked on 20 February 1943 with air support provided by I Fliegerkorps at Poltava, the IV Fliegerkorps at Dnepropetrovsk and by Fliegerdivision Donetz at Stalino with power ground-support forces. By 3 March three rifle divisions and XXV Tanks Corps had been decimated, killing an estimated 23,000 and netting over 9,000 Soviet PoWs. On 15 March the 4th Panzer Army and the II SS Panzerkorps captured Kharkov with Belgorod being recaptured on 18 March. The spring thaw prevented further fighting but pressure was relieved. The dominant feature in the East was now the huge salient round Kursk that was to become the battleground of the summer.

Kuban challenge

By November 1942 Army A (1st Panzer and 17th Armies) had advanced deep into the Elista steppes, along the line of the Caucasus mountains, and as far east as Mozhdok, some 120 miles (192 km) due west of the Caspian Sea. During the Stalingrad battles the front line was stabilised, before orders were received to pull back. On 1 January the Soviet South Front attacked towards Rostov to join the offensive in the south by the Trans-Caucasus Front which struck out towards Stavropol and Armavir. On 4 February 1943, the Soviets conducted an audacious

amphibious landing at the Myskhako region on the Black Sea coast, to outflank and cut off the 17th army's line of retreat towards the Taman peninsula on the line of the Kuban river. By March 1943, the Germans had withdrawn into the narrow peninsula, known as the Kuban bridgehead, and had set up strong defensive positions. The loss of the Kuban would threaten the Crimea which, if taken, would provide the V-VS with airfields within bomber range of the Romanian oilfields. The Luftwaffe was therefore forced to commit a strong contingent to the defence of the Kuban and during April-June 1943, ferocious air battles were fought.

Soviet forces were now bolstered with Lend-Lease aircraft such as P-39N/Qs, A-20Bs and Spitfire Mk VBs and for the first time, Soviet fighter units reached a standard approaching that of the Germans. In the battles of April 1943, the Soviets took terrible losses but for the first time in the history of air warfare in the USSR, the V-VS was not swept from the sky.

By July, attention had turned to the impending battles at Kursk, Belgorod and Orel and the Kuban theatre lost some of its intensity. On 14 September, the German 17th Army started its withdrawal from the Kuban to the relative safety of the Crimea with I Fliegerkorps having claimed 2,280 V-VS aircraft and 1,054 tanks since the start of the campaign. The V-VS alternatively had flown over 35,000 sorties to claim 1,100 German aircraft (800 in air combat).

Both Soviet and German high commands were aware that the summer battles would take place in the great Kursk salient. The German Army Groups 'Centre' and 'South' were to crush the Soviet forces within the salient in Operation Zitadelle (Citadel) scheduled for 12 June. With a victory at Kursk, the German army hoped once again to seize the initiative on the Eastern Front. During May and June over 900,000 troops, 10,000 artillery pieces and 2,730 tanks were readied for the last great Blitzkrieg of the war.

Above: Lend-Lease Spitfire Mk VBs are seen being readied for delivery to the V-VS at Abadan, Iran in 1943. Britain sent 2,952 Hurricanes, 143 Spitfire Mk VBs and 1,188 Spitfire Mk IXs to the USSR, but not all arrived.

Left: These Il-2m3 Shturmovik close-support aircraft on the Leningrad front in the summer of 1944 are possibly of the 277th ShAD of the 13th Armiya.

In an effort to reinforce ever-dwindling German stocks in the East, the mighty Me 323 Gigant was used to ferry supplies to the beleaguered troops. The Gigants belonged to I.-III. Gruppe of Transportgeschwader 5 which was formed in May 1943 and served, with mixed results, both in the USSR and the Mediterranean.

Kursk: The turning point

The German army gambled all on the great offensive to eradicate the Kursk salient in the summer of 1943, and to regain the initiative in the east. But it was to be yet another gross underestimation of Soviet strength, leading to a disastrous reverse.

The city of Kursk lies some 280 miles (445 km) south west of Moscow. By early summer of 1943 bitter fighting had rolled the front lines into two great salients, one German-held and jutting into Soviet territory in the Bryansk-Orel sector to the north of Kursk and the other Soviet-held and centred upon Kursk (bordered by Orel in the north and Belgorod in the south) in size some 150 miles (240 km) wide and 110 miles (177 km) deep. It was inevitable that the next conflict would be fought in this fiercely contested region. The leaders of both sides were keen for the other to attack, as a defensive stance seemed to offer the best chance for success. However, like so many times before, Hitler intervened and ordered his forces onwards. The date of 5 July 1943 was eventually set and Operation Zitadelle would consist of a maximum-effort strike aimed at wiping out the Soviet armies in the Kursk-Orel-Belgorod sector, straightening the front line, and regaining a measure of initiative. This was completely unlike the great offensives of 1941-42 which were aimed at breakthroughs deep into the Soviet Union. Victory was vitally important to both sides; the Russians needed a morale boosting win over the German armour while the Germans needed a summer win, as in the winter they tended to come out second best.

Pre-assault blitzes

However, by June 1943, the Germans were already running short on fuel. Quantities being delivered fell well short of those being used, with Fw 190s suffering especially. Furthermore, deliveries were hampered by the activities of partisans in the rear of Army Group 'Centre'. Some 268 locomotives, 1,222 freight wagons and 44 bridges were all destroyed in June.

As the build-up proceeded, both sides engaged in attacks on airfields. He 111H-6 bombers flew long-range penetration missions against strategic targets at Gorki, Saratov and Yaroslavl, while V-VS missions were mainly confined to the bombing of German airfields. An attack on 6 May saw 112 Il-4s and 156 Il-2s, covered by 166 fighters, claim 194 German aircraft on the ground and 21 shot down.

The great German offensive was planned for 5 July 1943 and on this beautiful summer morning, the Luftwaffe was preparing for the first air strikes of the campaign. However, it was the V-VS that struck first. At 03.30 the German Freya radars picked up a massed attack on the airfields of the VIII Fliegerkorps. Every Bf 109G-6 was scrambled and Fw 190A-5s of 1. Fliegerdivision diverted in from the Orel area in what was one of the biggest air battles of the war. Over 400 aircraft tangled in the skies above Belgorod and Kharkov and by 9.20, when the V-VS had retired, things seemed to be going well for the Germans, they had notched up 120 kills for minimal losses.

In the southern sector VIII Fliegerkorps covered the advance of the 4th Panzer Army towards Oboyan, Korocha and Prokhorovka, while to the north the 9th army rolled into the massed defences and anti-tank ditches towards Olkhovatka and Ponyri. A total of 47 German divisions was committed in Zitadelle against 1,300,000 Soviet troops in 109 rifle divisions, 3,600 tanks in 13 corps and over 20,000 artillery tubes. Moreover, the Soviet defences were prepared in depth over a distance of 25 miles (40 km).

Fighting was fierce and losses were high, a record 432 kills were claimed by 1. Fliegerdivision and VIII Fliegerkorps on the first day alone. II./JG 3 'Udet' performed especially well with Hauptmann Kurt Brändle claiming five

While not a popular aircraft with the western Allies, the Bell P-39 Airacobra was eagerly adopted by the Soviet forces (which received 4,924 examples), appreciating its strength and superlative performance at low altitudes. This P-39N was the mount of Major Alexandr I. Pokryshkin of the 16th GvIAP in the Kuban in summer 1943.

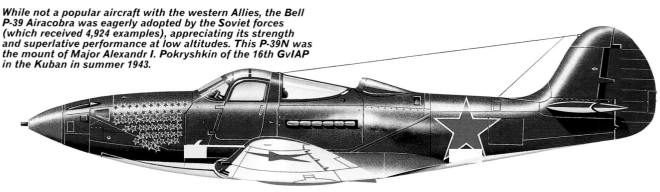

Left: A flight of Pe-2s prepares to sweep in on the enemy. This Soviet light bomber could be armed with bombs or aft-firing machine-guns and the 'Peshka,' which was built in massive numbers, exacted a major toll on the invading Axis forces.

Below: A pilot warms up the engines of his heavily armoured Hs 129B/R2 tank-buster of IV.(Pz)/SG 9. This Gruppe moved from Novo Krassnoye under I Fliegerkorps to Czernovitz under VIII Fliegerkorps in March 1944, and thence to Lysiatycze and Wintershausen – all retreats.

aircraft to reach his 151st kill and Oberleutnant Joachim Kirschner shooting down nine to reach his 150th. A record 12 were claimed by Hauptmann Johannes Wiese of 2./JG 52. Over-claiming as always was rife: the true losses of 5 July 1943 were probably 260 Luftwaffe and 176 V-VS aircraft.

Savage Soviet resistance caused the German offensive to flounder. In the air war, it was claimed that a total of 556 V-VS aircraft was destroyed against 854 German opponents during 5-8 July. Over the period of 5-6 July, the 9th Army pushed a mere 6 miles (10 km) south, but become bogged down after netting some 25,000 Russian PoWs. Luftwaffe efforts peaked at 3,000 sorties a day before stabilising at a more manageable 1,000, the majority by Ju 87Ds and fighters.

On 12 July, the greatest tank battle of the entire war was fought between the Soviet army's I and V Guard Tank Corps and elements of Army Detachment Kempf, the 4th Panzer Army and IV Panzerkorps, while to the north the Soviet West and Bryansk Fronts attacked the Orel salient. On 15 July, the Central Front launched its assault against the 9th Army towards Orel and Kromy, while on the following day the German armies commenced their withdrawal. A month of hard fighting lay ahead. The Soviet forces took Orel and Belgorod on 4-5 August and the flood gates opened. On 23 August elements of the Voronezh, Steppe and South-west Fronts took Kharkov to threaten the entire southern flank of von Manstein's Army Group 'South' and open the way for the massive Soviet autumn offensive in the Ukraine. For the German army, Zitadelle had failed with the sacrifice of the cream of the Panzerkorps. From

now onwards the bitter diet was to be constant and wearing retreats all the way back to the borders of the Reich; but this process was to take its time.

The impact of Kursk

The massive Kursk campaign was coincident with the Allied advances over Sicily and southern Italy and the dramatic escalation of attacks on the Reich by Allied heavy bombers. With the suicide of the Luftwaffe's commander, Generaloberst Hans Jeschonnek, Luftwaffe strategy changed with his successor, General der Flieger Günther Korten, who decided defence of the Reich took precedent over

foreign ventures and many units were drawn from the East and the Mediterranean area to Germany. It was also at this point that the Luftwaffe began the formation of a strategic bomber force, a wholly unnecessary venture that drew funds and supplies away from the more important fighter fleet. In the east, the relentless Soviet counter-offensive rolled on and the Germans were constantly pushed back. Soviet forces vastly outnumbered the invaders and by 6 November 1943, Kiev, the hub city of the Ukraine, was recaptured by the Soviets and the beginning of the end of the Great Patriotic War was in sight.

Axis allies in the East

It was not just the Germans making the ultimately suicidal charge into the Soviet Union. In the north, the Finns, eternal enemies of the Russians

reluctantly allied themselves with the Germans to stave off Soviet invasion. Further south, Bulgarians, Croats, Italians, Romanians and Ukrainians all

marched eastwards as part of the Axis. However, it was these allies that proved the weakest link in the German advance.

Ju 88A-4
Through May and June 1943, Finnish pilots ferried 23 ex-Luftwaffe Ju 88s to Finland for use by the Ilmavoimat. This aircraft served with 1. Lentue, Lentolaivue 44, based at Onntola late in 1943. The Ju 88s saw continuous service in support of Finnish forces until the acceptance of Soviet peace terms.

Ju 87D
The 6th Dive-Bomber Group of the Corpul 1 Aerian, Romanian Air Force, operated over the Kursk salient under VIII Fliegerkorps in the summer of 1943. The spatted wheel covers of the Ju 87 were often removed to prevent fouling by mud or snow.

Ilyushin Il-2/10 'Bark'/'Beast'

Il-2s depart from a forward base on a combat mission, probably in 1942. These early aircraft are ShVAK-armed single-seaters except for the one in the foreground which is fitted with VYa cannon (possessing longer barrels than the ShVAK).

Shturmovik

Outside Russia, the Il-2 and Il-10 remain, somewhat unbelievably, less well-known than other World War II types, although they were built in greater numbers than any other military aircraft in history.

During the 1930s, the Soviet Union placed great importance on creating survivable close-support and attack aircraft. Coupled with this was the fact that the Soviets possessed the world's best air weapons, including large-calibre guns, heavy recoilless cannon, hollow-charge, armour-piercing bombs and similar warheads fitted to air-launched rockets.

From the beginning of the decade, a succession of heavily armed attack aircraft appeared and in 1935 the Kremlin issued a requirement for a BSh (*Bronirovanyi Shturmovik* or armoured attacker) aircraft, specifically intended to knock out armoured vehicles and ground strong-points. By 1938 the OKBs of Sergei V. Ilyushin and Pavel O. Sukhoi were set in head-on competition. Both designers adopted a conventional low-wing, single-engined configuration, but Ilyushin's was ready much sooner, in the spring of 1939.

Designated TsKB-55, with the service designation BSh-2, it was powered by a large 1,350-hp (1007-kW) AM-35 liquid-cooled engine, and seated the pilot and radio operator/rear gunner/observer in tandem. The wing, hydraulic flaps and tail were of light alloy, but the lower part of the fuselage was made up of 1,543 lb (700 kg) of armour which covered the underside of the engine, coolant pipes, radiator, fuselage tanks and cockpits. Four 0.3-in (7.62-mm) guns were mounted in the wings outboard of the main landing gear legs, with a fifth in the rear cockpit, and four compartments in the centre section housed up to 1,323 lb (600 kg) of bombs.

Right: Pictured in 1944, these Il-2M3 two-seaters can be seen over the Eastern Front which, by this time, had been pushed beyond the frontiers of the Soviet Union and into countries such as Poland and Romania.

This Il-2M3 demonstrates the not-unusual decision to remove the rear cockpit canopy to give the gunner a free field of fire. It was also common for the gunner to have twin UB guns, though with reduced ammunition. The slogan 'mstitel' painted on the side means 'avenger'.

Right: The neat lines in which these Il-2s are drawn up (there are more than 65 illustrated) suggest that this was a formal occasion following the defeat of the Germans. The dedication 'Chapayev' painted on the fuselages may relate to a person or to the many towns of that name (which may have paid for them).

Left: Stalin threw his weight behind the Il-2 project. When production delays were occurring, he said that "The Red Army needs the Il-2 as it needs air or bread...this is my final warning."

Crash programme

Ilyushin was dissatisfied with the poor armament, and in tests the TsKB-55 showed, as predicted, poor stability. An improved second prototype, with the centre of gravity shifted slightly forward and with a larger tailplane, flew on 30 December 1939, but NII (State) testing in the summer of 1940 considered the good features outweighed by poor stability, range and general performance. Ilyushin therefore launched a 'crash programme' which in four months produced the TsKB-57. This was fitted with the 1,600-hp (1194-kW) AM-38, had an extra fuel tank instead of a rear cockpit, thicker and better distributed armour, two of the wing guns replaced by 20-mm ShVAK cannon and new underwing rails for eight RS-82 rockets. This was a much better machine, which reached 292 mph (470 km/h) and had good agility. Very large-scale production was then put in hand at three factories: in Moscow, at Fili to the north and at Voronezh to the south.

When the Germans invaded on 22 June 1941, 249 had been delivered and a few were in service, but this was far below target. By October, the Moscow and Fili plants had to be closed and their tooling and workers

evacuated far to the east, the chief new production centre being at Kuybyshyev. But output was slow to build up, and Stalin sent a telegram to the factory directors telling them that their performance was 'an insult'. In early 1942 the ShVAK guns were replaced by the much harder-hitting 23-mm VYa.

Later in 1942 the designation changed to Il-2M2 with the introduction of the 1,750-hp (1306-kW) AM-38F engines which improved all-round performance, even with an increase in armour to 2,094 lb (950 kg). Losses to fighters were severe, however, and it was not practical to provide adequate armour against fire from above and behind. Despite Stalin's reluctance to sanction any further modifications, Ilyushin was authorised to produce prototypes with a rear gunner, and these flew in March 1942. The gunner had a 0.5-in (12.7-mm) UB with 150 rounds and, differing from the original TsKB-55, was separated from the pilot by the amidships fuel tank.

Production was eventually sanctioned in October 1942 as the Il-2M3 – this new two-seater was in action on the Central Front by the end of the month.

Streamlining

Losses were immediately sharply curtailed, while casualties among Luftwaffe fighters increased. Production by this time was running at close to 1,000 per month, despite the introduction of a succession of minor changes which were mainly aimed at improving performance, which had fallen to a maximum speed of 251 mph (404 km/h). Thus, almost every part that could be better streamlined was modified, if this could be done without disrupting production. By mid-1943 maximum speed had improved to 273 mph (439 km/h) despite the continuing growth in weight.

Part of the weight growth was due to increased armament, which benefited from the superb products of the air weapon design staff. Most important was the new family of 1.45-in (37-mm) guns, unrelated to earlier weapons of this calibre and firing high-velocity ammunition fully capable of penetrating Pzkpfw V (Panther) and Pzkpfw VI (Tiger) tanks, except in a head-on attack. Additional types of bombs could be carried in the wing cells, while underwing loads were expanded to include the large 5.2-in/ 132-mm calibre) RS-132 rocket and boxes of 200 small PTAB anti-armour bombs.

In 1942 the first dual-control Il-2 appeared. Several more were produced by field conversion, and by 1943 small numbers were factory-built as the Il-2U, most with reduced armament. Another field modification resulted in the

Il-2T torpedo-carrier which, with the greatest ease, carried a 21-in (533-mm) torpedo. Altogether, at least 36,163 Il-2s had been built when production switched to the Il-10 in August 1944. By that time, monthly acceptances were running at the record level of 2,300, almost 16,000 being delivered in the first eight months of 1944 – the figure for the whole of 1943 had been 11,200. Whereas previously it had been difficult to gather Il-2s to form a trained regiment, by 1944 they were operating in corps strength, as many as 500 being committed at a time on a single localised area and generally leaving no vehicle able to move. The usual method of attack was a 'follow-my-leader' orbit which gave a long firing run from the rear of heavy armour, while individual aircraft dropped cluster or anti-armour bombs. To the Soviet forces the Il-2 was commonly known as the *Ilyusha*, but to the invaders it was soon the '*schwarz Tod*' (Black Death).

In 1943 the first foreign units began to receive Il-2 equipment. Subsequently, an estimated 3,000 were supplied to Polish, Czech, Yugoslav and Bulgarian regiments, while large numbers were supplied to China and North Korea in the post-war era. Several countries, including Poland and Czechoslovakia, applied their own local designations, while many Il-2s were modified in various ways with different equipment, weapons or a rear fuselage of fabric-covered welded steel tubes.

This Il-2M3 was serving at the end of World War II with the 3rd Attack Regiment (Szturmowego Pulk) of the 1st Mixed Air Corps, one of the first non-Soviet units to be equipped with the aircraft.

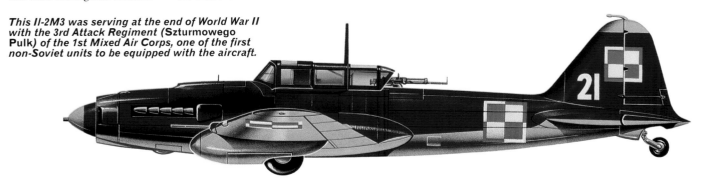

Retreat from Stalingrad

Ukraine and Leningrad

By the end of 1943, the Soviet war machine was in full swing. The initial shock of the German invasion and of the USSR's own inability to defend itself had passed: the Germans were in trouble.

After the monolithic battles of Operation Zitadelle and its aftermath, the Soviet armies in the south maintained their momentum, driving the Germans from the Don basin and liberating Kharkov, Melitopol, Zaporozlie, Krivoi Rog and finally, as a fitting climax, the city of Kiev on 6 November 1943. During October 1943 the Russian Voronezh, Steppe, South-west and South Fronts were renamed respectively the 1st, 2nd, 3rd and 4th Ukrainian Fronts. The strength of the V-VS air armies (VAs) in support of these ground formations was approximately 2,360 aircraft and the strength of an air army had risen to an average of about 700 aircraft, typically including Yak-1 and La-5FN fighters, Il-2m3 close-support aircraft, Pe-2 light day bombers, Il-4 medium night bombers and reconnaissance types. Some VAs were stronger, some weaker, according to the commitment on a particular battlefront. Above all the VAs were tactical organisations wholly dependent upon the front commander for day-to-day orders, being reinforced at times by autonomous units of the P-VO (Strany) and the Long-Range Aviation (ADD). Strategic bombing had played little part on the Eastern Front, either on the part of the V-VS or of the Luftwaffe: the air war remained one fought by fighters, close-support aircraft and medium bombers, while tactical reconnaissance played a very important role.

On Christmas Eve 1943 the 1st Ukrainian Front's 1st Guards and 1st Tank Armies debouched

westwards along the Kiev-Zhitomir road towards Berdichev and Kazatin on the front of the German 4th Panzer Army to open the Soviet winter offensive: overhead, under cloud bases of less than 330 ft (100 m), roared the Il-2s and La-5FNs of the 2nd VA. The Germans were soon in trouble: by 28 January some 56,000 men were trapped in the Cherkassy pocket between Lisyanka and Korsun Shevelienkovsky: hastily adapted Heinkel He 111-6 bombers and Junkers Ju 52/3m transports dropped 100-185 tons of supplies daily in bad weather and under constant pressure from Soviet fighters. The breakout from the Cherkassy pocket was made on 16 February, but only 30,000 men got away.

German air strength on the Eastern Front hovered around 1,800 aircraft in January 1944 (41 per cent of strength on all fronts) in opposition to some 11,000 V-VS aircraft.

Leningrad releived

Between January and March 1944 the 1st, 2nd, 3rd and 4th Ukrainian Fronts drove full tilt for the Bug river, and onwards to the great Dniester river that presented the last natural barrier before the Carpathian mountains and the

Guards Captain Igor A. Katgrov of the 3rd Guards IAP (Baltic Fleet) had the misfortune to fly this LaGG-3 in combat. The LaGG-3 was a truly awful fighter, but represented an important stop-gap in Soviet fighter capability.

border of Romania and the provinces of Moldavia. In the meantime pressure was reasserted on the sector of Army Group 'North' on the line Leningrad-Kholm-Demyansk.

On 14 January 1944 the Soviet's Leningrad Front opened its offensive in the north, partly driving east and partly probing towards encircled Leningrad. On the same day the Volkhov Front opened its assault on the flank of the German 18th Army towards Novgorod. Air support for the Leningrad Front was provided by

the 13th VA, while the Volkhov forces had the 14th VA: additional units were those of the 2nd GvIAK of the P-VO and the Red Banner Baltic Fleet (V-VS): total strength was around 1,200. The 15th VA was also available to support the 2nd Baltic Front's offensive. These forces opposed some 325 combat aircraft of Luftflotte I, including Bf 109G-6s and Fw 190A-5s.

On 19 January 1944 the Soviet 2nd Shock and 42nd Armies met near Krasnoye Selo, liberating Ropsha and cutting the road to

Ilyushin's Il-4 offered similar capabilities to the Luftwaffe's Heinkel He 111. These aircraft were photographed undergoing outdoor maintenance during 1943.

Rapid increases in the rate of Fw 190 production led to the type being widely introduced to Eastern Front Schlachtflieger during 1944. This aircraft, however, wears the markings of II Gruppe, JG 54.

Soviet fighter strength

By late 1943, the situation of the USSR had changed considerably from the early days of the German invasion, when Bf 109s faced ranks of inferior Soviet fighters such as the I-153. Now the Soviets could field massive numbers of potent new fighters, with expert and ferociously brave pilots at their controls.

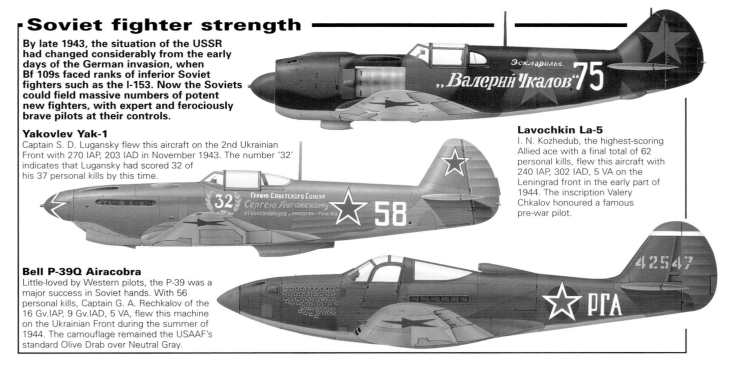

Yakovlev Yak-1
Captain S. D. Lugansky flew this aircraft on the 2nd Ukrainian Front with 270 IAP, 203 IAD in November 1943. The number '32' indicates that Lugansky had scored 32 of his 37 personal kills by this time.

Lavochkin La-5
I. N. Kozhedub, the highest-scoring Allied ace with a final total of 62 personal kills, flew this aircraft with 240 IAP, 302 IAD, 5 VA on the Leningrad front in the early part of 1944. The inscription Valery Chkalov honoured a famous pre-war pilot.

Bell P-39Q Airacobra
Little-loved by Western pilots, the P-39 was a major success in Soviet hands. With 56 personal kills, Captain G. A. Rechkalov of the 16 Gv.IAP, 9 Gv.IAD, 5 VA, flew this machine on the Ukrainian Front during the summer of 1944. The camouflage remained the USAAF's standard Olive Drab over Neutral Gray.

Novgorod; the 20th Army took Novgorod on the following day. During 21-29 January Puslikin, Lytiban and Chudove, were taken, to enable rail supplies to reach the beleaguered city of Leningrad for the first time since September 1941. Pressure was maintained with Luga, Staraya Russya and Porkboy being recaptured over the period 12-26 February 1944, with heavy losses to the embattled forces of Army Group 'North'. In the air the action was intense, and several V-VS units performed well: citations were given to the 275th IAD, and to the 9th and 277th ShAD. The 3. Fliegerdivision fought at great odds and lost a number of pilots.

Jagdflieger losses
Luftwaffe fighter superiority had been challenged over the Kuban and at Kursk in 1943, and by the spring of 1944 there were insufficient numbers of German fighters on the Eastern Front for the huge task of covering the various withdrawals: in March 1944 an average of 326 German fighters was available for combat along a 1,800-mile (2900-km) front from Lapland to the Crimea.

In spite of their fearful numerical inferiority the Jagdflieger continued to fight hard, with many pilots adding to their already substantial scores, while JG 51 'Mölders' scored its 7,000th combat kill on 15 September 1943.

In general, the Luftwaffe aces survived to fly day after day against overwhelming numbers of Yak-7Bs, Yak-9s, La-5FNs and MiG-3s: the quality of Soviet fighter opposition varied, but by early 1944 German pilots often

had hard fights on their hands against aircraft that matched the Bf 109G-6 and the Fw 190A-6 in performance and agility, and were aggressively flown. The replacement of the Ju 87D by growing numbers of Fw 190s eased the situation to a certain extent: in addition to their anti-tank and close-support work, many Schlachtflieger became adept at fighter-versus-fighter work.

By March 1944 the Soviet Ukrainian Fronts had advanced to a line running southwards from the Pripet Marshes, through Kovel to the Dnieper south west of Krivoi Rog. The Soviet spring offensive in this theatre opened on 4 March when the 1st Ukrainian Front attacked in the gap between the German 1st and 4th Panzer Armies: the 3rd Guards Tank Army headed south for Shepetovka and Proskurov. On the next day the 13th Army struck in the Lutsk-Dubno sector. To stem the rout Hitler ordered the establishment of fortified cities and towns, nominating Tarnopol, Proskurov, Kovel, Brody, Vinnitsa and Permovaysk among others: these fortresses became a marked feature in the months to come.

The huge tank battles that had characterised 1941-3 were gone: the Tigers and Panthers were now usually dug in, and fought defensive battles against the

columns of Soviet tank battalions before a hasty, and usually skillfully executed, withdrawal.

Ukraine liberated
During the period 25 March to 11 April 1944 the Germans were pushed back towards the line of the Dniester river, and narrowly escaped encirclement on a number of occasions: those at Tarnopol were less fortunate and out of a garrison of 4,000 only 53 men escaped. The last of the German troops crossed the Dniester on the night of 14 April and by the end of the month, when the Ukrainian Fronts ceased their advance, the liberation of the Ukraine was complete. The next crisis took place on 4 April 1944 when the 4th Ukrainian Front and the Independent Coastal Army struck at the Crimean-based German 17th Army from Perekop and Kerch, supported by the V-VS 4th VA and the 8th VA together with units of the ADD and ChF (Black Sea Fleet).

These forces faced 160 assorted German types (85 of which were serviceable). During the first 10 days 13,121 German and 17,652 Romanian troops were killed or captured and, by the first week of May 1944 when the mass evacuation commenced, some 64,700 men were still trapped at Sebastopol. The Soviet armies

secured the Crimean peninsula on 13 May, with the last Ju 52/3m and Me 323D transports leaving behind 26,700 Axis troops to fall into captivity: 250-300 German aircraft, the majority fighters, were lost in this short campaign.

Final preparations for the great Soviet offensive of the summer necessitated the securing of the northern flank in Karelia: the Soviet 21st and 23rd Armies were supported by the 13th VA and the 2nd Gv.IAK of the P-VO (Strany) amounting to 757 aircraft, which faced 360 aircraft of the Finnish air force (Ilmavoimat). Finnish fighters included Bf 109G-2s and Bf 109G-6s at Utti, Malmi and Immola. The Soviets invaded Karelia on 10 June 1944, following a massive air strike by the V-VS on the previous day, with the 21st Army crashing through the defences of the Finnish IV Corps. Hastily the Luftwaffe sent a small detachment with Ju 87D-5s, Bf 109G-6s and Fw 190A-5s to Immola, and these flew 940 sorties on 21 June in support of the Finns, but to little avail. Air combats proliferated with heavy losses to both sides. The key city of Viborg (Viipuri) fell on 20 June 1944, and thereafter the tempo subsided: an official cease-fire on 4 September brought the campaign to an end and Finland out of the war.

1 Lieutenant Mikko Pasila flew this Bf 109G-6/R6 during the last two months of fighting between Finland and the USSR. The aircraft was on the strength of 1/HLeLv 24 at Lappeenranta and is illustrated as it appeared in July 1944.

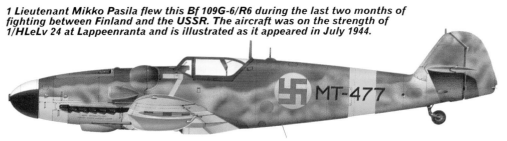

This Yakovlev Yak-3 was flown by René Challe, who commanded 4e and subsequently 1ère Escadrilles of the Normandie-Niemen Regiment. Having received the Yak-3 in July 1944, the regiment destroyed 119 enemy aircraft in a 10-day period in October 1944, proving the excellence of this low-altitude interceptor.

The drive to the Oder

The scale of the conflict on the Eastern Front may be guaged from the fact that the Axis had 164 divisions facing the Soviets; just 54 were stationed in France, with 27 in Italy and 40 in Norway and the Balkans.

Against a total Soviet V-VS air strength of 13,428 first-line aircraft the Luftwaffe disposed the following on 31 May 1944 (serviceability in parentheses): in northern Norway under Luftflotte V (Ost) 146 (120); in the Balkans under LwKdo Süd-Ost 262 (200), and on the Eastern Front under Luftflotten I, VI and IV a total of 2,360 (1,776), excluding the transport forces. With the Soviet armies massed on the Romanian borders in the Jassy-Kishinev sector, Hitler's greatest fear lay in the threat to the vital oilfields and refineries in the Ploesti complex, which were already under attack by the US 15th Air Force. This fear was reflected in the distribution of Luftwaffe units in the East: by June, out of a total serving on the Eastern Front of 2,085, the Romanian and Moldavian sector of Luftflotte IV held 845, including 670 fighters and close-support (Schlacht) aircraft in I and VIII Fliegerkorps. Luftflotte VI had 775 aircraft (405 bombers plus 275 fighters and close-support aircraft) within 1.

and 4. Fliegerdivision, IV Fliegerkorps and Fliegerführer 1 in the area north of the Pripet Marshes and extending northwards to Daugavpils.

Army Group 'Centre'

During May and early June Soviet military might in the area of Belorussia facing Army Group 'Centre' was stealthily increased for the first stage of the summer offensive along the Vitebsk-Minsk axis. Around 6,000 V-VS aircraft (including over 2,000 fighters) were concentrated for the support of the ground forces, including the potent Ilyushin Il-2M3 Shturmovik close-support aircraft and three new types – the Tu-2, the Yak-3 and the La-7.

On the morning of 22 June 1944 tanks of the 1st Baltic and 3rd Belorussian Fronts smashed into the 16th Army and 3rd Panzer Army to the northwest and southeast of Vitebsk: at Orscha and Mogilev the entire front erupted, while Soviet Il-4s, Tu-2s and Pe-2s plastered troop concentrations and airfields. A mere 40 serviceable Bf 109G-6s

and Fw 190s were on hand. On 26 June the Soviet tanks encircled 70,000 German troops to the south of Bobruisk, and plunged onwards to take Minsk on 3 July. Within 12 days Generalfeldmarschall Ernst Busch's Army Group 'Centre' lost no less than 25 divisions, with 130,000 out of the 4th Army's complement of 165,000 troops being killed or captured, as well as the 10 divisions of the 3rd Panzer Army. On 9 July 1944, with the fall of Vilna, Belorussia was cleared and the way opened into the plains of north eastern Poland. By now Army Group 'North' was under attack as Soviet armies took to

the offensive in the Baltic states; and to the south on 24 July Rokossovsky's left wing took Lublin and the Vistula river was reached on 26 July, while still farther to the south Konev's forces reached the river at Baranow some 130 miles (208 km) south of Warsaw. Then the front dramatically stabilized as German resistance hardened and Soviet lines of communication became overextended; but the advance of over 450 miles (720 km) within five weeks witnessed the decimation of Army Group 'Centre'. The operational effort of the V-VS during the period (5 July to 29 August) was 98,534

The Poltava Blitz – 21 June 1944

June 1944 saw the first shuttles by Boeing B-17s of the US 8th and 15th Air Forces to Soviet bases. But the arrival of B-17s and P-51 Mustangs of the 13th and 45th Wings at Mirgorod and Poltava on the afternoon of 21 June did not escape the attention of a lone He 177A-3 of IV Fliegerkorps (under Generalleutnant Rudolf Meister). An attack on Poltava was hurriedly prepared. To Minsk came KG 55 with 109 He 111H-16s under Oberst Wilhelm Antrup, and I-.III./KG 53 (111 Heinkels) under Oberst Fritz Pockrandt: I-.III./KG 27 were also available, with 72 Heinkels and six Ju 88S-1 pathfinders of I.-III./KG 4. At 20.15 the crews manned their aircraft, each He 111H-16 being loaded with incendiaries and two SC 1000 (2,205-lb) bombs. The first flares went down over Poltava at 00.30 on 22 June, and the Luftwaffe was permitted to display some of its old finesse. Some 200,000 Imp gal (909200 litres) of 100-octane fuel went up in flames, as did 47 Boeing B-17Gs, two Douglas C-47s and a single Lockheed F-5 Lightning; another 19 aircraft were damaged to varying degrees.

Fw 190s of 1944/45

An important type on the Eastern Front, especially in the ground attack role, the ubiquitous Fw 190A-8 also served alongside the re-engined 'Dora' fighter variant.

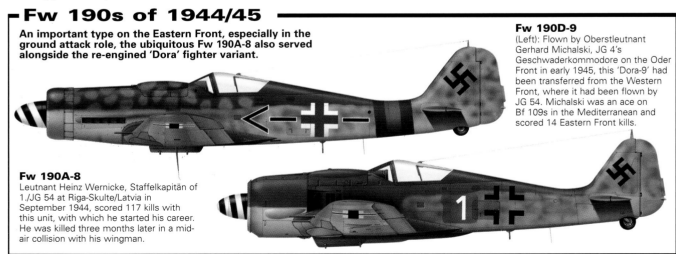

Fw 190D-9
(Left): Flown by Oberstleutnant Gerhard Michalski, JG 4's Geschwaderkommodore on the Oder Front in early 1945, this 'Dora-9' had been transferred from the Western Front, where it had been flown by JG 54. Michalski was an ace on Bf 109s in the Mediterranean and scored 14 Eastern Front kills.

Fw 190A-8
Leutnant Heinz Wernicke, Staffelkapitän of 1./JG 54 at Riga-Skulte/Latvia in September 1944, scored 117 kills with this unit, with which he started his career. He was killed three months later in a mid-air collision with his wingman.

V-VS La-7s on the offensive

Towards the end of the war Soviet fighter manufacturers were building aircraft that proved more than a match for the Luftwaffe opposition.

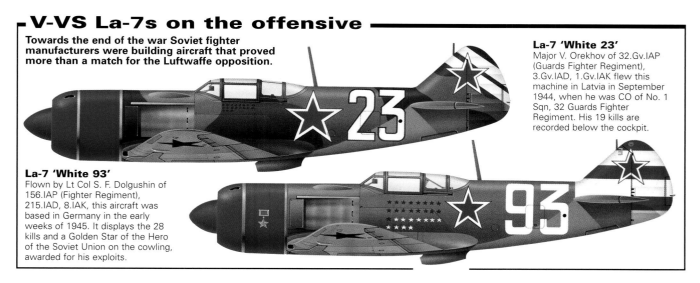

La-7 'White 23'
Major V. Orekhov of 32.Gv.IAP (Guards Fighter Regiment), 3.Gv.IAD, 1.Gv.IAK flew this machine in Latvia in September 1944, when he was CO of No. 1 Sqn, 32 Guards Fighter Regiment. His 19 kills are recorded below the cockpit.

La-7 'White 93'
Flown by Lt Col S. F. Dolgushin of 156.IAP (Fighter Regiment), 215.IAD, 8.IAK, this aircraft was based in Germany in the early weeks of 1945. It displays the 28 kills and a Golden Star of the Hero of the Soviet Union on the cowling, awarded for his exploits.

sorties, and over 1,500 enemy aircraft were claimed destroyed.

The Poltava raid (see box) proved to be the last major operation for IV Fliegerkorps, the resurrected strategic bomber force was disbanded on 16 September 1944. The Soviet offensive in the centre forced the transfer of VIII Fliegerkorps from Luftflotte IV to Luftflotte VI in July; 1,160 aircraft were based in the centre of the Eastern Front by mid-July 1944: 305 bombers, 375 strike aircraft, 50 night-strike aircraft, 215 single-engine fighters, 50 night-fighters, and 165 reconnaissance aircraft.

Balkans breakthrough

The great Soviet drive in the centre was held in two stages: the second offensive, known as the Lvov-Sandomir campaign, started on 13 July 1944.

Still reeling from the crushing blows in the centre, the Axis next suffered in the Balkans: the assault on the German Army Group 'South Ukraine' (ex-Army Group 'A') started on 20 August with the Soviet drive from Kishinev and Jassy. Soviet strength was 1,759 aircraft, aided by units of the V-VS ChF. The Romanian puppet regime was overthrown by a coup d'état on 23 August 1944, and this put paid to any hopes held by the Germans of securing their southern flank in the Balkans: 16 divisions were lost, cut off beyond the east bank of the Danube. The Soviet armies swarmed onto the

Romanian plains, sweeping aside all opposition: Galatz, Ploesti and Bucharest fell during 27-31 August, while the German position in the Balkans was rendered even more precarious by the capitulation of Bulgaria on 8 September.

Towards the end of October 1944 the 2nd Ukrainian Front had turned north to threaten Budapest in Hungary. Resistance here stiffened, but by December 1944 the Soviets had reached Lake Balaton and Budapest was encircled.

In this sector, in November 1944, Luftflotte IV remained with its Stab at Tavaros in western Hungary, with I and II Fliegerkorps subordinated. Units under the two Fliegerkorps were equipped with Fw 190F-8s and Ju 87D-5s. During the autumn and winter these small fighter and close-support forces fought a war against overwhelming Soviet air superiority in the Hungarian sector.

The drive to the Oder

By December 1944 the front line ran southwards from the Niemen river on the Baltic across Poland to Warsaw, and thence for hundreds of miles across open country to Budapest in Hungary. Having suffered the loss of some 840,000 men in the East and a further 393,000 in France and the West in the six months from June 1944, the German army faced a Soviet presence of 6,800,000 men

in 55 armies and six tank armies; against the Luftwaffe's 1,960 aircraft the strength of the V-VS amounted to 15,540 aircraft. The goals of the Soviet forces were Königsberg in East Prussia, and then the taking of the capitals of Prague, Vienna and finally Berlin.

The Soviet winter offensive started in mid-January 1945, earlier than planned due to the requests of Anglo-American leaders for pressure to be relieved in the west following the German offensive in the Ardennes. On the Soviet northern flank the 2nd and 3rd Belorussian Fronts were to attack Army Group 'Centre' in East Prussia, with some 3,000 aircraft of the 1st and 4th VAs in support, while in the centre the 1st Belorussian and 1st Ukrainian Fronts would advance westwards from the Vistula to liberate Poland, and advance to the line Bromberg-Poznan-Breslau. Some 4,770 Soviet aircraft were at the disposal of these forces: these would be opposed by the 1,060 aircraft of Luftflotte XI which formed the largest component of the Luftwaffe in the East at this time.

The campaign in East Prussia started on 13 January 1945, and met bitter resistance centred upon the fortress of Königsberg after good initial progress. The assault from the Warsaw-Sandomir axis started on 12-14 January in bad weather which negated much of the V-VS's effort. Warsaw was

taken on 17 January, by which time the 2nd and 16th VAs had flown 11,784 sorties against a mediocre Luftflotte VI in which 44 aircraft were lost in the air and 86 aircraft were destroyed on the ground. With the panache that had characterized offensives in the past, the 1st Belorussian and 1st Ukrainian Fronts were ordered to drive at full speed for the Oder: on 31 January 1945 the 5th Shock Army and 2nd Guards Army crossed the frozen Oder and established a bridgehead at Küstrin, an important railhead only 52 miles (84 km) due east of the Reich's capital. Farther to the south advancing Soviet armies crossed the Oder on the night of 21 January.

The Luftwaffe fought back savagely: during the latter part of January 1945, some 650 fighters (including Messerschmitt Bf 109G-0s and K-4s, and Focke-Wulf Fw 190D-9s) and over 100 close-support Fw 190F-8s were transferred from the Western Front to the Oder-Silesia theatre. But these had little impact against well-flown La-7s, Yak-3s and Yak-9Ds of the IAPs over the battle zones.

By 15 February 1945 Breslau had been invested, with massive Soviet strength consolidating on the line of the Oder. In the campaign from the Vistula to the Oder during January and February 1945 the Soviet armies fought their largest offensives of the war to decimate 31 German divisions and take 147,400 PoWs and 1,277 tanks. Operating in appalling weather the 2nd and 16th VAs alone put up 54,000 sorties to claim 908 enemy aircraft. By now there could be no salvation for Hitler and the Third Reich, for in the west the Allied armies were poised to cross the Rhine, while in the east the hour had struck for the final push to the great prize – Berlin.

Finished in an all-white winter colour scheme with high-visibility wingtips, this Lisunov Li-2 has a VUS-1 dorsal turret and skis fitted for operations in the harsh, and hostile, conditions.

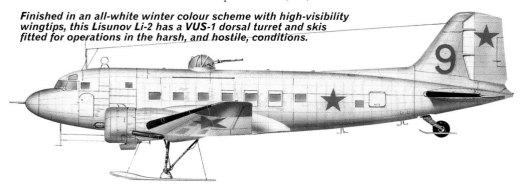

At the outbreak of war, only one Coastal Command squadron was equipped with the Hudson Mk I, nine had Anson Mk Is (illustrated), and one squadron was equipped with totally obsolete Vickers Vildebeest Mk IV torpedo-bomber biplanes.

Battle of the Atlantic

Air war at sea

The grave vulnerability of the UK to blockade by submarines was apparent during World War I, nevertheless, the UK was woefully ill-prepared to protect itself from the same threat in 1939.

In World War II Germany's most powerful advocate of all-out commerce warfare, to be conducted by U-boats against the UK, was Admiral Doenitz. Germany's naval forces were dwarfed by those of the Royal Navy and the French navy: the only means by which any balance could be attained was by massive U-boat production.

Even so, at the start of World War II, only 46 out of Doenitz's 56 submarines were ready for operations, of which the ocean-going Type VIIC numbered only 22. The strength of Germany's surface forces in 1939 amounted to two battle-cruisers (*Scharnhorst* and *Gneisenau*), three pocket battleships (*Deutschland, Scheer* and *Graf Spee*), eight cruisers, and 22 Z-class destroyers.

RAF Coastal Command

Despite the threat of the submarine menace to the almost total reliance by the UK on overseas commerce, RAF Coastal Command had received little new equipment. The Command strength on 1 September 1939 amounted to

16 squadrons with 265 aircraft, many of which were obsolete. Five squadrons were equipped with flying-boats, three with Sunderland Mk Is, and the remainder with Stranraers and Saro London Mk IIs.

Maritime reconnaissance and convoy protection were the prime roles of Coastal Command, allied with the tasks of protecting sea communications and attacking those of the enemy. After the first few weeks of war the tasks laid upon the Command increased in profusion: these included recce missions; fighter protection duties with Blenheim Mk IVFs and Hudsons fitted with the new dorsal turret; protection for fishing boats and naval mine-sweepers; and offensive patrols against U-boats and surface craft.

The selection of weaponry at the disposal of Coastal Command was unimpressive: the 50-lb (23-kg) and 100-lb (45-kg) antisubmarine Mk III bombs soon proved unreliable. Initially the only depth charge available was the RN's 450-lb (204-kg) Mk VII that dated back to 1918.

By July 1940 Coastal Command could muster 490 aircraft in 28½ squadrons, which included four with Beaufort Mk Is. As a torpedo-bomber the Beaufort was a major improvement on the Vildebeest although engine problems delayed its service entry.

In September 1939 Doenitz's U-boats sank 26 ships (135,552 gross registered tons: GRT) off British coasts and in the Western Approaches; in October 74,130 GRT were sunk, while in November, when the U-boats were hindered by foul weather, only 18,151 GRT went down. The period saw daring U-boat attacks on the RN's surface fleet: *U-29* sank the carrier HMS *Courageous* on 17 September and on the night of 13-14 October 1939, after penetrating into Scapa Flow, *U-47* sank HMS *Royal Oak*.

No easy targets

ASW became Coastal Command's most demanding commitment and successes against U-boats were very rare. The first U-boat sinking in which an aircraft of Coastal Command could take part credit took place off Brittany on 30 January 1940: damaged by HMS *Fowey* and HMS *Whitshed*, *U-55* was forced to scuttle after persistent attacks by a Sunderland of No. 228 Sqn.

Saro's Lerwick Mk I, here represented by a 209 Sqn example, was plagued by poor serviceability.

On 1 September 1939 the FAA had 232 aircraft, most of which could be considered as second-line in comparison with those of the RAF. The newest type in service was the Skua Mk II. The primary strike aircraft was the Fairey Swordfish Mk I biplane.

FAA duties

From the start of hostilities the FAA conducted anti-submarine patrols, with HMS *Ark Royal*, *Hermes* and *Courageous* in the north west and south west approaches under the Home Fleet. The carriers HMS *Furious*, *Glorious* and *Eagle* were stationed in the Atlantic, off Aden and in the East Indies respectively, with HMS *Albatross* in the Freetown sector. Early operations included those against the German supply ship *Altmark*. HMS *Furious* took part in the strikes in Narvik fjord in April, until relieved by HMS *Glorious* and HMS *Ark Royal*.

On 13 June 1940 *Ark Royal* sent a strike against the *Scharnhorst*: eight out of the 15 Skuas launched were shot down. The first torpedo strike on a German capital ship (*Scharnhorst*) was made without success on 21 June by Swordfish, whilst

Above: Of Coastal Command's aircraft only the Hudson Mk I could accurately release bombs or depth charges with the required spread or straddle across a submarine target.

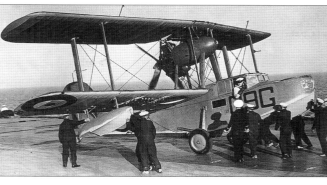

Right: Along with the Skua and Swordfish, the Fleet Air Arm flew reconnaissance types such as the Supermarine Walrus shown here and the Fairey Seafox.

throughout the period Skuas dive-bombed shipping off Bergen. During September and October 1940 *Furious* launched two strikes on Tromsö and Trondheim. After these operations it and HMS *Argus* were used to ferry US aircraft. With the loss of *Glorious* in June 1940, *Ark Royal* became the only available carrier in the Home Fleet.

Luftwaffe operations

At the start of the war the Luftwaffe's coastal reconnaissance and shipping defence force numbered about 228 aircraft, including Heinkel He 59Bs, He 60Cs and He 115A-1s, Dornier Do 18Ds and Arado Ar 196A-1s. One carrier, the *Graf Zeppelin*, was in existence but not completed.

In addition, 10. Fliegerdivision had been formed as a specialist fast bomber force with which to counter the RN on the high seas, and to attack it in its home ports. Initially only I. and II./KG 26 were assigned, with He 111P-2 bombers, and these started to assault coastal shipping, including fishing fleets, as early

This No. 240 Sqn Stranraer was photographed as it lifted off for a patrol in the period 1940-41. It has a 250-lb (110-kg) depth charge beneath each wing.

as September. On 26 September a Dornier of 2./KüFlGr 106 was sent by Marinegruppe West to reconnoitre the Great Fisher Bank area, where it sighted the Home Fleet's main force consisting of the battleships HMS *Nelson* and HMS *Rodney* and the carrier HMS *Ark Royal*: at 12.50 nine I./KG 26 He 111s were sent to intercept, these being joined by I./KG 30 Ju 88A-1 bombers. In the ensuing action four bombs straddled *Ark Royal*, or at least a ship identified as such, and the ship was reported to have sunk. *Ark Royal's* continued existence was then to the acute embarrassment of the Luftwaffe.

At 11.00 on 16 October I./KG 30 set off to attack Rosyth in the Firth of Forth: the Ju 88A-1s managed to inflict some damage on HMS *Edinburgh* and HMS *Southampton*, before being intercepted by the Spitfires of Nos 602 and 603 Sqns from Turnhouse, and No. 607 Sqn's Hawker Hurricanes from Drem. Two Ju 88A-1s were shot down. On the following day four Ju 88s attacked Scapa Flow where, in the face of heavy AAA fire, they

caused severe damage to HMS *Iron Duke*.

Mines and Condors

August 1939 saw General Coeler, an advocate of sea-mining, rise to the post of Führer der Luftstreitkräfte. His first attempts at getting authority for a mining force met little official attention, and so he formed his own small force. During the following month a few He 59B-2s started mining operations off East Anglian ports; these aircraft were later joined by faster Do 17Z-2s and He llIP-2s. Sinkings of shipping by mines laid by U-boats, E-boats and aircraft rose in number, however, losses were high as a result of the dangerous nature of the work; and British countermeasures, including the introduction of DWI (a covername, meaning Directional Wireless Installation) Wellington Mk IAs for the detection of magnetic mines, soon reduced the effectiveness of mining.

In November 1939, a reconnaissance Staffel was formed with the new long-range Fw 200C-0 Condor. In cooperation with KüFlGr 506, the Condors, now formed into 1./Kampfgeschwader 40, flew missions to the Faröes-Trondheim area on a regular basis to detect British naval reaction. The Stab and 1./KG 40 were forming at Oldenburg during this time with the definitive strike version of the Condor, the Fw 200C-1. By August 1940, the Condors were conducting numerous low-level attacks on unescorted shipping in the Western Approaches.

The fall of France and the German occupation of the Biscay ports revolutionised U-boat operations, with ocean- going Type VIICs now using the bases at Lorient, St Nazaire, Brest, La Pallice and Bordeaux, allowing them to range further into the Atlantic. The Führerweisung (Führer directive) of 17 August 1940, calling for unrestricted warfare against the UK, gave added impetus, and sinkings of merchant ships reached startling proportions. Doenitz now had sufficient numbers of U-boats at the Bay ports to resume the 'Wolfpack' tactics that had been attempted without success as early as October 1939. With his boats unhindered by enemy ships and aircraft, Doenitz also called for attacks by night and on the surface, where the U-boats could operate at speed without much chance of detection. In October 1940 Marinegruppe West, the command in charge of operations in the Atlantic, was largely responsible for the sinking of 63 ships totalling 352,000 GRT. Lacking aircraft of sufficient range to cover vulnerable convoys, Coastal Command was powerless, and even its subordination to the direct orders of the British Admiralty could do nothing to redress the situation.

With the United Kingdom now isolated and totally dependent upon the supply of oil, food, men and war material from overseas, the menace of the German U-boat now threatened its existence as a warring nation. Desperate measures were needed to combat this insidious danger.

This Do 18D-1 is finished in the 1939 colours of FFS (See). The type was used for reconnaissance and attack over the North Sea and off Norway in 1939 and early 1940.

One of the most important US aircraft to enter service with Coastal Command in 1941 was the Consolidated Catalina, which had a patrol endurance of over 15 hours.

Struggle for the sea lanes

By early 1941 Britain was starting to feel the full impact of U-boat and Fw 200 Condor attacks on its vital supply convoys. However, new technology and the introduction of long-range patrol aircraft helped Coastal Command close the 'Atlantic Gap'.

By the beginning of 1941 the severity of the UK's merchant ship losses in the Battle of the Atlantic was being felt. Hitherto merchant shipping strength had been made good by the redeployment of peacetime fleets, but now there was no further hope of meeting losses by this means: new ships were needed from the yards. Another doleful fact was that the U-boat establishment was being rapidly built up as the result of wartime construction programmes, and the supply far exceeded losses on operations. Combined with this was the corresponding shortage of Allied escort vessels.

For the British the threat of the U-boat menace was now clear. Training establishments devoted solely to anti-submarine warfare were set up, with the accent on the use of new weapons and tactics. New aids to detection were introduced. The primary detector, ASDIC (sonar), was improved and by July a long-range means of fixing W/T transmissions from U-boats was

being put into service, this being known as Huff-Duff. The main focus of U-boat and anti-shipping activity in 1941 was directed upon the convoys from Gibraltar and from the USA and Canada to the UK. In March 1941 the Luftwaffe formed two specialist reconnaissance and anti-shipping commands: Fliegerführer Atlantik, based at Lorient, operated over the Bay of Biscay and in the Western Approaches; and Fliegerführer Nord, based at Bodö, covered the northern sector.

Part of Fliegerführer Atlantik, KG 40, was based at Bordeaux-Merignac and Cognac with an average of eight Fw 200C-1 Condors available on a daily basis out of a strength of 20. The normal radius of the Fw 200 was 1,000 miles (1609 km), but 1,400 miles (2240 km) and an endurance of 14-16 hours was attainable with extra fuel tanks: normal bombload was four SC 250 250-kg (551-1b) bombs. On 9 February convoy HG.53 (Gibraltar-UK) was shadowed

and reported by *U-37*, and five Fw 200s of 2./KG 40 set off from Mérignac to rendezvous with the convoy. Five merchant ships were sunk by the Condors before they departed, with three others accounted for by *U-37*.

Condor strikes

In addition to shipping strikes, I./KG 40 flew shadowing patrols and a daily patrol on the route Merignac-Trondheim for spotting and weather reconnaissance. In February 1941 the bombers of IX Fliegerkorps and the Fw 200s of I./KG 40 sank a total of 27 Allied ships. But over the ensuing months losses, in particular with the He 111H-6 bombers of the new III./KG 40, rose alarmingly as merchant ships received heavy armament.

During the first half of 1941 it was primarily the threat from the U-boats, and to a lesser extent from the Condors, that caused the greatest concern to the Royal Navy and RAF Coastal Command. On 9 March RAF Bomber Command was ordered

to mount attacks on U-boat bases, construction yards, and industries associated with their manufacture. At this time Bomber Command posted Nos 107 and 114 Sqns to Coastal Command's control, as the first of many transfers. A new threat emanated on 22 March 1941 when the battle-cruisers *Scharnhorst* and *Gneisenau* docked at Brest for refit in the wake of a North Atlantic foray that had accounted for 22 ships. On the night of 30-31 March RAF Bomber Command started its offensive on these powerful ships at Brest, to which Coastal Command contributed in full: during an attack by Beaufort Mk Is of No. 22 Squadron on 6 April 1941, Flg Off Kenneth Campbell secured a hit on *Gneisenau* with a Mk XII torpedo. The Beaufort succumbed to Flak and crashed with the loss of the crew: Campbell was awarded a posthumous Victoria Cross for his gallantry. On 1 June the heavy cruiser *Prinz Eugen* joined the ships at Brest, and these

Above: A rearwards facing G.42 camera, fitted to a Coastal Command Whitley Mk V, captures one of the aircraft's depth charges exploding in the path of a U-boat in late-1941.

The Bristol Beaufort was undoubtably one of the hardest working types in Coastal Command service. The aircraft took a heavy toll on enemy seaborne and coastal units, but suffered heavy losses. Here, a line-up of Coastal Command Beauforts is loaded with mines.

Equipping eight operational Fleet Air Arm squadrons by mid-1941, the Fairey Fulmar was to play a vital and successful role in shadowing the Bismarck.

capital units, by their threat alone, occupied a major part of the Royal Navy's efforts.

Earlier, on 18 May, the powerful battleship *Bismarck* sailed from Gdynia in company with the *Prinz Eugen* on Operation Rheintibung. Their sailing was confirmed by a Martin Maryland of No. 771 Squadron, FAA. The Home Fleet sailed to intercept, with HMS *Victorious* (six Fairey Fulmar Mk Is of No. 800 and nine Fairey Swordfishes of No. 825 Sqns embarked) accompanying. After the loss of HMS *Hood*, *Victorious* launched a strike of nine Swordfish on 25 May, which secured a torpedo strike on *Bismarck's* armoured belt without damage. The Fulmars conducted shadowing patrols throughout the following day, when contact was lost, as a result of bad visibility, for the next 30 hours. On the morning of 26 May *Bismarck* was sighted by a Catalina Mk I and 45 minutes after this first contact, it ran foul of Force H, sent north from Gibraltar to assist in the search. Within this force, HMS *Ark Royal* embarked 24 Fulmars and 30 Swordfish: these were launched on an afternoon strike that went awry. Shortly after dusk another strike was flown off, with the Swordfishes attacking with the aid of airborne ASV.Mk II radar: two torpedo hits were made, the first doing no damage but the second putting *Bismarck's* steering gear out of action. Sailing an erratic course, but defending herself stoutly, *Bismarck* was finally sunk by surface ships at 10.40 on 27 May 1941.

Anti-ship strikes

The task of anti-shipping strikes on enemy coastal convoys was given to RAF Coastal Command in October 1940: the primary aim was to stop convoy traffic from Norway and Sweden to German ports, and in particular to Rotterdam, which served the Ruhr basin. During

the summer of 1940 Nos 22, 42 and 217 Sqns worked up on the Bristol Beaufort. But a task of such magnitude was too much for Coastal Command's limited resources, and by March 1941 No. 2 (Bomber) Group assisted by No. 11 (Fighter) Group had taken on the responsibility for 'Channel Stop', the operation designed to close the Straits of Dover to enemy traffic. Losses to Flak and enemy fighters were very high: between 1 April and 30 June 1941 No. 2 Group lost 36 Blenheims, with 52 Coastal Command Beauforts, Hudsons and Blenheims failing to return during the same period. As a result of these losses the anti-shipping strikes were reduced in number, while the accent on low-level bombing was lessened.

During the period 1 July to 31 December 1941 the RAF made attacks on 698 enemy ships, and made 41 known sinkings. A total of 123 aircraft was lost on these missions. The year of 1942 was but a few weeks old when, on 12 February 1942, the *Scharnhorst*, *Gneisenau* and *Prinz Eugen* made their daring passage of the Straits of Dover during their escape from Brest to German ports. In Operation 'Fuller', the British plan aimed at preventing such an escape, the Beauforts were given priority of

place. But such was the surprise achieved that the Beauforts of Nos 42, 86 and 217 Sqns were ill prepared. In time the Beauforts sorted out the various difficulties but, in the face of heavy fire and bad weather no hits were made and three were lost.

Additional aircraft

The strength of RAF Coastal Command rose from 564 aircraft at the start of the year to 676 on 1 July: new types in service included the Catalina Mk 1 and the Liberator Mk I (Very Long Range: VLR). These American types offered a dramatic increase in the Command's radius of action, but their numbers were small. Other aircraft in service as medium-range types included the Sunderland GR.Mk II flying-boat, the Wellington Mk IC and the Whitley Mk V.

By the summer of 1941 both the RAF's and Luftwaffe's patrol aircraft were equipped with Anti-Surface Vessel (ASV) radar. Trials were also in progress with a searchlight for the illumination of targets at night. Developed by Squadron Leader H. de V. Leigh as the Leigh Light, this equipment was to become essential to Coastal Command's night patrol aircraft.

Despite technical innovations, the successes for Coastal Command in 1941 were few. A

Catalina Mk I of No. 209 Sqn cooperated with naval forces in the sinking of *U-452* off Iceland on 25 August, and two days later, in an extraordinary episode, the crew of *U-570* surrendered to No. 269 (GR) Sqn's Hudsons, also off Iceland. Coastal Command's sole kill of the autumn occurred on 30 November, when a No. 502 Sqn Whitley Mk VII sank *U-206* in the Bay of Biscay: this was the first sinking of a U-boat achieved after ASV.Mk II contact.

On 14 December 1941, 32 ships set out from Gibraltar to England, with a heavy escort that included the escort carrier HMS *Audacity*: a converted German prize (the *Hannover* of 5,500 tons) which embarked eight Martlet fighters of No. 820 Sqn, FAA. These proved invaluable. On 17 December nine U-boats made their attacks, which endured on and off for the next four days. The losses were high with four U-boats sunk. In the course of these actions the Martlets downed two Fw 200s, but *Audacity* itself was torpedoed on the 22 December by *U-571* and lost. Despite the loss, this convoy was the first example of the use of round-the-clock air cover, from shore and shipborne aircraft, pioneering a tactic that would reap great benefits in 1942.

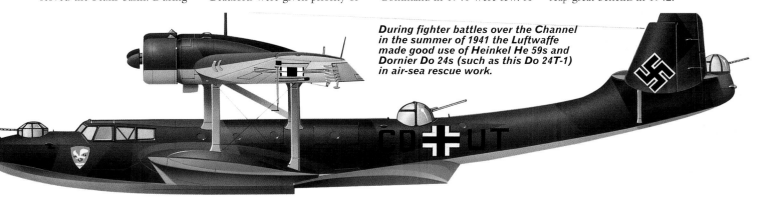

During fighter battles over the Channel in the summer of 1941 the Luftwaffe made good use of Heinkel He 59s and Dornier Do 24s (such as this Do 24T-1) in air-sea rescue work.

Liberators, such as this B-24D which was involved in the first Ploesti raid, were called upon to undertake some of the most dangerous and demanding missions of the war due to their great endurance, ruggedness and survivability.

Consolidated
B-24 Liberator

Despite being overshadowed by the B-17, the B-24 Liberator was, in fact, built in greater numbers than any other American aircraft of World War II, a remarkable feat for so large a machine.

The Consolidated B-24 Liberator is one of the best-known bombers of all time. The four-engined 'Lib', instantly recognisable in flight by its ultra-narrow Davis wing, fought almost everywhere and did almost everything during World War II. Yet men who flew the B-24 Liberator feel relegated to the shadows, eclipsed by the smaller and older bomber to which the Liberator is always compared, the B-17 Flying Fortress.

Four companies and five factories produced the Liberator in greater numbers than any other military aircraft ever manufactured in North America. The B-24 carried more bombs and went farther than the B-17, and Liberators also flew photo-reconnaissance missions and hauled cargo. The aircraft were a vital part of the crowded Eighth Air Force offensive against Germany and were sometimes alone fighting in the vast expanses of the Pacific. It is true to say that the war in China would have been lost but for Liberators transporting precious fuel into

A 15th Air Force B-24 heads home from a bombing mission over Europe. It can be seen here flying through the vapour trails of preceding formations returning to their bases in southern Italy.

China from India over the Himalayan 'Hump'.

A former Liberator pilot believes that the high-aspect 'fluid foil' wing patented by David R. Davis was the secret to success: "Without it", he says, "the Liberator wouldn't have been able to fly as far or as fast, nor carry as much as she did. Many of her virtues, as well as a good number of her faults can be traced directly to the wing: it gave the B-24 greater load-carrying capabilities than most other aircraft of her size, but also made her difficult to fly in formation. The wing helped make her faster but made her less manoeuvrable due to the [high] wing loading. It allowed her to fly farther, which made the B-24 the logical choice for Asia and the Pacific where missions were carried out at extreme ranges, and led to her being the only heavy bomber to be used in all theatres." Furthermore, says this pilot, the unique wing lent "grace and beauty to what admittedly became, in later models, a rather homely-looking aircraft". Even those who loved this bomber were rarely able to find beauty in it. Some called it, jokingly, "the packing box the B-17 came in".

A waist gunner on a Liberator draws attention to a message meant for inquisitive enemy fighter pilots: "If you can read this, you're too damned close."

Above: Serving for just four years, the B-24 had a mixed press. Described by some as the saviour of the Allied air forces, others referred it as a 'widow-maker', an object of pilots' fears. Some said that it was versatile and unmatched, others that it was ungainly and underpowered. While all these claims have some basis in reality, the B-24 made an indelible contribution to the war, devastating Axis targets.

Right: A number of Liberators were captured by the Germans during the war, and used for surveillance, transport and testing duties.

Development

At the beginning of World War II, the United States realised the need for a bomber that could strike further, drop more munitions and survive more punishment than the B-17. Even before this – in January 1939 – Major-General Henry H. 'Hap' Arnold, Commander-in-Chief, Army Air Corps, had foreseen the need for a bomber that could exceed 300 mph (483 km/h), with a range of 3,000 miles (4828 km) and a ceiling of 35,000 ft (10668 m). Apart from its unique wing, the Consolidated bomber was distinguished by a tricycle undercarriage, twin rudder and fin assembly, and a big, slab-sided fuselage that seemed spacious when compared to other bombers.

In 1942, an AAF (Army Air Forces) training manual on the Liberator told student pilots that 'the B-24, when properly used, has no equal in any air force. It has proved itself capable of delivering tremendous blows against the enemy over extremely long ranges, under unfavourable weather conditions and against heavy enemy opposition. If the gunners are properly trained, they can create havoc among enemy fighters.'

Short life

The Liberator was not fully developed when the war broke out, and essentially obsolete by the time it ended. At one juncture, the industrial heartland that produced almost 100,000 aircraft in 1944 was turning out a new B-24 bomber every 51 minutes, but the bomber was built more for immediacy than for durability and would be gone from service in only a few years.

Some said that the B-24 was hard to fly, demanding the best of a skilled pilot. Despite its roomy interior, the Liberator could seem cramped and, at altitude, it was always cold. On their worst missions, Liberator crews were battered about inside their cramped confines, numbed by bone-chilling temperatures, and stalked by flak and fighters. Still, a 'Lib' would often survive battle damage and bring its crew home, sometimes with its controls so badly damaged that the aircraft had to land on autopilot. As one crew member, searching for the essence of the B-24 Liberator, put it very simply: "This was the workhorse of all the bombers."

The Liberator was well prepared for fighter attacks, armed with various combinations of .50-cal. (12.7-mm) and sometimes .30-cal. (7.62-mm) machine-guns. Because of its greater capabilities, it was usually assigned the toughest, longest missions. The Liberator was one of the few land-based bombers used in the Pacific theatre because it could handle the long flights with no emergency landing fields available.

Many decades after the war, the grandson of a Liberator flier, First Lieutenant Charles T. Voyles, summarised everything about this bomber that mattered to his family. Never mind the wingspan or the bombload, he said: "The most important aspect of the B-24 to me is that my grandfather and nine of his brothers–in–arms climbed into their 'plane, nicknamed the *Phantom Renegade*, 30 times and risked their lives. They left homes, jobs, wives and children to go half way around the world to fight for what they believed in. The B-24 symbolises the dedication of a generation that is quickly passing away."

Artwork on B-24s was both colourful and plentiful and helped to increase morale and team spirit. This tired B-24J, 44-40973, **The Dragon and His Tail,** *was part of the 64th BS of the 43 BG in the Pacific theatre.*

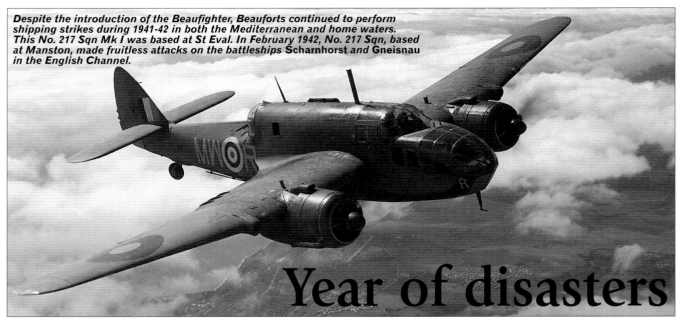

Despite the introduction of the Beaufighter, Beauforts continued to perform shipping strikes during 1941-42 in both the Mediterranean and home waters. This No. 217 Sqn Mk I was based at St Eval. In February 1942, No. 217 Sqn, based at Manston, made fruitless attacks on the battleships Scharnhorst and Gneisnau in the English Channel.

Year of disasters

On 7 December 1941, Japan attacked the US Pacific Fleet at Pearl Harbor, with the Axis declaring war on America three days later. With the world at war, U-boats were given a new opportunity for kills.

With the entry of the US into the war, Doenitz selected a force of 12 U-boats for operations off the American coast. From 16 December 1941 five U-boats departed Biscay ports for Operation Paukenschlag (drumbeat). First blood was drawn on 12 January when *U-123* sank SS *Cyclops* to the east of Cape Cod, and thereafter mayhem reigned. Air and sea escorts were weak, while the U-boats blasted ships only a few miles off the shores of the US. In February U-boat operations began in the Caribbean, aimed at sinking ships and shelling the oil refineries at Aruba and Curacao.

American ASW forces were inadequate along the US eastern coastline. With war in the Pacific now aflame, US involvement in the Battle of the Atlantic was seen as secondary. In January 1942 patrol and ASW work on the Atlantic seaboard was shared between the USN and the USAAF. The USN had few long-range aircraft and defences were restricted to Patrol Wing 3's four squadrons for coverage of the Gulf of Mexico and parts of the Caribbean. The US Army's 1 Bomber Command had only 46 aircraft fit for ASW work: these included B-17Es, B-18As and B-25Bs. Originally only the 2nd BG remained in January, but the 3rd, 13th, 45th and 92nd BGs became operational during February and March.

On 1 April 1942 US Navy ASW aircraft numbered 86, and those of I Bomber Command 84

along the Eastern Sea Frontier; several units were now based at Argentia, Newfoundland. The defences of the Gulf Sea Frontier were sparser: 19 US Army O-47s, together with two ASV.Mk II radar–equipped B-18As.

American successes

By May 1942 the USN insisted on all shipping being formed into convoys while in its operational area, and Doenitz's 'boats found it harder to reap the rewards that had once been won so easily, and moved away from the shores and into deeper water. On 1 March 1942 a VP-82 PBO Hudson sank *U-656* off Newfoundland in the first US airborne kill.

The specialist 1st Sea-Search Attack Group (SSAG) was formed on 8 June 1942, with its 2nd Squadron deploying B-18As with ASV.Mk II; in December the 3rd Squadron SSAG was formed with B-24Ds for trials with centimetric SCR-517 radar.

The total strength of patrol aircraft on 31 July 1942 was 141 USAAF and 178 USN aircraft, plus seven Goodyear F-4 blimps. Shipping losses in total amounted to 585,000 tons during the period from January to June 1942, and only 21 U-boats were sunk. Of these only six fell to US aircraft and escorts. Small wonder that this epoch was the second *Glücklichezeite* (happy time) for Doenitz's men. But with convoys in use and better escorts, the rich pickings were over.

Above: This U-boat was attacked by a Coastal Command Sunderland in the Bay of Biscay. The Sunderland's rear-facing cameras caught the lethal straddle of depth charges.

RAF Coastal Command

With a strength of 633 aircraft in 37½ squadrons on 1 January 1942, Coastal Command was committed to ASW work in the Bay of Biscay, in the North Atlantic, and from Gibraltar; at the same time, strikes on enemy shipping were flown at every opportunity. In the field of U-boat warfare the record was very disappointing in the first half of the year. This was due in part to a lack of U-boat activity in the theatres in which Coastal Command operated: despite constant patrols, UK-based units failed to score once. A breakthrough came in June 1942 when No. 172 Sqn started night patrols over the Bay with ASV.Mk II and the powerful Leigh Light: current German practice was to make the transit at night and on the surface. On 5

The flight deck of a No. 10 (RAAF) Sqn Sunderland, based at Mount Batten, Plymouth. In 1942, No. 10 Sqn was joined by another RAAF Sunderland anti-submarine unit, No. 466 Sqn.

In 1942, the US Navy's principal long- and medium-range patrol aircraft were the PBY-5 Catalina (left) and PV-1 Ventura, respectively. These examples operated over the Pacific Ocean from the Aleutian Islands.

July *U-502* was sunk by a Wellington GR.Mk VIII, the first kill so achieved.

Doenitz then took the extraordinary step of ordering transits on the surface by day in an attempt to clear the area as quickly as possible, and only four 'boats were lost between June and September. In addition, the U-boats now carried the Metox 600A (FuMB 1) device that could pick up ASV.Mk II transmissions. As the result of Metox, sightings in the Bay numbered two, whilst only one was obtained in October: this, however, resulted in the sinking of *U-216*.

Allied convoys to the Soviet Union via the Arctic Circle to Murmansk and Archangel started in August 1941, and continued throughout the autumn and spring of 1942. From Iceland Nos 269 and 330 (Norwegian) Sqns gave cover for the first 500 miles (800 km) and thereafter the ships and escorts were on their own. An awful threat also lay in the battleship *Tirpitz*, plus the *Scheer* and *Hipper*, which were stationed

at Trondheim. The FAA flew a number of strikes in the area: on 9 March, Nos 817 and 832 Sqns, FAA, flew their Albacores against *Tirpitz* to score two torpedo hits. This so alarmed Hitler that he ordered *Tirpitz* never again to put out when an Allied carrier was in the vicinity.

Convoy battles

Until March 1942 losses to German aircraft were minimal: that month Göering ordered Luftflotte V to devote greater energy to attacking the Russian convoys. Luftflotte V intervened against convoys PQ-13, PQ-14 and PQ-15 during March and April, claiming seven ships sunk. The major sea-air battles started after PQ-16 left Iceland on 21 May 1942, as PQ-12 left Murmansk. During the period 25-30 May PQ-16 came under attack from the Ju 88A-4s of KG 30, and the torpedo-bombers of I./KG 26. Seven out of the 35 merchantmen were sunk. The fact that PQ-16 got through however was too much for Hitler, and he ordered

that the next convoy was to be attacked by overwhelming forces of U-boats and aircraft.

During, the next few weeks the forces of Fliegerführer Lofoten and Fliegerführer Nord-Ost conserved their forces, and received reinforcement. Aircraft at their disposal consisted of 80 Ju 88A-4s; 45 He 111H-6 torpedo-bombers; BV 138B-1s, Fw 200C-4s and He 115C-4 torpedo-floatplanes.

This force was backed up by Ju 87B-2s and recce Ju 88D-1s. Recent operations had proved the tactics of mass torpedo drops, with the bombers approaching down-sun from out of the Arctic gloom, to comb the convoy's track whilst at the same time AA fire was distracted by the arrival of level-bombing Ju 88s: the mass torpedo attack was referred to as the *goldene Zange* (golden comb) tactic. The attack force numbered about 264 bomber and reconnaissance aircraft.

Loaded with equipment for Russia, PQ-17 consisting of 33 vessels, sailed from Iceland on 27 June 1942. It was not until 18.00 on 2 July that the first air attack took place, when eight He 115s made an abortive torpedo strike. The escort was already fully engaged in combatting numerous U-boat attacks. On 4 July the PQ-17 was attacked three times from the air. Late that evening, the escorting vessels were called off to counter a perceived surface threat, leaving the merchantmen to fend for themselves. The result was a massacre on a scale that exceeded

all of World War II's convoy battles. When the final count was taken 23 ships had been sunk.

A long period ensued before PQ-18 sailed. When it did, it was covered by USSR-based RAF fighters and ASW aircraft and sailed with a major escort force including HMS *Avenger* with its Sea Hurricane fighters. When the convoy finally reached Murmansk, some 13 vessels had been sunk, but the loss of 41 aircraft of Luftflotte V's limited forces was too much. It was the last major conflict in the Arctic seas, and thereafter, with Luftwaffe torpedo-bombers much needed in the Mediterranean, relative peace returned to these sullen and icy waters.

In July Doenitz ordered his U-boat packs to concentrate their efforts in the Atlantic Gap, beyond the range of Allied aircraft. In June U-boats sank 144 Allied ships (700,000 GRT), and Doenitz calculated that if an average of 800,000 tons of Allied shipping could be sunk each month, an Axis victory was certain. This average tonnage was not to be obtained throughout 1942, for the true figure was slightly less than 650,000 tons per month. Yet even this appaling statistic was a crippling rate of loss. Losses continued to mount into October, at which time the Allies were faced with the imminent landings of Operation Torch on the coasts of French North West Africa. In the minds of many Allied leaders a well-founded sense of foreboding reigned.

Atlantic adversaries

The Heinkel He 115 and Consolidated Liberator represented differing approaches to the maritime patrol task. The German floatplane design had the advantage of not being dependent on a shore base from which to operate, while the Liberator benefited from its origins as a heavy bomber and was bestowed with excellent range performance.

He 115C-1
Wearing improvised winter camouflage, this He 115C-1 served with 1./KuFlGr 406, based at Sörreisa, near Tromso, in 1942. This unit, together with 1./KuFlGr 906, carried out the first torpedo attacks on the ill-fated PQ-17 convoy.

Liberator GR.Mk I
Twenty Consolidated Model 32 patrol aircraft were supplied to the RAF in 1941. Converted to Liberator GR.Mk I standard, they were first issued to No. 120 Sqn at Aldergrove. With full main tanks, the Mk I had a patrol radius of 2,300 miles (3700 km). AM926, 'F-Freddie' of No. 120 Sqn, carries a ventral pack of four 20-mm cannon, and forwards and sideways-looking, ASU. Mk II radar.

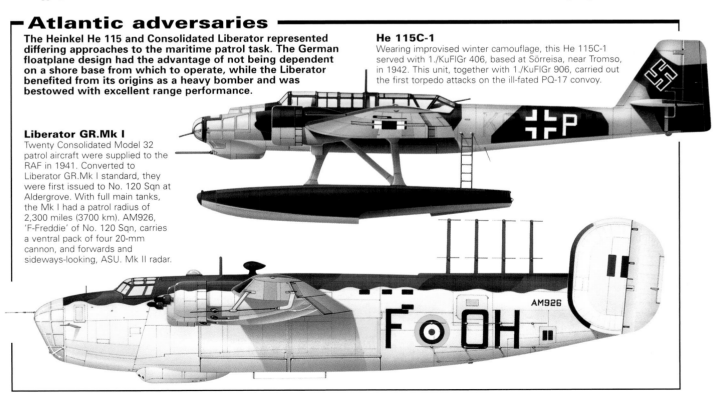

Defeat into Victory

A key element in the U-boat war was the CVE (escort carrier). As well as Wildcat fighters, which could ward off the Fw 200 long-range patrollers, the CVEs carried Grumman TBF-1 Avengers which hunted for U-boats.

During the course of 1942 the depredations of the U-boats had the Allies on the rack, but during the next year the tide of fortune was turned away from the Kriegsmarine.

On 8 November 1942 American and British land forces, conveyed by a huge concourse of shipping, landed on the shores of French North West Africa at Oran, Algiers and Casablanca. On the orders of the Befehlshaber der U-boote (Admiral Karl Doenitz), U-boats were transferred from the Atlantic and Cape Verde areas. The first U-boats arrived in the new theatre of operations as early as 11 November.

In anticipation of the Axis U-boat reaction off the shores of North West Africa, several units of RAF Coastal Command were sent to Gibraltar with Leigh Light-equipped Vickers Wellington GR.Mk VIIIs, Lockheed Hudson GR.Mk III/VIs, Catalina Mk IIBs and Short Sunderland GR.Mk IIIs. These bolstered the units equipped with Hudsons and Fairey Swordfishes already based on Gibraltar. Most, if not all, were equipped wifh ASV Mk II shipping detection radar equipment. Constant air patrols kept Doenitz's U-boats under great pressure throughout the Torch landings and the subsequent follow-up operations.

Following the initial activity after Torch and the firm establishment of Allied forces in North West Africa, BdU called off his U-boats on 23 December 1942 after the loss of seven in return for disappointing results. Operations within the range of

Allied shore-based aircraft were too risky in this theatre: Doenitz ordered a return to the Atlantic theatre.

The successful conclusion of the amphibious phase of Torch at once released huge numbers of Allied escort vessels for service in the North Atlantic and elsewhere. This factor, joined with the resolution to defeat the U-boat at all costs taken at Casablanca in January 1943, was instrumental in turning defeat into victory in the Atlantic during the course of the new year. Other considerations also came into play, including tighter command, better convoy routes and co-ordination, more efficient sea escorts, and greater numbers of very long-range (VLR) patrol aircraft.

As early as 29 April 1941, the British Admiralty requested the conversion of six C-3 Liberty hulls for fighter aircraft-carriers specifically for convoy protection: five of these conversions (HMS *Archer*, *Avenger*, *Biter*, *Dasher* and *Tracker*) came into service in 1943 with a usual complement of Grumman Martlets (Wildcats) and Fairey Swordfish.

The first Carrier Escort Vessels (CVE) produced for the United States Navy were the USS *Long Island*, *Charger*, *Bogue*, *Card*, *Croatan* and *Block Island*. Aircraft complement was a maximum of 16 Grumman F4F-4 or General Motors FM-1 Wildcat fighters and 12 Grumman TBF-1

Avenger bombers. British and American CVEs, and converted merchantmen known as Merchant Aircraft Carriers (MAC), were a vital complement to the Support Groups during 1943, when the Allies finally launched an all-out offensive against the German U-boat.

Maritime air forces

RAF Coastal Command remained committed to the primary task of U-boat patrols in the Atlantic, in the Bay of Biscay and in the Northern Transit Area (Farøes-Norway): its secondary task was a campaign against surface shipping with Bristol Beaufighters, Hudsons and Handley Page Hampdens. In the war against the U-boat the most vital aircraft were the VLR Liberator Mk I, IIIA and V, which equipped only three units at the turn of the year (52 aircraft). These, with a radius of 1,150 miles (2130 km), were the only aircraft able to close a portion of the 'Atlantic Gap' from bases in Iceland and Newfoundland. All were equipped with ASV Mk II and had additional tankage. By January 1943 these formidable VLR aircraft were backed by five squadrons of long-range (LR) types: Liberator GR.Mk V, Boeing Fortress GR.Mk IIA, and Handley Page Halifax GR.Mk II. The medium-range (MR) force included 13 squadrons of Hudsons, Whitleys and Wellingtons; 10 squadrons of Catalina Mk IBs and Sunderland GR.Mk I/IIIs were also available. Strike aircraft now included the Beaufighter Mk

VIC, TF.Mk X and Mk XIC, which replaced the Hampdens and Bristol Beauforts.

In 1943 the most important radar aids to come into service were the 10-cm ASV Mk III and Mk IV equipments, which could detect a U-boat on the surface at a maximum range of 12 miles (19.4 km). Once again U-boat crews were soon being surprised by enemy aircraft by day and night while on the surface, and a new phase of the anti-submarine war had commenced. The Leigh light (or American L-7 light) again rendered invaluable assistance in detecting the small target.

During 1942/43 the slow and cumbersome Hampdens and Beauforts gave way to the excellent Beaufighter in the units attacking German coastal shipping. The Mk VIC 'Torbeau', which entered service in November 1942, could carry a single Mk XV torpedo with little effect on performance.

American commitment

The threat of the U-boat menace forced the US Navy to maintain a strong complement of maritime aircraft based on the eastern seaboard of the United States, and at stations in the Caribbean, Brazil, Panama and Cuba, and on the island of Bermuda. The VLR types included the PB4-Y Liberator and PB2Y-3 Coronado. Long-range types included the Consolidated PBY-5 Catalina, the Martin PBM-1 Mariner, and the Lockheed PV-1 Ventura.

Notwithstanding the Allies' resolve with improved equipment and added strength, Doenitz still held the initiative in the Atlantic. In March 1943 came the climactic battle of Convoys HX.229 and SC.122, in which Doenitz claimed his greatest victory. A strong force of U-boats was concentrated ahead of the convoys in the area of 50° North and 40° West. The two great convoys, each assailed by a powerful force of U-boats, gradually merged into one, and in the course of the next four days 21 ships (140,842 GRT) out of the 98 which had sailed from New York were sunk by U-boats. Only one U-boat was lost when the battered convoys finally reached the area of air cover. For Doenitz and his crews it was a signal victory.

In the shadow of an impending defeat at sea the decisions taken at the March 1943 Washington Conference were significant. Firstly, a reorganised system of convoy and escort routing came into effect. Secondly, the command structure was tightened. Anti-submarine air units were strengthened on the American eastern seaboard, and to cover convoys arriving in the Mediterranean from the United States the Moroccan Sea Frontier was set up, initially with the 480th AS Group.

Battles in the Bay

The primary task of No. 19 Group, led by Air Vice-Marshal G. R. Bromet, was to attack surfaced U-boats in transit in the Bay of Biscay, a function that had been carried out since the early months of 1942. However, the results gained had been poor: only seven U-boat kills had been effected by RAF aircraft in the Bay up to January 1943. In February, however, U-boat crews began to experience surprise attacks by Allied aircraft fitted with the new, undetectable, centimetric radar. There now followed frantic efforts by the Germans to develop a new countermeasure.

Doenitz's crews came under constant pressure during Bay transits, and he now took the unprecedented step of ordering his U-boats to remain surfaced by day and to fight it out with AA armament. This tactic proved costly. During May 1943 RAF Coastal Command, now led by Air Marshal J. C. Slessor, made 98 sightings in the Bay and sank six U-boats in 64 attacks. These losses contributed significantly to what was an extraordinary change in fortune for Doenitz in the Atlantic.

Hoping to repeat the success of March, Doenitz concentrated his U-boats in the North Atlantic in April, but during that month the BdU could claim only 245,000 GRT for the loss of 15

*Above: **O**n the British escort carriers the Fairey Swordfish Mk II was the main strike aircraft. Here Fleet Air Arm officers check the nose fuse of a torpedo aboard HMS Battler in 1943.*

Below: Fernaufklärungsgruppe 5 at Mont-de-Marsan first used the Ju 290 for long-range patrols in October 1943. Equipped with FuG 200 Hohentwiel maritime search radar, the giants provided target information for the U-boats. This is a Ju 290A-5.

of his U-boats. Further convoy attacks met with stiff resistance from the escort carriers, and many U-boats were sunk.

May: the turning point

A maximum effort was made against convoy SC.130 between 15 and 20 May 1943 with four 'wolf packs' involved: the result was a disaster. Five U-boats were lost without the sinking of a single Allied ship. For Doenitz the losses against increasingly efficient aircraft and sea escorts were unbearable, and it transpired that SC.130 was the last convoy to be threatened seriously by his crews. On 24 May 1943 Doenitz ordered his U-boats out of the North Atlantic patrol beats either to base or to the southern sector where conditions were supposed to be quieter. On this day the Battle of the Atlantic was won and lost, for in just over eight weeks from a great victory, the Kriegsmarine's U-boat arm had ceded the initiative to the Allies.

Coastal Command support

Although it was the VLR Liberator, serving with the RAF, US Navy and USAAF, which was the aircraft which turned the tide of the Atlantic war in the favour of the Allies, there were numerous other converted bomber types employed on shorter-range missions. Many of these aircraft had earlier served with Bomber Command, but had been rendered surplus by the entry into service of more capable aircraft.

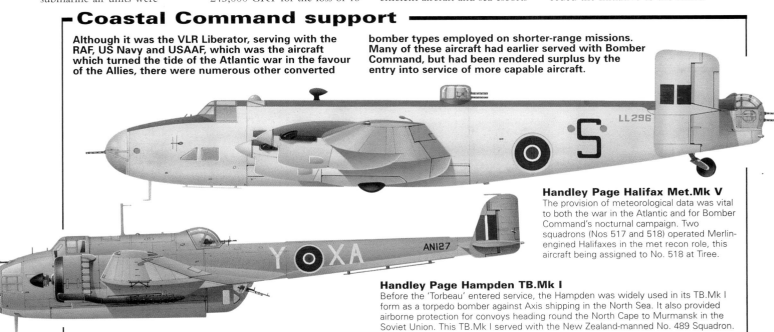

Handley Page Halifax Met.Mk V
The provision of meteorological data was vital to both the war in the Atlantic and for Bomber Command's nocturnal campaign. Two squadrons (Nos 517 and 518) operated Merlin-engined Halifaxes in the met recon role, this aircraft being assigned to No. 518 at Tiree.

Handley Page Hampden TB.Mk I
Before the 'Torbeau' entered service, the Hampden was widely used in its TB.Mk I form as a torpedo bomber against Axis shipping in the North Sea. It also provided airborne protection for convoys heading round the North Cape to Murmansk in the Soviet Union. This TB.Mk I served with the New Zealand-manned No. 489 Squadron.

Equipped with Avengers, to attack marauding U-Boats and F4F Wildcats (seen here), and to counter attacks by Luftwaffe patrol aircraft, the US Navy and Royal Navy (seen here) escort carriers made a major impact in reducing the horrendous losses suffered by Allied shipping in the Atlantic.

Triumph of the carriers

By the spring of 1943 the Allies were suffering unsustainable losses to Admiral Doenitz's 'wolf packs'. However, by the year's end, improved airborne radar, growing numbers of long-range patrol aircraft and, most importantly, the advent of escort carriers helped decimate the once powerful U-boat force.

This remarkable shift in fortunes, which gave the Allies the initiative in the Battle of the Atlantic, took many months to achieve. The first major triumph took place in May 1943, when an unsurpassed total of U-boats (41) was sunk. Maritime aircraft scored several successes during this month both in the Bay of Biscay and in the Atlantic ocean. The RAF and the US Navy, using Consolidated Liberators and Catalinas, were at last beginning to close the Atlantic Gap where so many ships had succumbed to U-boat attacks. But it was the appearance of escort and light carriers that set the seal on Doenitz's attempts to restore the balance at sea.

As early as March 1943, the 14,000-ton USS *Bogue* gave cover to convoys with her complement of Grumman F4F Wildcats and Grumman TBF Avenger bombers. The Royal Navy's HMS *Biter* and *Archer* entered operations in the Atlantic in April and May 1943 respectively: *Biter's* No. 811 Sqn shared in the destruction of two U-boats in May. *Bogue's* first kill took place on 22 May 1943 and her record, which was to be a remarkable one, showed what could be achieved against U-boat

packs with constant aerial cover. On 21 May, when *Bogue* was 520 miles (835 km) south east of Cape Farewell, *U-231* was attacked and damaged by TBFs to the extent that she had to set course back to Lorient. On the next day, another TBF chanced upon U-305 which was strafed forcing her to return to Brest. That afternoon *U-569* was located by *Bogue* some 20 miles (32 km) on the port quarter, and attacked by a TBF with four bombs. She crash-dived, and on surfacing later she received another dose from a TBF, which was circling directly overhead. After a terrifying plummet to 350 ft (94 m), *U-569* blew her tanks, rose to the surface and surrendered. It was *Bogue's* first kill, but she had located or attacked no less than four different U-boats.

In addition to 'conventional' weapons, the Allies received the first aerial homing (acoustic) torpedo in May 1943. This was the US-developed Mk 24, which

Beaufighter Mk VICs of RAF Coastal Command, launch a cannon and rocket attack on German escort vessels. The Beaufighter combined impressive armament with impressive performance.

was passed first to No. 120 Sqn, the RAF and to the USS *Santee* which embarked on her first Atlantic tour on 13 June. *Santee's* complement was VC-29, with TBF-1s and Douglas SBD-5 Dauntlesses. In addition to *Bogue* and *Santee*, the US 10th Fleet allocated the USS *Core* and USS *Card* to Atlantic operations in late June and July respectively. The four CVEs were to wreak havoc on the U-boat 'wolf packs' now centred in the Azores sector.

Bitter battles

Depredations by Allied aircraft on the U-boat transit routes in the Bay of Biscay in May had a salutory effect on Doenitz, who ordered crews to fight it out on

the surface with improved anti-aircraft guns. *U-441* set out from Brest on 8 June 1943 and to her misfortune she encountered on 12 June not a slow maritime patrol aircraft, but three Beaufighter Mk VICs of No. 248 Sqn, and after being severely strafed she was forced to put back to Brest. Despite the inherent difficulties of shooting from an unsteady platform, other U-boat crews reaped more success and several Allied aircraft were either shot down or crippled. From 12 June onwards the U-boats made group transits of the Bay using the mutual protection of Flak. The U-boats were often afforded fighter cover by the Junkers Ju 88C-6s of V/KG 40 based at

Equivalent to, but not as capable as the RAF's Sunderland, Blohm und Voss Bv 222s were used to conduct 'convoy hunting' patrols in the Bay of Biscay from their base on Biscarrosse lake.

Top: Armed with rockets, or as seen here a torpedo, the Bristol Beaufighter was a potent weapon against littoral targets such as Doenitz's U-boats transitting from their base into the Atlantic.

Above: In December 1942 the first of some 1,200 Lockheed PV-1s to be operated by the US Navy was delivered. The majority of Venturas were assigned to bomber rather than patrol squadrons.

Mérignac and Kerlin Bastard (Lorient). Units available in May 1943 included the Stab and III/KG 40 with Focke-Wulf Fw 200C-4 Condors at Cognac and Mérignac. In addition, a number of Fw 190A-5 fighters had been relocated by August to fend off wayward Coastal Command aircraft that ventured too close to the Biscay ports. In September the II/ZG 1, equipped with Messerschmitt Bf 110G-2 fighters, was installed at Lanveoc-Poulmic near Brest. The Gruppe fared badly against No. 10 Group's Spitfires in battles off Ushant, and by mid-October losses rendered the Gruppe non-operational.

On 24 May 1943 Doenitz ordered his U-boats south to get away from the troublesome North Atlantic and the Bay of Biscay. Two days later the 17-strong U-boat Gruppe lined up from north to south along the 43° West meridian athwart the crowded sea lanes from North America to the Mediterranean. But the US Navy was ready. In addition to the escort carrier USS *Bogue*, the USS *Card* went on her first convoy escort mission. The escort pattern provided by the TBF-1s and Wildcats consisted of round-the-clock surveillance to up to 250 miles (400 km) ahead and to the sides of the convoys. *Bogue* took up station with a westbound convoy on 1 June, and scored against the Gruppe on 5 June, when *U-217* was located some 63 miles (101 km) north west of the carrier and sunk by a TBF assisted by a Wildcat. One week later *Bogue* sank *U-118*

south west of the Azores. During June, American ships and aircraft accounted for five out of the 17 U-boats lost by Doenitz, and of these the Catalina-equipped VP-84 scored two. Four U-boat kills went down in the Bay of Biscay as more and more sea escorts ventured into this area, following Doenitz' withdrawal from the North Atlantic. U-boat crews were now fighting stoutly with their AA guns in actions that were costly to both sides. Then came the slaughter of July.

Allied successes

U-462, a tanker, was forced to return to port after a savage fight with aircraft on 2 July. In the next six days four U-boats were sunk in the Bay: Liberator GR.Mk IIIs of Nos 53 and 224 Sqns accounted for three, with the last falling to No. 172 Sqn. Between 7 and 9 July, the 1st and 2nd SSA Squadrons (US Army) and No. 179 Sqn sank three U-boats off Portugal and in the western approaches of the Mediterranean.

By this time two Staffeln of Ju 290s had begun regular patrols via Finisterre and Cap Ortegal to Gibraltar, and as far south as the Canaries, and to the Azores in search of convoys. Shorter patrols were operated by the Blohm und Voss Bv 138C-1s (plus a few Bv 222 flying-boats) from Biscarosse lake. These reconnaissance units enabled KG 40 to revert to the offensive role with the new Henschel Hs 293 radio-controlled glide-bomb (installed on Fw 200C-6 types) fitted with a 1,102-lb (500-kg)

warhead. The first success with the Hs 293 took place on 27 August 1943, when II/KG 100, on detachment from X Fliegerkorps with Do 217E-5s, sank HMS *Egret* off Cap Ortegal. During the autumn months several attacks on Allied shipping were made with these weapons, but losses were high.

The Allies did not have everything their own way. Luftwaffe heavy fighters operating in the Bay caused Coastal Command to lose on average one aircraft per day during the summer of 1943, and for this reason Beaufighter Mk VICs began to cover this area from No. 19 Group. Several combats ensued, with heavy losses to both sides.

The US Army Air Force was already heavily committed in all theatres of war, and for this reason it was relieved of its anti-submarine task on the disbanding of Anti-Submarine Command in October 1943.

American CVE groups continued to operate in the central sector of the Atlantic during October 1943. On 4 October a minor triumph resulted when *U-336* was sunk by a Liberator of VB-128 when east of

Cape Farewell, while VC-9 Squadron, based on USS *Card*, sank *U-460* and *U-422* to the north of the Azores. USS *Card* followed up her success with *U-402* on 13 October and *U-584* on the last day of October, while in the meantime USS *Block Island* despatched *U-220* off Flemish Cap on 28 October. In desperation Doenitz ordered direct transit across the Bay of Biscay, and during November and December numerous combats took place, with U-boat crews and Ju 88C-6s pitted against the Liberators, Sunderlands and Halifaxes of No. 19 Group, Coastal Command, and the PB4Ys of the US Navy's VB-103.

After the loss of 19 U-boats in November, bad weather and aggressive Luftwaffe fighter activity brought actions to a reduced state until 13 December, when No. 58 Sqn sank *U-391* in the Bay; she was one of only eight lost that month.

By the end of 1943, the sinkings of Allied merchant vessels were down to an average of 30 per month, representing about 130,000 tons, and these figures when compared to the grotesque losses of March 1943 when the Allies lost 120 ships (693,389 tons), give ample indication of the extent of Doenitz's defeat. From 1 May to 31 December 1943, losses amounted to 215 U-boats. For the Allies the year 1943 started in crisis with a defeat narrowly avoided in March, but strength and equipment had reached maturity to stave off defeat and reap victory during May. The ensuing battles there were the proof that never again would the menace of the U-boat threaten to engulf the Allied cause.

Serving aboard both US Navy and Royal Navy escort carriers, the Grumman Avenger proved deadly in the anti-U-boat role. This example served with No.846 Squadron at Machrihanish.

The final stages

From the end of 1943, Allied naval and air forces were dominant in the long and bitter struggle at sea. U-boats were being hunted all the way from their bases to the convoys, and new weapons and tactics meant that their chances of survival were not good.

Above: Allied strike aircraft wreaked havoc on German coastal shipping in the last two years of the war. This tanker has been set alight in the Skagerrak in October 1944.

Left: Beaufighters of RAF Coastal Command mob a German 'M-type' minesweeper. It had been escorting an eight-ship convoy off Borkum, in the Friesian Islands, on 25 August 1944.

In 1943, Grossadmiral Karl Doenitz lost 237 of his submarines, as compared to 87 in the year before. Allied shipping losses were more than halved, from 1,665 ships totalling 7,795,097 tons to 597 vessels of 3,220,137 tons. This German catastrophe was brought about by new Allied support groups, improved escorts, escort carriers, and well-equipped maritime air forces. Allied navies accounted for 67 U-boats, while 116 were sunk by Allied patrol aircraft, RAF Coastal Command sank 83 'boats, and a further 31 were claimed by US patrol aircraft, plus another two shared by American and British air units. Warplanes from American escort carriers sank 23 out of the 24 U-boats claimed by carrierborne aircraft.

At the beginning of 1944 the Befelshaber der U-Boote (Flag Officer submarines, or BdU) had 168 U-boats operational out of a total of 436 in commission, with about 60 at sea all over the Atlantic and into the Indian Ocean. Production was brisk, with 78 new boats commissioned in the previous quarter. Allied bombing of U-boat construction yards had not been effective even in reducing production, let alone halting it; crews were well trained and plentiful in supply. Even so, the U-boats were at a severe disadvantage, despite the recent introduction of new equipment such as the Schnorkel.

In January Doenitz sent 24 'boats to blockade the British western approaches, operating submerged for most of the time. The lack of air reconnaissance meant that they received few convoy reports, and the BdU later ordered the boats closer in to the Irish coast. This order was picked up by the British, who deployed hunter groups and aircraft reinforcements.

Allies meet the threat

The new AOC-in-C Coastal Command, Air Chief Marshal Sir William Sholto-Douglas, sent large numbers of aircraft to No. 15 Group in Ulster and Scotland. The U-boats began to attack on 27 January but RAF and US Navy patrol aircraft, together with the ships of the Royal Navy, were waiting.

On 26 February Doenitz had an audience with Hitler, bitterly accusing the Luftwaffe of failing to provide both reconnaissance, upon which he now relied almost totally, and escorts for the Bay transits. He also asked for the stepping up of production of the new high-speed Type XXI and Type XXIII U-boats. He received Hitler's sympathy but little else. On 22 March Doenitz called an end to the offensive: in two months 36 U-boats had been lost.

RAF Coastal Command's strike and torpedo bomber units continued to harry enemy shipping off Norway and in the North Sea during 1943-44. They were now equipped with rockets, armed with either 60-lb (27-kg) semi-armour piercing/high explosive or a 25-lb (11.30-kg) armour piercing warheads. The first mission with rockets was flown on 22 June 1943, and thereafter regular attacks took place.

Big-gun Mosquitoes

One unit was equipped with the de Havilland Mosquito FB.Mk XVIII fitted with a single 57-mm gun. No. 248 Sqn had little success until 25 March 1944, when *U-976* was sunk. The strike wings accounted for 13 ships (34,076 tons) in 1943, while the ageing Handley Page Hampden TB.Mk Is and Lockheed Hudsons secured another 19 totalling 50,683 tons, albeit with severe losses.

Allied forces landed on the shores of Normandy on the night of 5-6 June 1944, and the Channel was littered with shipping. BdU had 21 U-boats at Bergen and Trondheim, and nine Schnorkel boats at Brest and La Pallice. These were tasked against the invasion armada in the Channel, while seven older boats were sent to patrol the Lizard-Brest area. Nineteen others were to patrol the Bay in case of an invasion attempt in that sector.

Luftwaffe strength

Generalleutnant Alexander Holle's X Fliegerkorps had been

The Blohm und Voss BV 138 was known as the 'Flying Clog' because of the shape of its central hull. It was used extensively by the Luftwaffe: this example served at Trondheim with 1.(F)/SAGr 130 in the spring of 1944.

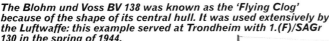

built up to 200-250 aircraft, including Focke-Wulf Fw 200C-6s, Heinkel He 177A-5s, Junkers Ju 88C-6s, Ju 88A-17s and Dornier Do 217K-2s. Much was expected of the Luftwaffe anti-shipping force, but in the event its record was extremely disappointing. Most operations were made by night because of Allied air superiority; losses were great, and the gains minimal.

By contrast, the U-boats fought back savagely during June and July, making maximum use of Schnorkel and heavy Flak defences, but they were pitted against very strong Allied coastal forces. The RAF had over 51 squadrons to seal the Western and Channel approaches, along with units of the Fleet Air Arm, the US Navy and the RCAF, all under Sholto Douglas.

The first U-boat attacks took place on the night of 6 June. Over the next four days, Coastal Command attacked 25 out of 36 U-boats sighted, while 18 fierce and separate actions were fought at night. Doenitz lost 48 U-boats from all causes in the course of June and July, many being destroyed in bombing attacks at home ports.

In late August, an era came to an end. With US forces advancing towards the Biscay ports, Doenitz gave the order to evacuate Lorient, Brest and La Pallice. The use of Schnorkel enabled most of the U-boats to make their escape to Germany and Norway.

After the PQ convoy actions of 1942, the Royal Navy's Fleet Air Arm was concerned mainly with operations in the Mediterranean and the Far East. Home Fleet actions were restricted to convoy escort in the Atlantic and on the Arctic and Gibraltar routes. Training and conversion were the main pre-occupations, and several new types became operational, including the Grumman Wildcat and Hellcat, and Chance Vought Corsair. The Supermarine Seafire still formed a large part of the Fleet Air Arm's inventory, while the Fairey Firefly and the Fairey

A Vickers Wellington Mk.XIV of No. 304 (Polish) Squadron, Coastal Command. From late 1943 the squadron operated almost exclusively by night, using Leigh Light-equipped aircraft.

A Heinkel He 177 Grief of KG 40 undergoes an engine change at Bordeaux-Merignac in the summer of 1944. German anti-shipping aircraft like this had little effect on the Normandy landings.

Barracuda became fully operational. By September 1943 the Fleet Air Arm was a powerful and well-equipped force, with 707 combat aircraft on strength.

The *Tirpitz* threat

The German fleet was still a problem in northern waters. While *Scharnhorst* had been sunk off North Cape on 26 December 1943, the massive *Tirpitz*, anchored in Kaafiord, remained a dire threat by its presence alone. The first and most successful carrier strike on the *Tirpitz* took place on 3 April 1944. The main strike force for Operation Tungsten was provided by Barracudas from HMS *Victorious* and *Furious*, escorted by Seafires and Corsairs, together with Hellcats and Wildcats from four escort carriers. Fourteen hits were recorded: *Tirpitz* was out of commission for the next three months. Further strikes in July and August were unsuccessful.

Sink the *Tirpitz*

In September RAF Lancasters of Nos 9 and 617 Sqns staged out of Yagodnik in north Russia, attacking the battleship with 12,000-lb (5443kg) 'Tallboy' bombs. A single hit pierced the forecastle, flooding the battleship. The crippled *Tirpitz* was moved to Haakoy island near Tromsø. The two RAF

squadrons made an abortive attack from northern Scotland on 29 October, before finally disposing of the battleship on 12 November. Bombing from 14,000 ft (4265 m), they made two massive hits that blew the ship's magazines and caused her to capsize with heavy loss of life.

The daily fare of RAF Coastal Command remained the constant round of shipping strikes and weary patrols in search of the Schnorkel-equipped U-boats operating from Kiel, Bergen and Trondheim and the Baltic. Few were sunk, and these were usually accomplished by surface escorts. But the effort by RAF Coastal Command was considerable: between 1 September and 31 December 1944, 9,216 sorties resulted in 62 sightings, 29 attacks and seven kills.

In January 1945 the first of the formidable Type XXIII U-boats (*U-2324*) sailed from Norway to join 19 conventional boats on station in British waters. The first blood of the new year was drawn by *U-1055* on 9 January, when it sank a freighter in the Irish Sea: in the course of the month six U-boats were lost in return for the sinking of seven Allied ships. In February 1941 U-boats sailed, but expertly handled sea escorts despatched 12 of them. March 1945 saw the loss of 15 U-boats in return for 10 Allied merchantmen and three escorts. Wing strikes by Nos 143, 235 and 248 Sqns were very successful in the Kattegat

and Skaggerak areas during April and May, and 10 U-boats were sunk by rockets and cannon fire, the last being *U-393* on 4 May 1945. A fitting end to the war was made by one of Coastal Command's oldest VLR squadrons, No. 86, when the unit sank *U-3503* on 5 May, and *U-1008* and *U-2534* in the Kattegat on the following day. Within 24 hours of this event Germany surrendered.

A costly struggle

The air war at sea in the Western hemisphere had been one of unprecedented bitterness and cost. At stake was the survival of Britain: the UK never came closer to losing the war than in the U-boat struggle in the Atlantic. The navies of all the Allied powers were involved, as were the considerable proportions of the respective air forces. RAF Coastal Command contributed in full throughout the war, sinking 183 U-boats out of the total lost to Germany of 783, and shared in the destruction of another 21. In addition 343 ships (513,804 tons) were sunk. But the cost was great: 5,866 pilots and crew members failed to return, with 1,777 aircraft written off or shot down in combat. The resilience of the German U-boat arm must be recognised; after the savage defeats of 1943 never once did it flinch in the face of Allied superiority at sea. Its casualties were frightening, but of the young volunteer crews there was never a shortage.

This Barracuda was photographed as it launched for the 3 April 1943 attack against the Tirpitz. The Fairey strike aircraft caused severe damage, but did not destroy the mighty ship.

Night bombing Early months

At the outbreak of World War II in September 1939 the primary instrument of UK air power lay with RAF Bomber Command and its meagre force of Blenheim, Hampden, Whitley and Wellington bombers.

The most capable bomber in RAF service at the outbreak of World War II was the Vickers Wellington. Faster than the Whitley and with a bigger bombload than the Hampden, the aircraft served with front line units until replaced by the new generation of four-engined bombers.

In September 1939 the operational strength of Bomber Command stood at 33 squadrons with some 480 aircraft. The war was only a few days old when No. 1 (Bomber) Group was transferred to France to form the Advanced Air Striking Force (AASF): few of the Battle Mk Is of this formation were destined to return to the UK. Therefore there remained some 23 squadrons based in England: six, equipped with Blenheim Mk IVs, six with Wellingtons, five with Whitleys and six with Hampdens.

Many lessons which had been available for consumption during the years of peace had been ignored by Bomber Command. The bombers lacked self-sealing fuel tanks and armour for the crew, while the rifle-calibre weapons were considered of sufficient potency to deal with fighter attack. The accent was on day bombing with the navigator relying on dead-reckoning

navigation with fixes from radio bearings, visuals and astro shots. The tenet, which held that a group of bombers flying in a closely packed formation could beat its way through any form of fighter opposition, was the first to be proved wrong.

Phoney war

With the outbreak of hostilities on 3 September 1939, both RAF Bomber Command and the Luftwaffe were restricted to attacking purely military targets at sea. While maintaining a policy of aircraft conservation, Bomber Command began a series of regular armed reconnaissances against the German fleet in the North Sea. It was not long before the vulnerability of daylight bomber formations became apparent in the face of fighter attack.

December 1939 saw a stiffening of resistance in German defences stationed on the North Sea coast with some 80 to 100 Bf 109Es and

Bf 110Cs. On 14 December Bf 109Es of II./JG 77 engaged 12 Wellingtons of No. 12 Sqn over the Schillig Roads, and downed five; a sixth crashed on the return to base. Then on 18 December came the climax. The Schillig Roads and shipping off Wilhelmshaven were once again the scenes of ferocious fighting: 24 Wellingtons of Nos 9, 37, and 149 Sqns were engaged by an estimated 40 or more Bf 109Es and Bf 110s in a running battle lasting over 40 minutes. The RAF force lost 10 shot down in fighter attacks, and another two in ditchings. The 50 per cent casualty rate was prohibitive, and the Battle of the Heligoland Bight was instrumental in the withdrawal of all RAF bombers from daylight operations, with the exception of those operating the Blenheim Mk IV. Bomber Command which was now committed to nocturnal bombing with all the problems that weather and navigation would inevitably involve.

Between September 1939 and May 1940, Bomber Command flew 861 anti-shipping (with 61 tons of bombs dropped) for the loss of 41 aircraft: apart from superficial damage to two pocket-battleships, the results were meagre.

Operations by all groups were stepped up when the Wehrmacht invaded Norway and Denmark on 9 April. The first attack on a mainland target took place on 11 April when six Wellington Mk ICs, escorted by Blenheim Mk IFs, were sent to

An RAF armourer checks a 250-lb (114-kg) bomb positioned in the bomb bay of a Bristol Blenheim. This twin-engined type suffered major losses on daylight raids.

attack the Luftwaffe base at Stavanger-Sola; three aircraft were bombed. This was followed by attacks on shipping and shore positions, with Sola, Bergen and Herdla coming under attacks by Blenheims by day and by Whitleys by night.

As for all the other commands in the air force, the war started in earnest on the morning of 10 May 1940, when the Germans invaded the Netherlands, Belgium and France: from the start the Battles of the AASF and the Blenheims of No. 2 Group were committed to attacks on communications, pontoon-bridges across the Maas and Meuse and on troop concentrations. In a matter of a week the Battles of the AASF had been annihilated, with No. 2 Group taking very heavy losses by day against Flak and the ever present Messerschmitts.

What has gone down in the annals of RAF Bomber Command was the start, albeit humble, of the strategic bombing offensive against the Reich on the night of 15-16 May 1940: 99 Wellingtons, Whitleys and Hampdens of Nos 3, 4 and 5 Groups were dispatched to

Flying sorties at under 200 mph (320 km/h), the Armstrong Whitworth Whitley was an easy target for Luftwaffe Bf 109 and Bf 110 fighters.

Above: The high morale of Bomber Command squadrons at the outbreak of war was quickly tempered by the heavy losses endured during the early daylight raids.

Below: The wreckage of a Hampden is inspected by German troops in the autumn of 1940. With little experience in night-bombing the effect of the early raids was minimal but did boost the morale of the British public suffering the effects of the Blitz.

Nicknamed the 'flying suitcase', the Handley Page Hampden, lacked sufficient defensive armament to ward off fighter attacks and suffered heavy losses during early daylight operations.

attack steel and oil targets in the Ruhr, primarily at Duisburg. On the night of 17-18 May oil storage tanks at Hamburg and Bremen were sought; on the next night damage was caused to the oil refineries at Misburg. On 18 June 1940 the selected targets in the Reich were widened to include aircraft factories, aluminium smelting plants, oil refineries and again, communications. However, only a fraction of the small forces (30-60 aircraft on major raids) released their bombs remotely near the selected target even in moonlight and in the face of minimal opposition. And therefore the damage sustained by German industry was inconsequential.

On the night of 11-12 June, marking Italy's declaration of war, Bomber Command sent 36 Whitley Mk Vs on a 1,350-mile (2175-km) round trip to the Fiat works at Turin as primary target. After refuelling in the Channel Islands the force hit bad weather over the Massif Centrale and severe icing. Out of the total sent, 23 turned back, 10 claimed to hit the primary or alternatives in Turin, and two from No. 51 Sqn bombed the Ansaldo works

and the docks at Genoa. Yet another lesson was learned; that of the effect of severe weather on heavily-laden bombers of relatively low performance.

Bombing Berlin

The most important raid during the Battle of Britain was the reprisal attack on Berlin, the first on the capital of the Reich by Bomber Command, on the night 25-26 August 1940. Eighty-one Wellingtons, Whitleys and Hampdens were sent in impossible weather conditions. Only 29 aircraft claimed to have bombed, with another 7 claiming to have been overhead but unable to identify their targets. Damage to the Reich's capital was slight, but the fury engendered by Hitler in a speech, where he called for immediate retaliation on London, was immediate: on 7 September 1940 the Luftwaffe turned its attention from attacks on Fighter Command's installations to London, thereby inexorably turning the tide of the battle in favour of the RAF.

An interim directive was issued to Bomber Command, on 21 September 1940, relieving all groups except No. 4 from anti-

invasion tasks. A high priority was placed on attacks on the oil industry, aircraft engine and component factories, communications, canals, U-boat construction yards and power stations in the Berlin area. On the night of 23-24 September 1940 some 119 bombers were sent to Berlin in adverse weather and despite severe engine and airframe icing, 84 claimed to have been bombed. Subsequent photo-reconnaissance revealed scattered groupings and minimal damage to the briefed targets.

A new directive issued at the end of that month called for the usual list of precision targets, but qualified their location by stating that they should be in the centre of well-populated town, and city centres: if results could not be gained on a precise target, then material and morale results would be achieved in flattening the surrounding area. The gloves were off, and well they might be with the savage night attacks on Coventry, Birmingham and Manchester as well as London. During November 1940 Bomber the Command raided Berlin, Essen, Munich and Cologne, and on each occasion the target was in the middle of a large built-up

area. Then, following some particularly devastating raids by the Luftwaffe, came the War Cabinet's directive to concentrate on German cities. The first of what was to be a continual series of area attacks was Operation 'Abigail' on the night of 16-17 December 1940.

Some 134 Wellingtons, Whitleys and Hampdens (plus four Blenheim Mk IVs) departed at dusk to attack the German city of Mannheim. Fourteen experienced Wellington crews started the attack with flares and 4-lb (1.8-kg) incendiaries, followed by the remainder which bombed in clear weather and moonlight over a duration of six hours: 103 attacked, dropping 89 tons of HE and over 14,000 incendiaries. Ten bombers failed to return. To the Germans the raid was as inaccurate as it was leisurely, with no particular target being hit: it was reckoned that 40 to 50 RAF bombers had taken part, and that the city had received probably 100 tons of HE and 1,000 incendiaries. Most of the damage was caused to the residential and commuter section of Mannheim. It was a strange way in which to wage a war.

No. 106 Squadron operated the Hampden Mk I between May 1939 and March 1942. This aircraft appears in the colour scheme adopted shortly after the initiation of night operations in 1940.

Avro Lancaster

Two Lancasters remained in airworthy condition 50 years after the end of World War II. This aircraft, PA474, was completed once hostilities had ceased, but has become the pride of the RAF's Battle of Britain Memorial Flight. In the late 1990s, it adopted the markings of No. 9 Squadron, a famous Lancaster unit.

A. V. Roe's Lancaster, designed under the supervision of Roy Chadwick, was to be the most successful of RAF Bomber Command's 'four-engined heavies' of World War II.

In response to the RAF's specification P.13/36 for a twin-engined medium bomber, Avro proposed and was contracted to produce the Rolls-Royce Vulture-engined Manchester Mk I which was to enter RAF service in 1940. However, the shortcomings of the complex powerplant meant that the Manchester's career would be a short one. In the heavy bomber category, the Handley Page Halifax was to be the RAF's preferred choice. Not to be outdone, Avro suggested that it could simply and quickly build an alternative – a four-engined Manchester derivative, the Manchester Mk III or Lancaster, as it was soon renamed.

New specification

Interested, the Air Ministry drew up a specification around the 'new' Avro design, requiring a 250-mph (402-km/h) cruising speed at 15,000 ft (4575 m) and a 7,500-lb (3405-kg) bombload capacity over a 2,000-mile (3218-km) range. The maximum range would be 3,000 miles (4827 km). The Manchester's large bomb bay, able to carry a variety of bomb types including a single 4,000-lb (1816-kg) 'Cookie', was retained.

A prototype flew on 9 January 1941. Impressed with its performance during testing, the Air Ministry cut Manchester production to just 157, ordering 454 Lancaster Mk Is instead. The first production example flew on 31 October 1941 and, on Christmas Eve, No. 44 Squadron at RAF Waddington became the first unit to receive four of the new bombers. On 3 March 1942 the type's first operational sortie – a mine-laying mission over the Heligoland Bight – was undertaken by the squadron.

Modifications

Throughout its service, modifications allowed the Lancaster to keep pace with the changing demands of the heavy bomber role. Defensive armament was improved and, most importantly, bombloads increased dramatically. The carriage of an 8,000-lb (3632-kg) 'Blockbuster' and, later, a 12,000-lb (5448-kg) bomb was soon necessary and, to cope with these new demands on the design, more powerful Merlin engines were fitted. In fact, most

Above: Night after night, the RAF set about destroying Germany's war-making potential. This Lancaster delivers a 4,000-lb (1814-kg) bomb and incendiaries. Some aircraft carried special equipment; the two aerials on this machine were part of an ABC (Airborne Cigar) radio-jamming installation.

Right: From early 1944, daylight raids were being carried out on French targets in preparation for the D-Day landings.

Lancasters were powered by Rolls-Royce's ubiquitous Merlin, the exceptions being the small batch of Mk IIs with Bristol Hercules radial powerplants. All other production used the Merlin, although these were often American-built Packard Merlins, introduced during 1942.

Other changes concerned the aircraft's defensive armament – different turret designs were introduced, along with heavier-calibre guns. Some aircraft were fitted with 'Village Inn', the Automatic Gun-Laying Turret, which sported a small radar set to improve the gunner's aim.

Lower loss rates

Contemporary statistics show how Lancasters proved their worth; by July 1943, 132 tons of bombs were dropped for every Lancaster lost on operations. The corresponding figures for Bomber Command's other 'four-engined heavies' were 56 tons for each Halifax and 41 tons for each Stirling. Some aircraft survived to successfully complete more than 100 sorties.

Perhaps the best known of these raids was that on a series of dams in western Germany, on the night of 16/17 May 1943. Modified aircraft of No. 617 Squadron, each armed with a 9250-lb (4196-kg) mine, succeeded in breaching two of the three dams targeted in a daring low-level sortie.

'Tallboy'

In 1944, No. 617's Lancasters undertook raids using a streamlined 12,000-lb (5448-kg) 'Tallboy' bomb on Saumur railway tunnel and, with No. 9 Squadron, on the German battleship *Tirpitz*, anchored in a Norwegian fjord.

The heaviest bomb of all entrusted to the Lancaster was the 22,000-lb (9988-kg) 'Grand Slam'. With one of these giant bombs aboard, the suitably-modified aircraft had a maximum take-off weight of 72,000 lb (32688 kg), compared to the 57,000 lb (25878 kg) of the Lancaster prototype.

Only the Hurricane and Spitfire fighters were built at a higher rate than the Lancaster during World War II (though the Halifax production rate was higher than that of the Lancaster until mid-1943). By the end of 1942, 91 Lancasters a month were being produced by five manufacturers in Britain and planning was well advanced for production in Canada.

From mid-1942 until VE-Day, the Lancaster had been RAF Bomber Command's main weapon in its nightly assault on German targets, equipping both the main force and Pathfinder Force (PFF). Of more than 7,300 Lancasters built, 3,345 were reported missing on operations, such was the intensity of their missions between 1942 and 1945, when 156,000 sorties were flown and 608,612 tons of bombs dropped. By March 1945, 56 squadrons were equipped with 745 examples of the type, another 296 serving with operational conversion units. Had the war continued, Lancasters would have joined the RAF's Tiger Force on sorties over Japan.

With the war over in 1945, most Lancasters were scrapped, but a few soldiered on, converted as Lancastrian airliners and freighters and as flying testbeds for new gas turbine engines. Others served as maritime reconnaissance aircraft with the RAF, and French and Canadian forces.

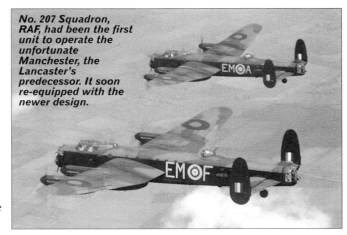

No. 207 Squadron, RAF, had been the first unit to operate the unfortunate Manchester, the Lancaster's predecessor. It soon re-equipped with the newer design.

The Canadian-built Lancaster Mk 10 served with the Royal Canadian Air Force well into the 1950s, mainly in the maritime reconnaissance role. This aircraft is one of three Mk 10-AR Arctic survey aircraft with nose-mounted radar. The RAF and French navy also operated maritime Lancasters after the war.

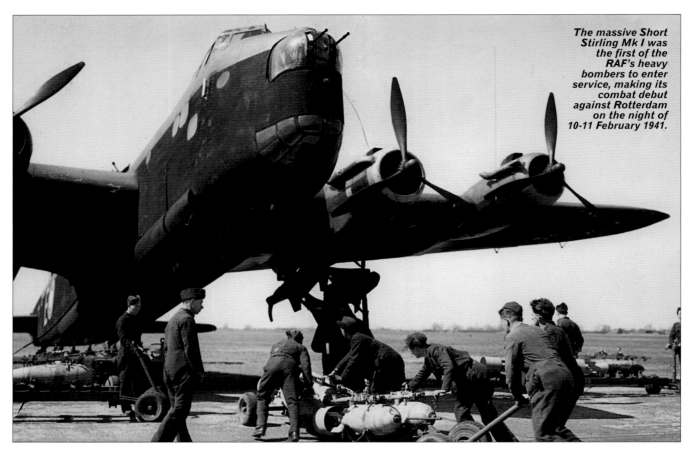

The massive Short Stirling Mk I was the first of the RAF's heavy bombers to enter service, making its combat debut against Rotterdam on the night of 10-11 February 1941.

Nadir of Bomber Command

1941 was to see an expansion of RAF Bomber Command's diverse operations, which ranged from leaflet dropping to the first stirrings of a genuine strategic bombing campaign. But events would call the very existence of the command into question.

In the course of 1940, Bomber Command's Vickers Wellingtons, Handley Page Hampdens, Armstrong Whitworth Whitleys and Bristol Blenheims had operated by day and by night against a wide range of targets: 21,089 sorties were flown (17,439 by night), resulting in 158 bombers lost in crashes, and 494 failing to return from operations.

On 15 January 1941 Bomber Command was directed to make precision night attacks on the German synthetic oil industry. Bad weather meant that only three raids were flown over the next six weeks. Despite numerous problems the first generation of heavy bombers made its debut. On the night of 10 February Short Stirling Mk Is of No. 7 Squadron attacked Rotterdam, two weeks later Avro Manchesters of No. 207 Squadron bombed the cruiser *Hipper* at Brest. On 10 March No. 35 Squadron's Handley Page Halifax Mk Is attacked the docks at Le Havre.

U-boat and Fw 200 Condor attacks on Britain's convoy supply lines were becoming the cause of serious concern. On 6 March 1941 Churchill issued the Atlantic Directive, stipulating an all-out offensive against the U-boat and the Condor at sea, in the air, at their bases, and in the yards and factories where they were constructed. These attacks, together with attacks on the battlecruisers *Scharnhorst* and *Gneisenau* at Brest, became a constant drain on resources.

Boeing Fortress fails

Attempts to use the new Boeing Fortress Mk Is of No. 90 Sqn by day proved unsuccessful, even though the aircraft were flown above 30,000 ft (9145 m), which was theoretically far above the capabilities of German fighters. The operational failure of the Fortress bemused the Americans, who set great store by Boeing's product. Blenheim Mk IV light bombers were being used for on 'Circus' operations over northern France, as

intruders, and on anti-shipping attacks from Norway to Brest.

Bad weather curtailed operations in winter, while long clear summer nights increased vulnerability. Twelve bombers failed to return from 1,030 night sorties in January; in June 1941 3,228 nocturnal sorties were flown, with 76 failing to return and 15 lost in crashes during recovery.

In 1939, night defence of the Reich was by the Luftwaffe's Flak arm. The 88-mm Flak 36 had a maximum effective altitude of over 20,000 ft (6095 m). Bf 109D-1 fighters were based at various airfields, and acted on a freelance basis: success

was minimal. By the summer of 1940 some 450 heavy Flak guns, backed by over 100 searchlights were arranged in batteries to cover the cities of Germany.

In the spring of 1940, Hauptmann Wolfgang Falck's 1./ZG 1 based at Aalborg (Denmark) started experimental night interceptions with the Bf 110C-1 Zerstörer. With the start of RAF attacks over the Ruhr, Goering ordered Falck to form the Nacht und Versuchsstaffel (night and experimental unit) at Düsseldorf. From this humble beginning grew the largest and most formidable night-fighter force ever.

Below: Vickers Wellington crews of No. 149 Squadron based at Mildenhall, Suffolk, board their aircraft for a night mission over Germany. The squadron played a prominent part in the early raids against Germany.

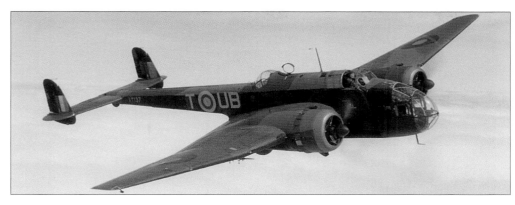

No. 455 Squadron was the first Australian bomber unit to form in Britain. Equipped with Handley Page Hampdens, its first mission was against Frankfurt on the night of 29-30 August 1941.

On 26 June 1940 Major Falck was appointed as Kommodore of Nachtjagdgeschwader Nr 1, which was to grow into a unit of four Gruppen operating a mixture of Messerschmitt Bf 110C-2, Junkers Ju 88C-2, and Dornier Do 17Z-10 types. The 1. Nachtjagddivision was formed on 17 July 1940 under Oberst Josef Kammhuber, with its headquarters at Zeist, near Utrecht. This command was subordinated to Luftflotte II.

Kammhuber Line

Originally searchlights and Flak were concentrated around the Ruhr and Lower Rhine areas. On the instigation of Kammhuber, the defences were redeployed into a line of box-like sectors stretching from Jutland to the south of Liège: this was to be called the Kammhuber Line by the British. A fighter orbited over a beacon behind the box of searchlights, attacking while the lights held an enemy bomber in their cones. This was known as *helle Nachtjagd* (*Henaja*, or illuminated nightfighting), and Oberleutnant Werner Streib of NJG 1 achieved the first Henaja kill on the night of 20 July 1940.

The Germans possessed good quality ground-based radars in 1940, but they were at least two years behind the British in the development of Airborne Interception (AI) radar. During the summer of 1940, experiments were conducted with the GEMA FuMG 80

(Freya) radar for rudimentary fighter interception. Freya sets were rapidly being installed at early-warning stations along the coastline of northern Europe. The first kill came on 2 October when the Freya station at Nunspeet, near Zwolle, guided Leutnant Ludwig Becker in a Do 17Z-10 to within 164 ft (50 m) of a Wellington, which he shot down. Eventually some 16 Freya sectors were created for so-called *dunkel Nachtjagd* (*Dunaja*, or dark night-fighting) over the coast.

In September 1940, I./NJG 2 was formed for night intruder work over RAF airfields in eastern England. Within weeks, the Gruppe took on charge the Junkers Ju 88C-4, which carried a crew of three and was armed with two 20-mm MG-FF/M cannon and three 0.31-in (7.92-mm) MG 17 machine-guns. Operations to harry returning RAF bombers immediately proved very successful.

Political interference

Kammhuber's attempts to increase the pace of intruder operations were blocked by Generaloberst Hans Jeschonnek, the Luftwaffe's chief of staff, who saw little need for such a diversion of resources. Finally, on 10 October 1941, German night intruder operations were stopped on the express orders of Hitler, and the Gruppe was posted to the Mediterranean.

At the time of the German invasion of Russia, on 22 June

1941, Bomber Command had around 1,000 aircraft in 49 squadrons. Eight squadrons of heavy bombers were either operational or under training, but serviceability was low. From June to December 1941 only about half of the 800 medium and heavy bombers were fit for operations, with the nominal nightly average dropping to as low as 60 on occasion.

Daylight raids

There were those in the Air Staff who believed that a return to daylight bombing might hold the key to victory over Germany. Luftwaffe defences in West were indeed at an all time low: in northern France and Belgium little more than two Geschwader remained.

There was growing scepticism from the War Cabinet about the accuracy and effects of raids on Germany and elsewhere. An analysis presented on 18 August 1941, was more depressing than

anyone had imagined: it confirmed that only 25 per cent of crews claiming to have reached the target by night actually did so; and in the haze of the Ruhr, only one in 10 dropped its bombs within 5 miles (8 km) of their target.

Pause in the offensive

In September the remainder of Bomber Command returned to attacks on Brest, and on the U-boat pens at Lorient and St Nazaire. With renewed demands on Bomber Command's resources from the Admiralty, and the RAF Middle East and Coastal Commands, the Air Staff decided to halt operations and declare a period of conservation for a renewed offensive in the spring of 1942.

Over the period from July to December, Bomber Command flew 14,833 night and 1,643 day sorties, in the course of which 605 bombers failed to return from operations and another 222 were otherwise destroyed: it was virtually the loss of the Command's establishment in five months. With Japan now in the war against the UK and the United States, and the Battle of the Atlantic intensifying, it was apparent to many that despite its benefit to home morale, Bomber Command had provided poor dividends for the resources invested. There were many voices calling for its dissolution. RAF Bomber Command faced crisis, not so much from the enemy as from the strident voices at home.

The Handley Page Halifax flew its first main strike against Germany on the night of 12-13 March 1941, when, in company with the Avro Manchester, the new bombers attacked Hamburg.

No. 37 Squadron RAF flew the first RAF bomber mission of the war on 3 September 1939. Losing five out of six aircraft on a single raid in December persuaded Bomber Command to switch from day to night bombing. This Mark IA aircraft entered service in April 1940, when the squadron was based at Feltwell, in Norfolk.

The year of trial

Several new types entered into service with Bomber Command in 1942, including the North American B-25C, designated the Mitchell II by the RAF. By March 1943, the medium bomber force comprised two squadrons of the type, as well as 15 squadrons of Vickers Wellingtons and three of Lockheed Venturas.

By early 1942, the USA was at war with Japan in the Pacific, and the Germans and Soviets were engaged in a death-struggle in Russia. Britain's major retaliatory weapon appeared to be Bomber Command, but ineffective tactical bombing campaigns up to that point had led to a crisis of confidence.

The Butt Report of August 1941 had instilled a lack of faith in Bomber Command's ability to strike targets in the Third Reich accurately. However, during the summer of 1941, an electronic aid to navigation named Gee Mk I had been produced. By February 1942, over 200 of Bomber Command's aircraft carried Gee, although it was acknowledged that Gee would soon be compromised by the Germans.

The close of 1941 saw Bomber Command during a period of conservation, while attacks, on the orders of the Admiralty, were maintained on the *Scharnhorst, Gneisenau* and *Prinz Eugen* at Brest. The escape of these capital ships on 12 February 1942 relieved Bomber Command of an irksome commitment. Events now moved fast. On 14 February the Command received a new directive calling for an offensive of unrestricted nocturnal bombing on targets in the Reich to capitalise on Gee.

The Gee campaign

Within a week of the new directive, Air Marshal Arthur T. Harris took up his post as the new AOC-in-C Bomber Command. Harris was firmly against the bombing of precise targets such as factories which if destroyed, might contribute materially to Germany's inability to wage war. His task was to bomb, and to bomb hard. The great industrial towns and cities of the Reich were to be erased brick by brick if

necessary, with a complementary fall in war production and the shattering of German civilian morale. He pursued these aims with tenacity.

Excluding five squadrons of Blenheims and Boston Mk IIIs, 44 squadrons were at Harris's disposal in February 1942, of which 38 were operational. Fourteen were equipped with heavy bombers, the remainder using the Wellington, Hampden and Whitley; on 22 February a nominal 300 bombers were combat ready. Of the heavy bombers the Manchester had proved to be a disaster; the operational ceiling of the loaded Stirling Mk I Srs 3 was limited; and the new Halifax Mk II Srs 1A was an improvement on the Mk I but performance was still low. The brightest star was the Lancaster Mk I, which was currently undergoing trials. To remedy the shortage of pilots, Harris dispensed with co-pilots, and ordered the fitting of auto-pilots on the heavy bombers; flight engineers were trained to assist the captain, while one member was trained to land the aircraft in an emergency.

Tactically, the growing efficiency of German night-fighters now ruled out the random and leisurely passage of bombers over the target.

KG 2 played an important role in the 'Baedeker' raids ordered by Hitler in April 1942, in retaliation for Bomber Command attacks. One of the units, Do 217E-4 is illustrated.

The first raid using new tactics took place on the night of 3-4 March 1942, against the Renault concern at Paris-Billancourt: the first wave of heavy bombers illuminated the target with flares, medium bombers in the second wave repeated, while all available Manchesters, Halifaxes and Wellingtons modified for the use of 4,000-lb (1814-kg) HE bombs brought up the rear.

The first major target of the Gee campaign was the vast concern of Krupp AG at Essen on the night of 8-9 March. With the serious failure of this attack, shortcomings in the new equipment and technique were revealed. A subsequent series of raids left the target virtually untouched. Obviously too much had been expected of Gee, although it remained a navigational aid of utmost significance.

Coastal targets with an approach aided by Gee Mk I remained a feasible proposition for reasonably accurate bombing, while out of the range of Gee lay the city of Lübeck on the Baltic; it served as a seaport of minor importance, it was lightly defended, and the houses were largely constructed with wood. Largely for these reasons it was

selected for attack to demonstrate the growing power of Bomber Command. Some 191 bombers released 300 tons of bombs to leave 15,707 people homeless: nevertheless, there was no wavering in civilian morale and the will to fight. Next Bomber Command struck out at Dortmund, Essen, Cologne and Hamburg before returning to another incendiary target, Rostock, on the night of 23-24 April 1942.

'Baedeker blitz'

In retaliation Hitler issued an order on 14 April 1942 calling for a resumption of air attacks on England with a more aggressive stamp than had hitherto been used. Cities, which if attacked would have the 'greatest possible effect on civilian life' were to be chosen. A large bombing force was established under Luftflotte III in France and Belgium and in keeping with Hitler's orders targets were to be cities with no particular industrial value, and usually of great beauty. The British soon called these attacks 'Baedeker' raids, after the famous 19th-century German tourist's guide to towns and cities. The first attack took place on the night of 23-24 April 1942 on the city of Exeter, but failed. On the

following night two waves of German bombers attacked with dire effects on the old cathedral city, for minimum losses.

Bath was attacked on two nights (25 and 26 April), followed by two raids on Norwich and one on York before April was over. During May the Luftwaffe attacked Exeter, Cowes, Norwich, Hull, Poole, Grimsby and Canterbury. The offensive continued throughout June, July and August, before finally petering out with an attack on Canterbury on the night of 31 October 1942, following a raid by 60 or more Fw 190s during the afternoon.

Throughout the summer offensive RAF Fighter Command put up a resilient defence with its night-fighters aided by GCI radars. In January 1942 the command fielded 10 squadrons of Beaufighter fighters with AI.Mk IV radar, and seven with Defiants, some of which carried AI.Mk VI. During that month No. 157 Sqn, based at Castle Camps, received the first Mosquito NF.Mk II, although technical problems delayed service its use until April, during which time the aircraft was fitted with AI.Mk V radar. The first of a new generation of radars, AI.Mk VII, was now received on trial: the first AI.Mk VII kill was achieved on 5 April and towards the autumn of 1942, the AI.Mk VIII was progressively installed in British night-fighters.

Although GCI was efficient, the controller was limited to one

interception at a time. In preparation for mass raids, Fighter Command therefore introduced a system not unlike that being currently developed by Kammhüber in Germany. Under the codename 'Smack', from December 1941 onwards, searchlights were redeployed into boxes: 36 in (90 cm) indicator searchlights were positioned in the forward 12 miles (19 km) of the belt, with a concentration of powerful 60 in (150 cm) lights in the Killer Zone of the belt, which illuminated targets for the orbiting night fighters.

Thousand-bomber raids

Improvement in weather and in serviceability enabled Harris to send a record 3,752 night sorties in April 1942, although losses were also the highest to date. Among the notable raids of this month was the daylight low-level attack by Nos 44 and 97 Sqns to the M.A.N. diesel factory at Augsburg, on 17 April.

The highlight of the summer was Harris's brilliant feat of putting over 1,000 bombers in one attack over the Reich. In reality three major raids, under the codename Operation Millenium, were made. Getting together this stupendous figure was a major feat of organisation. After one cancellation Cologne was the subject of attack on the night of 30-31 May 1942 by a total of 1,046 despatched. No less than 367 of the force were flown by students and instructors; 50

Blenheim B.Mk IVs of No. 2 Group and Army Co-operation Command also flew intruder sorties over Dutch airfields. Maximum emphasis was made on concentration of forces, with the Gee-equipped crews of Nos 1 and 3 Groups marking and making the first attack. Later it was found that over 250 factories had been either destroyed or badly damaged, 486 people were dead with 5,027 injured, and 59,100 rendered homeless. Some 42 bombers failed to return.

On the night of 1-2 June Harris sent 956 bombers to Krupp AG at Essen, and, after a period of bad weather, 1,006 bombers were sent to Bremen on the night of 25-26 June 1942.

No possibility of a repeat of Millenium was possible, for the forces available were not strong enough. But it pointed the way to greater things, and was of immense propaganda value.

The Kammhüber Line

Three night-fighting methods were in Luftwaffe use from September 1941; the most widely used was *helle Nachtjagd* (illuminated night-fighting) in which night-fighters operated in searchlight zones; in front and behind the zones were areas for *dunkel Nachtjagd* (dark night-fighting) in which ground radars played their part. Around the large cities a combination of the two (*kombiniertes Nachtjagd*) was used. Gradually, the three systems were merged into what became known as the Himmelbett.

By June 1942, the precious FuG 202 (Lichtenstein B/C) and FuG 212 airborne radars were

being fitted on a wholesale basis and by the summer of 1942 the skies over Germany were already becoming dangerous.

Crisis over

During July 1942 Bomber Command flew 10 major night attacks to inflict heavy damage on Wilhelmshaven, Hamburg, Duisburg and Saarbrücken, plus two daylight attacks to Danzig and Lübeck. Gee Mk I was already being jammed over Germany, and this put heavy dependence on moonlight and clear weather, which in turn brought losses from night-fighters. But the crisis of confidence in Bomber Command's raison d'être was over, and the command was now playing an important part in the war.

In the face of opposition from Harris, the Pathfinder Force was formed on 15 August 1942. Its duties were to find and mark a specific area for bombing by the Main Force.

Throughout the late summer months losses were heavy, but diminished after September 1942 as Bomber Command turned to operations indirectly connected with Operation Torch. Nevertheless, maximum effort daylight raids were mounted against Le Creuset on 17 October, and the Philips factory at Eindhoven on 6 December 1942.

The turn of the year saw the German forces on the defensive in North Africa after the defeat at El Alamein, and in the Soviet Union around Stalingrad, with a new sense of optimism pervading Allied strategy. Not least in this strategy would be the part played by Bomber Command and its new partner, the US VIII Bomber Command of the 8th Air Force, in the bomber offensive against Germany.

RAF night-bombers

In February 1942, at the nadir of the public's confidence in the RAF's bombing abilities, Arthur 'Bomber' Harris replaced Air Chief

Marshal R. E. C. Peirse as head of Bomber Command, and transformed British strategic air power into one of terrifying

strength and efficiency, despite inheriting mostly obsolete aircraft including the Halifax and Armstrong Whitworth Whitley.

Handley Page Halifax
Left: The first RAF squadron to equip with the Halifax was No. 35 (Madras Presidency) Sqn, which received the type in November 1940, and was tasked with service trials. The example illustrated failed to return from a raid on Nuremberg on 28-29 August 1942.

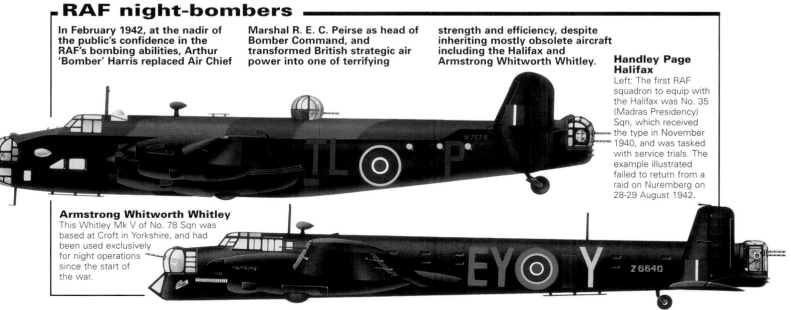

Armstrong Whitworth Whitley
This Whitley Mk V of No. 78 Sqn was based at Croft in Yorkshire, and had been used exclusively for night operations since the start of the war.

Declaration of intent

By early 1942, the USA was at war with Japan in the Pacific, and the Germans and Soviets were engaged in a death-struggle in Russia. Britain's major retaliatory weapon appeared to be Bomber Command, but ineffective tactical bombing campaigns up to that point had led to a crisis of confidence.

Above: Six thousand rounds of '50-calibre' ammunition and a pair of 2,000-lb (907-kg) HE bombs await loading aboard a B-17 bound for Germany in this posed publicity photograph taken at a station 'somewhere in England'.

Below: A typical RAF Bomber Command bomber of the period, 'A-Able' of No. 78 Sqn, RAF (and a veteran 10 operations) is a Halifax B.Mk II Series 1.

Following the crucial talks between Allied heads of state and their Combined Chiefs of Staff at Casablanca in January 1943, the respective commanders of RAF Bomber Command and the US VIII Bomber Command received a new directive outlining the future of the bomber offensive. 'Your primary object,' stated the directive, 'will be the progressive destruction and dislocation of the German military, industrial and economic system, and the undermining of the morale of the German people to a point where their capacity for armed resistance is fatally weakened.'

Priority targets

Targets for attack were listed in the following order of priority: German U-boat construction yards, the German aircraft industry, transportation, oil plants, and 'other targets in enemy war industry'. To Air Chief Marshal Sir A. T. Harris, commander- in-chief of RAF Bomber Command, this directive was but a re-affirmation of the area bombing directive of 14 February 1942, and he saw no reason to change his policies: area bombing held the key to victory in the future. No nation on earth would be able to continue the fight with the will and morale of the home population shattered by the

bombing of towns and cities. Many people thought differently, not least those in the Air Staff. In particular, American strategists had long been in disagreement with the RAF's policy of area bombing that had started as early as December 1940. Their reasoning was simple: attacks on civilian morale by aerial bombardment had met with few material results in this war, and they pointed at the resilience with which the British faced bombardment in 1940-41. So, in policy at least, there was to be a parting of the ways: the British stuck doggedly to nocturnal area bombing, aiming for a precision target but flattening the surrounding area as a by-product, while the Americans strove for pinpoint attacks on so-called bottlenecks (in other words Harris's 'panacea' targets) in German military, economic and industrial resources. In the event neither course was to win the war, but the contribution to victory was to be great.

Eaker aims for Germany

On 5 January 1943 General Carl A. Spaatz relinquished his post as commander of the 8th Air Force to Major General Ira C. Eaker, on his transfer to the Mediterranean theatre. By the winter of 1942-43 the US 8th Air Force in the UK bore all the hallmarks of a neglected force, as priorities in North Africa and the Pacific took pride of place. American losses rose from 3.7 per cent of sorties in November to 8.8 per cent in December 1942. Apart from tactical problems, VIII Bomber Command was troubled by low aircraft strengths: only 140 B-17Fs and B-24Ds were on establishment with the 91st, 93rd, 44th, 305th, 306th and 303rd Bombardment Groups (Heavy), with a 50 per cent availability. This situation was to endure until May 1943.

The tenet of US VIII Bomber Command was that of unescorted daylight precision bombing, and although U-boat

construction yards were assigned in the autumn of 1942, not one had been raided in the Reich. Perhaps Eaker felt that the 8th Air Force had not the strength or was tactically unfit to embark on long-range unescorted penetrations of German airspace, but initially he was to find that fighter opposition bore no relation to the ferocity and ingenuity of that provided by JG 2 and JG 26 over France. On the morning of 27 January 1943, the occasion of US VIII Bomber Command's first attack on German soil, some 50 to 75 Fw 190s and Bf 109G-1s of JG 1 rose to fight: primary target for the 91 B-17s and B-24s (91st, 303rd, 305th, 306th and 44th Bomb Groups), led by Colonel Frank A. Armstrong in the lead Fortress of the 306th Bomb Group, was the large Bremer-Vulkan Shiffbau AG at Vegesack (8 miles/13 km north west of Bremen). Cloud and the curcuitous route over the North Sea prompted the leader to head

Tinker Toy *was a B-17F of the 535th BS, 381st BG which gained a reputation as a 'jinx ship', three of its crew being killed and a number wounded over a six month period.*

for the alternate target, the Germania Werft at Wilhelmshaven. Flak and fighter opposition were both surprisingly ineffective.

The increasing efficiency of German fighter attacks, in particular the lethal head-on passes, forced VIII Bomber Command to take energetic action. By early spring extra armour was being carried in the B-17F and B-24D, whilst two or more 0.5-in (12.7-mm) Colt M2 machine-guns were installed around the Plexiglas noses. Since the winter of 1942-43 formation tactics had been radically altered: bombers now flew in tight combat boxes with squadrons stacked in vertical echelon to uncover as many dorsal and ballturrets as possible.

Battle of the Ruhr

While the 8th Air Force flew its first tentative raids over

B-26 Marauders began operations from England in May 1943, the 387th BG joining the fray in August. Initially employed at low level, the type suffered heavy losses and soon reverted to medium-level sorties such as this over occupied Europe.

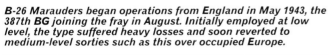

Germany, RAF Bomber Command resumed its nocturnal offensive on the Ruhr with greater strength than ever before, and with new aircraft and equipment. By February Harris had achieved his intermediate goal: strength had risen to 50 squadrons, including 35 equipped with the Lancaster B.Mk I, the Halifax B.Mk II, and the Stirling B.Mk III heavy bombers. Although Gee Mk I was being jammed over the Reich, the multi-frequency Mk II version offered some resistance. Two new navigation and bomb-aiming aids of the greatest importance were now being employed in the newly designated No. 8 (Pathfinder Force) Group under Air Vice-Marshal D. C. T. Bennett. These were named Oboe and H₂S.

Entering service in the Mosquito B. Mk IVs of No. 109 Sqn in December 1942, Oboe Mk I was based on the principle employing two ground stations, and a receiver in the aircraft. Range was limited, but it offered a bombing accuracy of within 120 yards (110 m) for a PFF Mosquito flying at 30,000 ft (9145 m) within a range of 250 miles (402 km) from the stations. The Ruhr therefore was just within range. Neither Oboe nor H₂S offered precision accuracy but they represented a considerable improvement on Gee- marking.

The directive to RAF Bomber Command, dated 4 February 1943, released Harris from the strictures of hammering at protected U-boat pens and freed

his forces for an all-out offensive on that great bastion of German industry: the Ruhr. The offensive started on the night of 5/6 March 1943, when 442 bombers were sent to Krupp AG of Essen (367 attacked). Using Oboe Mk I eight Mosquitoes of No. 109 Sqn dropped yellow TIs on the line of approach to a point 15 miles (24 km) short of the AP (Aim Point): from here 22 PFF backers-up marked the final approach with flares, and at Z-hour Mosquitoes dropped red TIs directly over the vast Krupps concern. German night-fighters and Flak shot down 14 RAF bombers, but the bomb pattern was a considerable improvement on that which had previously been attained on this elusive, and smog-ridden, objective.

During the phase known as the Battle of the Ruhr (5 March-28 June 1943), RAF Bomber Command launched 26 major raids on the Ruhr, including four on Wilhelmshaven, two each on Hamburg, Stuttgart and Nuremburg, and one each on Kiel, Bremen, Stettin, Munich, Frankfurt and Mannheim, all before the month of April was over. First priority fell to Essen, second to Duisburg, and third to Düsseldorf: by the end of June 1943 the command had dropped 34,705 tons of HE and incendiaries over Germany, for the loss of 628 bombers.

The 'Dam Busters'

Two raids in the early summer of 1943 bore testimony to the increasing skill of Bomber Command's crews. One demonstrated that bad weather was no longer a protective shield under which German cities could hide: on the night of 28-29 June, Oboe Mosquitoes sky-marked Cologne (with parachute flares) for the follow-up force of 540 Gee Mk II-equipped bombers. Severe damage was inflicted in this first effective instance of massed blind-bombing.

The great dams of the Eder, Sorpe and Möhne, which supplied hydro-electricity to the Ruhr, were the objectives of Operation Chastise by 19 Lancasters of No. 617 Sqn on the night of 16/17 May 1943. The force took off shortly

before 21.30 to attack the three great dams, and possibly a fourth if time permitted: the Möhne dam was attacked at 00.23, and breached after the fifth Lancaster had completed its low-level pass. The remainder of the Möhne force then flew to the Eder dam, which burst following a third pass at 02.00. Other Lancasters had proceeded independently to the Sorpe and the Schwelme dams, but their attacks failed. The losses amounted to eight aircraft: five crashed or were shot down en route, two went down over the dams, and the last was shot down on the return flight.

In Germany, the upsurge of Allied round-the-clock bombing in the spring of 1943 was recognised with a concern that was not matched by remedial action. Pride of place in the Luftwaffe's priorities remained the Soviet Union and then the Mediterranean theatres, where the vast majority of day fighter units were now stationed. But then the war had only just begun to tax the Third Reich's ability to fight. An important step forward was the fitting of FuG 25a (Erstling) IFF capability in both night and day fighters.

Summer battles

In April 1943 the US 4th, 56th and 78th Fighter Groups became operational with the Republic P-47C and P-47D Thunderbolts. But as a result of their low combat radius (175 miles;282 km), the P-47s were restricted to sweeps and escort operations over France. Meanwhile the forces of VIII Bomber Command were increased after the alleviation of pressure in the Mediterranean. The B-17s of the new 95th, 96th and 351st Groups became operational on 13 May, and the 94th on the following day, while the 92nd Bomb Group was at last released from its training commitment. Operations over Germany increased in tempo.

The Battle of Kiel on 13 June 1943 marked the beginning of intensive and sustained German fighter opposition to VIII Bomber Command's daylight penetrations of the Reich. In all, US VIII Bomber Command lost 26 bombers out of 182 credited with attacks on Kiel and Bremen this day. At last the severity of round-the-clock bombing was coming home to the Luftwaffe, but worse was to come.

Day-bomber offensive

The savage summer

'Round-the-clock' bombing of the Reich's targets began in February 1943. During summer 1943 the savagery of the Allied onslaught forced the Luftwaffe to defend its homeland with new energy.

In spring 1943 differences in British and American strategic bombing policies came to the fore. Bomber Command 'heavies' led by an increasingly efficient pathfinder force, were despatched almost nightly to the Ruhr cities and Germany as a whole. In June 1943 Bomber Command dropped a record 15,271 tons of bombs in 5,816 sorties, but the effort was not without cost: 275 bombers failed to return and 15 were destroyed in accidents. But the crisis of confidence in Bomber Command was past, Harris' policies drew widespread accord and results of the nocturnal bombing offensive appeared favourable despite casualties. The resources invested in Bomber Command seemed to be showing dividends.

With the Americans matters were different. Until May 1943 at least, Maj Gen Eaker's US 8th Air Force suffered a constant drain of resources without re-inforcement. Results of daylight precision bombing were meagre: weather handicapped accuracy, and standard GP bombs proved ineffective against U-boat pens in attacks that had consumed the lion's share of VIII Bomber Command's effort since October 1942. Early operations over France accentuated the need for adequate defences against German fighters. Eaker requested the establishment of a long-range escort fighter force as the direst necessity.

The recent casualty rate incurred over Germany meant a

The turbocharged Cyclone engines of the B-17 ejected massive amounts of vapour that froze on impact with the air. Here a combat wing trails vapour during a mission to Bremen on 20 December 1943. Crews hated these trails as they gave the aircraft's position away to marauding Luftwaffe fighters. In their initial forays to Germany the Fortresses were provided only with fighter cover over the enemy coasts, due to the shortfall in range of the VIII Fighter Command's P-47s.

B-17Fs of the 365th BS/305th BG flew from Chelveston from December 1942. Commanded by Col Curtis E. LeMay, the 305th pioneered formation bombing techniques.

revision in priorities: no daylight bombing campaign against the Reich could succeed until the Luftwaffe's fighter arm was defeated. A new bombing directive of 10 June 1943 stated the objective: the destruction of the German fighter arm as a task of the US 8th AF, to be concluded by April 1944 in conjunction with a Combined Bombing Offensive, and as an essential pre-requisite to an invasion of north west Europe.

'Blitz Week'

By 22 June 1943 VIII Bomber Command's strength had been raised to 13 groups. Fair weather towards the middle of July enabled Eaker to launch VIII Bomber Command's most intensive spate of operations to date: 'Blitz Week'.

On 24 July 1st BW attacked Heroya, Norway, whilst the 4th BW raided Trondheim and Bergen: one B-17F was the only loss. On the following day 323

B-17s set out to attack Hamburg and Kiel. The 1st Wing's sally to the Blohm und Voss yards at Hamburg received fierce opposition: fifteen B-17s were shot down, and four failed to return after attacking Warnemünde. The forces of LwBefhMitte were split up in order to face two attacks on 26 July, when 303 B-17s set out to bomb Hamburg and Hannover.

After a day's pause VIII Bomber Command sent 182 B-17s to Kassel-Bettenhausen and Oschersleben in what was the command's most distant penetration to date. The climax of 'Blitz Week' took place on the morning of 30 July 1943, when 186 B-17s were sent on a repeat visit to Kassel. Eight squadrons of P-47s provided withdrawal support. New drop-tanks allowed P-47s to reach the Dutch–German border, and combats went down from 30,000 ft (9145 m) to the 'deck': subsequent claims of VIII Fighter Command

Long-range Lockheed P-38s were at a premium in the summer of 1943, much needed in North Africa and the southwest Pacific. Texas Ranger, a P-38H Lightning, was flown by the 55th FG, which became operational at Nuthampstead in October 1943.

Above and right: ACM Harris was convinced that Germany's defeat could be brought about by mass devastation of cities and industry, with the inevitable collapse of civil morale and the complementary reduction in Germany's ability to wage war: his command had been forged for this purpose, with a massive force of Lancasters (pictured), Halifaxes and Stirlings.

amounted to 25 confirmed kills for the loss of seven P-47s.

In six days VIII Bomber Command had flown 1,672 sorties (1,047 credited) for the loss of 88 B-17s plus many more written off at base. It was proof that the command still did not have sufficient strength on hand to pursue a long period of intensive operations.

Operation Gomorrah

By May 1943 many of the secrets of the German early-warning and GCI radar systems were known to the Allies, and an all-out jamming campaign against Germany's radar network could begin. Authorisation for the use of 'Window' was given on 15 July 1943, and Harris, with the Battle of the Ruhr successfully concluded, used this opportunity to launch a devastating series of raids on Hamburg (Operation Gomorrah). On the night of 24–25 July Harris launched his first attack with the aim of the destruction of the Hamburg's repair, fire-control and air-raid warning systems by massive use of incendiaries. Within 150 minutes, 740 bombers (out of 791 despatched), unloaded 2,396 tons of incendiaries and HE on the

city. Throughout the attack crews dropped 'Window': the confusion in German defences was dramatic, and only 12 bombers failed to return. On the following night Bomber Command sent 705 aircraft to Essen; on night 27-28 July the bombers returned to Hamburg: 739 heavy bombers dropped 2,417 tons and with the convection brought on by conflagrations of over 1,000 degrees Celsius, fire-storms howled through the streets. Two follow-up attacks on Hamburg took place: on the nights of 30-31 July and 2-3 August 1943. The exact number of persons who perished in the bombing and fire-storms will never be accurately known. One source quotes 41,800 killed and 37,439 injured, many of whom succumbed later, plus the thousands listed as missing. Eighty-seven RAF bombers failed to return from Hamburg in the course of the raids: 3,095 sorties were sent, 2,630 were credited with bombing with the release of 8,621 tons of bombs, of which 1,426 tons were incendiaries. The Battle of Hamburg resulted in air defence units being drawn to the Reich from other theatres. By September 1943 over 60 per cent of the total strength of 1,646

fighters and 392 *Zerstörer* was established on airfields in Germany and the occupied territories.

Juggler and Schweinfurt

By August, with the 8th AF's strength at 16 operational B-17 groups, Eaker launched a major two-pronged mission deep into the heart of the Reich. Operation Juggler called for the 4th Wing to attack the vast Messerschmitt factory at Regensburg-Prüfening, before scaling the Alps and setting down in North Africa. 1st Wing would then attack Schweinfurt, its aircraft returning to bases in England. On the 17 August 1943 Eaker sent 376 B-17s on this dual mission: 127 4th Wing B-17Fs hit Regensburg, to lose 24 of their number; Schweinfurt was then bombed by 183 B-17s (230 sent) for the loss of 36. Allied fighter cover operated as far inland as Brussels and Eupen. Severe losses to JG 26 and I-IV/NJG 1 were effected by these fighters, but beyond their radius the B-17s came in for attacks of unparalleled savagery by over 300 German fighters drawn from all quarters of the Reich. The loss of 60 B-17s now set the pattern. A long pause

took place before VIII Bomber Command set out for targets in Germany: on 6 September 1943 a mission to Stuttgart failed in bad weather with the loss of 45 Fortresses, mostly to fighters. Over Emden on 27 September P-47s with new drop tanks were able to surprise German fighters to claim 21 kills for the loss of one P-47. But the fact remained that the supply of fighter groups and extra tanks was insufficient for the task of protecting VIII Bomber Command. On 2 October 1943 VIII Bomber Command launched a series of raids far into Germany: on this day 339 aircraft bombed Emden for the loss of two; the raid on Frankfurt and Wiesbaden on 4 October resulted in the loss of 16 bombers. The climax came on 14 October 1943 when a mission to Schweinfurt resulted in the loss of 60 B-17s, with five written off after landing and a further 145 more or less seriously damaged. The Luftwaffe lost 33 Bf 109Gs and Fw 190s, and four *Zerstörer*. For the Americans the losses were prohibitive, and Schweinfurt represented the crucifixion of unescorted daylight bombing, and a victory for the Luftwaffe.

Escort and defender

Throughout the course of August and September 1943, despite the opposition of the Führer and the almost total lack of response from Goering, top priority turned from the Russian and Mediterranean theatres of war to the defence of the Reich against invading Allied bombers and their attendant escort fighters.

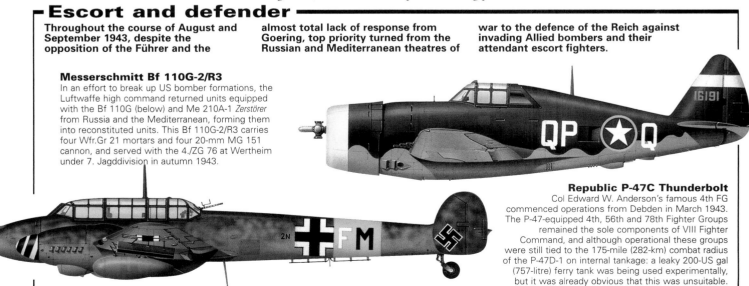

Messerschmitt Bf 110G-2/R3
In an effort to break up US bomber formations, the Luftwaffe high command returned units equipped with the Bf 110G (below) and Me 210A-1 *Zerstörer* from Russia and the Mediterranean, forming them into reconstituted units. This Bf 110G-2/R3 carries four Wfr.Gr 21 mortars and four 20-mm MG 151 cannon, and served with the 4./ZG 76 at Wertheim under 7. Jagddivision in autumn 1943.

Republic P-47C Thunderbolt
Col Edward W. Anderson's famous 4th FG commenced operations from Debden in March 1943. The P-47-equipped 4th, 56th and 78th Fighter Groups remained the sole components of VIII Fighter Command, and although operational these groups were still tied to the 175-mile (282-km) combat radius of the P-47D-1 on internal tankage: a leaky 200-US gal (757-litre) ferry tank was being used experimentally, but it was already obvious that this was unsuitable.

Battle of Berlin

With the Luftwaffe's victory over the US 8th Air Force in October 1943, Eaker was forced to abandon deep-penetration unescorted daylight raids pending the arrival of suitable long-range fighters. Harris, on the other hand, saw fit to launch a massive night bomber-offensive aimed ultimately at bombing Germany out of the war. The principal target was Berlin.

An ever-present hazard in the skies over Germany, apart from flak and fighters, was a potential threat from above; the bombs from aircraft in the upper levels of a bomber formation could cripple aircraft below if they drifted in formation. This 94th BG B-17 was lost over Berlin when its tailplane was hit by a 500-lb (227-kg) bomb. None of the crew escaped.

On 3 November 1943, Air Chief Marshal Sir Arthur Harris wrote a treatise addressed to Winston Churchill outlining RAF Bomber Command's past achievements and its future objectives: Berlin, the capital of the Reich, was to be the first priority in the forthcoming offensive, with Leipzig, Chemnitz, Dresden, Bremen, and others listed as secondary targets. He remarked disparagingly of recent American lack of co-ordination, their disastrous diversions such as the Ploesti raid, and at the siting of the recently formed US 15th Air Force far from centres of German war production in southern Italy. To Churchill, Harris addressed this dramatic message: 'We can wreck Berlin from end to end if the USAAF comes in on it. It will cost between us 400-500 aircraft. It will cost Germany the

war.' Harris had the means. Over 820 bombers, predominantly four-engined aircraft, were available for operations – Avro Lancaster, Handley Page Halifaxes and a few Short Stirlings.

Bomber equipment

By now the majority of main force bombers carried the Mk XIV (Stabilized Vector) bombsight, the multi-frequency Gee Mk II (TR.1355) for navigation, and metre-band H_2S Mk I radar. The heaviest bomb in use was the 12,000-lb (5443-kg) HC which was introduced in September 1943. No. 8 (PFF) Group continued to have pride of place in the allocation of the latest aids to navigation and marking: the 10-cm band Oboe Mk II and H_2S Mk III were superseding the older, and jammable, equipment. A new aid in use was Gee-H. It consisted of an airborne

transmitter plus Gee and two associated responder beacons based in the United Kingdom: the navigator obtained the phase-difference between signals, and thereby obtained an accurate fix.

In addition to 'Window', RAF bombers carried active and passive jamming equipment and tail-warners. But in this secret war of measure and countermeasure each side held only a temporary advantage before new equipment superseded the old. In tactical terms it was more vital than ever before to outwit the lethal German fighter reaction with elaborate diversions known as 'spoofs.' RAF Bomber Command flew its first spoof raid on night 22-23 September 1943 when the main force attacked Hannover, while a feint went to Osnabrück.

On 15 September 1943, the Luftwaffe's air defences were formed into two territorial fighter commands: one in the Reich and the other in the Western occupied territories. The production of fighter aircraft for the defence of the

Reich, although still second in priority to that of bombers, had, thanks to the efforts of Erhard Milch, increased: in July 1943 production peaked at 1,263 units, and thereafter fell to an average of 1,000 aircraft per month; few were new in design, and most were the standard types, including Messerschmitt Bf 110G-4, Junkers Ju 88C-6b and Ju 88R-1 types. A number of Dornier Do 217J-1, Messerschmitt Me 410B-1s and Heinkel He 219A-0 Uhu were also in service.

Use of wilde Sau and zahme Sau tactics enabled the Luftwaffe to recover from the 'Window' debacle with remarkable speed: now coming into service were new radars less susceptible to jamming. So, much to the consternation of Allied intelligence, the Germans were recovering their strength. They were on the defensive, but production was up, and training was booming albeit with the inevitable drop in standards.

Battle of Berlin

The assault on the Berlin primary commenced on the

The Handley Page Halifax B.Mk III entered Bomber Command service in early 1944. This No. 466 Sqn, RAAF aircraft carries the tail markings of an aircraft in No. 4 Group and is equipped with H_2S radar.

Left: The P-51 Mustang entered service in late 1943, initially with the 9th Air Force. 'GQ' codes on this P-51B Mustang indicate an aircraft of the 355th FS, 354th FG.

Below: The 55th Fighter Group began to replace its Lockheed P-38Hs with P-38Js in late 1943. These had much improved performance at altitude and were more useful to the 8th Air Force in the escort role.

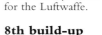

night of 18/19 November 1943, when 402 bombers out of 444 sent dropped 1,594 tons of bombs between 19.50 and 20.27; another force of 325 heavy bombers released 852 tons on Mannheim. It was the first occasion on which two major forces had raided, and only nine bombers failed to return. Further raids were made on the Reich capital over the following days.

Attacks followed the pattern set during November throughout the long, hard winter, when weather conditions were sometimes appallingly bad, until the night of 24/25 March 1944, when 726 bombers attacked Berlin with 2,230 tons: the loss of 73 bombers was a reflection on the efficiency of the German night-fighter force and the severity of the weather conditions. During the period described, Berlin suffered 16 major raids involving 9,111 sorties, and 208 harassing sorties by Mosquitoes on another 16 occasions: as the result of the major attacks RAF Bomber Command lost 492 aircraft failed to return and 954 damaged, of which 95 were written off after landing.

The Battle of Berlin and the

numerous major attacks on other objectives during the winter of 1943-44 was RAF Bomber Command's bitterest campaign of World War II, with losses rising to a peak of 314 failed to return and 38 written off in January during the course of 6,278 sorties over Germany. It was also a period when I. Jagdkorps' night-fighters fought back savagely. There was no dearth of trade in the nocturnal skies over Germany during this winter, and several aces, such as Lent, Streib, Jabs, Schnatifer, and others amassed high scores.

Enter the 15th Air Force

In November 1943 the US 15th Air Force, commanded first by Major-General James H. Doolittle and from January 1944 onwards by Major-General Nathan F. Twining, started operations from the complex of airfields around Foggia, in the heel of Italy. Strength grew rapidly from an original figure of about 930 operational aircraft in November, but low serviceability and difficult airfield operating conditions reduced the potential of this newly formed air force. The

strategic tasks laid at the door of the 15th Air Force included support for Allied armies in Italy, the weakening of German forces in the Balkans, and participation in Operation Pointblank, in addition to softening-up sorties to southern France in preparation for an eventual invasion. At first much was expected of Twining's command, with rich targets located in the 'soft underbelly' of the Festung Europa within range of its heavy bombers. But the distances to these targets, especially those in southern Germany, were great and weather and the mountainous Alps proved to be formidable obstacles. The 15th Air Force made its first major operational mission on 2 November 1943, when 139 B-17s and B-24s, operating from Tunisian bases and escorted on a section of the route by Lightnings, attacked the great Messerschmitt subsidiary at Wiener-Neustadt in Austria: 74 B-17s and 38 B-24s dropped 327 tons of bombs on the WNF concern with excellent results which were later estimated to have deprived the Luftwaffe of almost 250 Bf 109G-6 fighters over the following two months.

On 14 October 1943, as a climax after a fortnight of defensive operations against the US 8th Air Force, the fighters of 1. Jagdkorps shot down the majority of the 60 B-17s lost this day: the target was the ball-bearing factories at Schweinfurt in central Germany. Such losses were prohibitively high, and indeed for Eaker's command the casualties during October were horrendous: 198 bombers missing in the course of 2,159 sorties represented a peak of 9.2 per cent, and a loss rate

for US VIII Bomber Command that in the course of World War II was never to be surpassed. Collectively Schweinfurt meant the end of American aspirations in unescorted daylight bombing, and a victory, albeit temporary, for the Luftwaffe.

8th build-up

A unified command, later known as USSTAF (United States Strategic Air Forces), was formed under General Carl A. Spaatz in January 1944 to control the activities of the 8th and 15th USAFs, and to counter the political influence on the course of strategic bombing by both the AEAF and RAF Bomber Command. By February 1944, the 8th Air Force fielded 20 groups with the B-17G and nine with the B-24H and B-24J models, a force that at last was formidable.

Long-range fighters

October 1943 saw the new Lockheed P-38H-1-LO make its debut with the 55th Fighter Group and by February 1944, P-47 Thunderbolts reaching fighter groups were capable of matching German fighters in combat at all altitudes, and of escorting the heavies to as far afield as Hannover.

Without doubt the most dramatic debut, however, was that of the long-awaited Packard-Merlin-powered P-51B Mustang, which incorporated a superlatively efficient airframe with large internal tankage and the powerplant. Though the first examples were destined for 9th Air Force groups, the Mustang would soon join the ranks of the P-47 and Lightning of the 'Mighty 8th' in an all-out fight for air supremacy in the skies over the Reich.

The pilot of an Me 210A-1 of II./Zerstörergeschwader 26 jettisons his cockpit canopy as the aircraft's starboard engine blazes. The aircraft fell to a P-47 of the 61st FS, 56th FG on 11 December 1943.

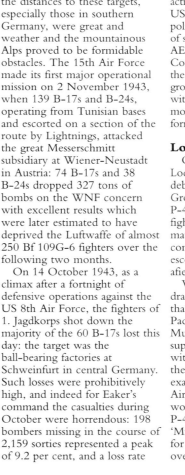

The battle for supremacy

A P-51B Mustang of the 334th Fighter Sqn, 4th Fighter Group cruises at altitude on an escort mission. With its impressive range the P-51 made a considerable impact on 8th Air Force bomber operations during 1944.

By early 1944, German fighters were waging a savage war against the USAAF by day and RAF Bomber Command by night. Though the fighting was on a scale unparalleled in the history of air warfare, the battle had yet to reach a climax.

General H. H. Arnold, the commanding general of the US Army Air Forces, knew that the task was very clear: defeat the Luftwaffe fighter arm within the few months remaining, or risk the cancellation of the invasion of North West Europe and thereby prolong the war.

Although the task of defeating the Luftwaffe was formidable, the USAAF was assisted by several hidden weaknesses in the opposing forces, particularly in the production and quality of fighters, engines and armament; the quality of fighter leaders; and both the quantity and quality of the new pilots.

Generaloberst Hans-Jurgen Stumpff succeeded Weise as commander of Luftwaffen-befehlshaber Mitte on 23 December 1943. It was immediately apparent to Stumpff's seasoned eye that the strength of Germany's fighter defences was critically weak: a serviceable strength of 480 day fighters was responsible for

defending a line from the Austrian/Hungarian border to the northern tip of Denmark, and against it were pitted some 1,500 B-17s and B-24s of the US 8th and 15th Air Forces backed by over 1,200 fighters, many now with a true long-range capability.

Luftwaffe pilots were in good supply, but quantity was being sacrificed for quality, and men arriving on the Staffeln had as little as 30 hours on type.

The night defences of Luftflotte Reich, on the other hand, had increased both in strength and efficiency: in December 1943 611 night-fighters, were on strength, with an average of some 400 serviceable: the effects of 'Window' jamming had been largely negated by the Lichtenstein SN-2 (FuG 220) airborne radar. Additional aids to homing included Flensburg (FuG 227) which homed onto the 'Monica' tail-warning radars of RAF bombers, and Naxos Z (FuG 350) which picked up

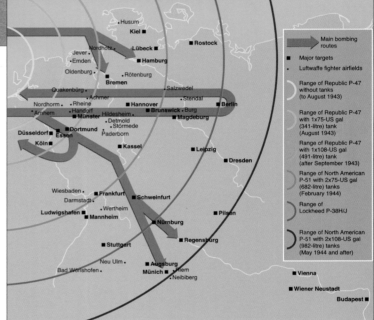

The main difference between the American bomber campaigns of 1943 and 1944 was in the steadily increasing range of USAAF escort fighters. By the end of 1944, Mustangs were escorting B-17s and B-24s deep into eastern Europe.

signals from the H₂S radars. The growing use of the 30-mm MK 108 cannon and the upward-firing *schräge Musik* installations on German night-fighters made them even more formidable.

Unfortunately for the Luftwaffe, Hitler and the Nazi hierarchy refused to recognise

the threat posed by the growing Allied bombing offensive. This was demonstrated in the reluctance to build more fighters at the expense of bombers, and to devote more energy into strengthening the defences of Germany. In January 1944, the Luftwaffe actually went over to the offensive.

Carpetbagger operations, dropping supplies to resistance forces in occupied Europe, were carried out by specially-tasked 8th Air Force squadrons. The first two Carpetbagger squadrons – the 36th and 406th Bomb Squadrons – were formed in late 1943. B-24J "Black Zombie" was assigned to the latter.

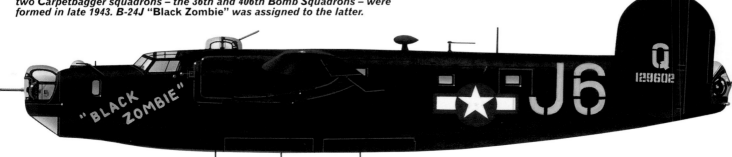

Left: This Messerschmitt Me 410A-2/U4 flew with 6./ZG 26 from Hildesheim in the spring of 1944. It is armed with a massive 5-cm BK 5 cannon for destroying Allied bombers. Twenty-one rounds were housed in the magazine.

Below: Waist gunners in a B-17 pose for the camera. In combat, the area beneath their feet would have been littered with spent cartridge cases.

Operation Steinbock

The offensive, named Operation Steinbock (Ibex), started with an attack by 227 bombers on the night of 21-22 January 1944, though little damage was inflicted. Twenty five bombers failed to return (RAF Mosquitoes claiming 16) and another 18 aircraft were lost in accidents. Attacks continued into April 1944, with dwindling strength and several losses, before Steinbock came to an ignominious end.

'Big Week'

Long-range deep-penetration attacks by Doolittle's US 8th Air Force were resumed against Germany on 11 January 1944. Weather posed a severe problem to both attacker and defender, but on 19 February clear weather at last gave Allied commanders the opportunity for which they had been waiting. Operation Argument was an all-out day and night bomber offensive aimed at obliterating German aircraft production. Launched on 20 February 1944, its epic battles became known as the 'Big Week'.

The great assault got under way on the night of 19-20 February 1944, when 823 RAF

A B-17G of the 452nd BG heads for Germany in February 1944. For the first time, the bombers were escorted all the way into the heart of Germany, thanks to the arrival of the P-51B Mustang.

bombers attacked Leipzig to lose a staggering 78 missing in action: on 20 February the US 8th Air Force sent 1,008 B-17s and B-24s, escorted by 661 US fighters to attack Leipzig, Poznan, Gotha, Brunswick, Halberstadt and Oschersleben. Luftwaffe pilots and observers were astonished to note American fighters penetrating as far inland as Brunswick: this area lay within easy range of the Mustangs, and many of the Thunderbolts were equipped with the new 150-US gal (568-litre) drop tanks.

At a stroke, the presence of the long-range US escort fighter upset the Luftwaffe's entire defensive strategy. For the American commanders, who were prepared to lose 200 bombers on a single mission, the losses in the Big Week were light: over 3,300 sorties by the 8th and 15th Air Forces resulted in the loss of 137 and 89 heavy bombers respectively, an overall average of 6 per cent.

For RAF Bomber Command the epic Battle of Berlin ended on 24 March 1944 after a winter of savage fighting. The losses had been severe, but well within the command's powers of recovery, but the Luftwaffe's night-fighter force was growing ominously

more deadly and proficient. There was no evidence of a collapse of the German nation's will to resist after the battering received by its capital city.

An attack by 795 bombers on Nuremberg on the night of 30-31 March 1944 cost the British 95 four-engined bombers, with a further 71 being badly damaged. In one night, Bomber Command lost more aircrew than Fighter Command did in the Battle of Britain. Nuremburg was the biggest night battle of World War II, and the total loss of over 13 per cent was too high even for the Air Staff and the imperturbable Harris, and thereafter the numbers of raids against the Reich fell. To his cost, Harris experienced the same defeat as had befallen the Americans over Schweinfurt in October 1943. For the Nachtjagdwaffe, it was a victory – but it was to be its last.

Duels over Germany

The conflict between USAAF and the forces of Luftflotte Reich during March and April 1944 came to a climax as the US 8th and 15th Air Forces struggled to gain air supremacy over Germany. The Italian-based 15th Air Force mainly attacked targets in Italy and the Balkans, with the occasional attack on Vienna, Klagenfurt, Steyr, Wiener- Neustadt and Graz.

The lion's share of the fighting was borne by the 8th Air Force

which, in March, had 20 groups of B-17Gs and 10 of B-24 Liberators; the fighter element consisted of seven P-47 groups, three with the P-38J, and three with the P-51B Mustang. US pilots were encouraged to be aggressive; dogfights starting well above 25,000 ft (7620 m) were followed down to the deck, with the returning fighters taking every opportunity to strafe. Here were none of the petty restrictions that had blighted RAF operations in 1941-43, and the bold tactics paid high dividends.

In the course of March 1944, Luftflotte Reich lost 309 fighters and 108 were damaged in combats – its total strength before replacement. The 8th Air Force lost 349 heavy bombers in 10,552 sorties, a 3.3 per cent casualty rate. The loss rate for US VIII Fighter Command was even lower, with 162 lost in 10,175 sorties.

During April 1944, when the strategic bombing forces were passed to the control of General Dwight D. Eisenhower for use in Overlord, the German attrition peaked, and by the end of the month air supremacy was in the hands of the US 8th Air Force. The back of Luftflotte Reich had been broken during the savage battles of February and March. This the Allied commanders knew, but their eyes were turned to another objective: the oil upon which the Wehrmacht depended.

North American P-51 Mustang

Above: To many pilots, the best P-51 variant was the P-51B. When fitted with the British Malcolm hood, it was lighter, faster, and had crisper handling than the bubble-hooded P-51D. The Iowa Beaut was a P-51B-15-NA of the 354th FS, 355th FG.

The P-51 Mustang was arguably the best operational piston-engined fighter ever built. With P-51s providing long-range escort, US heavy bombers could carry the war into the heart of the Third Reich with acceptable losses. Thus, the P-51 can justifiably claim its title as the fighter that won the war.

During World War II there were faster fighters than the P-51, more agile fighters than the P-51, fighters that packed a heavier punch, fighters that were more versatile and fighters that were built in larger numbers. Even among its US contemporaries, the Grumman F6F Hellcat turned more tightly, the Vought F4U Corsair was a better gun platform, and the Republic P-47 Thunderbolt was easier in a turning fight.

Few could claim that any other fighter was more important than the mighty Mustang, although an objective assessment might conclude that the Mustang had excessively high stick-forces, inadequate stall warning and vicious departure characteristics which severely constrained the aircraft's effectiveness.

The Mustang had a remarkable birth, being designed, built and flown (according to legend) in only 180 days. Even more remarkably, North American Aviation had originally been asked to produce Curtiss P-40s under licence for the RAF, and the young company had cheekily told the customer that it could design and build a superior fighter of its own design in the same timescale.

In its original form, the Mustang proved to be a superb performer at low altitude, and the early versions had successful careers as fighter-bombers and tactical reconnaissance aircraft. However, the performance of their Allison engines fell off dramatically at altitude, limiting the aircraft's usefulness in the pure fighter role. Even operating

The Mustang was flown by many of the United States Army Air Force's top-scoring aces in the European Theater of Operations. Exemplifying the breed was Captain Don Gentile, 336th Fighter Squadron, 4th Fighter Group, US Army Eighth Air Force, a remarkable fighter leader who scored 15.5 kills on Mustangs.

simply as a low-level fighter bomber and recce aircraft, the Mustang would deserve to be remembered as one of the great aircraft of history. But the success of the early Mustang was quite overshadowed by the achievements of the later versions.

The Mustang was entirely transformed through the replacement of its original engine by the Rolls-Royce Merlin. The

Left: The Mustang's cockpit has been compared to that of a high-class sports car, and for general all-round comfort, visibility and ease of operation, the P-51 was rated as being the best American fighter of World War II. These factors were very important during long-range bomber escort missions, for Mustang pilots had typically been airborne for several hours before engaging in combat.

Below: A gaggle of P-51s is framed by the starboard engines of a B-29 Superfortress bomber. The Mustang's long range made it ideal for long overwater missions, but the demands of the European theatre were such that only relatively small numbers of P-51s served in the Pacific. As the bombing campaign against Japan was stepped up, three P-51D fighter groups based on Iwo Jima took on Japanese fighters, allowing the B-29s to strike freely against industrial, military and civilian targets, with devastating results.

Merlin conferred the high-altitude performance which had been so lacking, while other modifications improved the aircraft's armament and the pilot's all-round view. With their new powerplant, the later Mustangs out-performed any other USAAF fighter, and the type was built in huge numbers and urgently rushed into service.

Although the aircraft was used in every theatre, and for a variety of roles, the Mustang found its métier escorting USAAF

Precious Metal *is typical of the many modified racing Mustangs still competing regularly in the US. These range from simple engine tweaks to complete rebuilds. This aircraft features a Cavalier Mustang tail, along with a streamlined, low drag cockpit canopy.*

bombers during their daylight raids over the Reich. With the arrival of the Mustang, the bombers could be escorted all the way to their targets, by a fighter capable of meeting aircraft like the Messerschmitt Bf 109 and Focke-Wulf Fw 190 on even terms. This kept bomber losses to an acceptable level, and allowed the USAAF and RAF to continue the round-the-clock bombing attacks which eventually brought the Third Reich to its knees.

The arrival of the jets rendered the P-51 obsolete in the fighter role, while its liquid-cooled engine and belly-mounted radiator made it too vulnerable for ground attack duties. Post-war, many operators preferred P-47 Thunderbolts to the Mustang, and

it faded from the scene. However, it served briefly in the defence of the continental United States and played a major combat role during the Korean War.Into the early 1970s, Mustangs were still in action in low-intensity conflicts over Central America.

The Mustang's exploits during World War II were more than enough to win it a prime position in aviation's hall of fame. Today, P-51s continue to dominate the unlimited air-racing scene, and are the most popular and sought-after warbirds.

Left: Boeing B-17Gs of the 532nd Squadron, 381st Bomb Wing set off into the morning sun for a raid over Germany. The red trim was adopted by the Group at the end of July 1944.

Below: The arrival of the Mustang changed the balance of power in the skies over Germany in 1944. These P-51Ds are from the 52nd Fighter Group, based in Italy at that time.

The oil campaign

In April 1944 Allied bombers prepared the way for Operation Overlord. However, the strategic campaign continued, with British and American attacks on Germany's vital synthetic oil industries.

Unless he was a man of exceptional experience, the young German fighter pilot of early 1944 found himself outmatched technically and numerically by his Allied opponents. The Luftwaffe had no answer to the long-ranged and aggressive US fighter escorts and supporting sweeps that accompanied every penetration of the Reich by day. The casualties suffered by the Jagdwaffe during early 1944 were high, and the loss of experienced men in Russia and the Mediterranean now began to tell.

Defence of the Reich

In the wake of 'Big Week', attempts were made to concentrate units within Luftflotte Reich. The overworked pilots had to defend areas from the Baltic coast through Berlin, central and southern Germany to Vienna. In fact the Bf 109 and Fw 190 units remained widely dispersed, save in the 'bomber alley' that ran from Brussels to Hannover, and beyond to Berlin. Between 400 and 500 fighters now faced over 2,800 Allied bombers and 1,500 fighters.

While Air Chief Marshal Sir Arthur Harris's RAF Bomber Command turned its attention to the enemy transportation system,

June 1944 saw the RAF return to daylight raids after a long absence. Allied escort fighters and a weak Luftwaffe fighter force made the skies much safer for Bomber Command.

the American air forces continued to attack aircraft production centres in Germany. Major-General J. H. Doolittle's US 8th Air Force now consisted of 31.5 groups of Boeing B-17Gs and Consolidated B-24Js. The VIII Fighter Command had risen in strength to 14 groups with the P-51B Mustang starting to replace the P-47. By May 1944 seven P-51 groups were operational, leaving four with P-47s and four with P-38J Lightnings. The US 15th Air Force operating out of Italy had received its first Mustangs in April.

Aggressive and confident US fighters sought out the Luftwaffe at all stages of their missions. Combats that started above 25,000 ft (7620 m) now were concluded in fierce dogfights at tree-top height,

On 15 April the 8th Air Force started 'Jackpot' strafing missions on airfields and communications in Germany and the occupied territories. Each group was assigned an area to work, but the missions were risky due to the intense flak: on this first day 32 fighters were lost.

Massive air battles continued over Germany through the rest of April. Luftflotte Reich lost 54 fighters during the raids on Oberpfaffenhofen and Landsberg on 24 April. But the Luftwaffe proved that it still had teeth during the Berlin attack of 29 April. In a series of skilfully controlled interceptions, 63 bombers and 10 fighters were shot down, for the loss of only 24 Fw 190s and Bf 109G-6s.

The 8th Air Force carried out 21 missions during April 1944, amounting to 14,380 sorties: bomber gunners claimed 397 fighters shot down with 114 possibles and 208 damaged. Losses peaked at 361 B-17s and B-24s, a rate of 3.6 percent. American fighters claimed a further 332 kills in the air and 493 on the ground for the loss of 148 of their own number. Actual Luftflotte Reich losses through all causes resulting from enemy action amounted to 580 lost and 193 damaged.

The oil campaign

By 1944 Germany was depended on the supply of synthetic fuel oil produced from coal to bolster the limited imports from Romania and Hungary. Synthetic oil plants were well scattered, but there were concentrations in the Ruhr and in particular in the Leuna-Leipzig area of Germany.

Production was booming: stocks over and above any strategic reserves rose from 280,000 tons in September 1943 to 390,000 in December, and to a peak of 574,000 tons by April 1944. The Germans anticipated Allied air attacks on such a vital, but vulnerable, industry: Leuna and the surrounding area was very heavily defended. The 14. Flakdivision had more than 380 heavy guns, many arranged in Grossbatterien of six or eight.

Oil targets

Attacks on oil targets started as early as May 1940, but a plethora of directives had turned both RAF Bomber Command and later the US 8th Air Force to other objectives. On 5 April the US 15th Air Force unofficially reopened the oil campaign with an attack on Ploesti: during late April General Carl A. Spaatz, the Commander of USSTAF, received permission to launch the 8th Air Force on the same objectives.

Before the opening of the campaign Luftflotte Reich had to contend with heavy attacks on Berlin (8 May 1944), and on Brunswick and Wiener-Neustadt

Lancasters at war, 1944

The Avro Lancaster flew its first missions in March 1942, and by 1944 it had become the backbone of the RAF's Bomber Command. It could carry a huge load over long distances, and by the time of the Normandy invasion it was flying daylight raids.

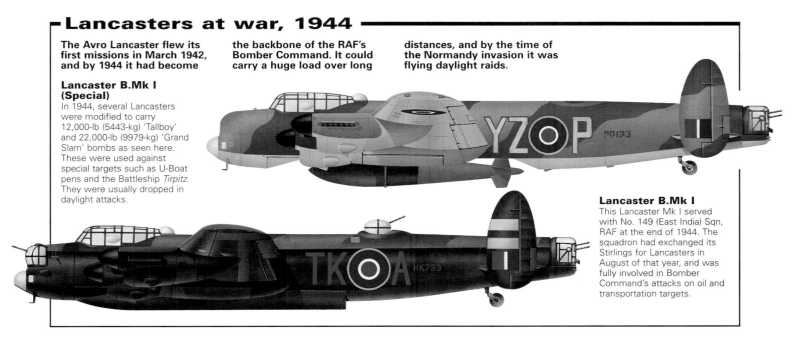

Lancaster B.Mk I (Special)

In 1944, several Lancasters were modified to carry 12,000-lb (5443-kg) 'Tallboy' and 22,000-lb (9979-kg) 'Grand Slam' bombs as seen here. These were used against special targets such as U-Boat pens and the Battleship *Tirpitz*. They were usually dropped in daylight attacks.

Lancaster B.Mk I

This Lancaster Mk I served with No. 149 (East India) Sqn, RAF at the end of 1944. The squadron had exchanged its Stirlings for Lancasters in August of that year, and was fully involved in Bomber Command's attacks on oil and transportation targets.

(10 May 1944), losing 51 fighters. On 12 May 1944 the 8th Air Force despatched its 1st, 2nd and 3rd Divisions to the oil centres at Leuna, Lückendorf, Zeitz, Böhlen, Brüx and Zwickau. The 952 bombers were supported by 21 fighter groups including 410 Mustangs, 201 Thunderbolts and 265 P-38 J Lightnings.

The 1st and 2nd Divisions lost 37 out of the 42 heavy bombers shot down on this day. But the damage they caused was crucial: Brüx ceased production, while output from Leuna was reduced by 60 per cent. The cost of

defending these vital targets was also high: Luftflotte Reich lost 73 aircraft destroyed.

On 28 and 29 May 1944 the 8th Air Force attacked Ruhland, Magdeburg, Zeitz and Leuna to inflict severe damage. The 224 Liberators of the 3rd Division hit Pölitz so hard that synthetic oil production at the plant ceased for two months.

The oil attacks, which continued over the summer, had a significant long-term effect on the Luftwaffe's ability to fight. By 22 June 1944 production of synthetic oil had been reduced by almost 90 per

cent. Output fell from 195,000 tons in May to 35,000 tons in July and only 7,000 tons in September 1944.

Strategic reserves had to be drawn on to allow the Luftwaffe to operate without restriction over the Reich and Normandy. But by August shortages began to bite, and grounding of all but the most essential combat units took place.

Bomber Command

Transportation targets to ease the invasion path were the objectives laid before RAF Bomber Command in the spring of 1944. Targets included marshalling yards, stations, junctions, tunnels, bridges and rolling stock factories.

As sortie numbers soared, loss rates fell. The nightmare of 314 heavy bombers being shot down in 6,278 night sorties during January 1944 had been overcome: 293 were lost in 13,592 sorties in June.

Losses to night fighters remained high, and low-level bombing brought more losses to light 20-mm and 37-mm flak around well-defended targets in France and Belgium.

On 3 May, heavy bombers raided 21 Panzerdivision's depot at Mailly-le Camp. Forty-two out of 362 were shot down, mainly by NJG 4 and III/NJG 5. On 10 May, 12 Lancasters out of 97 sent were lost during an attack on Lille.

Preparing the invasion

During the pre-invasion phase, RAF Bomber Command started to attack radar installations and gun positions between Domburg and Lannion, and after the landings of 6 June 1944, the command was called in regularly

to support ground troops and to attack V-1 sites.

On the night of 16-17 June 1944 RAF Bomber Command resumed intensive 'Crossbow' attacks on V-1 sites in France, before returning to area attacks, which now included a high proportion of oil targets, in Germany. An indication of the reduced power of the Jagdwaffe came on 27 August when 216 Halifax B.Mk IIIs of No. 4 (Bomber) Group, together with 27 Mosquitoes, strongly escorted by Supermarine Spitfires, attacked Homburg by daylight. Opposition to day attacks was negligible.

By September 1944 the Allied armies had secured all territory up to the German border, thus denying to Luftflotte Reich the vitally needed early-warning radars, advance GCI stations, observer posts and forward night fighter fields. RAF Bomber Command was now for the first time permitted to launch a wide range of spoof and main attacks. Only 96 heavy bombers were shot down in 6,428 night sorties during September, and 75 in 10,193 during October 1944.

Control of the skies

With control now in Allied hands, the great bomber forces were able now to operate at will with only the occasional burst of activity by the Luftwaffe to fear. Fuel was in critically short supply. The capable fighter leaders and experienced pilots had been used up during the great battles of 1943-44, leaving a force of freshmen of limited ability. Improved fighters like the Bf 109G-10 and Fw 190D-9 were good, but without experienced pilots not good enough to regain control of German skies.

Below: Bomber command provided massive support to Allied troops on the ground in Normandy in the summer of 1944. Here, a Halifax B.Mk III of No. 578 Squadron, RAF passes over the railway marshalling yards at Hazebrouck on D-Day.

Left: Douglas C-47s of the Ninth Troop Carrier Command load up on the evening of 5 June 1944. Within 24 hours, 1,600 Allied transports and 500 gliders delivered three complete airborne divisions to Normandy.

Below: A Martin B-26 Marauder of the 9th Air Force crosses the beach as it returns from a mission to disrupt German reinforcements.

Normandy

The Allies expected the Luftwaffe to react with furious energy against the D-Day landings. To their surprise, there was little effective opposition. The Luftwaffe had been drained over the previous year.

Almost exactly four years after the British Expeditionary Force had staged its near-miraculous evacuation from Dunkirk, the Allies once more set foot in strength on French soil when on 6 June 1944, under the supreme command of General Eisenhower, British, American and Canadian forces landed in Normandy. They did so with complete mastery of the air.

Preparation

For some months past, the RAF and USAAF had been preparing the way for the invasion. British and American heavy bombers, reassigned from the assault on Germany, were striking at key points in the French road and rail system to prevent the movement of reinforcements once the invading forces had landed. To this task was added the offensive against the flying-bomb sites in the Pas de Calais, while the fighter-bombers and light bombers of the 2nd Tactical Air Force struck at coastal targets. These included E-boat bases, radar stations, airfields and coastal gun batteries along the French coast. On the eve of the landings themselves the Allied Expeditionary Air Force comprised 173 squadrons of

fighters and fighter-bombers, 59 squadrons of light and medium bombers and 70 squadrons of transport aircraft; in addition to around 50 other support squadrons, there was also the might of RAF Bomber Command and the US 8th Air Force. In all, the Allies could count on close to 12,000 aircraft to support the invasion.

Operation Overlord

The assault on the French coast was a highly co-ordinated effort by the land, sea and air forces. As 145,000 men went ashore from the sea on the first day, considerable use was made of airborne forces, the US IX Troop Carrier Command's C-47s dropping large numbers of paratroops behind the American beachhead area, their task being to consolidate an area from which an advance could be made up the Cotentin peninsula to capture the port of Cherbourg. In the event, the American airborne operations were not wholly successful, the 82nd and 101st Airborne

Divisions being scattered over too wide an area to be fully effective. In the eastern sector, behind the British and Canadian beaches, the Stirlings, Albemarles, Halifaxes and Dakotas of the RAF's Nos 38 and 46 Groups dropped 4,310 paratroops and towed about 100 gliders to secure vital objectives such as coastal batteries, river bridges and road junctions.

Deception

As part of the elaborate deception plans undertaken to conceal the true location of the assault area during the night of 5/6 June a squadron of Lancasters (No. 617) had flooded the skies over the Channel far to the north east with 'Window'. The slow-moving cloud was designed to suggest on enemy radar an approaching invasion fleet. A similar operation was carried out by Halifaxes and Stirlings off Boulogne. These feints certainly played their part in discouraging the Germans from committing their reinforcements until the real landings had gained a powerful foothold in Normandy.

Throughout that first day, as more and more men and vehicles stormed ashore, the

Allied air forces put up an enormous umbrella of protective fighters to keep watch for the Luftwaffe. In fact, the German air force reacted slowly and sluggishly. On 31 May 1944 the strength of the Luftwaffe was 6,141 first-line aircraft and 934 transports. This was spread all over Europe, but the defence of the Reich took first priority in the allocation of fighters. Fifty three per cent of the Luftwaffe's interceptor strength was now based in Germany and Austria. All that was available to II Jagdkorps in France and Belgium, were 119 serviceable Focke-Wulf Fw 190A-8s and Messerschmitt Bf 109G-6s, 47 serviceable Bf 110G-4 night fighters and 55 Junkers Ju 88C-6 Zerstörers.

Massive assault

Only a small number of enemy air attacks developed and the damage caused by them was negligible. The Allies, on the other hand, recorded a total of 14,674 operational sorties on that first day, for the loss (mainly to flak) of 113 aircraft.

The initial assault phase ended with the delivery of 256 gliders to the inland dropping zones, carrying reinforcements to the

Clouds of smoke rise as the bridge over the River Loire at Tours is destroyed on 15 June 1944. Allied air attacks on such communications targets made German reinforcement of the battle front extremely difficult.

Fighters over the beaches

At the time of the Normandy landings, *Luftflotte* II had only 119 serviceable single-engined fighters in western France and Belgium. They were faced by an Allied air armada which could call on more than 5,400 front-line fighters, supporting 3,567 heavy bombers and 1,645 medium bombers.

Mustang Mk III
The six RAF Mustang squadrons were among the most successful of the 2nd TAF's fighter units. This example served with the Polish No. 133 Wing.

Fw 190A-8
A world-beater when introduced in 1941, the Fw 190A was outclassed by the time of the Normandy invasion. This example served with the *Geschwaderstab* of JG 26 at Lille-Nord in May 1944.

men of the British 6th Airborne Division. Heavy tank-carrying Hamilcar gliders were now used for the first time to bring the Tetrarch light tank into action.

For four days after D-Day the Allies were content to consolidate their beachhead as the tactical support Typhoons, Spitfires, Mustangs, Lightnings and Thunderbolts ranged over northern France, attacking road convoys and trains struggling to deliver German reinforcements to the battle area. Within 10 days more than half a million men had been landed on the Normandy beaches, scarcely troubled on their voyage from the UK by the Luftwaffe, thanks to the continuing efforts of the

2nd Tactical Air Force to pin the German aircraft to their bases. By 10 June, after only three days' work by the airfield engineers, the first landing strip on French soil had been completed and thereafter RAF Spitfires and Hawker Typhoons were able to operate close-up behind the land battle, the Typhoons in particular proving deadly with their rocket armament.

Operating from 'cab-ranks' stacked at 4,000 to 8,000 feet (1220 to 2440 m), the Typhoons were called in directly by radio-equipped forward air controllers. They repeatedly attacked panzer concentrations in the bocage (raised hedgerow country), and

were particularly useful in nailing dug-in 8.8-cm guns. For the Germans movement on the ground became fraught with hazard: the 2. SS (Das Reich) Panzerdivision had a tortuous journey from the Toulouse area to the battlefront, while the 989th Regiment took 19 days to come from Nice.

Luftwaffe reinforcement

Within one week of D-Day, II Jagdkorps had been reinforced by 998 fighters drawn from the Reich, Italy and Austria to bolster JG 2 and JG 26. The Jagdgruppen brought with them a number of Bf 109G-14s, which offered some improvement over the earlier models: in addition many Fw 190A-8s were fitted with boost override to improve performance. But these aircraft compared badly with the USAF's latest Republic P-47D-25RE and North American P-51D-1NA fighters, and with the 2nd TAF's Supermarine Spitfire LF.Mk IXs.

Luftwaffe pilot training hours were down to some 200 hours in all, with often only six hours on type being offered before posting to the front. What few of the aces remained were as always very dangerous, but in general Luftwaffe fighter operations over the Normandy front exhibited the hallmarks of inferior quality.

Normandy break-out

The Americans were the first to break out of the beachhead, striking north towards Cherbourg before the end of June, and west and south during July. By the middle of August the British 2nd Army and the Canadian 1st Army had

advanced south from Caen so that some 16 German divisions faced encirclement and annihilation at Falaise. After a week of pounding from the air and ground the bulk of the German 7th Army was decimated and the remainder in flight across France, all the while harried by the rocket-firing Typhoons, the Thunderbolts and Lightnings by day, and the Mosquitoes of the RAF's No. 2 Group by night. On 25 August Paris was liberated by its own citizenry and on 3 September the Welsh Guards swept into Brussels.

In the air the forces of Luftflotte III, which after 22 August 1944 was led by Generaloberst Otto Dessloch, had been unable to offer more than token support to the withdrawals. In combat operations alone this command lost 2,195 aircraft and 444 were damaged in the period from 1 June to 31 August 1944.

On to Germany

Many of the Luftwaffe's most experienced fighter pilots had been killed in the skies over Normandy. As if to concede Allied air superiority still further, OKL downgraded Luftflotte III's status to that of the Luftwaffenkommando West on 26 September 1944, under General Alexander Holle.

As they glanced at the situation maps, many Allied planners felt that the war would be over by Christmas 1944. Others, especially those who had first-hand knowledge of US battle reports of operations over Germany, especially those describing rocket- and jet-powered interceptors, were not so optimistic.

A P-47 Thunderbolt crosses the French coast at Mont St Michel, heading inland to support Patton's Third US Army in its drive on Rennes and Le Mans. The Allied break out from Normandy forced the Wehrmacht back beyond the Seine.

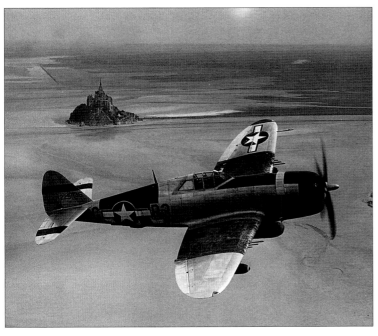

Autumn 1944

Allied forces suffered a number of setbacks after the headlong advance out of Normandy, particularly in the ill-fated Arnhem operation.

The destruction of German Forces south of Caen in mid-August 1944 was followed by the collapse of organised resistance throughout northern France. The Canadian 1st, British 2nd, and US 1st and 3rd Armies sped eastwards during the latter part of that month. Paris was liberated (partly from within and partly by Leclerc's 2nd French Armoured Division) on 25 August.

The British reached Brussels on 3 September and Antwerp on the following day. The US 3rd Army reached Verdun on 1 September, sweeping on to Metz and linking up with the US 7th Army as it advanced northwards having landed in the south of France on 15 August.

Headlong advance

During this great onrush the Allied air forces were constantly in action, as their ground echelons strove to establish and re-establish fresh bases close up behind the advancing armies. Before the crossing of the Seine, Mosquitoes, Mitchells, Mustangs, Bostons, Spitfires and Wellingtons of No. 2 Group attacked the ferries and barges at Rouen and elsewhere as German fighters attempted to interfere. These were engaged by No. 83 Group's Spitfires and the US 9th Air Force's P-47s and P-51s, which together claimed more than 100 of the enemy destroyed during the last week in August.

Early in the battle for Normandy, the RAF received another irksome commitment when the Luftwaffe commenced its belated and much vaunted V-1 campaign against London. The first V-1 to fall on British soil exploded at 04.18 on 13 June 1944 near Swanscombe, just west of Gravesend.

V-1 threat to London

The maximum speed of the V-1 was 497 mph (800 km/h), but in order to maximise range normal operating speeds were in the order of 348-410 mph (560-660 km/h). Gyro-stabilised, the

Above: Douglas A-20 medium bombers of the US Ninth Air Force hit enemy positions as the Allies force the Wehrmacht inexorably back towards the German border.

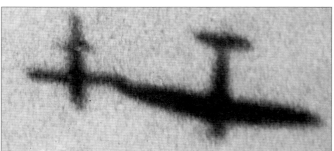

Right: A Spitfire on a 'Diver' patrol uses its wingtip to send a V-1 flying bomb out of control. Fighters accounted for 1,847 of the missiles, with AA fire destroying another 2,000.

V-1 maintained a constant heading until a timer cut the motor and applied full nose-down elevator to pitch the bomb into a 60° dive. The blast from this weapon was devastating.

Ground-based defences consisted of 40-mm Bofors and 3.7-in (94-mm) AA guns with radar prediction and, in the case of the heavy AA guns, new proximity-fused ammunition. Anti-aircraft artillery was located in a belt to the south of London, while Air Defence Great Britain's fighters operated over the Channel.

Fast fighters

The only fighters that could attain the V-1's pace were the Supermarine Spitfire Mk XIV, the Hawker Tempest Mk V, and the North American Mustang Mk III by day. The de Havilland Mosquito NF.Mk XIII and the Northrop P-61A Black Widow could also make successful intercepts by night.

The UK's first jet fighter, the Gloster Meteor Mk I, started 'Diver' operations from Manston under No. 11 (Fighter) Group on 2 August 1944, Flying Officer Dean shooting down the squadron's first V-1 two days later. When his cannon failed to fire, Dean flew alongside the V-1 and flipped the bomb over with his wingtip.

British Paratroops on their way to Arnhem. The ambitious operation almost succeeded, but suffered from poor luck, bad co-ordination and a shortage of air support.

Together the ADGB (Fighter Command after October 1944) and AA Command shot down 3,957 V-1s. Top-scoring pilot was Squadron Leader J. Berry DFC, who scored 61.33 while with Nos 3 and 501 Squadrons on Tempest Mk Vs.

Germany's first ballistic missile, the A-4 rocket (alias the V-2) first fell in the UK on 8 September 1944 at Chiswick,

West London. The last fell at Kynaston Road, Orpington, on 27 March 1945. There was no defence against these advanced weapons. In all V-1s killed 6,139 persons and injured 17,239, while the V-2 killed 2,855 and injured 6,268.

As RAF Bomber Command joined in attacks on German coastal garrisons from St Nazaire to Dunkirk, which had been

Updated veterans

A number of new fighters had been introduced as World War II progressed, but the two best fighters of 1939 were still in the front line at the end of the war. However, late variants of the Supermarine Spitfire and Messerschmitt Bf 109 were vastly more capable than their predecessors, being much faster and considerably more heavily armed.

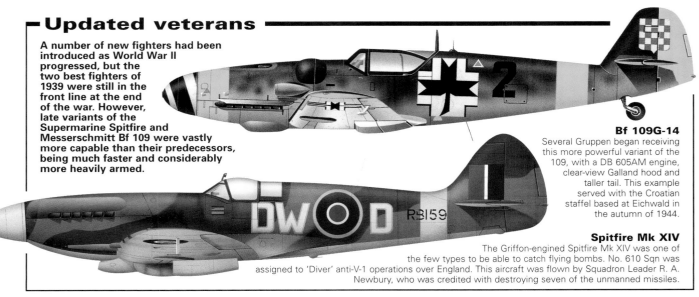

Bf 109G-14
Several Gruppen began receiving this more powerful variant of the 109, with a DB 605AM engine, clear-view Galland hood and taller tail. This example served with the Croatian staffel based at Eichwald in the autumn of 1944.

Spitfire Mk XIV
The Griffon-engined Spitfire Mk XIV was one of the few types to be able to catch flying bombs. No. 610 Sqn was assigned to 'Diver' anti-V-1 operations over England. This aircraft was flown by Squadron Leader R. A. Newbury, who was credited with destroying seven of the unmanned missiles.

bypassed by the advancing armies, the Dakotas, Stirlings and Halifaxes of RAF Transport Command were called on to mount the British airborne assault at Arnhem.

By early September 1944 the German army had retired to defence lines in the Netherlands, and along the fortifications, anti-tank ditches and wooded hills of the Siegfried Line. Despite their lengthy lines of communications, the Allies were determined to maintain the pace of the advance that had carried them from the Seine to Brussels in just under a fortnight. After much argument General Dwight D. Eisenhower, the supreme Allied commander, acquiesced to General Sir Bernard Montgomery's bold and imaginative plan to outflank the defences by crossing the lower Rhine, going on to advance into the north German plain.

In Operation Market the British 1st Airborne Division was to capture the bridge across the Neder Rijn at Arnhem, while American airborne forces secured the bridges to the south, at Grave, Veghel and Eindhoven. The drops were to be co-ordinated with Operation Garden, in which the British 2nd Army was to advance to Eindhoven and push northwards.

Market took place on the morning of 17 September 1944, The C-47s of the US IX Troop Carrier Command delivered the 82nd and 101st Airborne Divisions against targets on the Maas and Waal rivers, and the airborne troopers achieved their tasks without much difficulty.

"A bridge too far..."

To the north, at Arnhem, the DZs were too far to the west of the objective and progress was slow. By grotesque mischance the 1st Airborne Division was set down close to the crack II SS Panzerkorps. The 9th SS (Höhenstauffen) and 10th SS (Fründsberg) Panzer Divisions were resting after their exertions in France, and other top-quality infantry and tank battalions were re-equipping in the area.

On the first day 3,887 Short Stirlings, Armstrong Whitworth Albemarles, Handley Page Halifaxes and Douglas C-47 Dakotas with 500 Waco CG-4A, Airspeed Horsa Mk II and General Aircraft Hamilcar gliders participated in the drops and landings. They were supported by 1,113 Allied bombers and 1,240 fighters. Typhoons, P-51Ds and Republic P-47Ds were employed on flak suppression duties, and suffered heavy losses. It was a black day for the American 56th Fighter Group, which lost 16 out of 39 Thunderbolts.

Luftwaffe strikes back

Putting up 350-400 sorties per day, II Jagdkorps badly mauled the Allied transports, with II./JG 26's Focke-Wulfs shooting down a large number of C-47s. The bridge at Nijmegen had been secured, but the advance of the British XXX Corps became bogged down in increasingly bitter resistance. The admission of failure came on 25 September 1944, when the surviving paratroops pulled out of Arnhem. The RAF lost 55 aircraft and had 320 damaged by flak: one pilot of No. 271 Squadron, Flight Lieutenant D. Lord, was awarded a posthumous Victoria Cross for his sacrifice over the flak-ringed woods of Arnhem.

Mistel attacks

Elsewhere the Germans struck at the vital Nijmegen bridge over the Waal, now in British hands. The attacks included Mistels, unmanned Ju 88s packed with explosives with a piloted fighter mounted on top. These attacks failed to hit the bridge and during the last week in September the Spitfires of No. 83 Group claimed another 46 German aircraft.

Market Garden had been part of an Allied plan to cross the lower Rhine in force, liberate the Netherlands and outflank the Ruhr. To the south, the Americans were meeting with stiff resistance. By 18 November they had reached a line running along the borders of Belgium, Luxembourg and France.

Meanwhile the RAF had been supporting a major operation to clear the island of Walcheren at the entrance to the Scheldt, thereby opening up the great sea port of Antwerp. In a series of heavy raids from 3 October to 8 November, Bomber Command dropped almost 9000 tons of bombs. Over the same period the 2nd Tactical Air Force flew some 10,000 sorties, dropped 1500 tons of bombs and fired 11,600 rockets.

Although the Germans fought back hard in places, the skies over North West Europe in the late Autumn of 1944 were no place for a lone Luftwaffe pilot. Here, an Fw 190 falls victim to a marauding US fighter.

Boeing
B-17 Flying Fortress

The vast armadas of the US 8th Air Force, equipped mainly with the Boeing B-17, ranged far and wide over Germany and occupied Europe from 1942 to 1945. Bombing individual factories and other precision targets, they also whittled away at the fighter strength of the Luftwaffe in some of the largest and bloodiest air battles in history.

In 1934, the nature of the air battles to come could not have been foreseen. At that time, the only targets within the range of US bombers were in such unlikely places as Canada and Mexico. In the Depression, money was tight, and the new monoplane Martin Bomber appeared to be all that was needed.

But when the US Army Air Corps put out a request for a new multi-engined bomber, far-sighted engineers at the Boeing Airplane Company decided to interpret 'multi-engined' as meaning not two engines, but four. Admittedly, they did this mainly in order to achieve more

height over the target, but it had the effect of making the Boeing Model 299 significantly larger than its rivals.

First flight

Design began in June 1934, and the prototype made a successful first flight on 28 July 1935. The main purpose of the new bomber was to defend the United States by bombing an invasion fleet (the only plausible kind of target) and it was the nature of this mission, rather than heavy defensive armament, that resulted in Boeing registering the name 'Flying Fortress' for the new aircraft.

With a number of changes,

Top: Camouflage began to disappear from 8th AF Fortresses from January 1944. These are 381st Bombardment Group B-17Gs.

Above: Clear weather meant that good visual bombing results were possible, but made the B-17s obvious targets for flak gunners. These B-17Fs of the 390th BG are seen over Amiens/Glisy airfield in France during 1943.

especially to landing gear, armament and engines (930-hp/694-kW) Wright Cyclones instead of 750-hp/ 560-kW Pratt & Whitney Hornets), test Y1B-17s were ordered and delivered to the 2nd Bombardment Group at Langley Field in 1937.

Turbocharging

The 14th aircraft was built as the Y1B-17A, its engines fitted with General Electric turbo-superchargers, which increased its speed from 256 mph (412 km/h) to 311 mph (500 km/h) and raised the operating height to well over 30,000 ft (9145 m).

When the B-17B entered service in 1939 (in the teeth of US Navy opposition), it was the

fastest, highest-flying bomber in the world, ideal for the USAAC which was perfecting the art of daylight strategic bombing with large formations of aircraft with heavy defensive armament.

In December 1941, the month in which Japan bombed Pearl Harbor, the first large-scale production B-17 was entering service. The B-17E was a visually different model, incorporating the lessons learned in World War II in Europe. Its most striking change was the much larger tail, with a giant dorsal fin and long-span tailplane giving better control and stability at high altitude. The armament was completely revised to substantially increase the aircraft's

Providing adequate forward-firing defensive armament was always a problem with the Fortress, but was finally addressed in the B-17G. This variant was fitted with four 0.5-in (12.7-mm) machine-guns in two turrets (chin and dorsal, each with two guns), and two manually-operated 0.5-in (12.7-mm) cheek guns.

New roles were found for surplus B-17Gs post-war. This SB-17 carries H₂X radar under its nose and an air-droppable lifeboat for rescuing downed airmen. The US Navy also operated B-17s as early warning aircraft (as PB-1Ws) fitted with search radar.

In the chill of a February morning, ground crew at an 8th AF base at Framlingham, England stand by with fire extinguishers as a B-17G starts up prior to another daylight mission.

firepower. Further improvements in armour and equipment all helped to increase the gross weight to 54,000 lb (24494 kg), so that the cruising speed inevitably fell from 231 mph (372 km/h) to only 210 mph (338 km/h). Deliveries of this aircraft totalled 512.

The 'Mighty 8th'

With the B-17E and B-17F (the latter stressed to carry greater bombloads), the US 8th Air Force built up its strength in England. The first combat mission was flown on 17 August 1942 by 12 B-17Es of the 97th Bomb Group against a marshalling yard near Rouen.

This was the small beginning of the greatest strategic striking force ever created. It was to lead to a three-year campaign during the course of which 640,036 US tons of bombs were dropped on German targets, eventually achieving supremacy even over the heart of Germany in daylight, albeit at huge cost.

By far the most numerous B-17 model was the B-17G, the final

result of bitterly won combat experience. As well as being fitted with better armament, most G-models had improved turbochargers which actually increased the service ceiling to 35,000 ft (10670 m). However, as these bombers were so heavy, the cruising speed fell to 182 mph (293 km/h). This increased the time during which the gigantic formations were exposed to attack by the German fighters but, conversely, lengthened the period in which the B-17 guns could destroy enemy fighters.

Boeing built 4,035 B-17Gs, Douglas turning out 2,395 and Vega (a Lockheed subsidiary) 2,250 – a total of 8,680. In total, 12,731 B-17s of all variants were built, of which 12,677 were formally accepted by the USAAF.

B-17 operations were not confined to northern Europe. The type also served with the USAAF in the Pacific and Mediterranean theatres, although the Fortress's contemporary, the B-24 Liberator, with its longer range, was the preferred type, especially in the Pacific.

Modifications and a number of special Fortress variants appeared as the war progressed. Some 8th Air Force bomber aircraft were fitted with radar and electronic countermeasures equipment to improve survivability and bombing accuracy.

The YB-40 was a 1943 'escort fighter' conversion tested by the 8th Air Force. Armed with extra pairs of machine-guns and ammunition, and intended to fly in bomber formations, the YB-40 proved to be too heavy. Unable to keep up with the bombers, it was abandoned.

Reconnaissance and transport variants (the F-9 and C-108, respectively) were also used, though in comparatively small numbers. Perhaps the most unusual of the Fortress variants, however, was the BQ-7. This was a 'war-weary' airframe, filled with 10 tons of explosives and employed as a primitive form of guided missile on a limited (and

potentially hazardous!) basis by the 8th Air Force against targets in Germany.

Post-war, surplus B-17s found new roles, including air-sea rescue (equipped with an air-droppable lifeboat), airborne early warning (with a search radar installed) and drone launch/direction. 'Demobbed' aircraft flew as engine test-beds, crop sprayers and fire-bombers.

Probably the last Fortresses to be flown in anger were those secretly operated by the new state of Israel between 1947 and 1958. Other foreign air arms were also supplied with surplus American aircraft, mainly in South America.

A remarkable number of B-17s have survived, compared to other wartime bomber types, largely because they remained in use for so long after 1945. Of over 40 examples, 13 are in flying condition, a fitting memorial to the young men who flew the B-17.

Above: In spring 1941, a batch of 20 B-17Cs was assigned to the RAF, but these aircraft proved a failure in RAF service. However, the B-17F was used with more success by the RAF as the Fortress Mk II, and the B-17G as the Fortress Mk III, mainly with Coastal Command. The B-17G was also the chief heavy carrier of special electronics for the RAF Bomber Command's No. 100 Group.

Left: About 13 Fortresses were airworthy in 1998, including this aircraft, restored for the USAF Museum. Another 30 were displayed in museums.

Race for the Reich

Across the Rhine

Germany's last, desperate offensive in the west was followed by the Luftwaffe's last major action. Both the Ardennes offensive and Operation Bodenplatte achieved some initial success, but only at the cost of losing the cream of Germany's fighting forces.

Above: Major Glenn Eagleston taxis his P-47D along the PSP at Rosières-en-Haye in December 1944. Clearing weather meant that Allied fighters could be thrown against the Germans' surprise Ardennes offensive.

The Hawker Tempest V was one of the fastest fighters available to the Allies in the winter of 1944, and contributed to the gaining of air supremacy.

A break in the weather enabled transport aircraft to drop supplies to the beleaguered American 101st Airborne Division at Bastogne.

Following the failure of the Arnhem operation, the British 2nd TAF was fully engaged in supporting the operation to clear the Scheldt estuary. Farther to the south the US 9th Air Force's component of P-47s and Lockheed P-38s covered the battlefronts over Aachen during the assault, while the medium and light bombers of the US IX Bomber Command pounded German positions and communication targets. It was an autumn of stalemate, with conditions over the battlefronts being reasonably quiet even though great air battles continued to be fought between the US 8th Air Force and Luftflotte Reich. But it was not to last.

Ardennes Offensive

On 16 December, the 6th SS Panzer Army and the 5th Panzer Army mounted a massive surprise attack in the Ardennes. Driving between the US 9th and 7th Armies, the Germans penetrated some 60 miles (96 km) in under a week. The poor weather prevented large scale air action, but even without significant air support the

Americans were able to slow down, hold, and eventually push back the Germans. Among the enemy aircraft that did appear was the new bomber version of the Me 262.

The bad weather that had dogged Allied air operations during the Ardennes attack improved gradually during the last few days of 1944, and offensive action was resumed.

However, unsuspected by British and American intelligence, the Luftwaffe had for some weeks been planning a great set piece operation against the RAF and USAAF bases in northern Europe. The OKL believed that sufficient destruction could be caused to severely disrupt Allied operations, which would buy time to reorganise the defence of Germany.

Air attack

After assembling some 800 fighters and fighter-bombers of all types from all over the Reich, Operation *Bodenplatte* (Baseplate), was launched soon after first light on New Year's Day 1945. Jagdgeschwaders 1, 3, 6, 26, 27 and 77 attacked Allied bases at

Volkel, GilzeRijen, Eindhoven, Brussels, Ursel, Antwerp and Woensdrecht. JG 2, along with JGs 4 and 11 hit the bases at Asch, St Trond and Le Culot. JG 53 was targeted on the base at Metz-Frescaty. Surprise was almost universal.

Considerable damage was caused, and about 500 Allied aircraft were destroyed or later scrapped. However, the defence forces quickly recovered from the shock, and about 300 German aircraft were shot down or crashed on the way home.

Ultimate piston-engined fighters

By the last year of the war, fighters on both sides of the conflict had become bigger, faster and much more heavily armed than they had been only three years before. Speed had risen by over 100 mph, and most fighters (with the notable exception of American aircraft) fought with 20-mm and even 30-mm cannon rather than machine-guns).

Tempest Mk V
This Tempest Mk V was flown by Squadron Leader J. H. Iremonger's No. 486 Sqn RNZAF, based at Venlo in 1945. Most of the Tempest units escaped with little damage during the Luftwaffe's New Year's Day attack.

Fw 190D-9
Operated by II./JG 26 out of Nordhorn, this Fw 190D-9 took part in the attack on Brussels-Evère. The D-9 with its powerful Jumo 213 engine restored some of the performance advantage which had been lost to new Allied fighters.

As dawn broke on 24 March the 21st Army Group pushed across the Rhine. Spitfires, Tempests and Hawker Typhoons of Nos 83 and 84 Groups, 2nd TAF, were airborne on close-support and Flak-suppression duties, while the Thunderbolts of US XXIX TAC operated south of the Lippe river.

Below: A German's-eye view of the airborne element of the crossings. The 440 aircraft and gliders of Nos 38 and 46 Groups, joined by 243 Douglas C-47s of the US 52nd TCW, made the first drops over the Diersfordter Wald at around 10.00 hours.

But whereas the Allies were able to replace their losses within a few days — and relatively few aircrew were killed — the German losses, which included some 230 experienced aircrew, were little short of disastrous.

Indeed the folly of the operation had been voiced by many senior German commanders, but they were confronting Nazi leaders fanatically blind to the realities of Allied air supremacy and the inevitable grounding of the Luftwaffe through lack of fuel.

The advance to the River Rhine, the last major natural barrier confronting the Allies, was scheduled for February 1945. With the recent experience of Arnhem in mind, Allied leaders determined that there would be a softening-up period, with concentration on lines of communication, before the crossings and airborne landings were to be made. More to the point, they made sure that there were sufficient transport aircraft on hand.

Bombing continues
Meanwhile the strategic bomber forces continued to attack airfields, industries and oil, rail and road targets. Between January and March 1945 RAF Bomber Command flew 14,655 day sorties and nearly 40,000 by night, dropping over 120,000 tons of bombs and losing 521 aircraft, mostly to Flak. The losses, while high, were well within the command's replacement capacity. On 14 March 1945 the first 22,000-lb (9979-kg) Grand Slam bomb was dropped by a Lancaster B.Mk 1 of No. 617 Squadron.

Noteworthy attacks included the notorious Dresden fire-raid on the night of 13-14 February 1945: the first wave of 244 Avro Lancasters was followed by a second wave of 529 aircraft. Over 2,659 tons of HE and incendiaries were dropped on what was a supposed to be a centre of rail and road communications to the Oder front. In fact, the city was mostly full of refugees, and the loss of life was horrendous.

Bomb tonnages dropped by the RAF were now for the first time being exceeded by the US 8th Air Force. In March 1945 the 1st, 2nd and 3rd Bombardment Divisions flew 30,358 sorties (125 failed to return), and dropped 65,962 tons of bombs; the P-51s and P-47s of the 65th, 66th and 67th Fighter Wings put up 17,954 sorties, claiming 260 fighters in air combat while losing 95.

On 7 March the US 1st Army took Cologne, and as its advanced units approached the Rhine at Remagen they had the extraordinary fortune to find the Ludendorff bridge still intact. Elements of the US 9th Division were able to take the bridge, render the demolition charges harmless, and cross over to form a bridgehead on the East bank.

Rhine crossings
Attention now turned to the sector of the British 21st Army Group, where Operation 'Varsity', the crossing of the Rhine to the west of Wesel, was about to begin, At 23.25 on 23 March, as the first ground units prepared to cross the river, Bomber Command delivered an accurate and damaging attack on Wesel, which fell a few hours later to the 1st Commando Brigade. By this time British and Canadian troops were being ferried across the Rhine in Buffaloes and inflatable rafts under artificial moonlight.

This was followed by the largest airborne operation since D-Day. Light 20-mm Flak proved difficult to neutralise, and around 300 gliders were damaged and 10 were shot down. But by the end of the day, after 4,900 fighter and 3,300 bomber sorties, Allied troops were firmly established on the east bank of the Rhine.

Fall of the Reich

Petlyakov Pe-2s fly over the shell of the Reichstag in Berlin, as Infantry and Armour mount the final attack. Hard though they fought, the defenders had no answer to the sheer power of the Soviets.

By March 1945 the Allies were across the Rhine: in the east Hitler's armies faced massed Soviet strength on the Oder-Neisse line, while in the south battles were fought in Hungary. The Luftwaffe fought on, but its days were numbered.

Luftwaffenkommando West was annihilated after the failure of the Ardennes offensive. To the act of virtual suicide which was Operation Bodenplatte, were added the huge losses sustained in air battles with the US 8th Air Force in January. Thereafter wholesale transfers of fighters and close-support aircraft to the east left only a small force under LwKdo West. This was expected to counter the RAF 2nd Tactical Air Force, the US 9th Air Force, the US Tactical Air Force (Provisional) and the 1er Corps Aérien Français. In March fewer than 1,100 aircraft remained, although this included Arado Ar 234 and Messerschmitt Me 262 jets. Restricted by critical shortages of fuel, the Focke-Wulf Fw 190D-9 and Messerschmitt Bf 109K-4 fighters were limited to covering operations for the jet bombers and to the occasional mission against USAAF and RAF daylight raids.

Bombing continues

Throughout February and March 1945 Allied strategic bombing continued without serious hindrance from Luftflotte Reich, though there were isolated instances when the Fw 190A-8/R2s of the Sturmgruppen hit hard. The largest number of jets yet encountered came on 3 March 1945, when JG 7 put up 30 Me 262s against the Americans. Attacks by 50 or more became the norm over the next month.

Suicide attack

An isolated action by German fighters on 7 April has gone down in folklore: this was the last-ditch operation by 183 Fw 190s and Bf 109Ks of the so-called Sonderkommando Elbe, set up by the fanatical Oberst Otto Köhnke. Flying to the strains of martial airs played over the radio, the pilots of SdKdo Elbe were instructed to ram. How many actually did so remains a mystery: 137 German aircraft were lost, 70 pilots were killed, and only eight US heavies were brought down.

In the wake of heavy Allied attacks the Me 262s of IX Fliegerkorps were withdrawn to Prague, and finally to the Munich area where Adolf Galland's Jagdverband Nr 44 was operating.

In April 1945 RAF Bomber Command attained its peak strength of 1,609 combat aircraft. With the issue no longer in doubt the RAF effort dwindled, and in April 8,822 night and 5,001 day sorties were flown for the loss of 73 aircraft. The US 8th Air Force flew 17,437 sorties in April 1945, losing 108 heavies. The 8th Air Force's fighters flew 12,771 sorties, claiming 149 enemy fighters in the air and an incredible 1,791 destroyed on the ground by strafing, losing 99 aircraft in the process.

The Soviets started their drive on the Reich soon after the end of the Ardennes offensive. Eleven guards armies, five shock armies, six tank armies, and 46 infantry or cavalry armies supported by 13 air armies gave the Red Army commanders absolute superiority over the 200 German and Hungarian divisions

American troops examine an almost intact Me 262 captured at Stendal. German jets could have played a much more sigificant part in the final battles, had there been any fuel available.

Fighters over the Reich

Me 262A-1a/U3
The only area in which Germany had any superiority in 1945 was in reconnaissance, with jets like the Arado Ar 234 and the Messerschmitt Me 262 able to fly with near impunity when fuel was available. This aircraft of Einsatzkommando Braunegg flew over southern Germany in the last months of the war.

Lavochkin La-5FN
By the end of the war the best of the Soviet fighter pilots were very good indeed. This aircraft was flown at the beginning of 1945 by Captain Vitaliye Ivanovich Popkov, a squadron commander in the 5th Guards Regiment. In the last four months of the war Popkov took his score from 31 kills to 41, with a further 17 shared with other pilots.

An Me 262 flashes past a Mustang as the jet dives on another American fighter. Jets were vulnerable when enticed into dogfights with the more agile piston-engined fighters.

facing them. The only advantage Wehrmacht commanders may have had was the fear and hatred of the 'Mongol Hordes' so firmly implanted in the hearts of every Axis soldier.

Broad-front attack

Three fronts commanded by Marshals Konev, Zhukov and Rokossovsky, drove into East Prussia and Poland. In one week Soviet armies advanced along a 400-mile (640-km) front over a distance of 120 miles (193 km) towards the German frontier. By the end of January the Oder was in Red Army hands from the Carpathians to the north of Berlin, and on 31 January 1945 Zhukov's tanks reached Küstrin, only 52 miles (84 km) from the capital of the Reich.

In Hungary, fierce battles were fought by 2nd and 3rd Ukrainian Fronts when German and Hungarian armies tried hard to relieve the forces trapped in Budapest. However, the outskirts of Budapest were already under attack, and Soviet counterstrokes brought the offensive to a halt by 30 January. Over 400 aircraft had been amassed by Fliegerkorps I of Luftflotte IV. Unfortunately the Bf 109s, Fw 190s and Ju 87D-5s, Arado

Ar 66s, and Fiat CR.42s of the night harassment squadrons could do little to stem the tide.

The failure of the offensive prompted Hitler to withdraw the remains of Dietrich's powerful 6th SS Panzer Army from the Ardennes – not to the critical Oder front, but to Hungary to take part in the next offensive.

SS forces repelled

During March the SS put in an attack around Lake Balaton, in an attempt to preserve Germany's last remaining source of oil, but it was beaten back. By 19 March, the SS were fleeing back over the Austrian border towards Vienna, and by that time too, the armies of the Belarussian Fronts had fought their way across the Oder to the line of the River Neisse.

The British 21st Army Group and the US 6th and 12th Army Groups drove eastwards into Germany in the face of limited opposition. On 1 April the Ruhr was encircled. On 4 April the US 9th Army crossed the Weser, and reached the Elbe in a week.

Germany divided

When the Anglo-American allies and the Soviets joined forces on the Elbe, Germany was split in two. The Allied decision not to drive all out for Berlin was a subject of considerable controversy, and it was left to the Soviets to take the prize.

On the face of it, Berlin was formidably defended. An estimated 1,000,000 troops, 10,400 guns, 1,500 tanks and more than 2,000 aircraft of Generaloberst von Greim's Luftflotte VI were available. But

the Soviet V-VS mustered more than 7,500 combat aircraft. These included Petlyakov Pe-8, Tupolev Tu-2 and Ilyushin Il-4 bombers, and Ilyushin Il-2m/3 Shturmoviks. Fighters included Yakovlev Yak-3s, Yak-7B and Yak-9DD, and Lavochkin La-5FN and La-7s.

On the night before the offensive the 18th Air Army flew 743 sorties on Letchin, Langsof, Werbig, Seelöw, Friedersdorf and Dolgelin: thick fog hampered close-support efforts on the scale planned. The Soviet bombers returned on the night of 16 April to attack the roads behind the front, while a major battle took place on 18 April over Berlin. On 19 April Lieutenant Colonel Ivan N. Kozhedub, the V-VS's leading ace, scored his 61st and 62nd kills (two Fw 190s). By 20 April the Oder defences had been broken, despite an all-out effort of some 1,000 sorties per day by Luftflotte VI, and the 1st Belorussian Front advanced to encircle the city.

The fighting now became increasingly savage. Konev's forces reached the Spree on 17 April 1945: another German counterattack in the Cottbus-Spremberg area was held despite an effort by 100 or more 190F-8s and Ju 87Ds.

Berlin surrounded

On 20 April the 2nd Belorussian Front completed the encirclement of Berlin by striking across the Oder under cover of the 4th VA. Vicious fire-fights took place on the outskirts of the city and in the Frankfurt-Gilben pocket.

On 30 April 1945, during the battle for the Reichstag parliament buildings, Adolf Hitler committed suicide. On the morning of the following day the Red Banner flew from the topmost pinnacle of the Reichstag. Berlin surrendered on 2 May, and Germany's unconditional surrender was signed six days later. The war against the Third Reich was over.

Messerschmitt Me 262 Schwalbe

Fighting 'Stormbird'

Young German gunners, huddled around their light 20-mm and 37-mm flak weapons, could be excused for a slight lack of attention to their task at their first sight of the Messerschmitt Me 262s on the snow-covered expanses of Rheine-Hopsten air base in 1944. In every sense the sleek, shark-like fuselage, mottled ochre and olive green and beset with razor wings from which hung the huge turbojets, was a portent of the future.

The noise, the high-pitched whine and howl of the Jumo 004B-1 turbines, the swirls of snow, the hot paraffin-tainted blast: all were of a different time. This was the present, however, and, beset by Allied air superiority on all sides, black-helmeted pilots, crouched forward in the narrow cockpits of their Messerschmitt Me 262A-2a fighter-bombers, code-named *Sturmvogel* ('Stormbird') by the Luftwaffe, anxiously scanned the overcast skies for the first signs of the diving Hawker Tempests, North American P-51s or Supermarine Spitfires, as they coaxed throttles

and jabbed brakes prior to take-off. Flak gunners trained their pieces along the approach paths, watched for the red Very lights that would bring them to instant action, and heard the thunder of the departing jets.

With such machines, how could Germany lose the war in the air? Such a thought must have raced through minds. The job of a flak gunner is humble, and he and his comrades could have had no insight into the extraordinary train of events and decisions that were instrumental in the denial in quantity of Germany's most potent air weapon of World War II. In the

heady days of 1941, when the Messerschmitt Me 262 series was born, not one person in the Third Reich could foresee the desperate need for an outstanding aircraft with which

to wrest air supremacy from the hands of the enemy. The Heinkel concern was already deeply involved in the development of a fighter powered by the new reaction-

Above: Four months after the Me 262A-1a fighter entered service, in April 1944, the Me 262A-2a (also known as the Me 262A-1a/Jabo) fighter-bomber entered the fray against targets in northern France. This example carries the usual pair of 551-lb (250-kg) SC 250 bombs; the A-2a differed from the fighter solely in having pylons and bomb-fusing equipment fitted.

Top: Seen at Lager-Lechfeld in the late summer of 1944, this Me 262A-1a was on strength with Erprobungskommando (EKdo) 262, the operational test detachment established in late 1943. Standing on the wing is believed to be Leutnant Fritz Müller, who later achieved ace status on the type, while flying with JG 7.

Among a number of Me 262 variants that failed to see more than experimental service was the Me 262C-1a Heimatschützer I ('Home Protector I'), fitted with a rocket motor in the rear fuselage to boost climb rate. The C-1a could reach 38,400 ft (11704 m) in 4½ minutes. In V186 (pictured) Oberstleutnant Heinz Bär, CO of III./EJG 2 and one of the top scorers on the Me 262, scored a kill over a P-47 in early March 1945, shortly before the aircraft was destroyed on the ground by an Allied fighter sweep.

Above: The Me 262 was at its most vulnerable during take-off and landing; it was during this low-speed regime that Allied pilots claimed most of their kills over the fighter, though they needed to down the jet before it reached the protection of flak batteries protecting its base.

Below: An American GI guards the engineless remains of a Schwalbe, abandoned in a German forest in the last weeks of the war. By the end of April 1945 only JV 44 and III./JG 7 were still operational. JV 44 was finally overrun by US armour on 3 May.

turbine engines when, on 4 January 1939, the Augsburg-based Messerschmitt AG received orders from the German air ministry (RLM, or Reichsluftfahrtministerium) to produce specifications for a similar type of aircraft. Two plans were drawn up by a team led by Dipl Ing Waldemar Voigt, one for a twin-boom configuration and the other for a pod-and-boom design. Neither of the two then-existing turbojet designs was considered to be powerful enough for a single-engined fighter, and as a result Voigt was forced to resort to the design of a twin-engined aircraft.

Heinkel had already turned to twin engines with the development of the promising He 280 series powered by the six-stage axial-flow BMW P.3302 engines, and Germany's first definitive jet fighter, the Heinkel He 280 V2 prototype, lifted off from Rostock-Marienehe's runway at 15.18 on 30 March 1941 with Fritz Schäfer at the controls. (Within six weeks of this maiden flight, the UK, too, flew its first jet aircraft: powered by a Whittle-designed W.1X centrifugal-type turbojet of 860-lb (3.82-kN) thrust, the Gloster E.28/39 took to the air on 15 May.) At Augsburg, work had proceeded slowly on the design of what at first bore none of the hallmarks that graced the Heinkel product, or gave any hint of the

fineness of line that was a characteristic of Messerschmitt's piston-engined fighters.

This ugly duckling, known as the Me 262 V1 was taken into the air for the first time on 18 April 1941, powered by a piston engine. The jet engines for the Me 262 V1 eventually arrived from Spandau in mid-November 1941, being BMW 003s each of 5.39 kN (1,213 lb) static thrust. On his first flight with the BMW 003s, Wendel suffered a double flame-out shortly after take-off and was forced to put the aircraft down with some damage.

Fortunately, an alternative to the touchy BMWs was available – Junkers' Jumo 004. By August 1941, the Jumo 004 was giving 1,323 lb (5.88 kN) static thrust, and many of the earlier problems had been cured. Jumo 004s were installed on the Messerschmitt Me 262 V3, first flown on the morning of 18 July 1942. Henceforth the fortunes of the Messerschmitt Me 262 were to rise at the expense of its nearest rival, the Heinkel He 280, which suffered a series of setbacks until its eventual cancellation in March 1943.

Service test pilots of the Erprobungsstelle (test establishment) at Rechlin showed interest in the Me 262 from its earliest days. The experienced Major Wolfgang Späte had already reported his enthusiastic findings when the General der Jagdflieger, Adolf Galland, flew the Me 262 V4 on 22 May 1943 and become unequivocal in his praise for this revolutionary aircraft. A production order for 100 followed at the end of the month.

In the meantime, on 17 August 1943 the US 8th Air Force's attack on Regensburg destroyed much of the embryonic Me 262 production lines, forcing Messerschmitt AG to move its jet development centres to

Oberammergau, near the Bavarian Alps. The delay occasioned by the move was increased by a chronic shortage in the supply of skilled labour, and production slipped by many months.

By the autumn of 1943, Germany was on the defensive in the USSR and Italy, and was being subjected to furious aerial assault by day and by night. Therefore, nobody could have been surprised when many senior commanders, including Hitler, mooted the concept of the Me 262 as a fighter-bomber as opposed to an interceptor, for the idea was tactically sound. The Me 262 could carry up to 2,205 lb (1000 kg) of bombs with uncomplicated conversion work completed within two weeks per unit.

So, from that day the Messerschmitt Me 262 was destined to play a dual role, that of a fighter-bomber and that of a pure air-superiority fighter. Neither the role nor the aircraft could by then have had any influence on the outcome of the war. It was too late to start a major production scheme, as oil and aviation kerosene, precious alloys, and skilled airframe and engine specialists were all at a premium. The Messerschmitt Me 262 had been recognised in its full potential, but too late in the war.

Over the period March 1944 to 20 April 1945, the Luftwaffe took delivery of 1,433 Me 262s, but for the Allies the impact of this fine aircraft was largely psychological. On inspection after the war's end, it was acknowledged that in design of airframe and engine the Messerschmitt Me 262 was years ahead of aircraft of other nations, and its secrets permitted the Russians and the Anglo-Americans to accelerate development of jet fighter and bomber aircraft to the magic of Mach 1.0 and beyond over the ensuing years.

Avia S.92 'Turbine'

Major components for the Me 262 were produced in German-occupied Czechoslovakia during World War II, the large Avia factory building airframe parts, while other dispersed facilities supplied, among other things, engine parts. By the end of the war a considerable stockpile of engines, airframes and other spares existed and it was decided that these would be used to produce aircraft for the newly reformed Czech air force. The Jumo 004B-1 engine was copied by Letecke, as the

M.04, while Avia continued its airframe work, producing an S.92 prototype, based on the Me 262A-1a (left). This aircraft made its first flight on 27 August 1946 and was followed by three CS.92 two-seat trainers (above) and a further three S.92s. The third of these latter machines was the first accepted by the air force, in 1947; by the early 1950s eight aircraft equipped the 5th Fighter Flight. Plans to develop the Me 262 (including fitting BMW 003 engines in place of the Jumo 004s and redesigning the fragile nosewheel undercarriage) and produce further aircraft for the Yugoslav air force were cancelled after the Soviet MiG-15 became available for local production.

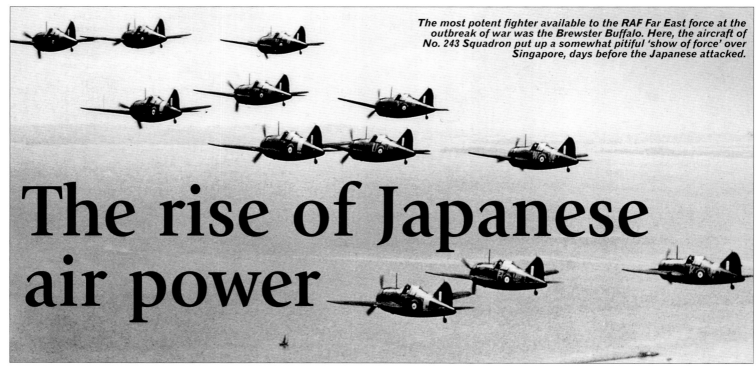

The most potent fighter available to the RAF Far East force at the outbreak of war was the Brewster Buffalo. Here, the aircraft of No. 243 Squadron put up a somewhat pitiful 'show of force' over Singapore, days before the Japanese attacked.

The rise of Japanese air power

Operations by the Japanese air services in Manchuria and China provided invaluable combat experience for the Pacific war, which began in 1941. This advantage was initially overlooked by the British, Dutch and Americans – at their cost.

Throughout the latter part of the 19th century and early part of the 20th, Japan rose meteorically in industrial and economic fields. It had become a fully industrialised nation with a powerful navy and army, both of which had subordinate air services. Like Britain, Japan had no oil and few natural resources, and was almost totally reliant on maritime trade to fuel its burgeoning economy and to feed its 100 million-plus people. Between 1895 and 1918, the Japanese empire grew through the annexation or acquisition of Sakhalin, Formosa, Korea and large areas of the Pacific. Much of this territory had been gained through conflicts with both China and Russia – which would provide the opposition for more serious conflicts in the 1930s.

These began openly in September 1931, when the Japanese army invaded Manchuria in just five weeks; supported by Nieuport 29, Salmson 2, Mitsubishi 2MB1 and Kawasaki KDA-2 aircraft of the army air arm. There was no aerial opposition from the Chinese, so the Japanese aircraft were restricted to bombardment and reconnaissance sorties.

Soon after, in January 1932, it was the Imperial Japanese Navy's turn to go to war, during the Shanghai invasion. Nakajima A1N1s and Mitsubishi 2MT1-4s flying from the carriers *Hosho* and *Kaga*, together with Kawanishi E5K1 floatplanes, supported the action and encountered a few Chinese fighters. Despite stout resistance, Shanghai fell on 4 March.

Relations between China and Japan remained tense for the next

Above: The Mitsubishi G3M was the IJN's principal land-based bomber in 1941 – the force was being augmented by a growing number of the larger G4Ms. The G3M saw much action over China.

few years, although no major conflicts broke out until 1937. By this time China itself had began to rise economically and militarily. To pre-empt any future aggression and to protect its interests, Japan struck on two fronts in August: one force arriving by sea at Shanghai and striking north and west, while another headed south from Manchuria.

Japanese fighters

In the air over the north, the Japanese employed Kawasaki Ki-10 fighters, Kawasaki Ki-3 bombers, Mitsubishi Ki-1 bombers and Nakajima Ki-4 reconnaissance aircraft, while in the south, Mitsubishi G3M1 bombers made raids from Japanese territory. The Chinese, as ever, put up a stoic defence, although the advance ground on, forcing Chiang Kai-Shek back into the mountains at Chungking. New equipment in the form of Nakajima Ki-27 fighters, Mitsubishi Ki-15 reconnaissance aircraft and Mitsubishi Ki-21 bombers made an appearance, but on the Chinese side the air force, under the guidance of Captain Claire Chennault, began operating Polikarpov I-15s, I-153s and I-16s, together with Tupolev SB-2 bombers. These inflicted growing losses on the Japanese. In the event, unable to win decisively on the ground, Japan turned to an economic blockade of China, and it was this factor, among others, which led to the expansion into Southeast Asia which was a prelude to the outbreak of war in the Pacific.

Before that, however, the Japanese were to fight a brief

Nakajima's Ki-27 fighter was exceptionally agile but was well matched by the Polikarpov fighters it met over both China and the Nomonhan. In the latter conflict the Japanese claimed that 1,260 Soviet aircraft had been downed.

Above: Predecessor of the Zero, the Mitsubishi A5M was the standard IJN carrier-based fighter in 1940. This example of the 14th Flying Group is seen over China.

Below: Soviet pilots relax in front of a Polikarpov I-16 during a lull in the fighting during the Nomonhan Incident. This was fought over disputed land in the Khalkhin-Gol river valley.

and bloody battle against Soviet forces in the Nomonhan region. Here, Ki-27s battled it out with I-153s and I-16s, while Tupolev TB-3 and Mitsubishi Ki-30 bombers were in constant action. The result was inconclusive.

Southern expansion

The dramatic successes of the German army in Europe during 1940 persuaded Japan to ally with Germany and Italy. France and Britain were the dominant colonial powers in Southeast Asia and, when faced with Japanese military aggression, both were too weak to do anything other than to accede to Japanese demands. In late June 1940, Japanese troops landed at Haiphong in the French colony of Tonkin; the French could offer no resistance and agreed to the establishment of Japanese army air bases in the country. The British had to agree to the closing of the Burma Road.

The bases in French Indo-China allowed Japanese bombers to strike against Chiang Kai-Shek's Chinese forces, but also threatened British holdings, including the jewel of the region – Singapore. As well as furthering the stranglehold on China, Japan looked to control Malaysia, Borneo, Java and the

Philippines. This would secure a good source of raw materials, including the all-important oil. When Japan established bases in southern Indo-China, directly threatening Singapore, US President Roosevelt froze all Japanese assets in the US and terminated oil supplies. War on a major scale with Britain, the United States and the Dutch East Indies was now virtually unavoidable.

The Japanese were well-equipped for the coming action in what it termed the Southern Area, and its pilots were battle-hardened. The Japanese army had received the Nakajima Ki-43 Hayabusa fighter, Kawanishi Ki-48 light bomber and the excellent Mitsubishi Ki-46. The navy had re-equipped with Aichi D3As, Nakajima B5Ns and Mitsubishi A6Ms on its carriers, and with Mitsubishi G4M bombers for land-based operations. In the A6M, the Japanese had undeniably the best fighter in the theatre by a considerable margin, and one which would sweep the victorious Japanese imperialists all the way to the shores of Australia. The first phase of this action was a six-pronged attack on Allied positions from Siam to Hawaii, including a pre-emptive attack on the US fleet at Pearl Harbor.

Fighters in the Far East

In the late 1930s both Japanese and Soviet air arms were equipped with stubby, radial-engined fighters. Although they were not as fast as the sleeker, inline-engined monoplanes being fielded in Europe, they were far more agile. As the Pacific war progressed, this attribute was largely negated by the use of fast, slashing attacks in which the faster machine would not be drawn into turning fights with these nimble but slow aircraft.

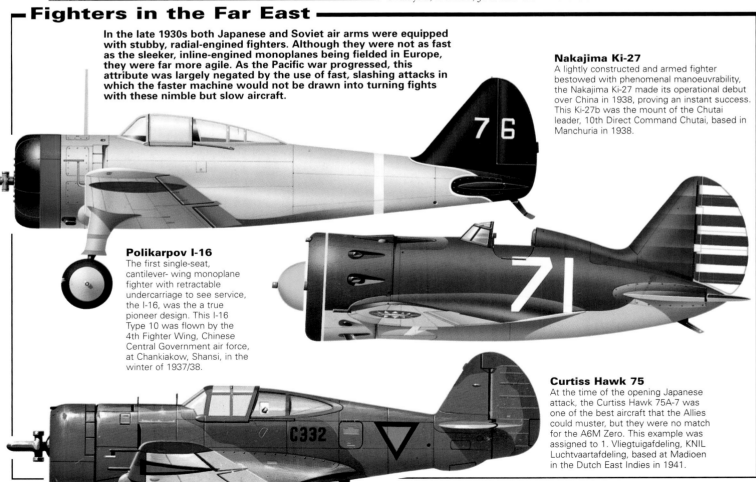

Nakajima Ki-27
A lightly constructed and armed fighter bestowed with phenomenal manoeuvrability, the Nakajima Ki-27 made its operational debut over China in 1938, proving an instant success. This Ki-27b was the mount of the Chutai leader, 10th Direct Command Chutai, based in Manchuria in 1938.

Polikarpov I-16
The first single-seat, cantilever- wing monoplane fighter with retractable undercarriage to see service, the I-16, was the a true pioneer design. This I-16 Type 10 was flown by the 4th Fighter Wing, Chinese Central Government air force, at Chankiakow, Shansi, in the winter of 1937/38.

Curtiss Hawk 75
At the time of the opening Japanese attack, the Curtiss Hawk 75A-7 was one of the best aircraft that the Allies could muster, but they were no match for the A6M Zero. This example was assigned to 1. Vliegtuigafdeling, KNIL Luchtvaartafdeling, based at Madioen in the Dutch East Indies in 1941.

Dawn of the rising sun

America's Pacific Fleet was taken completely by surprise by the Japanese attack on Pearl Harbor. With the US still licking its wounds, the Japanese war machine was free to roam across the Pacific.

The timing of the Japanese air, naval and amphibious operations against Malaya, Siam, the Philippines and Hong Kong was dictated to a large extent by the fact that it was the custom of the US Pacific Fleet to be at anchor in Pearl Harbor (Oahu) on a Sunday morning. The Japanese high command gambled all on a series of operations designed to neutralise American and British air and sea power in the Far East and Pacific theatres, before proceeding with the establishment of their Greater East Asia Co-Prosperity Sphere. Having established this, and formed a defensive wall around it, the Japanese hoped to

be in a position to seek peace terms, for their industries could not match those of the USA.

The schedule of the operations was as follows: 02.15 (Tokyo time, 8 December 1941), the landings by the 25th Army at Kota Bahru; 03.25, the Hawaiian operation (Pearl Harbor); 04.00 the landings in the Kra isthmus at Singora and Patani; and at 08.30 the invasion of Hong Kong by the 38th Division. Subsidiary operations were to include the occupation of Guam, Wake, Tarawa, Nauru and Makin (Gilbert Islands) in the Pacific Ocean.

The Strike Force earmarked for Pearl consisted of the carriers

Kaga, Akagi, Hiryu, Soryu, Zuikaku and *Shokaku*. By 03.00 on 7 December (Western date), Oahu was bearing 180° at a distance of 200 miles (320 km).

By 05.45 the A6M2 CAP was airborne, with Nos 1 and 2 Attack Forces launching shortly afterwards. Primary targets were the ships anchored in Pearl

In the air and on the ground at Pearl Harbor, the USAAF lost 71 aircraft, the USMC lost 30 and the USN 60; 2,403 personnel were killed, and 1,176 wounded.

Below: This wartime map shows the disposition of US craft at Pearl Harbor. Both Pearl and nearby Waikiki were geared more for Christmas celebrations than for repelling an attack.

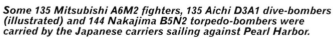

Some 135 Mitsubishi A6M2 fighters, 135 Aichi D3A1 dive-bombers (illustrated) and 144 Nakajima B5N2 torpedo-bombers were carried by the Japanese carriers sailing against Pearl Harbor.

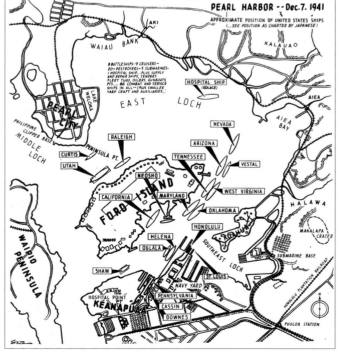

A6Ms and B5Ns prepare to launch against Pearl Harbor. Nine A6M2s, 15 D3A1s and five B5N2s were shot down in the attack, a small price to pay for the results gained.

Harbor roads and in 'Battleship Row', while the A6M2s and D3A1s were used on CAPs and strikes on the airfields at Wheeler, Hickam, Ewa, Kanehoe and Ford Island. The US Army's new SCR-270 radar spotted the incoming force at 07.02 from Opana station; operators thought it was an exercise, informed the duty officer, who informed the relevant channels, but it was too late. By 07.50 the attack had started in conditions of almost total tactical surprise. Torpedoes struck the battleships USS *West Virginia*, *Arizona*, *Oklahoma*, *Nevada* and *Utah*, and the cruisers *Helena* and *Raleigh*; these, as well as the battleships USS *California*, *Maryland*, *Tennessee*, and the repair ship USS *Vestal*, were also hit. Less damaging blows were inflicted on the USS *Pennsylvania*, the cruiser USS *Honolulu* and the destroyers USS *Cassin*, *Downes* and *Shaw*. The 'carriers USS *Enterprise*, *Saratoga* and *Lexington* were all absent from Pearl and escaped attack.

Wake and Guam

Japanese forces, centred at Truk in the Carolines, were responsible for covering the occupations of the Wake, Guam, and Gilbert Islands. Only at Wake was there stiff resistance, where Major Devereux and his USMC detachment managed to hold out for almost three weeks. As early as 8 December, Mitsubishi G3M2s had destroyed seven Grumman F4F-3s on Wake, killing 23 Marines. The G3M2s were back the next day to bomb Wake, Wilkes and Peale Islands. The first amphibious landing, on

10 December, was beaten back with support from the three surviving F4F-3s. Impatient to force a conclusion, the Japanese diverted *Hiryu* and *Soryu*, en route to Kure from Oahu, to the scene. Heavy air strikes by D3A1s and B5N2s covered the final invasion, and the gallant USMC garrison surrendered on 23 December 1941.

Siam and Malaya

The Japanese invasion fleets were first located by a No. 1 Sqn RAAF Hudson at 14.00 on 6 December, while they were sailing 82 miles (133 km) east south east of the southern tip of Indo-China. Hudsons and Catalinas were sent to plot the course of the convoys, but were thwarted by bad weather. Mitsubishi Ki-21s and Kawasaki Ki-48s were active, however: Singapore was raided at 04.00 on 8 December, other damaging attacks taking place at Butterworth, Sungei Patani, Penang and Alor Star. By that evening, the Japanese 5th and 18th Divisions were ashore at Singora and Patani, with the Takumi Butai heading inland from Kota Bahru.

At 17.35 on 8 December Admiral Sir Tom Phillips' battlegroup, Force Z (including the 35,000-ton battleship HMS *Prince of Wales* and the 32,000-ton battle-cruiser HMS *Repulse*) sailed from Singapore to search out and destroy the Japanese invasion fleets. No air cover was available. When approximately 80 miles (128 km) due east of Kuantan, on 10 December, Force Z came under attack. In precise and co-

ordinated attacks, G3M2s and G4M1s, making bombing and low-level torpedo runs, hit both the *Repulse* and the *Prince of Wales* time and again: the former sank at 12.33, the *Prince of Wales* going under 47 minutes later. The sinking of Force Z ended effective Royal Naval participation in the Malayan campaign.

In Hong Kong, the isolated British garrison surrendered on 25 December. By the end of December the British situation in Malaya was strained beyond limits. Advancing down the eastern seaboard of Malaya, Japanese forces broke the Perak river defences on 26 December, took Ipoh on 28 December, and were in Kuala Lumpur by 11 January 1942. With Nakajima Ki-43 (Type 1) and Ki-27b (Type 97) fighters, Japan maintained air superiority over the threadbare RAF and RAAF forces, the arrival of Hurricane Mk IIAs in January making little impact. British and Empire forces crossed the Johore Straits into Singapore island on 31 January, enduring continual Japanese attacks. On 15 February 1942, the British forces in Malaya surrendered. In the campaign of 73 days, one of the most disastrous in British military history, over 9,000 British and Empire troops had been killed and 130,000 captured. Japanese casualties were 9,284, of which 3,000 had been killed in action – and 92 Japanese aircraft had been lost as against 390 of the British and Australian air forces.

Luzon and Mindonoo

About 160 US and 29 Filipino aircraft of US Air Forces Far East (USAFFE) in the Philippines were combat-ready on the morning of 8 December 1941, when the first Japanese air strikes came in. The first attack took place far to the south, at Davao, where B5N2s and Mitsubishi A5M4s made a surprise raid; this was followed by raids on Baguio and Tuguegaro, in northern Luzon, by Ki-49s and Ki-21s. At 12.45, after fog lifted at their home airfields, G3M2s and G4M1s, escorted by A6M2 fighters, delivered devastating attacks against the Manila airfield complex.

Bombing attacks on the FEAF in the Philippines on 8 December 1941 wiped out 108 aircraft, leaving only 17 B-17s and fewer than 40 P-40Bs. This dwindling force fought at odds over the following weeks, that witnessed Japanese landings at Aparri (10 December 1941), Vigan and Legaspi (11 December), Davao (20 December), Lingayen Gulf (21 December), and at Lamon Bay (24 December), by which time the remnants of FEAF had retired to Australia. Manila fell on 2 January 1942. Under the orders of Roosevelt, General MacArthur left the Philippines on 12 March, leaving Major General J. M. Wainwright in command of US and Filipino forces. They held out in the narrow Bataan peninsula until 9 April 1942, when 78,000 men went into Japanese captivity.

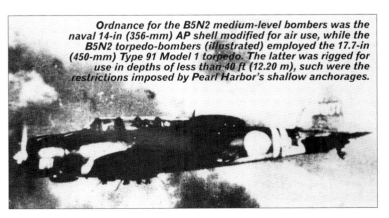

Ordnance for the B5N2 medium-level bombers was the naval 14-in (356-mm) AP shell modified for air use, while the B5N2 torpedo-bombers (illustrated) employed the 17.7-in (450-mm) Type 91 Model 1 torpedo. The latter was rigged for use in depths of less than 40 ft (12.20 m), such were the restrictions imposed by Pearl Harbor's shallow anchorages.

Flying from Saigon, Mitsubishi G3M2s sank Repulse *and the* Prince of Wales *using torpedoes. The G3M2 remained the backbone of the IJN's land-based strike force for several months before the G4M became widely available.*

Mitsubishi
A6M Reisen 'Zeke'

Few aircraft in history had as much mystique built around them as the Zero. Following its combat success in China, and during the early stages of the Japanese campaign in the Pacific, Allied airmen became convinced that the Japanese fighter was invincible.

The Zero dominated the early years of the war in the Pacific. With its superb agility and exceptionally long range, it gave Japanese naval forces almost guaranteed air superiority. From 1943 the tide turned against the Zero, with the introduction of more capable Allied fighters.

The Mitsubishi A6M is perhaps more popularly known as the Zero or Zero-Sen, a contraction of its full designation (it was officially the Rei Shiko Kanjo Sentoki – Type Zero Carrier Fighter). The Zero is remembered as being one of the great fighters of World War II, though it was never the invincible and faultless aircraft demonised by Allied air forces during the early years of the war.

The A6M was certainly fast when it entered service, and extremely agile, but these undoubted attributes were achieved despite having relatively little engine power. Thus the designers of the Zero had to do everything possible to reduce weight, and this meant a structure so light as to make it vulnerable to even the lightest calibre enemy armament, with little armour and a relatively light punch.

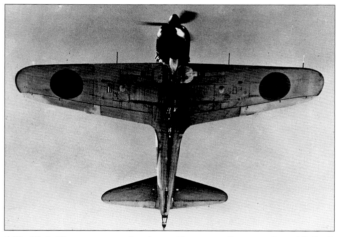

Allied intelligence scored a dramatic coup when an almost intact A6M2 force-landed in the Aleutian Islands in June 1942. It was shipped to NAS North Island in San Diego for thorough evaluation. At last, the myth of the Zero's invincibility had been broken.

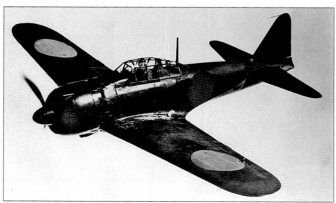

The Zero possessed a level of manoeuvrability which was far in excess of any contemporary Allied fighter. It could out-turn even the Grumman F6F Hellcat, but was hampered by poor diving ability and woefully inadequate armour protection.

While the Zero was fighting ill-trained Chinese airmen and similarly inexperienced volunteers, flying inferior fighters like the Polikarpov I-15 and I-16, it was almost unbeatable. But even during the early years of World War II, when folklore has it that the Zero was 'invulnerable', small numbers of aircraft were despatched by 'inferior' Allied types, including the Hawker Hurricane, the widely disparaged Brewster Buffalo, and even the unwieldy Bristol Blenheim bomber. Eight Zeros were shot down during the Pearl Harbor operation.

Overall, the Zero did enjoy an impressive degree of superiority over Allied aircraft in the first few years of the war, and this was reflected by its highly favourable kill:loss ratio. The Zero won its reputation in these early encounters, and such was the measure of its early superiority that its reputation lasted long after the aircraft had lost its edge.

The Zero was never able to gain mastery over the Grumman F4F Wildcat, whose heavier armament and robust construction compensated for its slightly inferior performance and

agility. Allied fighters had gained in weight (like the Zero), but engine improvements had brought about massive improvements in performance and agility. The Zero was being overtaken and would soon be thoroughly outclassed by almost all of its competitors. Thus, against the F4U Corsair and Spitfire, the Zero enjoyed only superior turn performance, and against the Grumman F6F Hellcat even this advantage was severely eroded at higher speeds. The superiority of the Hellcat over the Zero was most conclusively demonstrated at the Battles of the Philippine Sea and Leyte Gulf in 1944.

Design weaknesses

By the end of the war the Zero's weight had increased through essential improvements which addressed a handful of the type's weaknesses. Engine development had been slow, and performance improved very little between the first and last variants of the aircraft. In fact, the major late-war version, the A6M5, was actually slower than the A6M2,

but was slightly faster climbing. This weakness was well recognised even by the Zero's designers. Replacements for the Zero had been put in hand as early as 1940, but prototypes of more advanced aircraft like the J2M Reisen and A7M Reppu took many years to emerge, and proved disappointing when they did so. Thus, the Zero served on

after it should have been replaced, and its ability to do so, in the face of increasingly superior opposition, was a tribute to the versatility and adaptability of the aircraft. The aircraft remained in very large-scale production until the end of the war, and some 10,449 were built, making it the most numerous of Japan's wartime fighters.

By the end of the war the Zero was teetering on the brink of complete obsolescence, fit only for Imperial Japan's last, desperate gamble – the kamikaze offensive. Today, the Zero is remembered for its early successes – and has gone down in history as one of the great classic fighters of World War II.

Of nearly 10,500 Zeros built, just two examples survive in airworthy condition. The A6M5 (top) is currently operated by the Planes of Fame Museum in Chino, California, and retains its orginal Sakae engine. The remaining example (pictured below) is the Confederate Air Force's A6M2, which saw combat over the Solomon Islands with the 5th Carrier Division on the carrier Zuikaku. Ironically, it is now fitted with an American engine and propeller.

Allied reversals
Runaway victories

The Grumman F4F Wildcat was the principal fighter available to the US Navy until 1943. At Coral Sea in 1942, the F4Fs found it difficult to contain the superior Mitsubishi A6M Reisen.

The spring of 1942 saw the continuation of Japanese victories in Southeast Asia. Their success was due primarily to the fact that the Allies had been weak, ill-prepared and divided. This weakness, accentuated by few reinforcements, continued to be exploited.

Illustrating Japanese aerial dominance during the opening months of the Pacific war are these Mitsubishi G4M1s heading for a target in New Guinea. This type began to replace the same company's G3M as the navy's major land-based strike and torpedo-bomber in 1942.

On 10 January 1942 the Allied Command known as ABDA (American, British, Dutch, Australian) was set up, with Air Chief Marshal R. E. C. Peirse (RAF) as the leader of the air component. The force could only scramble together about 310 combat aircraft. The last RAF aircraft from Singapore flew to Sumatra on 10 February, where surviving units were formed into No. 225 (Bomber) Group and No. 226 (Fighter) Group, centred on P.I and P.II airfields near the Palembang oil refineries. American presence was limited to the 7th BG's B-17Es and

LB-30s, the 43rd BG and the main part of the 19th BG. Additionally, the US 17th Pursuit Group, with its Curtiss P-40Es, formed at Surabaya.

The second phase of the Japanese campaign in the East Indies got underway, with naval operations being covered by the Japanese navy air force's 22nd Flotilla, and the Japanese army air force's 3rd Hikoshudan flying cover. The Japanese plan in the West was for one force to thrust through Davao, Jolo, Dutch Borneo and several smaller islands until they arrived at Bali. In the East, another task force led an assault on the Celebes and

southwards via Manado and Ambon Island to Timor.

The campaign started on 11 January 1942 with landings at Tarakan and Manado. On 24 January, simultaneous landings were made in Borneo and the Celebes. The western group opened its attack with a paratroop landing by JAAF Lockheed WG-14s, backed by Ki-21s capturing airfields and

vital refineries. The battered elements of Nos 225 and 226 Groups retreated to Java and joined the remnants of ML-KNIL (Dutch East Indian air force) and the USAAF. The Japanese landings at Timor severed the last air route to the embattled theatre from Australia. The last great air battles over Surabaya on 19-21 February saw the end of ABDA (Air) and the

The 'Flying Tigers' (more formally known as the American Volunteer Group) in China under Claire Chennault operated Curtiss Hawk 81A-2s, scoring many famous victories over – superior – Japanese aircraft. This example was flown by Henry Geselbracht of the 2nd Sqn, AVG, based at Toungoo in February 1942. Note the Chinese insignia under the wings.

One of the most historic raids of the war took place on 18 April 1942 when a force of 16 North American B-25B Mitchells took off from the carrier USS Hornet to bomb targets in mainland Japan. The physical results were minimal, but the effect on morale was supreme.

Before the introduction into service of the Grumman TBF Avenger, the prime torpedo-bomber was the Douglas TBD Devastator. These aircraft are preparing for a strike from the deck of USS Enterprise. They belong to squadron VT-6, with the Wildcats of VF-6 spotted further forward on the deck.

command was disbanded the following day. Japanese forces swept the seas south of Java, attacking shipping and achieving total air superiority. Within eight days, the Netherlands East Indies government surrendered.

The Japanese also struck southeast to secure the Bismarcks and gain territory in northern Papua New Guinea. On 20 January Rabaul was attacked by 120 Mitsubishi A6M2s, Aichi D3A1s and Nakajima B5N2s. The pitiful RAAF forces put up a gallant fight, but were unable to halt the damage to Rabaul's installations. On 23 January, 5,300 Japanese troops landed at Rabaul, soon securing the port and airfield at Kavieng. Rabaul was an important gain for the Japanese as it meant that it could be used as a launch point for future attacks on Australia. However, this meant that Allied forces at Port Moresby, on southern Papua were now within striking distance. The Allied bastion was constantly harried by 'Zekes', but these were just about kept at bay by RAAF P-40Es.

In January 1942, the Japanese navy's aircraft-carrier strength of nine ships dwarfed that of the US Pacific Fleet, which only had four in-theatre. This was cut to three on 11 January when the *Saratoga* was damaged by a torpedo and forced back to Pearl Harbor.

First US carrier strikes

The threat of Japanese invasion prompted Admiral Nimitz to launch a series of air strikes on the Marshall Islands. On the morning of 1 February, Task Force 8 hit Roi, Kwajalein and Maloelap at dawn. The strike achieved little, with four SBD-3s shot down, USS *Chester* damaged and the *Enterprise* just managing to avoid being hit by a crashing Japanese bomber. On 20 February, the *Lexington* undertook attacks on Rabaul, and Wake and Marcus were struck by the *Enterprise* on 24 February and 4 March, respectively. The most successful strike took place against Japanese ships and troops on 10 March at Lea and Salamaua. Four transports and several smaller vessels were sunk.

The most famous raid was the daring strike by members of the 17th Bomb Group, led by Lieutenant Colonel J. H. Doolittle, on the Japanese mainland. Sixteen modified B-25Bs with increased fuel capacity took off from the *Hornet* and made strikes on Tokyo. The actual effects of the raid were minimal, but the shock factor unnerved the Japanese and raised the spirits of the Americans.

Australia was the next target for the Japanese and a series of attacks were made on Darwin. A destroyer and several other ships were destroyed, plus RAAF and USAAF fighters and bombers. Java soon fell, and with it came savage attacks on evacuating civilians and military personnel alike. From there, the Japanese then thrust into the Indian Ocean, where the target was Ceylon. The attack on Colombo harbour took place on 5 April with B5N2s, D3A1s and Reisens and these were opposed by only a small force of RAF/FAA aircraft. The strike was a success, with a merchantman and a destroyer

sunk, and many Allied aircraft downed. More strikes were made on the south of Ceylon, with the carrier HMS *Hermes* sunk.

Siam was captured by the Japanese at the end of 1941 and, from here, attacks were made on Rangoon. A series of daylight attacks by massed forces achieved little damage for high losses and, for a while, assaults were made only at night. Nevertheless, this was the first occasion on which the Japanese had suffered heavy losses, proving that they were not invincible.

However, Japanese forces in the region were increased and Rangoon eventually fell on 8 March 1942, with Toungoo following on the last day of the month. A steady stream of reinforcements ensured that Japanese expansion continued and, by 29 April, the Japanese had cut the Burma Road at Lashio; Mandalay fell in May 1942 and, just over one week later, the 55th Division had advanced to the Chindwin. India lay beyond, but monsoon rains halted the Japanese impetus.

Early adversaries

Fuelled by expansionist ambitions and fanatical zeal, the Japanese forces swept through the Pacific, pushing back anyone in their way. It was not until the USA pushed more and more fighters into the region that the Nipponese advance was stemmed.

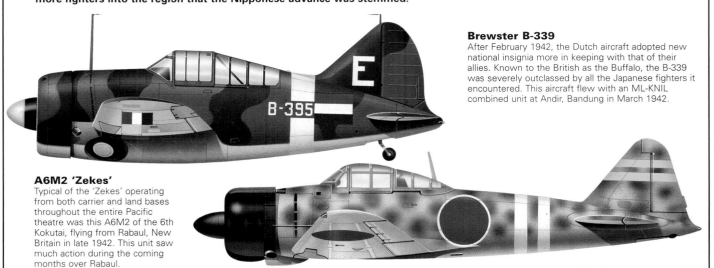

Brewster B-339
After February 1942, the Dutch aircraft adopted new national insignia more in keeping with that of their allies. Known to the British as the Buffalo, the B-339 was severely outclassed by all the Japanese fighters it encountered. This aircraft flew with an ML-KNIL combined unit at Andir, Bandung in March 1942.

A6M2 'Zekes'
Typical of the 'Zekes' operating from both carrier and land bases throughout the entire Pacific theatre was this A6M2 of the 6th Kokutai, flying from Rabaul, New Britain in late 1942. This unit saw much action during the coming months over Rabaul.

Midway
Point of no-return

At cost to itself, the US Navy trumped the Japanese bid to secure Port Moresby in the Battle of the Coral Sea. Less than one month later, Admiral Nimitz's pilots sank four carriers at Midway to cripple Japanese naval air power, so turning the tide of war.

The crews of torpedo squadron VT-6 board their Douglas TBD-1 Devastator aircraft prior to launch for the Battle of Midway. Flying from the USS Enterprise, only four of these aircraft were to return to their carrier in the wake of heavy fighting.

By 1 May 1942 the Japanese were congratulating themselves on achieving all the aims set before them the previous December. In six months they had ripped through Siam, Malaya, Burma, Borneo, Java, Celebes and now the Philippines. They had captured 340,000 Allied troops, sunk numerous enemy vessels and downed hundreds of enemy aircraft. The forces of Imperial Japan were at the peak of their efficiency and future plans now envisaged the extension of Japanese power to Midway, the Aleutian islands and beyond to

Australia via Port Moresby in Papua. Vice Admiral Inouye was in charge of *Mo-Sakusen* (Operation Mo), namely the occupation of the Solomons and Port Moresby, and the fleet included a massive transport group, a support group which had the seaplane tender *Kamikawa Maru* and fighter support and a covering group with the carrier *Shoho* plus three heavy cruisers.

This flotilla was to head down the Solomons chain and sweep north west to Port Moresby. Meanwhile, the carriers *Zuikaku* and *Shokaku* were to counter US moves and sweep east of Santa

Isabel and San Christobal. Supporting these fleets were A6M2s, G4M1s and H6K4s based at Rabaul, Simpson, Tulagi and Tonelei.

However, a major development in code-breaking had meant that Nimitz had learned of 'Mo' and so was able to take pre-emptive action. Task Force 17 was hastily set up and it consisted of warships of the USN and RAN and the *Yorktown* and *Lexington*.

The first stage of Operation Mo began on 3 May with the landings at Tulagi. *Shoho* was

then detached to join the Port Moresby invasion groups. The following day, *Yorktown*'s air group struck Tulagi in response. The Battle of Coral Sea started in earnest on 7 May, with a Japanese air strike taking out the USS *Sims* and the oiler *Neosho*. However, the first round had already gone to the Allies, with the *Shoho* coming under attack by the *Yorktown*'s air group. The SBDs, armed with 1,000-lb (454-kg) bombs and torpedoes, eventually sank the carrier. *Yorktown* and *Lexington* then proceeded to make attacks on the

These Douglas SBD Dauntless aircraft are about to make a second run on a Japanese ship (seen burning on the right of the photograph). The dive brakes can clearly be seen, as can the fins of the bomb under the fuselage.

Below: The type which delivered the fatal blow to the USS Yorktown was the Nakajima B5N torpedo-bomber. It went on to sink many other important ships.

A Consolidated PBY-5A Catalina kicks up the mud as it lands back at Amchitka in January 1943. The island had been recaptured from the Japanese only days before, and this enabled the Americans to attack the enemy base at Attu.

Shokaku to force it to withdraw to Truk. Meanwhile, B5N2s and D3A1s from the Japanese carriers made attacks on the *Lexington*, which was hit by a torpedo, but nevertheless managed to continue recovering aircraft before being ripped asunder by an internal explosion. The crew were forced to abandon ship and 'Lady Lex' was scuttled. Both sides had suffered heavy air losses: 80 Japanese and 66 American aircraft had been downed during the first ever major carrier battle in the Pacific.

Extending influence

Japanese offensive strategy, following the tide of runaway victories, continued to concentrate on the consolidation of assets gained. However, the capture of Midway was also important, while the failure to capture Port Moresby added impetus to the operation. The occupation of Midway was to be preceded by a diversionary attack on the Aleutians while the Midway invasion took place.

The Northern (Aleutians) Force under Vice Admiral Hosogaya consisted of over 30 warships and auxiliaries, supported by the 2nd Carrier Strike Force consisting of the light and heavy carriers *Ryujo* and *Junyo*, respectively. A distant support force comprised a further light carrier and support ships. On 3 June Japanese aircraft struck Dutch Harbour, damaging oil facilities and destroying two PBY-5s. However, returning from this mission, an A6M2 was hit by a stray bullet in the fuel lines and so put down on Akutan island. The pilot broke his neck, but the aircraft was intact and was found by an American team. The Reisen was shipped to San Diego where it was evaluated, gathering invaluable intelligence on Japanese capabilities.

The Japanese fleet heading for Midway was led by a strong force of battleships and cruisers and consisted of 227 aircraft, borne by four carriers. Once more, though, American signals intelligence had revealed invaluable data on the invading fleet and Task Force 17 again readied itself for war. USS *Yorktown* was hastily patched up and the American force consisted of 232 carrier-mounted aircraft and a further 119 at shore bases.

PBY-5 reconnaissance aircraft picked up the invading fleet 700 miles (1125 km) west of Midway. The first strike package

was noted at 05.45 the following morning and a little later the fleet was spotted 160 miles (257 km) north-west of Midway. All American aircraft were sent aloft, fighters orbiting to counter the strike, and the B-17s, B-26As, TBF-1s and Vindicators set off to find the carriers. Japanese B5N2s and D3A1s first hit installations at Sand and Midway at 06.33 and their escort A6M2s decimated the defending VMF-221. The SBD-2s and SB2U-3s of VMSB-241 also suffered heavy casualties, with 13 aircraft failing to return. B-17Es also failed to score any hits on the wildly-turning carriers. Admiral Nagumo was then informed of the presence of an unexpected American carrier force and the Japanese aircraft were then forced to re-arm with torpedoes. By this time, the first TBD-1s had begun their torpedo assault on the carriers. They were immediately set upon by a swarm of A6M2s, which slaughtered 35 of the 41 aircraft. VT-3, VT-6 and VT-8 were all obliterated although, as the Reisens were landing, a fleet of dive-bombing SBD-3s, each armed with 1,000-lb (454-kg) bombs, struck the carriers. *Akagi*, *Kaga* and *Soryu* were all badly hit, though the undamaged *Hiryu*

managed to launch sufficient aircraft to mount a retaliatory strike on the *Yorktown*. After a series of hits, the carrier had to be abandoned. SBD-3s from *Enterprise* then found the *Hiryu* and sunk it. With this, the battle ended and the effects on the Imperial Japanese Navy were catastrophic: four heavy carriers and one cruiser sunk, 332 aircraft lost and 216 invaluable pilots dead. The Americans lost one carrier, a destroyer and 150 out of 307 aircraft.

War in the Aleutians

Meanwhile, further north east, the war for the Aleutians raged. The Japanese naval air arms were opposed by the US 11th Air Force which had B-24Ds, B-25s, B-26As, P-38Fs, P-39Ds and P-40Fs. From June to October 1942 both sides fought against each other and the weather. Islands changed hands and early Japanese gains soon fell prey to American amphibious assaults By August 1943 the Japanese forces had finally withdrawn from the island of Kiska and the Aleutian theatre once more became one of minor importance.

Although replaced in the fleet by the Grumman F4F Wildcat, the Brewster F2A Buffalo still served with the Marine Corps squadrons. This F2A-3 was on the strength of VMF-221, based at Ewa on Hawaii, shortly before the removal of the red and white tail stripes.

Mitsubishi
G4M 'Betty'

The 'Flying Cigar' appellation is fully justified in this view of a G4M1. Built in larger numbers than any other Japanese bomber, the type saw considerable success in long-range bombing duties.

So lightly protected that it was known to US fighter pilots as 'the Honorable One-shot Lighter', the G4M (codenamed 'Betty' by the Allies) tried to get too much range from too small an aircraft. Despite this, it was by far the most important Imperial Japanese Navy bomber, seeing action throughout the Pacific.

Probably the rock-bottom moment of World War II for the British was 10 December 1941, when the Japanese, whose aircraft were as all knew copied from Western designs but made of bamboo and rice paper, sank two of the Royal Navy's greatest warships (HMSs *Prince of Wales* and *Repulse*) by air attack. What could have done such a thing? The only answer seemed to be the ancient Yokosuka B4Y biplane torpedo bomber. Only later was it realised the great battleship and battle-cruiser had been sent to the bottom by Mitsubishi G3M and G4M long-range bombers. The latter was totally unknown to the Allies, because nobody had read the reports on it sent back from China; they had not read the reports on the Mitsubishi A6M fighter, either, and this was an even bigger shock.

In the context of the war in the Pacific a Japanese twin-engined bomber was unlikely ever again to be more than a thorn in the side of the Allies. At the same time a front-line force of more than 2,000 aircraft flown with immense courage and determination could hardly be ignored, and on occasion 'Betty' did inflict damaging blows. It must be remembered that this modest aircraft, with a much lower gross weight than (for example) a B-25 Mitchell, was used for missions which really demanded a four-engined 'heavy', a type that the Imperial Japanese Navy elected to develop too late to see service during World War II.

Development begins

Development of the G4M began with the issue, in September 1937, of a

Though the much improved G4M2 was available from 1942, engine shortages kept its predecessor, the G4M1 (pictured), in production until early 1944.

Unbeknown to the Royal Navy at the time, the G4M made its debut against Allied forces when a number joined G3Ms in attacking and sinking Royal Navy battleships on 10 December 1941. Here IJN personnel load a torpedo aboard a G4M1.

specification (known as a 12-*shi* specification, because it was in the 12th year of Emperor Hirohito's reign) for a new long-range bomber to succeed the very successful G3M. The latter had gone into action over China in July, and had delighted navy officials by having a combat range in excess of 2,300 miles (3700 km).

Not unnaturally the Koku Hombu (navy air HQ) considered it would be possible to do even better, though it suggested that Mitsubishi should use just two engines of 1,000 hp (746 kW) each. Other numerical demands were a speed of 247 mph (398 km/h), a range with a 1,764-1b (800-kg) torpedo or similar bombload of 2,299 miles (3700 km) and all-round defensive guns needing a crew of seven to nine.

It was soon evident to Kiro Honjo, leader of the bomber design team at Kagamigahara, that the task could not be done

on the stipulated power. It was essential to use engines in the 1,500-hp (1119-kW) class, and the company's engine division happened to have a promising new two-row engine, the Kasei (Mars), that fitted the bill admirably. The rest of the aircraft almost designed itself, the general layout (especially the forward fuselage) being closely similar to the army's Ki-21 bomber produced at the company's main Nagoya plant. Where the new bomber, which was given the designation G4M, differed from most previous single-fin twin-engined machines was that there was a gun position in the extreme tail. As a result the rear fuselage did not taper in the usual way, and this gave rise to a most distinctive shape that immediately resulted in the G4M's popular name of 'Hamaki' (cigar). Aerodynamically it was perfectly acceptable, though Honjo was unable to achieve the long-span wing he wanted, for maximum

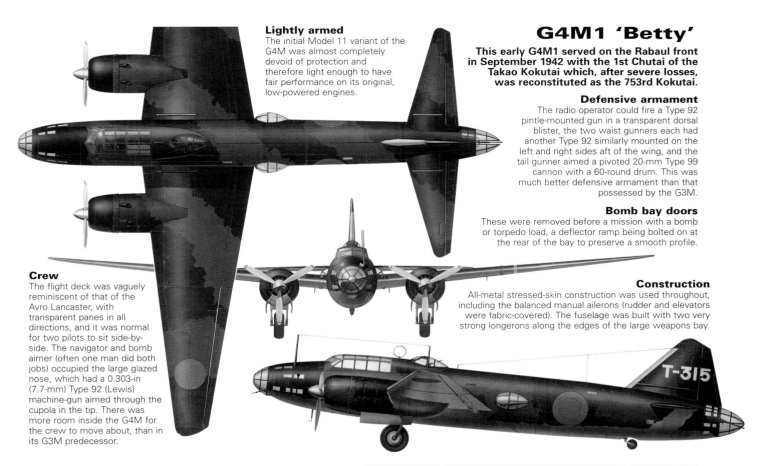

Lightly armed
The initial Model 11 variant of the G4M was almost completely devoid of protection and therefore light enough to have fair performance on its original, low-powered engines.

G4M1 'Betty'

This early G4M1 served on the Rabaul front in September 1942 with the 1st Chutai of the Takao Kokutai which, after severe losses, was reconstituted as the 753rd Kokutai.

Defensive armament
The radio operator could fire a Type 92 pintle-mounted gun in a transparent dorsal blister, the two waist gunners each had another Type 92 similarly mounted on the left and right sides aft of the wing, and the tail gunner a pivoted 20-mm Type 99 cannon with a 60-round drum. This was much better defensive armament than that possessed by the G3M.

Bomb bay doors
These were removed before a mission with a bomb or torpedo load, a deflector ramp being bolted on at the rear of the bay to preserve a smooth profile.

Crew
The flight deck was vaguely reminiscent of that of the Avro Lancaster, with transparent panes in all directions, and it was normal for two pilots to sit side-by-side. The navigator and bomb aimer (often one man did both jobs) occupied the large glazed nose, which had a 0.303-in (7.7-mm) Type 92 (Lewis) machine-gun aimed through the cupola in the tip. There was more room inside the G4M for the crew to move about, than in its G3M predecessor.

Construction
All-metal stressed-skin construction was used throughout, including the balanced manual ailerons (rudder and elevators were fabric-covered). The fuselage was built with two very strong longerons along the edges of the large weapons bay.

G6M escort fighters

As the previous-generation G3Ms were met with much tougher resistance over China, notably from the American Volunteer Group, and the decision was taken to modify the G4M with heavy gun armament instead of bombs and send them in formation with the G3Ms. The result was that the first 30 production machines were G6M1s, or Type 1 Wingtip Convoy Fighters. The bomb bay was sealed, the dorsal gun removed, and the beam guns replaced by a single Type 99 cannon which could be swung on an arm to fire to either side. Two more Type 99s were mounted in a new ventral gondola, one firing ahead and the other to the rear. Thus four cannon could be brought to bear on attacking fighters, and the nose machine-gun was also retained. With a crew of 10 and 21 drums of ammunition the G6M1 was a sluggish performer, and cruising speed was actually slower than that of the G3Ms after the latter had dropped their bombs. Survivors were taken off operations and converted first as G6M1-K trainers and finally as G6M1-2L paratroop transports.

In this view of early G4M1s on a bombing mission, it is possible to see the space left by the deleted bomb bay door. Note also the gun blisters on the fuselage flanks.

range, and was forced for reasons of structural strength to use a strongly tapered wing of modest span (25 m/82 ft compared with a 20-m/5.6-ft length of fuselage).

Katsuzo Shima made the first flight on 23 October 1939. The new G4M was outstanding from the start, and the only visible change needed was to increase the height of the vertical tail. By

1940 Mitsubishi's Nagoya factory was all set to build what in most respects (notably excepting the question of vulnerability) was the best twin-engine bomber of the day. But by this time the Koku Hombu had come to the questionable conclusion that the first aircraft off the line should be completed as escort fighters! In late 1940 production of the

G4M1 bomber, or Type 1 Attack Bomber Model 11, at last got under way, 13 trials aircraft being followed by the first for the navy inventory in April 1941. By June 1941 the Kanoya Kokutai had become fully operational in China and completed 12 combat missions in that month. Another Kokutai went into action in August, and by the time of Pearl Harbor on 7 December 1941 the Imperial Japanese Navy had 120 G4M1s in its front-line inventory. Of these 97 were with the 21st and 23rd Air Flotillas on Formosa, while 27 Kanoya Kokutai aircraft were switched to the Saigon area to attack the British fleet. These were the aircraft which, with G3M2s, sank HMS *Prince of Wales* and HMS *Repulse*, opening attacks on the following day on US airfields in the Philippines. By 19 February 1942 Japanese forces had overrun a huge geographical area, and the G4M1s were bombing Darwin in northern Australia.

From early March 1942 the G4M1s hammered at Rabaul, Port Moresby and other New Guinea targets. Opposition by the scattered and initially demoralized Allies gradually stiffened, and even though the Allied fighters (initially Curtiss P-40Es of the No. 75 Sqn, RAAF) had a hard time against the A6M2s, if they got near a G4M the bomber went up like a torch. It had been known from the start that, to meet the severe range requirement, the G4M must lack armour and self-sealing tanks. As the situation appeared likely to get worse, the Model 12 bomber was quickly produced with various arrangements of rubber sponge and sheet to protect the tanks, and CO_2 extinguishers were added. The side blisters were replaced by flat gunnery windows, the tail gun was put in a blunter position with a large vertical wedge-shaped opening, and Kasei 15 engines were fitted to give better altitude performance, above the effective ceiling of 40-mm AA fire.

Several identifying features of an early production G4M1 are visible on this example, including three-bladed propellers, an oval crew door in the rear fuselage and limited nose glazing.

Fortress Rabaul

One year of recovery enabled the United States to go onto the offensive, starting at Guadalcanal. The Solomons and the Bismarcks, dominated by the Rabaul bastion, were the scene of attrition for the Japanese navy.

Above and below: Sweeping across Karas harbour in Dutch New Guinea, one of these Douglas A-20Gs is caught by flak and plunges, out of control, into the sea. This scene was to be repeated many times throughout the Pacific war as American light bombers pounded Japanese defences.

The character of operations in the South West Pacific Area (SWPA) was changed on 21 July 1942 when the Japanese put 2,000 troops ashore at Buna to launch an offensive against Port Moresby via the tortuous Kokada Trail. But the savage fighting of this arena was overshadowed on 7 August when 9,000 US Marines were landed at Tulagi and Guadalcanal in the Solomons under the cover of air groups from USS *Saratoga*, *Wasp* and *Enterprise* of Task Group 61.1. Air strikes at Tulagi decimated an A6M2-N unit on the ground and US troops overran the garrison, which fought to the death. At Lunga Point, across the narrows, men and equipment went ashore at Guadalcanal without any hindrance. The Americans' objective was to capture a recently constructed airfield and to secure a base in the Solomons from which the heavily-defended Rabaul and the Japanese axis in the Bismarcks

could be threatened.

Rear Admiral Yamada's 25th Air Flotilla soon responded and the 5th and 6th Koku Kushu Butais took off from Rabaul, setting course for Lunga Point. However, the force was spotted by American forces and F4F-4s of VF-5 and VF-6. Total casualties were 11 Wildcats and one SBD-3 against 14 G4M1s and D3A1s and two A6Ms. A further strike the following morning saw another force of G4M1s hit the convoy at Lunga, but it only managed to sink a transport and damage a destroyer at much cost to itself.

Over the next five months, the Japanese navy made every effort to dislodge the US Marines' hold on Guadalcanal. An increasing number of units was fed into Rabaul and Kavieng and, as early as September 1942, the headquarters of the 11th Koku-Kantai (air fleet), under Vice-Admiral Nishizo Tsukahara, was transferred from Tinian to Rabaul to oversee operations. On 9 August, Japanese troops were landed on

Guadalcanal by destroyers, cruisers and transports and engaged the 1st Marine Division in some of the fiercest fighting of the war. Bereft of air cover following the withdrawal of T61.1, the defence of the island fell to the F4F-4s of VMF-223. At sea, naval engagements intensified with the Battles of Savo Island, Eastern Solomons and Santa Cruz being of significance, with both sides losing carriers and scores of aircraft.

The climactic battles of October 1942 saw the first signs of exhaustion in the Japanese air

and land forces. On Guadalcanal, the Americans built up their forces, with USAAF P-38Fs, P-39Ds and P-40s aiding the SBD-3s, TBF-1s and F4F-4s in pushing back the Japanese. The *Enterprise* was back in action in November, its air groups sinking the battleships *Hiei* and *Kirishima* on 12 November. Suffering their first major land defeat of the war, the Japanese evacuated their forces from Guadalcanal between 4 January and 9 February. This American victory coincided with activities in the Papua sector, where the Japanese had been driven from Buna and forced to flee along the coast to Lea and Salamaua. Thus the threat to Port Moresby was relieved. In the battle for Guadalcanal, the Japanese navy had lost a carrier, 23 ships and about 350 aircraft, along with the cream of its pilots and air crew. However, the balance of carrierborne air power, now recognised as the decisive factor in the Pacific war, still lay with the Japanese, despite its losses. As of 9 November 1942, the first-line strength of the JNAF was 1,721 aircraft, of which 465 were carrier-based. Primary strike

As the war neared Australia, the RAAF began to play a greater part in the conflict. Among its weapons were the Bristol Beaufort torpedo-bombers which were to see much action in the anti-shipping role. Many of these were based in northern Australia.

In the Allied build-up to the landings at Lae, the US 5th Air Force commenced an all-out campaign against the JAAF in the Wewark area. On 17 August 1943, B-17s, B-24s and B-25s attacked the airfields with cannon and para-frag bombs and, after the two-week blitz, the airfield was littered with wrecks. The decimation of the 4th Kokugan's aircraft paved the way for that autumn's invasion, which resulted in the western flank of Rabaul being captured.

aircraft were the ageing Aichi D3A1s and Nakajima B5N2s. Improvements to the A6M fighter gave it a temporary ascendancy over the F4F-4 and P-40, but time was running out. Land-based bombers of the JNAF were restricted to the G4M1 'Betty' and the G3M3 'Nell', while the twin-engined J1N1 Gekko 'Irving' was just entering service.

Front-line strength of the Japanese Army Air Force amounted to 1,642 aircraft, consisting of Ki-43 fighters, Ki-48 light bombers and Ki-46 fast reconnaissance aircraft.

New equipment

During 1943, the Americans finally began to turn the tide against the Japanese. The Imperial empire had failed to gain a significant victory in over a year and many of its most experienced crews and troops were dead. In the production of aircraft alone,

the Japanese could not hope to match the Americans. US forces also provided longer and more in-depth training for their pilots, while their equipment, such as the F4U Corsair, F63F-3 Hellcat and SB2C Helldiver coupled with the new 'Essex'-class carriers, provided the USN and USMC with a technological superiority.

Fighting in the Solomons

Units serving in Guadalcanal came under a Commander Air Solomons (ComAirSols) who, though changing, was usually a USMC officer. The first formations were F4F-4s and SBD units of the USN and USMC. VMF-223, 224 and 232, VMSB-231, VS-5 and VB-6 had all come to Henderson Field by 30 August 1942 and they were joined here by the USAAF's 67th Fighter Squadron's P-400s. As units were worn out, they were simply replaced, but five

Medals of Honor were awarded to USMC pilots.

In November 1942, the decimated JNAF 25th Air Flotilla was withdrawn to Japan and taking its place were elements of the 21st and 22nd Air Flotillas from the Marshalls and the Marianas. The 26th Air Flotilla was now located on the southern tip of Bougainville with A6M3s, D3A2 dive-bombers and G4M1 bombers. Aircraft strength at Rabaul was kept at around 220, while about 120 were based at Bougainville.

ComAirSols was backed by the US 13th Air Force with B-17Fs making raids, anti-shipping strikes and mine-laying sorties all over the region. The F4U-1 also entered service with VMF-124 and it was the first Allied fighter to out-match the dreaded A6M in combat.

Rising Allied air superiority was most notably illustrated on

3 March 1943 when RAAF Beaufighters and American B-17s, B-25s and A-20s smashed a Japanese sea convoy so badly that, out of 16 ships, only four destroyers escaped. Throughout 3-4 March, major air battles were fought, with the Japanese suffering heavy losses in return for three P-38s and a single Fortress.

Admiral Yamamoto flew to Rabaul on 3 April 1943 and launched a campaign known as Operation 'I-Go', aimed at destroying Allied air power in the Solomons. On 7 April, 110 A6Ms and 67 D3As attacked shipping off Guadalcanal and Savo Island. ComAirSols countered with 76 fighters, including RNZAF P-40Ns. Intervening air battles continued until 18 April. US cryptographers had found out that Yamamoto would be arriving at Ballale and so 18 P-38s, with hand-picked crews, were sent to intercept. At 09.35, the Lightnings sighted two G4M1s with an escort of A6M3s north west of Kahili. The two 'Bettys' were downed, as were several of the 'Zekes' and one P-38 failed to return. Admiral Mineichi Koga was named as Yamamoto's successor.

Japanese air power

Japanese offensive operations against the Allies often suffered due to the limited abilities of the Imperial bomber fleet, even new types like the Ki-49. The most serious problem was that many of the bombers had unprotected fuel tanks and insufficient armour – aircraft such as the G4M1 received the nickname 'Flying Lighter' from Allied pilots due to the ease of setting them alight.

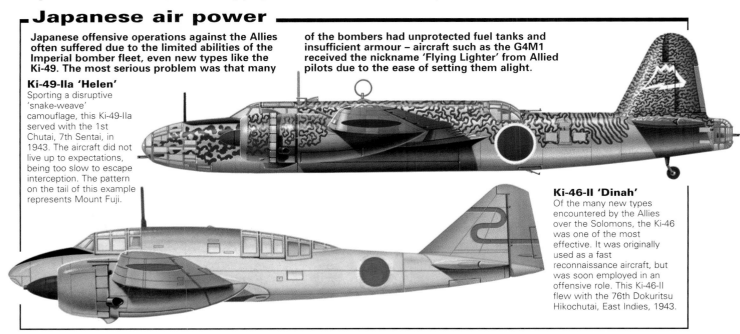

Ki-49-IIa 'Helen'
Sporting a disruptive 'snake-weave' camouflage, this Ki-49-IIa served with the 1st Chutai, 7th Sentai, in 1943. The aircraft did not live up to expectations, being too slow to escape interception. The pattern on the tail of this example represents Mount Fuji.

Ki-46-II 'Dinah'
Of the many new types encountered by the Allies over the Solomons, the Ki-46 was one of the most effective. It was originally used as a fast reconnaissance aircraft, but was soon employed in an offensive role. This Ki-46-II flew with the 76th Dokuritsu Hikochutai, East Indies, 1943.

Pacific drive

A Nakajima J1N1 Gekko 'Irving' burns after a failed attack upon the escort carrier USS **Coral Sea**, during operations off Saipan, in the Marianas, in June 1944. By the close of 1943, the aircraft carrier group had become the key component of US air power.

For the Allies, towards the end of 1943, the tortuous path to Japan lay via New Guinea and the Philippines, and along the atolls of the Central Pacific.

Air units of the JNAF in the South East Area in August 1943 included five Kokutais with A6M3s and new A6M5 Model 52 fighters; two with D3A1s and a small number of D4Y2 Suisei 'Judy' dive-bombers; three G4M1-equipped units; and four Kokutais with E13A1s, F1M2s and H8K flying-boats. Savage fighting was experienced during the build-up of the Allied landings in New Georgia; Admiral Koga committed the Hiyo's and Junyo's air groups to Kahili and Ballale as part of the 6th Air Attack Force under Commander Mitsugu Kokufuda. From 20-22 August 1943 the Japanese withdrew from the New Georgia islands, while units of ComAirSols moved into the airfields of Munda, Bairoko, Ondonga and Segi Point. On 14 September ComAirSols, aided by units of the RNZAF, 5th and 13th Air Forces, commenced

pre-invasion bombing of Buin, Kara, Kieta, Ballale, Buka, Bonis and Kahili airfields on Bougainville. Rabaul, already frequently hit, was the subject of a massed bombing campaign by Kenney's US 5th Air Force starting on 12 October 1943. Repeat raids were made on 13, 18 and 29 October, and on 2 November. Three days later, Sherman's Task Group 58.3 (USS Saratoga and USS Princeton) launched 52 Hellcats, 23 TBM-1s and 22 SBD-5s to strike at Rabaul. These were met by 60-70 'Zekes' from Tobera and Vunakanau. The US Navy mounted another strike on 11 November. Following this, Koga was forced to pull out the air groups of the 1st Kokusentai, which had been sent to Rabaul on the first of the month: in two weeks of action, 43 out of 82 A6Ms, 38 out of 45 D3A2s, and 34 out of 40 B5N2s had been destroyed. All the Allied efforts

against Rabaul had been conducted with the aim of covering the landings at Cape Torokina (Bougainville) on 1 November 1943. From bases on Bougainville, Rabaul lay within range of the F4U-1 Corsairs of VF-17 and units of the US Marine Corps which quickly established ascendancy over Kusaka's remaining fighter forces. Throughout December 1943 and January 1944, Rabaul was attacked frequently, its ailing defences once again being stiffened on 22 January by the air groups of the Junyo, Hiyo and Ryuho (62 A6M5s, 18 D4Y2s

and 18 B6N2 Tenzan torpedo-bombers). But events in the mandated territories, in the wide Pacific, now bore influence. Elements of the 25th and 26th Air Flotillas, consisting of 50 or more 'Zekes', defended Rabaul against a raid by 145 TBF-4s, SBD-5s, F6F-3s and Corsairs for the last time on 19 February 1944. On the following day, on the orders of Admiral Mineichi Koga, Rabaul's air units flew to Truk in the Carolines, leaving Rabaul with no aircraft.

The Central Pacific drive, as finalised in the 'Quadrant' conference of August 1943, started on 1 September 1943 with the occupation of Baker Island, to the east of the Gilberts, and the air strikes on Marcus. These operations saw the debut of the new F6F-3 Hellcat, with a 20-mph (32-km/h) margin over the JNAF's latest A6M5 fighter. Although not as manoeuvrable, the F6F-3 possessed durability and firepower that were to pay handsome dividends. Another new type entering service was the SB2C-1 Helldiver, a heavier and less adaptable replacement for the SBD-5 Dauntless. The legendary F4F Wildcat, in its General Motors FM-1 model, continued to serve in the smaller CVE carriers. In preparation for the campaign in the Gilbert Islands, Vice Admiral R. A. Spruance's US 5th Fleet gathered the largest carrier force yet seen, amounting to 11 carriers in all, with 703 aircraft. Standard equipment was the F6F-3, the SBD-5 and the Grumman TBF-1 Avenger. First blood to the F6F-3s occurred during the Baker Island operation on 1 September, when three Kawanishi H8Ks were shot down on reconnaissance missions.

Operation 'Galvanic'

The first enemy-held atolls selected for amphibious assault in Operation 'Galvanic' were Betio (Tarawa) and Makin; target date was 19-20 November 1943. US Navy aircraft mauled the JNAF 22nd Flotilla at its bases in the Marshalls before 'Galvanic', while sundry targets were attacked by

Flying through a barrage of defensive fire, a Nakajima B6N Tenzan 'Jill' torpedo-bomber attempts an attack on the USS Yorktown during the raid on Truk in the Caroline Islands.

Above: Countering the submarine threat posed to the continual Allied re-supply convoys, the Avenger, with its useful endurance, was employed on convoy protection patrols.

Above: The P-38 Lightning (as well as this F-5B) arrived at Isley Field, Saipan, in July 1944. The return of US aircraft to the Marianas, within striking reach of the Japanese mainland, marked the beginning of the end of the Pacific war.

US 7th Air Force B-24Hs based at Funafuti. During the carrier strikes on Roi, Maloelap and Mille in the Marshalls, the F6F-3s effectively dealt with the A6M3s, while the overhead CAP warded off most of the determined low-level attacks by Mitsubishi G4M2s and the new Nakajinia B6N2 Tenzan torpedo-bombers from Roi-Namur.

With D-Day on 1 February 1944 for the landings on Roi and Kwajalein (Operation 'Flintlock'), to be followed on 18 February by Operation 'Catchpole' (the invasion of Eniwetok), the US fast carriers went to task on Japanese air strength in the Marshalls. Of the 150 serviceable JNAF aircraft available on 27 January, not one was left in fighting condition by the time of the various landings.

Of more dramatic effect, however, was the air strike on

Truk, the Japanese bastion in the Carolines and the supply base for Rabaul and Eniwetok. On 17 February 1944, at the airfields of Moen, Eten, Param and Dublon in Truk Lagoon, the rump of the 24th and 26th Air Flotillas (plus added reserves) amounted to some 155 serviceable A6Ms, G4M2s, B6N2s and D3A2s, together with floatplanes and transports, and 180 aircraft under repair. At dawn on that day 72 F6F-3s were sent aloft to take out Truk's air strength. Belated radar warning enabled only 53 A6Ms to get into the air, which engaged the Hellcats. About 30 'Zekes' were shot down in combat, and all but four F6F-3s returned to the carriers. This strike was followed by 18 TBF-1s with 500-lb (227-kg) and 300-lb (136-kg) fragmentation bombs in an attack on Moen, Eten and Param. The first and only counter-attack took place in early evening when six B6N2s slipped through the CAP to gain one torpedo hit on the *Intrepid*. By the end of the following day, Task Force 58 had accounted for over 200,000 tons of shipping and destroyed 252 Japanese aircraft.

The US strike on Truk, together with the loss of vital bases in the Gilberts and Marshalls and the reduction of Rabaul, forced the Japanese to tighten the defensive line to the Marianas, eastern Carolines and the Paulaus. The hub of JNAF power was concentrated upon the Marianas.

Defeat of the JAAF

MacArthur's landings early in 1944 were aimed at completing the cordon around Rabaul, and to this effect operations against Green Island (15 February), the Admiralty Islands (29 February) and Emirau (20 March) took place. Kenney launched a renewed offensive on 4th Kokugun's bases at Boram, Wewak, Dagua and But on 11 March in preparation for Operation Reckless, in which troops were to be landed some

300 miles (485 km) up-coast. Up to and including 27 March, the 5th Air Force and the RAAF paid constant visits to Wewak and its satellites. JAAF fighter reaction was meagre, the maximum being 40-50 Ki-43s and Ki-61s along with a small number of Nakajima Ki-44s which scrambled from Dagua and Boram on 11 March. On 25 March Teramoto withdrew his headquarters from Wewak to Hollandia where, at the airfields of Sentani and Cyclops on the same day, PR coverage revealed the existence of about 260 aircraft.

Hollandia success

The Hollandia 'blitz' opened at dawn on 30 March when 57 Liberators, with a top-cover of P-38Js, plastered Hollandia's airfields. The raid was repeated on the following day, and finally on 4 April 1944, when 66 B-24Ds dropped 492 1,000-lb (454-kg) GPs on Hollandia, Cyclops and Sentani, followed by attacks from 96 Douglas A-20Gs and 76 B-25Js. As a result of these ferocious assaults, the back of 4th Kokugun was broken in New Guinea for all time; Itabana was relieved of his command, and the headquarters of the 4th Kokugun was forced to retire to Manado (Celebes).

Troubled only by the small force of G4M2s, based at Sorong, Jefman and Samate in the western extremity of New Guinea, MacArthur was able to proceed with his timetable of amphibious landings without hindrance: Hollandia and Aitape were invaded on 22 April 1944, Wakde and Biak on 17 and 27 May respectively, and Sansapor on 30 July. Bypassing Halmahera, the forces of the South West Pacific Area made their penultimate leap before the invasion of the Philippines, setting forces down on Morotai on 15 September 1944. The line of Allied bases in New Guinea was now secure, and the active campaign in New Guinea was at an end.

This view of a Japanese airfield, resplendent with a 'greeting' to the enemy airmen above, was photographed by Maj. Gen. Willis H. Hale, USAAF, during a mission over the Palau Islands.

By 1943 the Hellcat was replacing the Wildcat on larger USN carriers, although VF-11 continued to operate the F4F-4 from Guadalcanal. This example, flown by Lt(jg) William Nicholas Leonard, was used to down a pair of Zeros on 12 June 1943.

The first of the Lend-Lease Catalinas to enter RAF service were 170 Mk IBs (similar to PBY-5 standard). This example is fitted with ASV Mk II radar and was allocated to No. 202 Squadron, based at Gibraltar.

Consolidated PBY Catalina

Multi-role patrol 'boat

The greatest of all flying-boats, the Catalina proved to be one of the most versatile and enduring aircraft ever built. Active in all theatres of World War II, the PBY outlived its proposed replacement and earned its place in the annals of air warfare.

The Consolidated Catalina (known to its manufacturer as the Model 28) was one of the slowest combat aircraft of World War II; wags said its crews needed a calendar rather than a stopwatch in order to rendezvous with a convoy. Flown in 1935, it was no longer young even at the outbreak of war, and the US Navy had already ordered a next-generation flying-boat (the Martin PBM) to succeed it. But the well-loved 'Cat' happened to be rather hard to beat. In 1938 it had been recognised by the Soviet Union as superior to

anything created by their own designers, and it was built there under licence throughout the war. More than that, the original US machine blossomed forth in many new versions which, to the end of the war, outsold all the newer replacements. More Catalinas were built than any other flying-boat or floatplane in history.

Development

The genesis of the PBY, as the aircraft was known to US forces, lay in a 1933 requirement by the US Navy for a new long-range patrol flying-boat. At that time

the principal aircraft in this category was the Consolidated P2Y, designed at Buffalo by Isaac M. 'Mac' Laddon, a gifted seaplane engineer and a director of Consolidated Aircraft. To meet the new demand, he cleaned up the P2Y by giving it an almost cantilever wing, mounted above the shallow but broad hull on a central pylon housing the flight engineer. The wing differed from that of the P2Y by having a regular centre-section and tapered outer panels, all of stressed-skin all-metal construction (ailerons were fabric- skinned). A unique feature was that the wingtip floats were mounted on pivoted frames which could be retracted electrically so that in flight the floats formed the wingtips. The hull, likewise all metal, was quite different from that of most large 'boats in being all on one deck, with a broad semi-circular top. In the bow was a mooring compartment, and transparent

sighting window with a venetian blind giving sea water protection. The bow cockpit was a turret with large all-round windows in production aircraft, and a machine-gun above. Two pilots sat side-by-side in the wide cockpit, with large windows all round. Aft of the wing were left and right gunner's stations, each with a sliding hatch. Unlike the P2Y the tail was clean and simple, with the horizontal tail mounted well up the single fin. The powerplant switched from Cyclones to the new two-row Pratt & Whitney Twin Wasp, neatly cowled on the centre-section with cooling gills and driving Hamilton variable-pitch propellers.

With the massive order for 60, Consolidated had plenty of work to support its 2,000-mile (3220-km) move to San Diego in southern California, where the weather was fine throughout the year. In October 1935 the XP3Y made a non-stop flight of almost 3,500 miles (5633 km) from Coco Solo to San Francisco. It then went on to participate in the dedication of the giant new San Diego plant on 20 October, before returning to Buffalo to be modified to PBY standard with a broad rounded rudder, de-icer boots on all leading edges (with pull-out steps up the leading edge of the fin), full armament and combat equipment. It flew again in March 1936 and reached US Navy squadron VP-11F at the same time as the first production machines in October 1936. Unquestionably this was the best patrol flying-boat in the world at that time.

In July 1936 Consolidated received a contract for 50 PBY-2s with all four wing racks stressed to 1,000-lb (454-kg) loads and with 0.5-in (12.7-mm)

This PBY-1 is seen taxiing out, possibly at NAS Pensacola. A crewman is on the wing, waist hatches are open, and the pilot has full up-elevator and full left aileron. The biplane is an N3N Canary.

guns in the waist positions. In November 1936 an order followed for 66 PBY-3s with R-1830-66 Twin Wasps uprated from 900 to 1,000 hp (671 to 746 kW), and in December 1937 a contract followed for 33 PBY-4s, all but one with large bulged transparent blisters instead of lateral sliding hatches for the beam gunners and with 1,050-hp (783-kW) engines. Two more PBYs were sold in 1937 to explorer Dr Richard Archbold, who named them *Guba I* and *Guba II* (Motu word for a sudden storm). *Guba II* spent an arduous year in New Guinea, finally making the first flight across the Indian Ocean to survey the route known in World War II as the 'horseshoe route' on which hundreds of military and BOAC Catalinas were to fly. It then crossed Africa and the Atlantic, the first aircraft to circle the globe near the Equator. *Guba I* was sold to a Soviet expedition led by Sir Hubert Wilkins, flying 19,000 miles (30600 km) through the worst weather in the world, fruitlessly searching for S. A. Levanevskii, who vanished near the North Pole on 13 August 1937. So outstanding was the Model 28 in this work that the Model 28-2 was put into production at Taganrog on the Azov Sea as the GST (civil transport version, MP-7), over 1,000 being used in World War II with 950-hp (709-kW) engines in Polikarpov I-16-type shuttered cowlings and with Soviet equipment and armament.

British interest

Another Model 28-5 (PBY-4) was bought by the British Air Ministry and tested at Felixstowe as P9630, proving so outstanding that it was adopted as a standard boat for Coastal Command. Named Catalina Mk I – a name later adopted by the US Navy – the first RAF variant was similar to the latest US Navy type, the PBY-5 with 1,200-hp (895-kW) R-1830-92 engines, an order for 200 of

which had been placed on 20 December 1939. No flying-boat – in fact no large US Navy aircraft – had ever been ordered in such quantities, and the vast open-ended British orders called for massive extra capacity. British officials helped to arrange for licence-production by Canadian Vickers at Cartierville (Montreal) and Boeing of Canada at Vancouver. The San Diego plant also much more than doubled in size and was joined by a larger plant a mile down the road, building B-24s.

On 22 November 1939 Consolidated flew a PBY-4, rebuilt as the XPBY-5A with retractable tricycle landing gear. This excellent amphibian conversion was a great success and had only a minor effect on performance. The final 33 PBY-5s were completed as PBY-5As, and another 134 were ordered in November 1940. At the time of Pearl Harbor (7 December 1941), the US Navy had three squadrons of PBY-3s, two of PBY-4s and no fewer than 16 flying the new PBY-5. Before sunrise on that day, a PBY crew spotted the periscope of a Japanese submarine at Pearl Harbor, marked it with smoke and guided the destroyer USS *Ward*, which sank it – the first US shots of World War II – over an hour before the air attack began. By this time a further 586 PBY-5s had been ordered, and the export list had risen to 18 for Australia, 50 for Canada, 30 for France and 36 for the Netherlands East Indies. In 1942 another 627 PBY-5As were

The PBY-1's defensive armament comprised one 0.3-in (7.62-mm) machine-gun in the bow turret and one similar weapon in each waist position. A further 0.3-in (7.7-mm) machine-gun could be fitted in the tunnel position in the bottom of the hull.

added, of which 56 were to be OA-10s for the USAAF, used for search and rescue. The first Lend-Lease batch for the RAF comprised 225 non-amphibious PBY-5Bs (Catalina Mk IBs), 55 of which were retained by the USN, followed by 97 Catalina Mk IVAs, fitted in Britain with ASV Mk II radar. RAF Catalinas usually had a Vickers K (VGO) machine-gun in the bow and twin 0.303-in (7.7-mm) Brownings machine-guns in the waist blisters.

Pacific action

From the time of the devastating Japanese attack on Pearl Harbor, the Catalina was by far the most important US patrol aircraft. In the northern campaign along the Aleutians, many Catalinas had to make overloaded downwind take-offs in blizzards at

night, with ice over the windscreen. The PBY was the first US aircraft (other than the obsolete Douglas B-18) to carry radar. It fulfilled diverse missions including those of torpedo-bomber, transport and glider tug. Perhaps the most famous of all Catalinas were the Black Cat PBY-5A amphibians which, painted matt black, roamed the western Pacific from December 1942, finding Japanese ships of all kinds by radar at night and picking up Allied survivors from ships and aircraft in boats and dinghies. In addition to radar, bombs, depth charges and fragmentation grenades, the Black Cats often carried crates of empty beer bottles whose eerie whistling noise deterred Japanese gunners, making them look for what they imagined to be unexploded bombs.

Above: The esteem in which the PBY was held is typified by this image of four US Navy patrol squadrons lined up in San Diego as part of the 1938 Warner Brothers film 'Wings of the Navy', starring Olivia de Havilland and George Brent.

Left: In November 1939 Consolidated first flew the XPBY-5A. This was converted with tricycle-type undercarriage from a PBY-4 and was the first of the amphibian variants (denoted by the 'A' suffix).

Iwo Jima to Okinawa

The islands of Iwo Jima and Okinawa represented the final stepping stone for the Americans before the attack on Japan itself. The Japanese fought desperately, throwing air and surface forces into ultimately futile suicide attacks against the invaders.

By January 1945 US fleet dispositions were being made for the capture of the island of Iwo Jima, just 760 miles (1223 km) south of Tokyo itself and roughly the same distance north of Saipan. The principal naval force was Task Force 58 (the Fast Carrier Force) comprising five task groups consisting of 11 fleet carriers and five light carriers plus 100 battleships, cruisers and destroyers.

The importance of Iwo Jima lay in its position directly under the route of the B-29s that were based in Saipan and making raids on Japan. Observers on Iwo Jima could launch interceptors from

Iwo Jima or the homeland itself to stop the bombers. If the island was captured, it could be used by the USAAF as a base for fighters to escort the B-29s.

To cover T.G. 52, T.F. 58 sailed to within 60 miles (97 km) of Tokyo, launching strikes on the capital, downing about 40 enemy aircraft and harassing Japanese shipping.

On 19 February, the Fast Carrier Force struck the island with a big gun bombardment from two battleships and strikes by Helldivers, Avengers and Corsairs. Meanwhile, the home-based Japanese aircraft did not interfere with the invasion force off Iwo Jima until the evening of

Above: The assault force for Iwo Jima (Task Group 52.2) contained no fewer than 1,000 ships with 12 escort carriers, embarking a total of 226 Wildcats and 138 Avengers.

Top: A USAAF B-24M Liberator departs the flaming beachheads of Iwo Jima, with Suribacji Mountain in the background. B-24s and B-25s proved invaluable in softening up the opposition, attacking targets with bombs and rockets.

19 February, due to the fear of the marauding T.F. 58. By the time the Japanese aircraft did arrive, some 40,000 Marines had gone ashore and the Japanese aircraft were heavily engaged by American fighters and anti-aircraft fire.

On 21 February, the *Saratoga*, along with three destroyers, was detached from T.F. 58 to cover the amphibious forces and at about 17.00 hours, was attacked by six Japanese suicide aircraft. Two were hit by AAA, but hit the ship's sides where the bombs exploded; the bomb from a third aircraft struck the forward end of the flight deck, a fourth also hit the flight deck, a fifth hit the starboard side of the ship, and the sixth aircraft was shot down. Two hours later, a further five suicide aircraft hit the carrier. Yet the old carrier survived; with 123 dead or missing and 192 injured, and 42 of its aircraft destroyed or jettisoned, it was ordered to

retire from the area for refits and, after only two months, returned to active service.

That same evening, the escort carrier *Bismarck Sea* was hit by two suicide aircraft; just as its captain issued the order to abandon ship, it was torpedoed and went down with 218 of its crew, 19 Wildcats and 15 Avengers.

In an effort to prevent further suicide attacks, the Fast Carrier Force was detached north to Japan on 23 February, but poor weather prevented carrier strikes and so the the Force reconnoitred Okinawa for the impending attack. Within a fortnight, Iwo Jima had been captured, no further significant Japanese air attacks having troubled the land or naval forces, while aircraft from the escort carrier *Anzio* had sunk two Japanese submarines.

During the invasion, T.F. 58 and T.G. 52 were estimated to

This classic pose captured the moment when the US Marines claimed Iwo Jima. In fact, the US flag had been raised six hours previously, but the moment was recreated for the camera.

The Japanese fought desperately to defend their territories. On 11 May, the carrier Bunker Hill *was hit by bombs and suicide aircraft; it was saved, however, though not before losing 389 of its crew.*

and destroy as many transport ships as possible before being overwhelmed by American forces. However, the immense ship was detected as it left its home waters, shadowed by Mariner flying-boats and attacked by 280 aircraft from T.F. 58, including 98 Avenger torpedo aircraft. Inevitably, the *Yamato* succumbed, but only after being hit by 10 torpedoes and five bombs, taking to the bottom 2,498 of its crew; with it went an accompanying light cruiser with 450 men.

have destroyed 393 aircraft in the air and 200 on the ground. US Casualties amounted to 95 aircrew and 143 aircraft. However, a key base had been secured within fighter range of Japan and without any irreplaceable losses among the vital American carrier task groups.

The end in sight

The invasion of Okinawa, an island which lies midway between Formosa and the southernmost part of the Japanese mainland, involved an assault and support force second only to that thrown against Normandy 10 months previously, but far exceeding that operation in terms of distances and logistics involved. Once more, the 5th Fleet's Task Force 58 would provide the naval muscle in the assault and its protection.

Before the fleet sailed from Ulithi to the south-west of the Marianas, the fleet-carrier *Randolph* was hit by a suicide aircraft and was put out of action, with the loss of 27 men. On

14 March, T.F. 58 sailed north to attack air bases in Japan where the majority of suicide units was thought to be based. However, warned of the impending attack, many of the Japanese aircraft were withdrawn out of range of the carrier aircraft. Meanwhile, the carrier aircraft had found and attacked Japanese warships in their home waters, causing damage, especially to the light carrier *Ryuho*. Pre-occupation with these attacks allowed a number of Japanese bombing raids to take off, the aircraft making for Task Group 52.2, where *Wasp* was hit and badly damaged, with 102 men killed and 269 injured. However, the remaining crew managed to extinguish the fires and, within an hour, the carrier was recovering its aircraft. Almost simultaneously, the fleet carrier *Franklin* suffered two bomb hits which started massive fires. In an epic sea rescue only 55 miles (90 km) off Japan, the carrier was saved, though 832 of its crew perished.

In attacks over Japan the Task Force claimed the destruction of

432 enemy aircraft during 18-19 March, and the following day the American ships withdrew as further attacks by suicide pilots began to cause damage to the *Enterprise*. Two days later the *Franklin*, *Enterprise* and *Wasp* left the combat area for repairs.

On 23 March the assault on Okinawa started, with air strikes by T.F. 58's carrier aircraft and a bombardment by 10 battleships which lasted a week. The invasion was to be supported by 13 fast carriers, six light carriers and 18 escort carriers, between them embarking more than 1,000 aircraft. A further 10 escort carriers were loaded with replacement aircraft and USMC fighters to be based on Okinawa.

When the landing assault on Okinawa was launched on 1 April, the Japanese responded by ordering the opening of Operation Tengo, a concerted suicide assault by surface and air forces. No fewer than 4,500 aircraft would be involved in suicide and conventional attacks on the Americans. The most extraordinary element of this operation was the sailing of the super-battleship *Yamato* from Japan on 6 April, it being intended to penetrate right to the Okinawa invasion beaches

A hard battle

The conquest of Okinawa itself took three months and involved one of the greatest combined naval/air campaigns ever fought. The early part of April was marked by sustained conventional and suicide attacks. On the same day that *Yamato* was sunk, the American carrier *Hancock* was badly damaged while, on 11 April, the recently repaired *Enterprise* was again hit, as was *Essex*.

When the Okinawa campaign was officially declared ended on 2 July 1945, it was calculated that the Japanese had launched some 34,000 sorties by 6,000 aircraft, many of them suicide attacks. The US forces claimed to have shot down 2,336 aircraft for the loss of 790 of their own. American naval losses amounted to 33 ships sunk and 119 severely damaged. Obviously, the Japanese suicide attacks posed a serious threat in all operations of 1945, but such were the enormous reserves and resources available to the Americans that the losses, grievous though they were, could be shrugged aside, and never in fact endangered the campaign.

Japanese aircrew on standby with a Mitsubishi G4M 'Betty', This aircraft was one of a batch modified to carry the Ohka piloted missile and was designated G4M2e. Its reduced top speed and poor handling made it an easy target.

Below: **Information, please,** *a reconnaissance P-38J-20-LO, accompanies napalm and rocket-armed F4Us for an attack on Kushi-Take in central Okinawa in June 1945. The P-38 carries cameras and a crewman in the Plexiglas-nosed belly tank.*

These USAAF Republic P-47 Thunderbolts are seen leaving on a routine patrol shortly after the capture of an island in the Marianas chain.

Leyte and the Philippines
Decisive naval battles

Japanese naval power was finally defeated during the Battle of Leyte Gulf. With superiority of the skies assured, US Navy and USAAF aircraft were able to support the successful landings on the Philippines.

Great US forces were assembled for the Marianas invasions (Operation Forager) with D-Day for Saipan on 15 June, and W-Day for Guam and Tinian on 18 June 1944. Once again, the task of wiping out JNAF air power fell to Mitscher's Task Force 58 with 896 aircraft. Starting on 12 June, Mitscher's F6F-3s flew massed fighter sweeps over 1st Koku-Kantai's airfields on Guam, Saipan and Tinian, shooting down 81 enemy aircraft in the air and destroying 29 on the ground on the first morning.

To carry out Operation 'A-Go', the Japanese navy's last attempt to seize the initiative from the US Navy, Admiral Ozawa's 1st Mobile Fleet sailed on 13 June to head north east into the broad wastes of the Philippine Sea. The *Chitose*, *Chiyoda* and *Zuiho* sailed with the Van Force which included the great battleships *Yamato* and *Musashi*. The rest was split into 'A' Force (*Taiho*, *Shokaku* and *Zuikaku*) and 'B' Force (*Junyo*, *Hiyo* and *Ryuho*). The last great carrier battle of the war was about to be joined.

Warned of Ozawa's approach from the San Bernardino Strait by submarine contacts, Mitscher decided to avoid the old strike-counter-strike concept, and to await the Japanese air attacks with overwhelming defensive forces. On 19 June 1944 the first strikes were launched: from the decks of the *Chitose*, *Chiyoda* and *Zuiho*, 43 A6M2s, seven B6N2s and 14 escorting A6M5s roared into the air. This strike was intercepted by the F6F-3s of VF-15 at 70 miles (115 km) while other Hellcats waded in; in return for one hit

Introduction of the 'Divine Wind'

The threat of imminent invasion of the Philippines called for a desperate remedy. Japanese pilots and crews began acts of self-sacrifice to perpetuate the memory of the Divine Wind (*kamikaze*) that, centuries ago, had saved Japan from conquest from across the seas by a savage Mongol horde. This new, but supremely effective, form of air warfare involved suicide attacks on the principle of one man for one ship. Vice Admiral Takijiro Onishi suggested that the 201st Kokutai's pilots form so-called *Kamikaze Tokubetsu Kogekitai* (Divine Wind Special Attack Air Units) at Mabalacat. The first successful *kamikaze* operation was made by four A6M5s against TF 77.4 off Leyte on the morning of 25 October; heavy damage was inflicted on the *Santee* and the *Suwannee*. In

the forenoon six more A6M5s appeared and went down in 70° dives: three were seen to dive on the *Kalinin Bay*, one on the *Kitkun Bay*, and another struck the *St Lô* (above left) with such devastation that it broke up and sank within 30 minutes. The attacks struck fear into US fleet commanders and the tactic soon claimed several more US ships, including the aircraft-carriers USS *Essex* (left) and USS *Princeton* (above right). The initial success of the *kamikaze* attacks ensured that such methods continued for the duration of the war.

Left: A USAAF B-25 Mitchell of the Far East Air Force attacks a Japanese light destroyer off the Philippine coast in early 1945. The burning hulk of another vessel is visible in the background.

Below: Possibly the finest Japanese fighter of the war, the Nakajima Ki-84 'Frank' proved a match for American fighters, but suffered in action due to a lack of combat-experienced pilots.

on the USS *Dakota*, the F6F-3s and the US Navy's lethal 40-mm AA guns shot down 42 of the first wave. It was an early indication of the way in which the battle would go. US submarines now played their part and, as waves of JNAF aircraft left the decks, torpedoes thudded into the *Taiho* and the *Shokaku*, to take both out of the battle; they sank later in the day. Ozawa launched four strikes on 19 June, totalling 373 sorties, losing the shattering total of 243 aircraft, with another 33 severely damaged in the greatest air battle of the Pacific war. Retiring towards Okinawa on 20 June, Ozawa's forces were caught by a TF 58 strike of 85 F6Fs, 77 SB2Cs and 54 TBF/TBM-1s, which succeeded in sinking the *Hiyo*, and severely damaging the *Ryuho* and *Chiyoda*; returning after dark, and critically short of fuel, 80 US aircraft were ditched or lost in crashes. However, the risk had been worth this expenditure. The air groups of the 1st Mobile Fleet had been totally decimated during the fighting of 19-20 June, the same fate befalling the shore-based elements of 1st Koku-Kantai. By August 1944 the Marianas had been secured, and the ex-Japanese airstrips were in the process of being enlarged to take the Boeing B-29s of the USAAF for the bombing offensive against Japan.

Introduced in 1944 to counter the B-29 bombing raids, the Kawasaki Ki-45 KAIc night-fighter featured two obliquely-firing 20-mm cannon and a single 37-mm forward-firing cannon.

Having lost 50 per cent of its strength in the Marianas, the 1st Koku-Kantai was transferred to Nichols Field, near Manila in the Philippines, to join the 26th Air Flotilla. The strength of the forces had risen to about 500 A6M5s, G4M2s, D4Y2s and B6Ns by early September. The existence of this force was to be short-lived. During the pre-invasion air strikes by TF 38 from 9-14 September 1944, JNAF strength was decimated. By 30 September, the 5th Base Air Force had fewer than 100 serviceable aircraft.

Heavy dogfighting

On 12 October Halsey's air groups attacked the airfields on Formosa, where some 630 aircraft of the 6th Base Air Force and the JAAF's 8th Hikoshidan were based. The F6Fs met a 200 or more aircraft reaction over Formosa, to claim over 100 enemy aircraft in return for 30 of their number. The JNAF admitted the loss of 492 aircraft in the following week's fighting while the JAAF's losses amounted to 150; the destruction of the carrier air groups left only 52 A6M5s, 28 A6M7s, 29 torpedo-bombers and seven D4Y2s on the *Zuikaku*, *Zuiho*, *Chitose* and *Chiyoda* – both the 5th and 6th Base Air Forces were reduced to shadows.

It was in this parlous state that the JAAF's 4th Kokugun and the

JNAF faced the arrival of a massive armada of warships and transports which appeared at dawn off the beaches of Leyte on the morning of 20 October. In the biggest amphibious operation to date, the first of 200,000 men of the US 6th Army were placed ashore at Leyte. Close air cover was provided by some 500 aircraft of Task Force 77.4. The US 3rd Fleet (Admiral Halsey) had the usual task of distant cover, with 1,074 F6Fs, SB2Cs and TBFs on nine fleet carriers and eight CVLs of Mitscher's TF 38, distributed within four task groups.

Allied land-based air assets comprised the Far East Air Force (FEAF), to which the US 5th and 13th US Air Forces were subordinated. The strength of FEAF was 2,500, with another 420 contributed by the Royal Australian Air Force; the heavy bombers were B-24H/Js, the P-38L and P-47D formed the bulk of the fighter forces, while medium and light bombers were B-25s and A-20s. However, until Morotai's airfields could provide bomber support to the Leyte beachhead, FEAF's strength would be negated.

In four dispersed and confused battles over the period from 23-26 October, the Japanese navy came to the end of its career as a fighting entity. The aim of Operation Sho-1 as commenced on 18 October after a series of false starts, was the annihilation of the US forces off Leyte. Four task forces were employed; three as attackers, and one as a decoy.

In the greatest naval battle of the war, fought over 24-26 October 1944, both carrier- and land-based air units clashed in a series of fierce naval engagements. The conflicts ended in a decisive victory by the US 3rd and 7th Fleets over the Imperial Japanese Navy, which lost three battleships, all four aircraft-carriers, 10 heavy and light cruisers, and 11 destroyers; 288 aircraft were also lost.

Following its withdrawal to Ulithi, elements of the 2nd Koku-Kantai (6th Base Air

Force) flew to Manila on 23 October. Three days later, all JNAF units, numbering some 400 aircraft, were remustered under the newly-formed 1st Combined Base Air Force. Fresh units were equipped with A6M5s, D4Y2s and D3A2s, and other types included Nakajima N1K1 and Mitsubishi J2M3 fighters.

For the first time since its drubbing in New Guinea, the JAAF performed well and fought hard in the defence of the Philippines, taking full advantage in the initial stages of US weakness over the Leyte beachhead. The strength of the 4th Kokugun was raised to some 400 aircraft, of which 200 were serviceable. Arriving from as far afield as Japan, Burma, and Sumatra, the units were fresh, and relatively well equipped, having received Ki-44 and Ki-84 fighters and Ki-67 bombers.

The JAAF flew maximum-effort sorties during and after the Leyte landings. On 27 October the US Army completed repairs to the Tacloban fighter strip, and it was with some relief that P-38s of the US 7th and 9th FS arrived from Morotai. The severity of the air fighting in October and November 1944 equalled that over Rabaul and Bougainville in 1943. From 27 October-31 December, over 1,033 separate attacks were made on Leyte, the US V Fighter Command claiming 314 enemy aircraft destroyed for the loss of 16 pilots.

General Krueger's 6th Army spearheaded the massive invasion operation in Lingayen Gulf (Luzon) on 9 January 1945, supported by the US 3rd and 7th Fleets. *Kamikaze* strikes abounded, starting on 3 January with a hit on the oiler USS *Cowanesque*. Scores of vessels were damaged in vicious suicide attacks that continued until 13 January. Thereafter, the campaign in Luzon began: Manila fell on 3 March, while final mopping-up operations lasted until July 1945.

The ubiquitous RAF operational aircraft throughout the last three years of the war was the Hawker Hurricane. The most common version was the Mk IIC, which featured four 20-mm cannon and long-range tanks.

CBI theatre

Below: Designed to have enough armour, armament and speed to operate without fighter cover, the Nakajima Ki-49 proved to be underpowered and did not live up to expectations. These Ki-49s of the 3rd Chutai, 95th Sentai, served over north-east China during the summer of 1944.

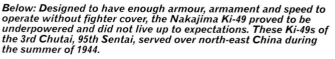

While the British played a minor role in the events taking place in the Pacific, it was in mainland Asia where RAF and Commonwealth forces came to the fore, battling the Japanese into an eventual retreat.

After months of limited advance and counter-offensive in northern Burma, the Japanese embarked on their last major offensive in March 1944, thrusting towards Assam in the northwest. Now re-formed as Long-Range Penetration Groups (LRPs), the British-commanded Chindits were parachuted into the jungle behind enemy lines at Indaw on 5 March and, after overland reinforcement, began construction of a number of landing strips (of which 'Broadway' was the most important); within a week 9,000 Allied troops had been flown deep into enemy-held territory. However, when the Japanese launched an attack against the airfields being used to fly supplies over 'the Hump' into China, they also destroyed 'Broadway', together with most of the RAF fighters based there.

In the course of the Japanese advance, the defended towns of Kohima and Imphal were surrounded and besieged. By June it seemed that Imphal would be forced into surrender but, just in time, General Slim's 14th Army managed to reach and break through the Japanese perimeter. Within days, the withdrawal of the enemy had turned to rout, as RAF, SAAF and USAAF fighters and fighter-bombers began a year-long operation to destroy the Japanese forces in Burma.

By that time (July 1944), Air Command, Southeast Asia, commanded by Air Chief Marshal Sir Richard Peirse, had grown to a total of 90 squadrons, of which 26 were American (flying P-38s, P-40s, P-51s, B-24s, B-25s and C-47s), four were Indian (flying Hurricanes), one a Canadian squadron with Catalinas and one a South African squadron with Venturas. The remaining 58 were of the RAF, flying Thunderbolts, Spitfires, Hurricanes, Beaufighters, Mosquitoes, Wellingtons, Liberators, Sunderlands and Catalinas.

As the new advance (somewhat cautious at first) began, and the Allied forces found abundant evidence that the Japanese army was far from invincible, a heightened morale gripped the Allied aircrews. Combat procedures and weapons, hitherto confined to the European war, were adopted. The dreadful napalm weapon, found so effective in the jungle, came into use, as did Air Support Signals Units for the control of 'cab ranks', the patrols by fighter-bombers over the battlefield.

When the 1944 monsoon season arrived in July, all effective operations by the Japanese air force in Burma ceased. By then, the Allies were closing up to the Irrawaddy, and their air forces, particularly the long-range Liberators, concentrated on the enemy supply lines to prevent a build-up of reinforcements.

Enter the B-29

The object of Operation Matterhorn, which began in India in early 1944, was the establishment of a strategic bomber force, equipped with B-29s, in India with advanced

No. 607 'County of Durham' Squadron Mk VIII Spitfires rest at Imphal as a USAAF B-25 prepares to take off in the background. Though encounters with the enemy were initially rare, by mid-1944 the Spitfires were engaged in the fight for air supremacy with the Japanese army. From early 1945, the unit turned to the fighter-bomber role, supporting Allied armies in Burma.

Left: Known by the Japanese as the 'Whispering Death', the Bristol Beaufighter Mk X was supremely effective in the low-level strike role, principally against jungle river traffic.

Below: No. 681 Sqn, RAF, based at Dum Dum, India briefly flew Mosquito PR.Mk IV and Mk IX aircraft between September and December 1943 before handing them over to No. 684 Sqn. In February 1944, the first Mk XVIs arrived, including this aircraft (NS787/M), probably photographed at Dum Dum.

bases in China from which targets in Manchuria and Kyushu (Japan) could be attacked. To command these heavy bombers, the JCS established the 20th Air Force, with General H. H. Arnold as its executive. The first B-29 of the 58th Bomb Wing landed at Chakulia, near Calcutta, on 2 April 1944, to start working up in the new theatre. In China, in the Chengtu complex, airfields had recently been constructed by over 700,000 labourers to house the giant bombers for their raids to Japan. The first mission took place on 5 June 1944, when 98 B-29s struck the Bangkok Makasam marshalling yards. In the following month, attacks took place only at night, with the first daylight raid not taking place until 7 July, when 18 B-29s bombed the JNAF air bases at Sasebo, Omura, Ota, Omuta and Tabata. By the end of the month, enemy opposition in the shape of Ki-43s and Ki-44-IIbs was being encountered and on 29 July, five out of 80 B-29 aircraft were downed when attacking the Showa steel plant at Anshan.

Over the following months, the B-29s were sent up against a range of targets from engine and airframe factories to Japanese shipping, and along the way they encountered the latest Ki-84 Hayates and J2M3 Raiden types, but in general the B-29s displayed the ability to defend themselves well and losses remained low. Up to 30 March 1945, when the command ceased operations, 49 missions had been flown in 3,058 sorties, expending 11,477 tons of bombs. The results were meagre, but much experience in operating this superlative bomber had been gained.

The end in sight

Back in Burma, by the end of the rains in November, when the advance southwards resumed, the Japanese could muster no more than 125 aircraft in the entire theatre. In the North Shan States efforts were made to open the Burma Road from Mandalay to China as a Chinese Expeditionary Force fell on and captured Wangting on 21 January 1945, supported by aircraft of the

USAAF in China. Exactly two months later, the northern capital of Mandalay fell to the 14th Army as the Chinese fought their way southwards through Lashio and Hsipaw. Throughout this campaign, the needs of more than 350,000 fighting men were supplied by the Dakotas of the Combat Cargo Task Force, an achievement which, having regard to the harsh weather conditions, hazardous terrain and a desperate enemy, was acknowledged by Slim as the vital component of the 14th Army's victory. Even when a sudden Japanese thrust menaced Kunming in distant China, the Dakotas were quickly switched to fly 25,000 Chinese troops, their guns and pack animals across the 'Hump' to meet the threat.

The advance southwards from Mandalay was double-pronged along the great rivers, the Irrawaddy and the Sittang, while XV Corps advanced down the coast, leapfrogging islands until Taungup was reached and captured on 28 April. Occasionally, Ki-43 fighters tried

to interfere, but these were always quickly overwhelmed by the ever-present Spitfires, Hurricanes and Thunderbolts. Soon there was no remaining usable base or airstrip available to the Japanese aircraft, and all air opposition evaporated.

Trapped

The great seaport of Rangoon was itself captured after a sea landing by XV Corps on 2 May, and four days later a link-up was achieved with IV Corps which was advancing down the Sittang. Trapped in the Burmese hinterland lay some 20,000 Japanese troops, sick and hungry yet fanatically determined to break eastwards across the Sittang into the mountains of Indo-China. In 10 days of concerted action by Allied tactical aircraft, the RAF alone flew more than 3,000 sorties and dropped 1,500,000 lb (680400 kg) of bombs and napalm, killing 10,000 of the enemy. By the end of July the Japanese had been defeated throughout Burma.

Above: No. 356 Squadron was based at Salbani, India from January 1944 to July 1945. As well as bombing Japanese bases, mining, meteorological flights and supply-dropping were all duties undertaken by this unit.

Lacking the agility of other Japanese fighters, the Nakajima Ki-44 followed a more Western approach and proved fast and stable, with good climb and dive properties. This is a Ki-44-IIb, flown by the CO of the 85th Sentai from Canton in China during 1944.

Grumman F6F Hellcat

Proving to be an outstanding fighter with the US Navy during World War II, the Grumman-designed F6F Hellcat was mass-produced at a rate unequalled by any other aircraft manufacturing programme and went on to turn the tide against the attacking Japanese hordes.

The bright blue, spirited Grumman F6F Hellcat is rarely named on any shortlist of aviation's greatest flying machines, but that is only because the Hellcat has never been given the credit it deserves. Not as fast as a Mustang, not as manoeuvrable as a Zero, lacking the peppiness of a Yakovlev, and by no measure as advanced as the Vought F4U Corsair – which had begun its life on the drawing board at an earlier date – this sturdy and functional product of the 'Grumman Iron Works' did nothing more than to turn the tide of the Pacific air war.

The Hellcat was one of the few aircraft to need minimal changes during flight test and development, moving quickly from drawing board to combat. This is how one naval aviator described the creation of the Hellcat: "A questionnaire was sent to all Navy and Marine Corps pilots in mid-1942 asking them what they would like in the way of design, manoeuvrability, horsepower, range, firepower, and the ability to operate off an aircraft-carrier. The naval aviation people went to Grumman and presented them with what they learned;

thus was born the F6F Hellcat." The questionnaire was very real, and it meant a lot to hard-pressed naval personnel aboard carriers at sea that their opinion was being sought, but in fact this occasion was the improvement of the basic Hellcat design rather than its beginning. In truth, the Hellcat had been designed after the Japanese attack on Pearl Harbor (on 7 December 1941) had brought the US into the war. Nor was the Hellcat, as is often claimed, a direct response to

Japan's Zero. The Hellcat owes its origin to Grumman company model proposals in 1938 to improve the XF4F-2 Wildcat. However, after considering modifications to this design, engineers decided instead to begin work on a new aircraft – the F6F Hellcat.

Heavyweight fighter

Literature has described the Vought F4U Corsair as 'back-up' insurance against the Hellcat when, if anything, the reverse was true: Grumman forged ahead to ensure that the Navy had a high-performance fighter if the Corsair was delayed. The Corsair did run into developmental problems and, accordingly, the Hellcat was the first to fly from carriers. The latter was intended to be a heavyweight and had enormous strength to enable it to survive against Japanese fighters armed with cannon. However, many thought that the Hellcat was the right aircraft with the wrong engine. The initial production version of the Hellcat needed changes because of this, although these were only minor. In an era in which American industry was unchallenged as the

This F6F-5 awaits launch aboard the USS Bennington, poised for more action against Japanese targets. Almost all the major air combats in the Pacific from 1943 were dominated by the Hellcat.

*Above: Finished in the **US** Navy's 1943 scheme of non-specular blue-grey graduating to a light grey-blue around the base of the fuselage, these F6F-3s bear the markings of Navy Squadron VF-8. Hellcats continued to serve with the Navy until 1954, after which they were used for several more years in the target drone role.*

Right: The only other operator of the F6F during the war was the Fleet Air Arm, flying the type over Norway, the Mediterranean and the Far East. The unusual way in which the undercarriage folded backwards into the wings is well illustrated in this view.

world leader, there were other problems involved in building the Hellcat, including inadequate plant space at Bethpage. In spring 1942, therefore, Grumman bought up thousands of steel girders from New York city's dismantled Second Avenue 'el' (elevated railway) and World's Fair pavilion to help build a new Bethpage plant.

Grumman and the Navy improved the Hellcat as the war progressed, in much the way that any aircraft receives improvements over time. In the case of the Hellcat, however, there was little to improve and changes were minimal. At one juncture, an improved windshield resulted from US Navy complaints that dust was accumulating between the curved windshield and the bulletproof transparent plate. In what might have represented a bigger change to the Hellcat, consideration was given to fitting the aircraft with a bubble

canopy, but the idea was rejected because it would have dramatically decreased the aircraft's production rate.

So, although there were six variants in the Hellcat series by the end of the war, the fighters were so similar that it was all but impossible to tell them apart. All in all, a total of 12,275 Hellcats were manufactured by Grumman between June 1942 and November 1945.

Hellcat at war

The F6F first saw combat in the Pacific in 1943 and was soon involved in island-hopping campaigns in which many dozens of Navy fighters routinely battled similar numbers of Japanese aircraft. Hellcats are not usually remembered for fighting in Europe, but they did see limited action during Allied landings in southern France in 1944. In one celebrated air engagement, three Heinkel He 111 bombers were downed by F6Fs. The Hellcat was flown

by the Navy's top Pacific aces; Captain David McCampbell, the Navy's all-time ace of aces (with 34 kills), shot down nine aircraft in a single mission on 24 October 1944.

Early plans for licence production of the Hellcat by Canadian Vickers never bore

fruit, and the only foreign user of the Hellcat during World War II was Britain, which had once planned to name the aircraft the Gannet. Among the many actions carried out by British Hellcat pilots were strikes against the German battleship *Tirpitz*.

*Above: The 10,000th Hellcat, an F6F-5, was delivered to VFB-87 aboard the USS **T**iconderoga in May 1945. During construction, a bucket was hung upon its tail and used by Grumman workers for the collection of money for the squadron; $700 was collected in all.*

Left: At least 120 ex-USN Hellcats were supplied to France's Aéronavale for use in Indo-China, and survivors later served in North Africa.

The DB601-powered Kawasaki Ki-61 Hien fighter was preferred equipment for aces, including Shogo Takeuchi (over 30 kills). With little JAAF/JNAF co-operation, ill-planned interception tactics and antiquated radar stations, however, the Japanese defences could not cope with massed raids by high-speed, high-flying and well-armed B-29s.

The fall of Japan

With the Empire crumbling, the Japanese tried desperately to stave off the Allied advance, throwing everything they had into the fray. However, Allied technological advances, most notably in the shape of the atomic bomb, meant that the end was inevitable.

The aim of securing Iwo Jima was to establish advanced bases for the US 20th Air Force operating against Japan from the Marianas. Softening-up operations against Iwo Jima started in August 1944, Saipan-based US 7th Air Force B-24Js flying regular attacks. Prior to the invasion in February 1945, TF 58 of the US 5th Fleet carried out the first major carrier strike on Japan. On 16 February, 125 miles (200 km) south-east of Tokyo, the first fighter strike took off. F6F-5s and F4U-1s fought about 100 A6M5s, N1K1s and J2M3s over Chiba, and claimed 40, while

other air groups roamed over Tokyo and the Kanto Plain; at 11.30 SB2C-3s struck at Ota and Koizumi airfields. The strikes were repeated on the next day. TF 58 flew 2,761 sorties to claim 341 enemy aircraft in the air and 190 on the ground: 60 US aircraft were shot down, and 28 were lost in accidents.

D-Day for Iwo Jima was 19 February, and bitter fighting lasted well into March before the island was secured. During this time Teraoka's Honsbu-based

3rd Koku-Kantai used many of its 400 aircraft on conventional and *kamikaze* attacks on the US 5th Fleet to sink the escort carrier USS *Bismarck Sea* and damage USS *Saratoga*. The invasion of Okinawa, Operation Iceberg, was preceded by carrier strikes by TF 58 and the British TF 57. Landings took place on 1 April 1945, and the campaign lasted until 22 June. Allied shipping came under sustained attacks by Formosa and Kyushu-based *kamikaze* units. Out of 36

Below: Following the capture of Iwo Jima, former Saipan-based P-51Ds moved to new bases on the captured island. These examples carry long-range fuel tanks to escort B-29s over Japan.

Right: Whereas high explosives were needed to devastate the cities of Europe, incendiaries were more effective against the paper houses of Japan – more Japanese perished from the effects of the latter than from the two atomic strikes.

Left: The explosion of the 9,000-lb (4050-kg) Fat Man *plutonium-based nuclear bomb over Nagasaki resulted in the deaths of 73,884 people. It was not just the scale of the destruction or the number of casualties that was so shocking, but the fact that a single weapon could have such power, both immediately and in the lingering effects of fallout.*

Above: As the victorious Allied fleet swept into Tokyo Bay for the Japanese surrender, it was escorted by an immense fleet of American fighters and bombers.

ships sunk and 368 damaged to varying degrees, Japanese suicide attacks claimed 26 and 164 respectively. Allied aircraft losses totalled 763. The Japanese navy fought its last battles, the most spectacular being Operation Ten-1 (Heaven-1) of 7 April 1945 when TF 58's air groups sank *Yamamoto*, one cruiser and seven destroyers. The losses of the JNAF and JAAF were enormous: from 1 April to 1 July 1945 the navy lost 2,585 aircraft on *kamikaze* and conventional operations, and the JAAF lost 4,225. Another 1,020 aircraft were destroyed on the ground.

On 12 October the first B-29 of the 73rd Bomb Wing (VH) arrived at Isley Field on Saipan. The first mission to Japan was flown on 24 November, when 111 B-29s were dispatched to the Nakajima-Musashi No. 11 engine plant near Tokyo.

In the ensuing months XXI BC grew in proficiency, striking at Musashino, Kobe, Nagoya and Akashi in daylight precision attacks. The next wing to arrive on Tinian, the 313rd BW, started operations in February. By this time XXI Bomber Command was under the experienced Maj. Gen. Curtis E. LeMay, who introduced the practice of devastating nocturnal incendiary raids with M69 bombs. Tokyo was attacked by 334 B-29s drawn on the night of 9-10 March 1945. A high wind caused a conflagration that ultimately burned out 18.5 sq miles (47.9 km²), killing 83,793 and injuring 40,918 people. Devastation of a similar nature was visited upon Nagoya, Osaka, and Kobe – huge areas of Japan's four greatest cities were incinerated.

In April XXI Bomber Command was turned over to the support of the Okinawa campaign, and undertook raids on airfields in Kyusbu. P-51D Mustangs of VII Fighter Command escorted the B-29s over Japanese targets for the first time on 7 April. The first of many successful sea-mining missions by B-29s was flown on the night of 27-28 March. B-29 losses to Japanese fighters were consistently low: 13 B-29s were shot down by fighters in 3,487 sorties in April 1945.

Preparations for the invasion of the Japanese homeland were commenced at an early stage: the southernmost island, Kyusbu, was scheduled for invasion on about 1 December 1945 (Operation Olympic), and that of Honshu on about 1 March 1946 (Operation Coronet). In addition to 2,300,000 regular troops in Japan, there were some 28,000,000 local volunteer levies. The JNAF and JAAF still had about 5,350 aircraft plus a similar number of *kamikaze* aircraft based in the Empire, with another 1,800 in China and Manchuria. Moreover, negotiations aimed at securing a surrender were fruitless.

It was in these circumstances that President Truman sanctioned the use of the A-bombs. It was mostly a political decision, not a military one, and the intention was to shock the Japanese into surrender before the USSR declared war on Japan. It had already been recognised that the Soviets would pose the next threat to world stability and fear of the bomb would hopefully keep the USSR from advancing into Japan. However, it was also realised that any invasion of the Japanese home islands would result in tremendous loss of life, both Japanese and Allied, and so the decision to drop the atomic bomb was made.

At 08.15 on 6 August 1945 a single B-29 of the 509th Composite Group released *Little Boy* from an altitude of 31,600 ft (9650 m) over Hiroshima, eradicating 4.7 sq miles (12.2 km²) of the city and killing instantly 118,661 people. Three days later, another nuclear bomb fell on Nagasaki. On 15 August 1945 Emperor Hirohito, against many of his advisors' wishes, broadcast the humiliating decision to surrender.

Below: The Japanese surrender was officially carried out by emissaries on behalf of Emperor Hirohito and the Japanese government aboard USS Missouri *on 2 September 1945. Officially, the war had lasted six years and a day, although some fighting would carry on for several months, and one elderly Japanese soldier, hiding out on a remote island, did not surrender until 1985!*

Above: No. 356 Squadron, RAF Liberator ground crews celebrate the war's end. RAF and USAAF B-24s played a pivotal role in the war against the Japanese, performing transport and reconnaissance duties as well as the more traditional bombing missions.

Index